THE
SONG
OF
SONGS

The publisher gratefully acknowledges the generous contribution to this book provided by the General Endowment Fund of the Associates of the University of California Press.

THE SONG OF SONGS

A NEW TRANSLATION
with an Introduction and Commentary

ARIEL BLOCH AND CHANA BLOCH

Afterword by Robert Alter

UNIVERSITY OF CALIFORNIA PRESS
Berkeley   Los Angeles   London

University of California Press
Berkeley and Los Angeles, California

University of California Press, Ltd.
London, England

First Paperback Printing 1998

Reprinted by arrangement with Random House, Inc.

Library of Congress Cataloging-in-Publication Data
Bible. O.T. Song of Solomon. Hebrew. 1998.
  The Song of songs : a new translation with an introduction and
commentary / Ariel Bloch and Chana Bloch.
      p.   cm.
  Contains Hebrew text and English translation of the Song of
Solomon.
  Originally published: New York : Random House, c1995.
  Includes bibliographical references and index.
  ISBN 0-520-21330-0 (pbk. : alk. paper)
    1. Bible. O.T. Song of Solomon—Commentaries.   I. Bloch, Ariel A.
II. Bloch, Chana.   III. Bible. O.T. Song of Solomon.
English. Bloch-Bloch.   1998.
  [BS1483.B56   1998]
  223'.9077—dc21   97-34743
                                                                       CIP

Printed in the United States of America

09   08   07   06   05   04   03   02   01
     12   11   10   9   8   7   6   5   4

Book design by Carole Lowenstein

The paper used in this publication meets the minimum requirements of
ANSI/NISO Z39.48-1992 (R 1997) (*Permanence of Paper*). ∞

Contents

For our sons,
Benjamin and Jonathan,
with love

Acknowledgments

In the course of our work on the Song of Songs, we have come to appreciate the truth of the Jewish saying, "From all my teachers have I learned." Any interpretive study dealing with the Hebrew Bible must take account of generations of scholarship. This is particularly true for a text like the Song, which has elicited a wealth of exegesis from antiquity to the present day. Our scholarly debts are recorded in the Commentary and the Bibliography.

Here it is a special pleasure to thank the many friends and colleagues who have helped us. Everyone we turned to responded with uncommon generosity, and we wish to acknowledge our deep appreciation. If we have inadvertently omitted anyone's name, we hope to have expressed our gratitude in person.

Robert Alter championed this undertaking from the start. He read the translation with us, line by line, discussing problems of interpretation, and commented on the Introduction, "In the Garden of Delights." His support has meant a great deal to us. Stephen Mitchell helped with his subtle criticism and steadfast encouragement. In fact, it was he who first suggested over lunch one day that we collaborate on a new translation of the Song. The project seemed immediately appealing; at that time, we had no idea it would engage us both for years.

Our heartfelt gratitude to Sally Belfrage, Josephine Carson, Stanley Moss, Shirley Kaufman, Chana Kronfeld, and Peter Dale Scott, who read the translation closely at various stages; their criticism enabled us to come closer to the spirit of the Song. Our thanks also to Marilyn Chandler, Shirley Kaufman, and Cynthia Scheinberg for their comments on the Introduction. Most of all, we are grateful to Anita Barrows, who followed the translation and Introduction in draft after draft; we have benefited immeasurably from her poetic intuition, her critical acuity, and her unstinting generosity.

JoAnne Bernstein, David Biale, Daniel Boyarin, Kenneth Cohen, Julius Held, Thomas Rosenmeyer, Andrew Stewart, and David Winston answered queries in their respective fields. Michael Fox, Moshe Greenberg, and Carol Meyers corresponded with us about specific points. Indran Amirthanayagam, Yael Chaver, Michael Chyet, Betsy Dubovsky, Stuart Friebert, Tess Gallagher, Joanna Harris, Richard Moore, and Susan Rattray offered suggestions or advice. With their lively skepticism, the participants in the Bible study group chaired by Jacob Milgrom constituted an ideal sounding board. We are also obliged to the editors of *Equinox, The Forward, Judaism, The Iowa Review,* and *Poetry,* where some of these lyrics and portions of the Introduction and Commentary first appeared.

We have been fortunate in our agent, Georges Borchardt, who offered wise counsel and staunch support, and in our editor at Random House, Jason Epstein, whose enthusiasm for this project was an inspiration to us.

We began the translation at Yaddo in 1990, and the Introduction and Commentary at the MacDowell Colony in 1992. Both of these artists' colonies offered us comfortable working conditions in idyllic surroundings. They even provided the deer in the field and the little foxes—an unexpected gift.

Finally, we wish to thank each other. This project was truly a collaborative effort. We worked together on the translation, debating—sometimes fiercely—the meaning of the Hebrew text and the multitude of possibilities offered by English; then Chana wrote the Introduction and Ariel the Commentary, each of us consulting with the other and editing the other's many drafts. Neither one of us could have completed this work without the devoted assistance of the other.

ARIEL BLOCH and CHANA BLOCH
Berkeley, spring 1994

IN
THE
GARDEN
OF
DELIGHTS

T HE SONG OF SONGS is a poem about the sexual awakening of a young woman and her lover. In a series of subtly articulated scenes, the two meet in an idealized landscape of fertility and abundance—a kind of Eden—where they discover the pleasures of love. The passage from innocence to experience is a subject of the Eden story, too, but there the loss of innocence is fraught with consequences. The Song looks at the same border-crossing and sees only the joy of discovery.

The poem is set in early spring, with its intimations of ripening. The rains of the winter season have just ended, the vines are in blossom, the air is alive with scents and birdsong. Since the poem speaks through metaphor, this setting reveals something essential about the lovers, who live in harmony with the natural world. The images of spring reflect their youth, and the innocent freshness of their passion.

The woman appears to be very young, probably just past puberty. Her brothers call her their "little sister" and think of her as a child—"We have a little sister / and she has no breasts," they say—though she is more grown-up than they admit: since by her own account her breasts are developed, she has reached sexual maturity (8:8–10).[1] The Shulamite, as she is called, is presented in relation to her close family, her mother and her brothers, as well as a group of young women, the daughters of Jerusalem. She and her lover meet secretly in the countryside at night and part at daybreak, so it is clear that they are not married.

For centuries, exegetes have considered their relationship chaste, ignoring the plain sense of the Hebrew. The word *dodim*, which occurs six times in the Song, including the opening verse—"Your *dodim* are better than wine"—is almost always translated as "love," though it refers specifically to sexual love.[2] Moreover, the metaphors of feasting

---

[1] Compare Ezek. 16:7–8: "Your breasts were well-formed. . . . I saw that you had reached the age of lovemaking" (*'et dodim*). See Moshe Greenberg, *Ezekiel, 1–20*, vol. 22 of *The Anchor Bible* (Garden City, N.Y.: Doubleday, 1983), pp. 270, 276–77.

[2] Song 1:2, 1:4, 4:10 (twice), 5:1, 7:13; compare Prov. 7:18, Ezek. 16:8, 23:17. Unless otherwise specified, references to the Bible are to the standard English translations; occasionally the numbering differs from the Hebrew by a verse or two.

suggest fulfillment, particularly when they are in the perfect tense, and the verb "to come into" or "to enter" often has a patently sexual meaning in biblical Hebrew:

> I have come into my garden, . . .
> I have gathered my myrrh and my spices,
> I have eaten from the honeycomb,
> I have drunk the milk and the wine. (5:1)

All this strengthens our conviction that the sexual relationship between the two lovers is not just yearned for—as has often been assumed—but actually consummated. In this respect, our understanding of the Song differs crucially from that of most commentators in the past, and indeed some even in our own day.

How can a poem so voluptuous be so full of innocent delight? For one thing, since it relies on metaphor rather than explicit statement, the language of the Song is restrained and delicate even where it is most sensuous. And because the lovers seem new to love, tender and proud and full of discovery, their words have a kind of purity—a "cleanly wantonness," in the phrase of the seventeenth-century English poet Robert Herrick.

In the Bible, written for the most part from a male point of view, women are by definition the second sex. History is traced through the line of the fathers, as in the priestly genealogies ("And Enoch begat Methuselah"), and the typical formulas for sexual relations ("he knew her," "he came in unto her," "he lay with her") make the woman seem passive and acted upon. But in the Song, where the lovers take turns inviting one another, desire is entirely reciprocal. Both are described in images that suggest tenderness (lilies, doves, gazelles) as well as strength and stateliness (pillars, towers). In this book of the Bible, the woman is certainly the equal of the man.

Indeed, she often seems more than his equal. Most of the lines are hers, including the first word in the poem—"Kiss me"—and the last. As a rule, she is the more forceful of the two; her lover describes her as 'ayummah, "daunting" (6:4, 10). Only the Shulamite makes dramatic statements about herself: "I am dark, and I am beautiful!" (1:5), "I am a wall / and my breasts are towers" (8:10), and only she commands the elements: "Awake, north wind! O south wind, come, / breathe upon my garden" (4:16). She isn't shy about pursuing her lover: she goes out into the streets of Jerusalem at night to search for him—bold and unusual behavior for an unmarried woman (3:1–4, 5:6–7). She finds him, and makes it perfectly clear that she intends to keep him: "I held him, I would not let him go / until I brought him to my mother's house" (3:5).

Her invitations to love are more outspoken than his: "Let my lover come into his garden" (4:16); "There I will give you my love" (7:13); "I would give you . . . / my pomegranate wine" (8:2). She is the one who takes the initiative in their lovemaking: "I awakened you," she reminds him with some pride (8:5). In 6:11–12 he goes down to the walnut grove in an expectant mood ("to see if the vine had budded"), and there, to his surprise, she anticipates and rewards him. When she asks him to be true to her forever—"Bind me as a seal upon your heart" (8:6)—she phrases the wish in her own characteristically emphatic way.

It is the Shulamite who pronounces the great truths about love:

> For love is as fierce as death,
> its jealousy bitter as the grave.
> Even its sparks are a raging fire,
> a devouring flame. (8:6)

And she is the one who teaches that love must not be roused carelessly:

> Daughters of Jerusalem, swear to me
> by the gazelles, by the deer in the field,
> that you will never awaken love
> until it is ripe. (2:7, 3:5, 8:4)

The wisdom here may sound like Ecclesiastes ("Everything under the heavens has its time and its season: . . . a time to embrace, and a time to refrain from embracing," 3:1, 5) but the spirit that informs it is very different: not a bleak determinism but the inner logic of the passions. And the voice is her own—urgent, insistent, filled with awe at love's power.

The Shulamite's lively presence has been obscured by two millennia of translations and interpretations that, for the sake of propriety, have presented her as a sweet young thing, chaste and demure and properly bridal. In most translations (the King James Version is a notable exception), she wears a veil, a reading not supported by the Hebrew. That incongruous veil, like the fig leaf of Renaissance painting and sculpture, is a sign of the discomfort of the exegetes. When we lift the veil from her face, the Shulamite is revealed as a passionate young woman, as spirited and assertive as Juliet.

Apart from the Shulamite, women are given an unmistakable prominence in the Song. There is no mention of a father or a "father's house," the usual biblical term for "family," while mothers are referred to repeatedly. The Shulamite is her mother's favorite (6:9); when she speaks of her brothers, she calls them, in the Hebrew, "my mother's sons" (1:6); she wishes her lover were as close to her as a brother "who nursed at [her] mother's breast" (8:1). She brings her lover home to her "mother's house," perhaps to signify a more binding relationship (3:4, 8:2). She declares that she awakened her lover in the very place where his mother conceived and gave birth to him (8:5). Even King Solomon's mother appears in the poem, crowning her son on his wedding day (3:11). Though the history of the tribe is shaped by the fathers, the traditions of love, in the Song at least, are handed down by the mothers.

The daughters of Jerusalem act as a kind of chorus, a foil to the Shulamite and an audience. She addresses her feelings about love to them, and turns to them for help; they are invoked, and perhaps even present, during some of the couple's intimate dialogues. Like the young women who accompany Jephthah's daughter in her mourning, or the women of Bethlehem who come out to greet Naomi, the daughters of Jerusalem represent the social milieu in which the lovers move, answering their need for public testimony and public validation. The young man's companions, mentioned briefly in 1:7 (and perhaps 5:1 and 8:13), may serve a similar purpose, though unlike the daughters of Jerusalem they are given no voice in the poem. The lovers in the Song are certainly unlike the many star-crossed couples of other literary traditions who languish in tragic isolation.

The brothers and the watchmen provide whatever friction there is in the poem. From the beginning, the Shulamite's brothers are watching her; as one would expect in a biblical text, they are their sister's keepers. In 1:6 we learn that they have rebuked her, possibly for her sexual behavior—that is, if "guarding the vineyard" is understood metaphorically. The enigmatic "Catch us the foxes" (2:15), which has been assigned to a variety of speakers, belongs most plausibly to the brothers; in their proprietary way, they are worrying about the young "foxes" who may be despoiling "their" vines (the vineyard is associated with the Shulamite throughout the poem). Later they consider how to deal with their little sister when she is old enough for suitors (8:8–9). We are not surprised that the Shulamite has the last word in these deliberations (8:10).

When the watchmen first come upon the Shulamite in the streets of Jerusalem at night, they seem harmless enough, but later they assault her physically (3:3, 5:7). Whether or not this incident reflects reality, its primary purpose in the poem is to create dramatic tension. By their opposition, the brothers and the watchmen provoke the Shulamite to reveal her resolve and assurance in love. And their presence serves as a contrast to the sweet flowing milk and honey and myrrh, which to some readers might otherwise seem cloying.

Despite the brothers and watchmen, the Song has none of the dark complication of many familiar love stories. For Romeo and Juliet, love is wedded to loss and death; for Tristan and Isolde, or for Heathcliff and Catherine, love itself is a form of suffering. The word "passion" comes from the Latin *patior*, "to suffer," and passionate love is often regarded as a consuming disease, its symptoms being (in Sappho's diagnosis) a fluttering heartbeat, a burning sensation, a drumming in the ears, a cold sweat, paleness, and trembling. But apart from one episode of rapid heartbeat (5:4), the lovers in the Song exhibit few of the usual symptoms. They don't suffer love, they savor it.

The Song has its moments of anxiety or yearning, to be sure, but the prevailing mood is one of celebration. Hopelessness is not among its charms. The young, in each other's arms, sing a sensual music, their theme the transforming experience of falling in love. Like the blossoming wildflowers, they take no thought for the morrow. Sufficient unto the day is its own delight.

The lovers are fervent, impetuous, filled with an unwavering headlong intensity. "Take me by the hand, let us run together!" in 1:4 proclaims their exuberance. Hyperbole is their natural language. Dramatic and self-dramatizing, the Shulamite sings out:

> Let me lie among vine blossoms,
> in a bed of apricots!
> I am in the fever of love. (2:5)

And her lover matches her extravagance:

> Oh come with me, my bride,
> come down with me from Lebanon. . . .
> from the mountains of the leopards,
> the lions' dens. (4:8)

A moment later, they are tender and playful with each other; they vie in the gallantries of praise; she interrupts him lovingly to complete his thought. He in particular is fond of affectionate epithets: "my love," "my friend," "my sister, my bride," "my dove," "my perfect one." Both of them delight in the sound of the first person plural: "our bed," "our roofbeams," "our rafters," they say, "our wall," "our land," "our doors," taking possession, as a couple, of the world around them.

Shakespeare was right about lovers: they have such seething brains, such fantasies. To be in love is to be caught up in the power of fantasy. "Be like a gazelle," the Shulamite commands (2:17), as if the words themselves had the power to transform reality. In her mind her lover can as easily become a king. When she calls him "the king," or when he calls her "nobleman's daughter," they are dressing up in borrowed robes, playing at King-Solomon-and-his-court. And though they seem, at least from this distance, convincingly pastoral, it may be that they are only playing at being shepherds; apart from 1:7–8, the images of pasturing (2:16, 6:2–3), like those of the vineyard, are erotic double entendres. Perhaps, like Marlowe's Passionate Shepherd, or Shakespeare's Rosalind, they are really just lovers in shepherds' clothing.

Jerusalem is at the center of their world ("Shulamite" probably means "woman of Jerusalem"), but the geography of their imagination reaches from the mountains of Lebanon to the oasis of Ein Gedi, from Heshbon in the east to Mount Carmel on the sea—the four points of their compass. The garden of delights in the Song is a fantasy garden, filled with precious and exotic spices:

> flowering henna and spikenard,
> spikenard and saffron, cane and cinnamon,
> with every tree of frankincense,
> myrrh and aloes,
> all the rare spices. (4:13–14)

Henna and saffron grew in ancient Israel, but myrrh, cinnamon, and cane probably did not, while frankincense, aloes, and spikenard were imported from faraway Arabia, India, Nepal, and China.[3] With what abandon these lovers inhabit their fantasies! But that is precisely what makes them seem so convincing. The Song of Songs offers us an imaginary garden—with real lovers in it.

[3] Yehuda Feliks, *Song of Songs: Nature, Epic and Allegory* (Jerusalem: Israel Society for Biblical Research, 1983), pp. 22–26.

ELSEWHERE IN THE BIBLE, nature is the mirror of God, reflecting His power and sublimity, and man, that paragon of animals, is glorified as the crown of Creation:

> You have made him master
> over all the works of Your hands,
> You have set the world at his feet.
> (Ps. 8:6; compare Gen. 1:28)

The notion of man's preeminence was very likely formed in reaction to the neighboring pagan cultures with their animal gods, and it is as rooted in biblical thought as the archetypal oppositions of day and night, light and darkness, sea and dry land. But in the Song the name of God does not even appear, and there is no opposition between human and animal, no hierarchy, no dominion. Nature is the mirror of the human lovers.

The lovers discover in themselves an Eden, thriving and abundant, a Promised Land of vines and fig trees, pomegranates, wheat, milk and honey. The poet's metaphors keep shifting between the actual landscape, suffused with erotic associations, and the landscape of the body. The Shulamite waits for her lover in a garden, but she herself is a garden; the two of them go out to the fragrant vineyards to make love, but she herself is a vineyard, her breasts like clusters of grapes, and their kisses an intoxicating wine.

The Song is filled with wonder for what the poet Denise Levertov calls "animal presence." When the lovers are compared to animals, it is in tribute to their beauty and undomesticated freedom. Both lovers have dovelike eyes, and both are associated with deer and gazelles. At moments they seem almost transformed into those graceful creatures. The Shulamite, hiding behind a wall, is a rock dove in the craggy ravines (2:14); the young man bounding over the mountains is a gazelle, a stag (2:9). When she asks him to "be like a gazelle, a wild stag" (2:17, 8:14), she is sweeping aside the biblical hierarchies, and we are reminded that animals were once venerated for their power and beauty. It is not by chance that the Shulamite asks her friends to swear "by the gazelles, by the deer in the field." In an oath, precisely where we might expect to find the name of God, we find instead the names of two animals that are frequently associated with the lovers. This oath makes plain the secular boundaries of the lovers' world. Divinity lives within them and their landscape; the earth is all of paradise they need to know.

KING SOLOMON is a central figure in the lovers' fantasies, not a character in the poem, as commentators once assumed. His reign is invoked as a symbol of legendary splendor that enhances and ennobles the two young lovers. The account of Solomon in the Book of Kings, even if largely historical, appears to incorporate elements of legend. Solomon "exceeded all the kings of the earth in riches and in wisdom" (1 Kings 10:23). He controlled the caravan trade in gold and spices, and his merchant fleet brought back sandalwood, precious stones, gold, silver, ivory, apes, and peacocks (9:26–28; 10:11, 14–15, 22). He imported horses from Cilicia and chariots from Egypt for sale to the kings of the Hittites and Aram, while building his own force of twelve thousand horses and fourteen hundred chariots (10:26, 28–29). Women he imported, too, one might say—from the Moabites, Ammonites, Edomites, Phoenicians, and Hittites—for his harem of seven hundred wives and three hundred concubines (11:1–3). He was a master builder, famous for the Temple in Jerusalem; his elaborate palace complex boasted a separate dwelling for the daughter of Pharaoh, the most politically consequential of his wives (6:38–7:1, 8). His throne was made of ivory overlaid with the finest gold: "Nothing like it was ever made in any kingdom," and all his drinking vessels were of gold: "None were of silver; nobody valued silver much in the days of Solomon" (10:18–21). One can almost hear the chronicler's gasp of admiration.

Now, kings are regarded with a skeptical eye elsewhere in the Bible, and wealth is often suspect. The "Law of the King" in Deuteronomy 17:14–20, apparently formulated with Solomon in mind, stipulates that a king shall not "multiply" horses, wives, silver, and gold (listed, yes, in that order). The author of Kings admits that Solomon's love of foreign women led to idolatry and the dissolution of the kingdom (1 Kings 11:1, 4, 9–11). And in the Book of Ecclesiastes, the king contemplates his vast possessions—gold and silver, herds and flocks, houses, gardens, vineyards, orchards—with the weariness of the jaded connoisseur, and declares them all "vanity" (2:4–11).

But in the Song, King Solomon is a sign and a wonder. Whenever the poet alludes to queens and concubines, horses and chariots, the cedars of Lebanon, gold, ivory, and spices, the reader is imaginatively invited into

King Solomon's court. The geographical range of the Song suggests the extent of his empire, which stretched from the Red Sea to the Euphrates. Even the formulas of counting—threescore queens, fourscore concubines, a thousand pieces of silver, ten thousand men—owe something to the rhetoric of glorification in the Book of Kings. The Song lingers appreciatively over that world of opulence—that is, until the final lyrics, when wealth and possessions are weighed in the balance by the two lovers, and found wanting. The Shulamite scorns the wealthy fool who would try to buy love (8:7), and her lover grandly dismisses the king along with his vineyard, and his need to keep watch (8:11–12). Solomon in all his glory, as Jesus will later say, is eclipsed by the lilies of the field. In the Song, even that magnificent king is no match for the lovers, who feast in splendor.

A POEM about erotic love would seem out of place in Holy Scripture, particularly if one's point of reference is the antipathy to sexuality in the New Testament. But sex is no sin in the Old Testament. As a matter of fact, sexual attraction is counted as one of the wonders of the world in the Book of Proverbs:

> Three things I marvel at,
> four I cannot fathom:
> the way of an eagle in the sky,
> the way of a snake on a rock,
> the way of a ship in the heart of the sea,
> the way of a man with a woman.
> (Prov. 30:18–19)

The image in Genesis of man and wife "cleaving" to each other and becoming "one flesh," at once mythic and anatomically precise, sees that union as healing the primal wound of separation (Gen. 2:23–24). It is a husband's duty to provide food, clothing, and "conjugal rights" ('onah) to his wife (Exod. 21:10). And since fertility is a central concern—God's blessing over Adam and Eve is "Be fruitful and multiply" (Gen. 1:28)—sex within its ordained bounds is almost a sacred calling.

In images that recall the Song, the Book of Proverbs recommends erotic pleasure as a remedy against temptation, a way of keeping a good man out of trouble:

> Drink water from your own cistern,
> fresh water from your well. . . .
>
> Let your fountain be blessed;
> take delight in the wife of your youth,
> a loving doe, a graceful gazelle.
>
> Let her breasts fill you with pleasure,
> be entranced always by her love.
>
> (Prov. 5:15, 18–19)

And even the skeptical speaker of Ecclesiastes sees love as a God-given consolation for the dreariness of existence:

> Go eat your bread with joy, then,
> and drink your wine with a merry heart,
> for God has already approved what you do.
>
> May you always be clothed in white
> and never lack oil to anoint your head.
>
> Enjoy life with a woman you love
> all the fleeting days that are granted you
> under the sun,
> all your fleeting days.
>
> For this is your portion in life,
> to repay your toil here under the sun.
>
> (Eccles. 9:7–9)

But sex is sanctioned only in marriage; on this point the Old Testament laws are unequivocal. Outside the pale of marriage there are only crimes and punishments, catalogued in exhaustive detail. A young woman was assumed to be a virgin when she married; according to Deuteronomy, her parents had to produce the proof of her virginity (that is, the bloodstained garment) before the town elders in the event that her husband accused her. In the absence of such evidence, she could be stoned for "playing the whore in her father's house" (Deut. 22:13–21). This severe penalty is typical of the laws regulating sexuality—though, of course, the laws do not tell us how people actually behaved. And it is worth noting that sex between unmarried people, though hardly approved of, is not considered a flagrant transgression like incest and adultery (the technical term for such offenses is *gilluy 'arayot*, "uncovering someone's nakedness").[4] If a

---

[4]Rachel Biale, *Women and Jewish Law* (New York: Schocken Books, 1984), p. 175. This attitude was maintained by the rabbis; *see* pp. 191–2.

man forced a young woman to have sex with him, he was required to marry her, paying the bride-price of fifty shekels of silver to her father, and forbidden to divorce her (Deut. 22:28–29). At issue here is not premarital sex but property: an unmarried woman's sexuality was the property of her father, and a married woman's, of her husband.

The perils of sex are dramatized in the Book of Proverbs. In one passage, an adulterous woman goes after her poor victim in the city streets at night, kissing him openly and seducing him with honeyed words:

> I have spread my couch
> with dyed Egyptian linen,
> sprinkled my bed
> with myrrh, aloes, and cinnamon.
> Come, let us drink our fill of love,
> let us make love all night long!
> (Prov. 7:16–18)

This passage may remind us of the Song in its naming of fragrant spices and the association of wine and lovemaking, but while it makes plain the irresistible appeal of sex, it is intended, of course, as a stern warning.

In the prophetic books, the whore and adulteress are contemptuous metaphors for Israel. Hosea, Jeremiah, and Ezekiel conceive of the covenant between God and Israel as a marriage—or rather, when Israel goes astray, as a marriage on the rocks, with God as the wronged husband and Israel as the unfaithful wife—and their images for illicit sexuality bristle with revulsion.[5] There is an element of horror at female sexuality in Jeremiah's picture of Israel as a she-camel "snuffing the wind in her lust; who can restrain her when she is in heat?" (Jer. 2:23–24). Certainly, Ezekiel's talk of donkeys and stallions (23:20) makes the very notion of sex seem degrading.

The biblical narratives openly acknowledge the role of sexuality in human existence. Samson and Delilah, David and Bathsheba—tales like these have led sober citizens to declare the Bible unfit reading for children. Women behave with a surprising boldness in some of these stories. Tamar, dressed as a prostitute, tricks her father-in-law, Judah, into sleeping with her; Ruth anoints herself, puts on her best clothing and lies down at the feet of Boaz on the threshing floor at night (in one interpretation, she seduces him). But for all their sexual aggressiveness, Tamar

---

[5]Hosea 1–3, Jer. 2–3, Ezek. 16.

and Ruth are interested only in perpetuating the family line. They make themselves whores for the sake of heaven, one might say; they are not sexual beings but the handmaidens of history.

It is possible that the unconstrained relation between the young lovers in the Song is not so remote from daily life in ancient Israel as one might think. The biblical laws, after all, are prescriptive, and they do not necessarily reflect reality. Still, we must be as tentative in drawing inferences about social behavior from literature as we are from the legal codes. The Song is after all a work of the imagination, a work unique in its unabashed celebration of erotic love. Its theme is the wonder of a woman with a man—an unmarried woman, with no concern about perpetuating the family line and no motive but pleasure. In it, eros is its own reward. One might be tempted to call the Song subversive, were it not the least polemical of books. No wonder the pious exegetes of synagogue and church were so quick to marry off the young lovers.

THE LANGUAGE of the Song is at once voluptuous and reticent. "Let my lover come into his garden / and taste its delicious fruit" (4:16) is characteristic both in what it boldly asserts and in what it chooses to leave unexpressed. We can appreciate its restraint by comparing this verse with, say, the invitation of Inanna, the goddess of love and fertility, to Dumuzi in the sacred marriage rite of Sumer: "Plow my vulva, my sweetheart."[6] In the Song, sexuality is evoked primarily by metaphors such as the vineyard and garden, mountain of myrrh, hill of frankincense, a mound of wheat edged with lilies, the sweet fruit of the apricot tree. The Shulamite describes her lover as a shepherd pasturing among lilies (2:16, 6:2–3); he anticipates an erotic encounter by saying he will go to the mountain of myrrh (4:6). The use of metaphor that both reveals and conceals has the effect of enhancing the Song's eroticism, while the suggestive play of double entendre suffuses the whole landscape with eros.

In celebrating love and lovers, the Song proclaims the power of the imagination. The verb *damah* ("to be like") occurs with particular frequency; in one of its conjugations, *dimmah*, it means "to liken, to

---

[6]S. N. Kramer, trans., "Sumerian Sacred Marriage Texts," in *Ancient Near Eastern Texts Relating to the Old Testament*, ed. James B. Pritchard, 3rd ed. (Princeton: Princeton University Press, 1969), p. 643.

compare," but also "to conjure up a mental image, to imagine, to fanta-
size." The lover imagines the Shulamite as a mare (the verb here is
dimmitik, 1:9) and a palm tree (*dametah*, 7:8); she imagines him as a
gazelle or a stag (*domeh*, 2:9), and tells him to "be like" a gazelle or a
stag (*demeh leka*, 2:17, 8:14). In using these verbs, as Robert Alter has
observed, the poet is "flaunting the effect of figurative comparison,"[7]
deliberately calling attention to the workings of simile and metaphor,
and by extension, the workings of the imagination. We have already
noticed the role of fantasy in the Song. It is often hard to tell what is real
and what imagined; for that reason, many readers have found the poem
to be dreamlike, with a freedom of movement, a dizzying fluidity, that
conveys the intoxication of the senses.

Similes and metaphors from nature alternate with images from art
and architecture in the four formal set-pieces where the lovers single out
for praise the parts of each other's bodies; these poems belong to a genre
often referred to by the Arabic term *wasf*. The images are not literally
descriptive; what they convey is the delight of the lover in contemplating
the beloved, finding in the body a reflected image of the world in its
freshness and splendor.

There is a striking Egyptian example of the form almost a thousand
years older than the Song, which may have been known in ancient Israel:

> One alone is [my] sister, having no peer:
>   more gracious than all other women.
> Behold her, like Sothis rising
>   at the beginning of a good year:
> shining, precious, white of skin,
>   lovely of eyes when gazing.
> Sweet her lips [when] speaking:
>   she has no excess of words.
> Long of neck, white of breast,
>   her hair true lapis lazuli.
> Her arms surpass gold,
>   her fingers are like lotuses. . . .
> Lovely of [walk] when she strides on the ground,
>   she has captured my heart in her embrace.[8]

[7]Robert Alter, *The Art of Biblical Poetry* (New York: Basic Books, 1985), p. 193.
[8]Michael V. Fox, *The Song of Songs and the Ancient Egyptian Love Songs*
(Madison: University of Wisconsin Press, 1985), p. 52; from poem no. 31. Fox makes
a good case for the possible transmission of Egyptian love poetry to ancient Israel.

This genre was to have a long history. It later became a favorite of the troubadour poets and the Elizabethan sonneteers, but Shakespeare effectively put an end to it with his satirical "My mistress' eyes are nothing like the sun."

If the first *waṣf* (4:1–7) seems fairly conventional in its itemized account of the young woman's body, each of the others is given an inventive twist. In 5:10–16, the Shulamite offers an impassioned description of her lover's uniqueness in response to the daughters of Jerusalem, who have asked what makes him so special, the framework of question and answer adding a note of dramatic urgency. In 6:4–10, the allusions to King Solomon's court, and the hyperbolic comparisons, invest the form with a mythic grandeur. Here the expected simile or metaphor about the eyes is replaced by an exclamation, "Your eyes! Turn them away / for they dazzle me" (6:5), and the final verse is couched as the extravagant tribute of Solomon's court:

> Every maiden calls her happy,
> queens praise her,
> and all the king's women:
>
> "Who is that rising like the morning star,
> clear as the moon,
> bright as the blazing sun,
> daunting as the stars in their courses!" (6:9–10)

Finally, in 7:2–7, the Shulamite is dancing as the audience cheers her on: "Again, again!" (7:1). This time the traditional order of praise, from the head down, is reversed: starting appropriately with her graceful dancing feet, the Shulamite's body, in intimate detail, is surveyed in her lover's gaze. Reading these four *waṣfs* together, we can appreciate both the homage paid to convention and the poet's virtuoso variations.

Though the Song is not a drama, as some critics have assumed, it is dramatic in effect, since many of the poems are either monologues spoken in the presence of an audience or dialogues between the lovers. In 1:15–17 and 2:1–3, where the lovers admire one another, part of the pleasure of the dialogue is in their quickness and verve as they outdo each other in praise. In 7:8–11 the dialogue is handled with great charm and imaginative freedom. The young man is confessing to the Shulamite how she once seemed to him inaccessible, a lofty palm tree:

> I said in my heart,
> Let me climb into that palm tree
> and take hold of its branches.

> And oh, may your breasts be like clusters
> of grapes on a vine, the scent
> of your breath like apricots,
> your mouth good wine—

when she interrupts him with a knowing endearment, completing his sentence:

> That pleases my lover, rousing him
> even from sleep.
>
> I am my lover's,
> he longs for me,
> only for me.

That playful interruption beautifully captures the intertwining speech of lovers.

Though most of the Song is devoted to the lovers' words, the poet also lets us hear their inner voices. What the young man confesses in the passage just quoted are his secret fantasies: how he daydreamed, how he yearned from afar. We hear the lovers musing aloud about their inten-tions: "I must rise and go about the city, / . . . till I find / my only love" (3:2); "I will hurry to the mountain of myrrh, / the hill of frankincense" (4:6). The refrain "His left hand beneath my head, / his right arm / hold-ing me close" (2:6, 8:3) is a moment of inwardness, a rapt meditation compounded of memory and desire. The Shulamite's emotions are the subject of 5:2–8, when, ardent and impatient, the young man comes to her door at night. She coyly pretends reluctance, though her heart is beating fast. As soon as he leaves, she is filled with regret and longing: "How I wanted him when he spoke!" With economy and precision, the poet evokes passion, coquetry, self-reproach, and yearning, letting us see the tension between the Shulamite's feelings and her words.

The lovers take turns seeking one another: he invites her or "goes down" to her (2:8–13, 5:2–6, 6:2, 6:11); she goes looking for him or invites him (3:1–4, 5:6–7, 7:12–14). They move from desire to anticipa-tion to fulfillment and back to desire; sexual consummation, expressed in 5:1 and 6:12, is an episode in the poem, not its grand finale, and it doesn't appease their hunger for very long. A number of strategically placed refrains punctuate the Song:

> I am in the fever of love. (2:5, 5:8)
>
> His left hand beneath my head,
> his right arm
> holding me close. (2:6, 8:3)

> Daughters of Jerusalem, swear to me. . . . (2:7, 3:5, 5:8, 8:4)
>
> My beloved is mine and I am his. (2:16, 6:3; cf. 7:11)
>
> Who is that rising from the desert! (3:6, 8:5; cf. 6:10)

The incremental repetition of refrains and motifs such as these, and the densely exfoliating metaphors, have the effect of binding the lyrics to one another, reinforcing the impression of artistic design.

The lovers' relations to each other and to the daughters of Jerusalem, the brothers, the mother, and the watchmen add up to a kind of "plot," like the narrative thread in a Schubert song cycle. There is a perceptible symmetry between the first and last chapters: in both we hear about Solomon (1:5, 8:11–12), the vineyard (1:6, 8:11–12), the brothers (1:6, 8:8), and the lovers' companions (1:3–4, 1:7, 8:13). The Shulamite's spirited response to her brothers in 8:10 resolves the tensions implied in 1:6, 8:8–9, and perhaps 2:15. The elements of a plot are available, and we can hardly help wanting to link them, though plot seems the least of our poet's concerns. The Song of Songs is a sequence of lyric poems, episodic in its structure—not a narrative, and not a drama. The so-called gaps and discontinuities in the text are problematic only for those who attempt to read it as one or the other.

The Song doesn't begin at the beginning, and it doesn't have a "proper" ending. It starts at a pitch of intensity that implies an already existing erotic relationship. And it doesn't conclude, as some might have wished, with the dramatic declaration of 8:5–7, scored for trumpets and high-sounding cymbals. Instead, it ends quietly, with the Shulamite's "Run away!" (Hebrew *beraḥ*, "flee") in 8:14:

> Hurry, my love! Run away,
> my gazelle, my wild stag
> on the hills of cinnamon.

This resonantly open ending reveals the poet's delicacy of touch. We know the lover will return, as he did after the Shulamite's almost identical words in 2:17:

> Run away, my love!
> Be like a gazelle, a wild stag
> on the jagged mountains.

Like a musical da capo, the parting in 8:14 inevitably implies another meeting. The lack of closure at the end of the poem has the effect of prolonging indefinitely the moment of youth and love, keeping it, in Keats's phrase, "forever warm."

THE SONG OF SONGS is a work of subtlety and sophistication, remarkable for its artistic control and elegant finish. Because of its consistency of characterization, themes, images, and poetic voice, it asks to be read as a unified sequence.[9] The Song is set in springtime, in the city of Jerusalem with its outlying vineyards and pastures. The two lovers are recognizably the same throughout, as are the daughters of Jerusalem, the mother, the brothers, and the watchmen. Eros is celebrated as the most powerful of human pleasures; other conceptions of love—as irrational and destructive, say, or spiritually improving—are not even contemplated.

It is of course conceivable that the Song was composed by a school of poets sharing certain values and recurring motifs, like the poets of courtly love. And one might imagine, too, that its unity and consistency were the work of a redactor who collected love poems of others, stringing them together with refrains and repetitions and multiple cross-references. But it is equally plausible, and rather more attractive, to assume that the Song was the work of a poet—one who, as so often in the Bible, would have found it perfectly natural to incorporate quotations and adaptations of material already in circulation. Indeed, if a redactor was responsible for shaping the poem as we now have it, then he or she was a literary artist of the highest caliber, and fully deserves to be called a poet.

Some scholars, pointing to the shifts of scene or image or address, have argued that the Song lacks cohesiveness and cannot be regarded as a unified work of art. There are those who see it as an anthology of love poems in a variety of genres—lyrics of yearning or fulfillment, poems in praise of the beloved, duets of mutual praise, etc. A more extreme view takes it to be a patchwork of epigrammatic poems, some of which merely "fill up space in one column of the scroll so that a new, longer poem can begin in a new column."[10] This approach bears the stamp of nineteenth-century biblical scholarship, which was typically concerned with breaking the text down into its constituent units. We have only to

[9]Among those who argue persuasively for this view are Roland E. Murphy, "The Unity of the Song of Songs," *Vetus Testamentum* 29 (1979): 436–43; and Fox, *Song of Songs*, pp. 202–26.

[10]Franz Landsberger, "Poetic Units Within the Song of Songs," *Journal of Biblical Literature* 73 (1954): 212.

compare the Song with such anthologies as the Psalter and the Book of Proverbs to see just how unified it is. The Song is more of a piece too than Ecclesiastes, which purports to be the work of a single author and encompasses a variety of material, from prosaic to gnomic to high poetic.

It makes no sense to judge lyric poetry by the standards of logical discourse, requiring a systematic progression from A to B to C and thence to a conclusion, with every link soldered firmly into place, as some exegetes do. None of the poems in the Bible would fit such a model. Even a short lyric like the Twenty-third Psalm brings together disparate elements: "He makes me lie down in green pastures" and "You spread a table for me in full view of my enemies," shifting abruptly from shepherd to host and from the third person to the second. Apparently the biblical poets had a more flexible notion of unity and structure than many scholars have recognized.

One source available to the poet may have been folk lyrics or secular love poems performed at banquets and festivals and transmitted orally for perhaps hundreds of years. Indeed, much of the poetry in the Bible originated in the oral tradition, and circulated in the mouths of the people long before it was written down.

Singing to the accompaniment of flute, timbrel, or lyre was as much a part of the good life in ancient Israel as drinking wine or anointing oneself with fine oils; we know this in part from the scathing denunciations of the prophets. Ezekiel, for one, hopeless about ever getting through to the rich and pampered, compares himself with bitter irony to "a singer of bawdy songs who has a sweet voice and plays skillfully."[11] One would like to know what was sung on festive occasions; perhaps something like 5:1 in our poem, which has been called a drinking song:

> Feast, friends, and drink
> till you are drunk with love!

And it may be that some version of 3:11 was sung at weddings before it was incorporated into the Song. But there is no way of knowing which lyrics would have circulated in this fashion, or to what extent they were modified by our poet.

The prominence of women in the Song, and the unusually sympathetic rendering of a woman's perspective, has led some readers to wonder

[11]Ezek. 33:32; cf. Amos 6:5–6, Isa. 5:11–12, 24:8–9.

whether the author might have been a woman. This question is being asked with increasing frequency about many of the anonymous works of antiquity, particularly those that reveal a sensitive understanding of women characters. For example, there has been much speculation (some of it rather irresponsible) about whether "J," one of the major prose documents of the Pentateuch, was written by a woman.[12] In the case of the Song, the question arises naturally, since women are associated to some extent with poetry and song in the Bible. Women traditionally sang songs of victory (1 Sam. 18:6–7; compare Exod. 15:20–21) and mourning (2 Chron. 35:25, Jer. 9:17–22), probably composing them as well. The rousing victory poem in Judges 5 was attributed to Deborah; though this may have come about because Deborah was a great political leader, the very fact of the attribution is of some significance. One would suppose that professional women singers (*šarot, mešorerot*) also sang love songs, particularly when they performed at banquets and festivals (2 Sam. 19:35, Eccles. 2:8, Ezra 2:65). Whether or not they composed love songs is anyone's guess. A poet would not have had to be literate. Most of the population was illiterate; it is only in the modern age that we associate literary composition with writing.

It is possible, then, that some of the individual lyrics of the Song were composed by women, or that a woman poet was the author of the final version. This is a hypothesis that will appeal to many readers today. Perhaps it would help to explain why the Song is so remarkably different in spirit from much of the Bible. But ultimately, it must be said, there is no way to determine the gender of an author on the basis of style or content. Any statement about the gender of our poet is necessarily conjectural—and as impossible to verify as whether the poet was young or old, from Jerusalem or the countryside, from the north or the south.

IT WAS A COMMON PRACTICE in antiquity to attribute works of literature to eminent figures from the past—the Torah to Moses, for example, and many of the Psalms to David. In this way the Song of Songs, the Book of Proverbs, and Ecclesiastes all came to be associated with

[12]Harold Bloom and David Rosenberg, *The Book of J* (New York: Grove Weidenfeld, 1990). See the review by Chana Bloch, "Shakespeare's Sister," in the *Iowa Review* 21 (1991): 66–77, and the other pieces in that issue's "Forum on *The Book of J*," pp. 11–86.

Solomon, who was known as a poet and a sage: according to the Book of Kings, he was the author of three thousand proverbs and a thousand and five songs (1 Kings 4:32). The stages of Solomon's literary career were worked out by Rabbi Jonathan, who deduced that the Song was an early effort: "When a man is young he composes songs; when he grows older he makes sententious remarks; and when he becomes an old man he speaks of the vanity of things."[13] The biblical view of Solomon as a poet, and son of a poet, which persisted until the nineteenth century, is captured in a stanza of English doggerel:

> King David and King Solomon lived very wicked lives,
> with half a hundred concubines and quite too many wives.
> But when old age came creeping on, they both were filled
>   with qualms,
> so Solomon wrote the Proverbs, and David wrote the Psalms.

No one takes the attribution in 1:1 seriously today, though some scholars still date the Song early, linking the images of wealth and luxury, and the joyous spirit of the poem, to the Golden Age of Solomon, "the only really happy reign of an Israelite king"[14]—as if happiness were the exclusive property of the tenth century BCE. Like many great leaders, Solomon became a figure of legend, and the stories about him continued to flourish long after his time. In Ecclesiastes, probably a work of the third century BCE, he is presented as the type of the most fortunate man; in the Hellenistic age, Solomon with his riches and wisdom came to be regarded as a kind of Jewish counterpart to the Ptolemaic kings.[15] The Talmud, later, contains tales about Solomon's mother, his wedding day, his magnificent throne, and the like, all fanciful elaborations of the biblical text.[16] The Song uses extrabiblical mate-

---

[13]Maurice Simon, trans., "Canticles Rabbah," in vol. 9 of *Midrash Rabbah*, ed. H. Freedman and Maurice Simon (1930; reprint, London: Soncino Press, 1983) p. 17.

[14]M. H. Segal, "The Song of Songs," *Vetus Testamentum* 12 (1962): 483.

[15]Francis Landy, *Paradoxes of Paradise: Identity and Difference in the Song of Songs* (Sheffield: Almond Press, 1983), p. 29; Martin Hengel, *Judaism and Hellenism: Studies in their Encounter in Palestine during the Early Hellenistic Period*, trans. John Bowden (London: SCM Press, 1974), vol. 1, pp. 129–30. Hengel speculates about the fascination with Solomon in the Hellenistic age and later, citing the many writings attributed to him. Apart from the Book of Proverbs, Ecclesiastes, and the Song, these include the Psalms of Solomon, the Wisdom of Solomon, and the Testament of Solomon. Hengel suspects the intention was to demonstrate the antiquity and superiority of Jewish wisdom to that of Greece.

[16]Louis Ginzberg, *The Legends of the Jews* (Philadelphia: Jewish Publication Society, 1909–38), vol. 4, pp. 125–76; vol. 6, pp. 277–303; compare Matt. 6:29.

rial about Solomon and treats it as if it were familiarly known. In 3:11, for instance, Solomon's mother crowns him on his wedding day, yet neither the crowning nor the wedding appears in any of the biblical texts, suggesting that the poet was drawing on the folklore tradition. The references to Solomon, then, do not exclude a date of composition long after the Solomonic age.

The most reliable criterion for dating the Song is language. After the Babylonian Exile in the sixth century BCE, Hebrew gradually came to be replaced by Aramaic as the major language of communication in Palestine. Hence the Aramaic portions in the late Old Testament books of Ezra and Daniel, and the traces of Aramaic even in the Greek New Testament. Historically, the language of the Song represents a transitional stage between classical Biblical Hebrew and the Hebrew of the Mishnah, a collection of oral law edited around 200 CE, which likewise shows the imprint of Aramaic.

If a language changed at a constant rate, the date of the later biblical texts could be assessed with some accuracy by measuring their Aramaic content—a kind of linguistic carbon dating. Although this method is imprecise, it gives us a fairly reliable gauge of how far along Hebrew was in the process of change when the Song came to be written down. The following are examples of forms and expressions either patterned after or influenced by Aramaic:

> *'eykah* in the locative sense, "where" (1:7)
>
> *šallamah* "lest" (1:7), after the Aramaic *di le-mah*
>
> *'ad 'še-* "before, until, while" (1:12), corresponding to the Aramaic *'ad di*
>
> *rahiṭenu* "our rafters" (1:17) from the root *rhṭ*, as in *rehṭā* in Syriac (a language belonging to the Aramaic family)
>
> *berotim* "cypresses" (1:17), as in the Syriac *berutā*, for the Hebrew *berošim*
>
> *miṭṭato še-li-šelomoh* (literally "his bed that is to Solomon," 3:7); this syntax occurs only here in the Bible, but becomes standard in Mishnaic Hebrew
>
> *'aḥuzey ḥereb* "skilled in warfare" (3:8), after an Aramaic idiom
>
> *me'av* referring to the surface of the belly (5:14), as in the Aramaic *me'ohi* (Dan. 2:31), rather than to the entrails, as in Hebrew

The frequency of Aramaisms, reflected not only in vocabulary but also in morphology, idiom, and syntax, clearly points to a late date.

Like the Mishnah, the Song contains many new Hebrew words that do not appear in earlier texts or that replace older words:

> *naṭar* "to guard" (1:6, 8:11–12), used for the older *naṣar*
> *kotel* "wall" (2:9) for *qir*
> *ḥarakkim* "crevices" (2:9)
> *setav* "winter, rainy season" (2:11)
> *pag* "unripe fig" (2:13)
> *semadar* "blossoms or blossoming of the grapevine"
>   (2:13, 15, 7:13)
> *ṭanneṗ* "to soil, dirty" (5:3)
> *qevuṣṣot* "hair, bunches of hair" (5:11)
> *ginnah* "garden" (6:11)
> *'omman* "craftsman" (7:2) for *ḥaraš*
> *mezeg* "mixed wine" (7:3)
> *sugah* "surrounded by" (7:3)

More than any other text in the Old Testament, the Song appears to reflect the vernacular idiom; one scholar calls it "the first text in the Bible that makes spoken Hebrew fit for literature, including poetry."[17] Some examples:

> *še-* becomes an all-purpose conjunction, largely replacing the relative *'ašer* ("who, which," etc., 1:7, 3:1–4, 3:11, 4:1–2, 6:5), *ki* ("that," 1:6, 5:8) and *ki* ("because," 5:2, 6:5), and forming compound conjunctions, *'ad še-* (1:12, 2:7, 2:17, 3:5, 8:4) and *kim'aṭ še-* ("no sooner than," 3:4).

> The masculine form replaces the feminine in the plurals of pronouns and verbs (2:7, 3:5, 4:2, 5:3, 6:6, 8:4).

> There is a major change in the tense system: the perfect becomes the regular tense for the narrative past, replacing the classical *waw*-conversive.

Finally, there are words of Persian or Greek origin in the Song, *pardes* "orchard" (4:13), from which the English "paradise" is derived, and the enigmatic *'appiryon*, "pavilion, palace[?]" (3:9). All these factors taken

---

[17]Abba Bendavid, *Leshon Miqra u-Leshon Ḥakamim* (Biblical Hebrew and Mishnaic Hebrew) (Tel Aviv: Dvir, 1967), vol. 1, p. 74. The only exceptions to these innovative tendencies are the deliberately archaizing uses in 1:1 *'ašer li-šelomoh*, 3:11 *ṣe'eynah u-re'eynah*, 4:11 *tiṭṭoṗnah*, and 6:9 *va-ye'aššeruhah . . . va-yehalleluhah*.

together—the Aramaic influence, the similarity to Mishnaic Hebrew, the influence of the spoken idiom, the foreign loan-words—suggest that the Song was written down in post-Exilic times, most likely in the Hellenistic period, around the third century BCE.[18]

A Hellenistic date raises some intriguing questions about the relation of the Song to Greek literature and art. After Palestine came under the sway of Alexander in 332 BCE, Greek culture began to be widely diffused there. Greek was the language of administration and commerce, and was known to the upper classes. Thirty Hellenic cities were established, most of them along the Mediterranean coast or near the Sea of Galilee, and were settled by Greek officials, soldiers, and merchants. In a jumble of languages—Hebrew, Aramaic, Greek—a new culture began to evolve, an eclectic mélange of East and West. The precise extent of Greek influence in the early Hellenistic period is the subject of some debate, given the fragmentary nature of the evidence. According to one authority, the works of the Greek poets and philosophers were available in Palestine, and "the man who wished to acquire Greek learning could probably achieve his object to a certain degree in the Greek towns of the country."[19]

Scholars have long pointed out parallels between the Song and the pastoral idylls of Theocritus, court poet to Ptolemy Philadelphus at Alexandria in Egypt, who wrote in the first half of the third century BCE. Among the examples usually cited are the reference to a dark beauty, the comparison of a graceful woman to a horse, and the image of foxes raiding a vineyard,[20] but the affinities go beyond this handful of slender correspondences, which may well have come from the common stock of Mediterranean culture. The Song resembles Greek pastoral poetry in its central conceit—the lovers as shepherds in a setting of idyllic nature—and its celebration of innocent pleasures in highly sophisti-

---

[18]See H. L. Ginsberg, "Introduction to the Song of Songs," in *The Five Megilloth and Jonah* (Philadelphia: Jewish Publication Society, 1969), p. 3; Fox, *Song of Songs*, pp. 186–90.

[19]Victor Tcherikover, *Hellenistic Civilization and the Jews*, trans. S. Applebaum (Philadelphia: Jewish Publication Society, 1959), p. 114.

[20]For Song 1:5, compare Idyll X.26-27: "Charming Bombyca, all call thee . . . sun-scorched, and I alone, honey-hued"; for Song 1:9, compare Idyll XVIII.30-31: "As some . . . Thracian steed [adorns] the chariot it draws, so rosy Helen adorns Lacedaemon"; for Song 2:15, compare Idyll I.48-49: "one [fox] goes to and fro among the vine-rows plundering the ripe grapes," and Idyll V.112-13: "the foxes with their bushy tails that come ever at evening and plunder Micon's vineyard." These translations are from A. S. F. Gow, ed. and trans., *Theocritus* (Cambridge: Cambridge University Press, 1950), vol. I.

cated art. As in pastoral, the lovers exist in a world of leisure and delight, untroubled by the wind and the rain of a real shepherd's life, a world conjured up by the poet's idealizing imagination. The Song is informed by an entirely new sensibility, unique in the Bible. Given the temper of the times, it is possible that the poet of the Song had some knowledge of the themes of Greek poetry, just as the author of Ecclesiastes seems to have been aware, in a general way, of questions debated by the Stoic and Epicurean philosophers.

One can more confidently assume borrowing in areas that were commonly accessible, such as the visual arts. We know that Attic pottery decorated with Dionysiac scenes has been found at a number of archaeological sites. And what would our poet have seen on a visit to the coast cities of Ptolemais (Acre), Joppa (Jaffa), Ascalon (Ashkelon), and Gaza, or to Marissa, Scythopolis (Beth She'an), or Gadara, with their buildings and shrines, gymnasia and theaters? A statue of a nude Aphrodite was found a few decades ago in the area of Mount Carmel.[21] The nude Aphrodite was "an astonishing novelty" in Hellenistic art.[22] While archaic and classical Greek sculpture explored the beauty of the unclothed male body, the female form was draped, with very few exceptions. It is only with the work of Praxiteles—in particular, his much-imitated Aphrodite of Knidos (ca. 350 BCE)—that the female nude comes into its own as a subject of Greek sculpture. There is nothing comparable in Jewish art, given the Second Commandment (Exod. 20:4), which effectively ruled out the physical representation of the human body. One can imagine what it would have meant for a Hebrew poet to see for the first time, in a public setting, the sculpture of a nude body—and a woman's body, at that. The lyrics in the Song praising the lovers' physical beauty may well owe something to the encounter with Greek art. As in the case of Greek pastoral poetry, the argument does not rest on exact correspondences, and here again we are, of course, in the realm of conjecture.

[21]Elias J. Bickerman, "The Historical Foundations of Postbiblical Judaism," in *The Jews: Their History, Culture, and Religion*, ed. Louis Finkelstein, 3rd ed. (New York: Jewish Publication Society, 1960), vol. 1, p. 93. See the photograph of a nude Aphrodite found at Mount Carmel, dated fourth to third century BCE, in Cecil Roth's article "Art: Antiquity to 1800," in *Encyclopedia Judaica*, 1971 ed., vol. 3, col. 510. The evidence is unfortunately limited because the Maccabees in their iconoclastic zeal destroyed pagan sites, and the Romans carted away much of artistic value; moreover, many sites are yet to be excavated.
[22]R. R. Smith, *Hellenistic Sculpture* (London: Thames and Hudson, 1991), p. 79.

A Hellenistic date for the Song is a hypothesis, and it is still controversial. In ancient history, there are no certainties, and more questions
than answers. But it is clear that much of the Song is anomalous in the
biblical context, and calls for explanation: the concern with the private
life as opposed to the public and communal, the frank interest in
sexual experience, the idealization of pastoral innocence, the aesthetic
appreciation of the human body. All of this would suggest that the
Song was composed in a Hellenized atmosphere.

READERS TODAY often ask, with some puzzlement, how the Song ever
managed to "get into" the canon of Holy Scripture. It is, after all, an
emphatically secular book: the name of God is never once mentioned.
Nor is there any reference to Israel's history, or to the national themes
that figure so importantly in the rest of the Bible. The erotic joy of the
two lovers, the human body presented as an object of admiration, the
beauty of nature appreciated for its own sake—all seem out of place in
the Bible.

We tend to think of Holy Scripture as a single volume, soberly bound
in black, with each verse numbered, and with cross-references up and
down the margins. But in ancient Israel, "the Bible" was a collection of
scrolls written on papyrus and stored in a room or cave. The Song was
first written down in an age when literacy was not yet widespread and
copying by hand laborious; the perishable papyrus needed to be carefully stored if it was to survive in the harsh Near Eastern climate. Under
such conditions, no work of literature could last very long unless it
had acquired a devoted following, an audience that would wish to preserve it.

Most people assume that the criteria for canonization were strictly
religious, and that they reflected an orthodox point of view. In fact the
Hebrew Bible, an anthology of works composed over the period of
nearly a millennium, is a very heterogeneous collection. The word
"Bible" comes from the Greek *ta biblia*, meaning "the books," appropriately a plural noun. Not every book meets the test of piety: Job and
Ecclesiastes, for example, challenge the fundamental beliefs that human
beings are the crown of Creation, or that evil is punished and virtue
rewarded, yet they found a place in the canon. Some books may have
been preserved for reasons of national pride, or because they were
numbered among the literary treasures of the Jewish people—the Song,

in this instance, because it is one of the most beloved works of ancient Hebrew literature.

There is barely any evidence about how the canon of the Hebrew Bible was formed: who made the decisions, what criteria were employed, and when the canon was closed. Scattered bits of information in the Apocrypha, Pseudepigrapha, Talmud, and Midrash, and in writers like Josephus, are cryptic and ambiguous. The Song is found in the third section of the Hebrew Bible—the *Ketubim* ("Writings" or Hagiographa), a miscellany including Wisdom literature, poetry, and history—that was granted canonical status centuries after the Torah and the Prophets. The scholarly consensus is that the canon was probably closed sometime before the end of the first century CE; many scholars believe that at the Council of Jamnia in 90 CE the rabbis simply gave their sanction to writings that had already been accepted as authoritative.

There was apparently some controversy about admitting the Song to the canon, as there was about Ecclesiastes and the Book of Esther. Rabbi Akiva (d. 135 CE), who read the Song allegorically, insisted that there had never been any doubt about its canonical status:

> God forbid! No man in Israel ever disputed the status of the Song of Songs . . . for the whole world is not worth the day on which the Song of Songs was given to Israel; for all the writings are holy, but the Song of Songs is the holiest of the holy.[23]

From this denial of denials, we may conclude that there were still reservations about the Song even in his day.

It may be that the attribution to Solomon in the title (1:1) was a factor for admission to the canon. A book believed to have been written by one of Israel's admired kings, and preserved for a thousand years, would certainly have been difficult to exclude. (That this attribution was added by an editor, possibly for the express purpose of preserving the book, was recognized only much later.) It is generally assumed that the allegorical interpretation of the Song, which may have gained currency around this time, played a role as well.

On the other hand, it is entirely possible that the allegorical interpre-

---

[23]Mishnah, Yadayim 3:5, as translated in Sid Z. Leiman, *The Canonization of Hebrew Scripture: The Talmudic and Midrashic Evidence*, 2nd ed. (New Haven: Transactions of the Connecticut Academy of Arts and Sciences, 1991), p. 121.

tation and the final imprimatur of the rabbis came after the Song had already attracted a popular following. We know that secular or even pagan customs of holidays like Passover or Christmas were often sacralized by the religious authorities because they were widely established in popular practice. It is not hard to imagine a similar process at work in the official reception of the Song, bestowing upon this most secular of books an aura of sanctity. At all events, by virtue of its place in the canon, the Song demanded interpretation. The Jewish and Christian exegetes, an imaginative and industrious lot, had their work cut out for them.

FOR A BOOK of only eight chapters, the Song has elicited a prodigious volume of commentary. There is hardly a line of the Song that does not present some difficulty, and no other book of the Bible has called forth such wildly divergent interpretations.[24] The difficulties arise in part from the compactness and concentration of the poetic form. While the narrative prose of the Bible is fairly straightforward and accessible, biblical poetry is compressed and elliptical, sometimes to the point of unintelligibility. The language, too, is very often obscure. The Song has an unusually high proportion of *hapax legomena* (words occurring only once), as well as rare words and constructions. A hapax is almost as frustrating for the interpreter as a <u>lacuna:</u> even where the context provides some clues, it is difficult to establish the precise meaning of such a word. Verses like "King Solomon built an *'appiryon*" (3:9) or "your *šelaḥim* are an orchard" (4:13) or "a king is caught in the *rehaṭim*" (7:6) must finally remain a riddle.

a cavity
gap —
empty space
missing part

Actually, the Song itself is a kind of hapax, for it is the only example of secular love poetry from ancient Israel that has survived. Other love poems must have been composed in biblical times, including poems about courtship, marriage, or unrequited love, but if they were written down at all, they have since vanished. There is something to be learned

[24]For a more detailed summary of the history of exegesis, see H. H. Rowley, "The Interpretation of the Song of Songs," in his *The Servant of the Lord and Other Essays on the Old Testament* (Oxford: Basil Blackwell, 1965), pp. 197–245; Marvin H. Pope, *Song of Songs*, vol. 7c of *The Anchor Bible* (Garden City, N.Y.: Doubleday, 1977), pp. 89–229; and Roland E. Murphy, *The Song of Songs* (Minneapolis: Fortress Press, 1990), pp. 11–41.

by comparing the Song with poems from ancient Egypt or Hellenistic Greece, but because it is one of a kind, the Song is in many respects an enigma.

Early audiences would have had no trouble understanding the Song in its literal sense; even in rabbinic times there were those who still understood it in this way. Rabbi Akiva warned, "Whoever warbles the Song of Songs at banqueting houses, treating it like an ordinary song, has no portion in the World to Come,"[25] the emphatic prohibition making it perfectly clear just what people were doing, and where. Rabbi Simeon ben Gamaliel (late first century CE) recounted that twice a year, on the fifteenth of Av and the Day of Atonement, the young women of Jerusalem would dress in white and go out to dance in the vineyards, calling out to prospective husbands, "Young man, lift up your eyes and see what you would choose for yourself," and reciting verses from the Book of Proverbs and the Song of Songs.[26] These rabbinic passages are the earliest testimony we have about the popular understanding of the Song. For the young men in the banqueting house, or the young women in the vineyard, the Song needed no interpretation, whatever the theologians were saying.

But the theologians prevailed: for twenty centuries, the Song was almost universally read as a religious or historical allegory. The allegorical interpretation found its first great champion in Rabbi Akiva, who taught that the Song was about the love of God and the people of Israel, an interpretation elaborated in various ways by Jewish commentators such as Rashi (d. 1105) and Ibn Ezra (d. 1168). The Church Fathers, following Origen (d. 254), applied this reading to the relations between Christ and his Bride the Church, or Christ and the soul of the believer. For the rabbis and Church Fathers the "spiritual" meaning is inherent in the text; to read it as "carnal" is to miss its deeper truth. They found support in the Old Testament metaphor of God's marriage to Israel and the New Testament image of Christ as a Bridegroom[27]—though nothing in the Song itself calls for such an interpretation.

The rabbis and the Church Fathers were committed to an allegorical interpretation, moreover, because in their world the very fact of sexuality had become problematic. The rabbis associated the *yeṣer ha-raʿ* ("evil impulse") primarily with sexuality; on the other hand, they never saw

---

[25]Tosefta, Sanhedrin 12:10, as quoted in Fox, *Song of Songs*, p. 249.
[26]Mishnah, Taʿanith 4:8, as quoted in Fox, *Song of Songs*, p. 229.
[27]Isa. 54:5, Jer. 2:2, Hosea 2:14–20; Matt. 9:15, 25:1–13, John 3:29.

celibacy as an ideal, but instead advocated marriage and "the sober duty of procreation."[28] The Church Fathers were rather more extreme: Origen took Christ literally—not allegorically, alas!—and made himself a eunuch for the kingdom of heaven's sake; Jerome (d. 420) believed that a man who too ardently desires his own wife is an adulterer; Augustine (d. 430) wistfully imagined procreation in Eden, when the body obeyed the will without the vexation of lust. These men genuinely believed that in reading the text allegorically they were serving a higher purpose. They sought to spiritualize the Song, to purge its mortal grossness, the way some Greek philosophers interpreted away the carnality of the Homeric gods, or Philo converted the legends of Genesis into a series of philosophical and moral truths. This kind of exegesis requires considerable ingenuity and linguistic acrobatics, and some of its more extravagant "findings" now seem very curious: the Shulamite's two breasts as Moses and Aaron, or the Old and New testaments; her navel as the Great Sanhedrin or the order of holy preachers.

Allegories that reconstructed the intimate passion of the lovers as political or religious history now seem particularly misconceived. The Targum, a seventh-century paraphrase in Aramaic, saw in the Song an account of God's relations with Israel from the Exodus till the coming of the Messiah. Luther read it as Solomon's thanksgiving to God for his divinely ordained and peaceful kingdom; one twentieth-century exegete read it as an Essene manifesto, with the Pharisees playing the role of watchmen. And as recently as 1992 a Jesuit theologian wrote a commentary arguing that the Song is "a text in code" about "the restoration of the Davidic monarchy in Judah after the exile." A major discovery of his is a "hitherto unsuspected" meaning of the word "love." Commentators have invariably understood this word to refer to the affection between the lovers, a reading he finds "reductionist" and "sentimental." On the basis of his study of the treaty literature of the ancient Near East, he concludes that "love" is a technical term for the sociopolitical alliance between the house of David and the Jewish community.[29] One cannot help thinking of those learned, old, respectable scholars in Yeats's poem who "shuffle" and "cough in ink" as they annotate the lines of the young Catullus.

[28]David Biale, *Eros and the Jews: From Biblical Israel to Contemporary America* (New York: Basic Books, 1992), pp. 40, 43–44.
[29]Luis Stadelmann, *Love and Politics: A New Commentary on the Song of Songs* (New York: Paulist Press, 1992), pp. 2, 16, 23.

In the abundance and generosity of the Song, a lily is a lily is a woman's body is a man's lips is a field of desire. The allegorists, intent on delivering a spiritual equivalent for every last physical detail, read the Song as if they were decoding a cryptogram. From their perspective, of course, they were not imposing an arbitrary reading but searching out the hidden soul of the text. The allegorical interpretation now seems to us constrained and often absurd, but it may well have played a vital role in safeguarding the text. When we remember how many great works of antiquity have been lost—the poems of Sappho, for example, have come down to us only in fragments—we must be grateful for the protective wrap of allegory, if indeed it helped to preserve the Song intact.

The Song fared better at the hands of the mystics, Jewish and Christian, who honored its literal meaning as symbolic of the human longing for union with God. The *Zohar* (a mystical commentary on the Pentateuch written in the late thirteenth century) speculated about intercourse between the male and female aspects of God, believing that this could actually be influenced by the way in which human sexual relations were conducted; for this exalted purpose, the Cabbalists were encouraged to have intercourse with their wives on Sabbath eve.[30] Christian mystics like Bernard of Clairvaux in the twelfth century, or St. Teresa of Avila and the poet St. John of the Cross in the sixteenth, contemplating the love of God and the soul, found in the Song a source and inspiration for their ecstatic spirituality. St. Bernard, who wrote eighty-six sermons on the first two chapters of the Song, set the tone: "O strong and burning love, O love urgent and impetuous, which does not allow me to think of anything but you. . . . You laugh at all considerations of fitness, reason, modesty and prudence, and tread them underfoot."[31] The mystics read the Song allegorically, to be sure, but they remained true to its intensity and passion, its emotional power.

All along, there were those who favored a literal interpretation, though they had to pay dearly for their views. Theodore, Bishop of Mopsuestia (d. 429), who read the Song as a poem by Solomon in defense of his marriage to Pharaoh's daughter, was condemned in his own day, and again after his death by the Second Council of Constantinople in 553—sufficient deterrent for any commentator with

[30]Gershom Scholem, *Major Trends in Jewish Mysticism* (1941; 3d rev. ed., New York: Schocken Books, 1961), pp. 225–35; Biale, *Eros and the Jews*, pp. 109–13.

[31]"Sermon 79," in *Bernard of Clairvaux: On the Song of Songs*, trans. Irene Edmonds, Cistercian Fathers Series, no. 40 (Kalamazoo, Mich.: Cistercian Publications, 1980), p. 137.

like inclinations. Among the Protestant Reformers, the humanist and Bible translator Sebastian Castellio considered the Song a "lascivious and obscene poem in which Solomon described his indecent amours";[32] Castellio thought it had no spiritual value and should be excluded from the canon. For this and other offenses, he was forced to leave Geneva.

As the allegorical approach lost ground at the end of the eighteenth century, Protestant exegetes began to expound the literal sense, while attempting in one way or another to defend the Song against charges of indecency. In the Victorian era, some commentators who supported the popular "dramatic theory" spun out of the poem a scenario with three principal characters: King Solomon, a beautiful country maiden, and her shepherd-lover. The King carries the maiden off to Jerusalem, and tries to convince her to exchange her humble station for a life at court, but the Shulamite, a paragon of virtue and devotion, steadfastly resists his blandishments and remains true to her rustic swain. This soap opera is embellished with a complicated plot line and a moral purpose, neither of which has any foundation in the text. One famous scholar of Semitics, the author of an influential introduction to the Old Testament, defended this interpretation—"the triumph of plighted love over the seductions of worldly magnificence"—as having "real ethical value," lending the Song "a purpose and an aim," thereby saving it from the reproach of being "purely sensuous."[33] So much for Victorian sermonizing. But even in our day there are exegetes who take an apologetic stance. Although the Song is no longer seen as the "erotic effluvia of the unchaste Oriental mind which calls a spade a spade,"[34] there are still commentators who prefer to think of the lovers as a married couple, or who declare their love unconsummated.

A new theory was advanced at the turn of the century, based on research by the Prussian consul in Damascus, who saw the Song as a collection of poems like those sung at peasant weddings in Syria. In festivities lasting for seven days, the bride and bridegroom were crowned as king and queen, and their beauty proclaimed in formal songs

[32]According to Calvin's account, quoted in Roland H. Bainton, "The Bible in the Reformation," in *The Cambridge History of the Bible: The West from the Reformation to the Present Day*, ed. S. L. Greenslade (Cambridge: Cambridge University Press, 1963), pp. 8–9.

[33]S. R. Driver, *An Introduction to the Literature of the Old Testament* (1913; reprint; Cleveland: Meridian, 1956), p. 445.

[34]Max L. Margolis, "How the Song of Songs Entered the Canon," in *The Song of Songs: A Symposium,* ed. Wilfred H. Schoff (Philadelphia: Commercial Museum, 1924), p. 9. Margolis is characterizing the views of his contemporaries in 1924.

of praise; war songs were sung, and the bride performed a sword dance. But the "wedding-week theory" doesn't really fit the details of the Song: though the young man is addressed as "king," the woman is never called a "queen"; the dance in 7:1 is not a sword dance, and apart from 3:11, the poem has nothing to do with a wedding ceremony. Still, it is conceivable that popular customs such as those in Syria may have had their analogue in ancient Israel, and may shed light on the composition of some of the Song's lyrics. And this theory at least recognized the love of ordinary mortals as the subject of the Song.

More recently, scholars have associated the Song with Near Eastern fertility rites that were celebrated with music and ecstatic poetry in Sumer from the third millennium BCE, and later adopted by the Akkadians, the Canaanites, and, some believe, the ancient Hebrews. Each spring the king and a priestess, representing Dumuzi and Inanna (Tammuz and Ishtar), would participate in this "sacred marriage rite" for the purpose of restoring life to nature.[35] Some of the images and motifs in the ancient Mesopotamian poems, detached from their original ritual context, may indeed have left their traces on the Song; an example of such an image is "Your right hand you have placed on my vulva, / Your left stroked my head."[36] But fertility, the central concern of the cultic rite, is of no concern in the Song. And since the prophets emphatically denounced the fertility rites of Israel's neighbors, it is unlikely that the Song would have found its way into the canon if it had anything to do with the copulation of the gods; human kisses were problem enough for the rabbis.

The commentaries on the Song are, as Polonius might have said, the best in the world, whether literal, philosophical, ecclesiastical, allegorical-historical, comical-allegorical, or tragicomical-mystical-eschatological. They define the subject of the Song variously as the love of God and Israel, Christ and the Church, or Christ and the believer's soul; the chaste love of the Virgin Mary; the marriage of Solomon and Pharaoh's daughter, or of the active and the passive intellect; the discourse of Solomon with Wisdom; the trials of the people of Israel; or the history

[35]The clearest explanation may be found in Samuel Noah Kramer, *The Sacred Marriage Rite: Aspects of Faith, Myth, and Ritual in Ancient Sumer* (Bloomington: Indiana University Press, 1969), pp. 49–106.

[36]Ibid., p. 105. See also the Mesopotamian clay plaque of lovers embracing in a similar posture in Diane Wolkstein and Samuel Noah Kramer, *Inanna, Queen of Heaven and Earth: Her Stories and Hymns from Sumer* (New York: Harper and Row, 1983), pp. 43, 187.

of the Church—and that's only a partial list. Commentators have praised the Song for teaching chastity, fidelity, and virtue, or denounced it as lewd and injurious to morals. Of course, every reading of the Song necessarily bears the imprint of the interpreter's time, personal outlook, and taste. But whatever its ideological bias, this voluminous scholarship has advanced the understanding of the text, and no student of the Song can afford to ignore it.

In some respects, the Song seems very accessible to readers now, more so than it has been for some two thousand years. The Shulamite, with her veil off, is a figure all of us recognize, and we find the frankness about erotic love more natural than did earlier audiences. In our day it is the innocence of the Song, its delicacy, that has the power to surprise. Perhaps that very innocence is one source of the poem's continuing attractiveness. To read the Song is to recover, through the power of art, a freshness of spirit that is now all but lost to us. The Eden story preserves a memory of wholeness and abundance from the beginning of time; the prophets look forward to a peaceable kingdom at the End of Days. The Song of Songs locates that kingdom in human love, in the habitable present, and for the space of our attention, allows us to enter it.

About the Translation

THE TRANSLATION presented here follows the Masoretic (or established) Text of the Leningrad Codex, the oldest extant manuscript of the entire Hebrew Bible (early eleventh century CE), which is reproduced in the standard editions of the *Biblia Hebraica*. We have taken into account variant readings in the major translations of antiquity—the Greek Septuagint, the Syriac Peshitta, and the Latin Vulgate—which occasionally reflect manuscript traditions differing from the Masoretic Text. Since the Masoretic Text of the Song is very reliable, we have found it necessary to emend only one verse, 6:12.

Like most contemporary translations, we print the Song as poetry (the King James Version prints it as prose). In dividing the Song into separate lyrics, we have followed the internal logic of the text as we see it, taking note of changes of speaker or scene; the grapevine ornament marks the beginning of each new lyric. We sometimes differ from other translators in determining where one poem ends and another begins. For example, we separate 3:6 from 3:7–11 because, contrary to what is generally assumed, 3:6 is not a question, and 3:7 not an answer. Line breaks and stanza divisions reflect our understanding of the poem and our judgments about the demands of English verse. The Hebrew and English are presented on facing pages, the Hebrew in lines of verse corresponding to the English, along with chapter and verse numbers, as a help to the reader who wishes to compare our translation with the original or with other translations. The Hebrew includes the traditional cantillation marks.

For the sake of clarity, four typefaces are used in this translation to indicate the different speakers: roman for the young man, and italics for the young woman; boldface roman for the brothers, and boldface italics for the daughters of Jerusalem. Although there are no formal indications in the Hebrew text assigning the verses to different speakers such as one finds in many translations ("The Shulamite speaks," "The shepherd-lover replies"), the text itself often supplies clues about who is speaking. For example, the participants in a dialogue are usually identifiable because Hebrew distinguishes gender formally in the second person: *hinnak yapah* (feminine) versus *hinneka yapeh* (masculine), both of which mean "You are beautiful" (1:15–16). In some cases the identification of the speaker depends on one's interpretation of the context. Exegetes and translators therefore differ widely in assigning verses such as 2:15, 3:6, 3:7–11, 5:1b ("Feast, friends"), 6:11–12, 7:10b ("That pleases my lover") and 8:5a ("Who is that"). The reader is invited to consult the Commentary for our rationale in identifying the speakers of these verses.

Our highest priority has been fidelity to the spirit of the Hebrew text; for that reason our translation is by no means a free re-imagining of the poem. Every line in the English is based on scrupulous research, explained in detail in the Commentary. At the same time, as one would expect in a poetic translation, we have chosen to translate freely when a word-for-word rendition would have been awkward, pedantic, or untrue to the spirit of the Song. In such cases, the reader will find the literal sense recorded in the Commentary. On a few occasions we have adopted a felicitous phrasing that we admired in the King James Version, the Jewish Publication Society Bible, the New English Bible, or the translations of T. Carmi, Marcia Falk, Peter Jay, and Diane Wolkstein; such borrowings are noted in the Commentary. More frequently, however, we will be found to differ, sometimes substantially, from the commonly accepted readings.

The Song is one of the most enigmatic books in the Bible. Line by line and word by word, it is far more obscure and problematic than a reader of English might suppose, in part because it contains a higher proportion of rare locutions—the technical term is *hapax legomena*—than any other book of the Bible. A few examples, explained at greater length in the Commentary, will suggest how we went about deciphering the text.

In resolving interpretive cruxes, our practice has been to look first to the internal evidence of the Song itself. Since the Song is consistent in its language and imagery, words or expressions or grammatical constructions in one chapter often help to interpret difficulties in another. For example, the notion of "spreading" implied in *repidato* (3:10) elucidates the rare verb *rapped*, which we understand as "to make or spread a bed" (2:5). Similarly, the notion of height implied in *dagul* "towering" (5:10) suggests a possible meaning for *nidgalot*, literally "the elevated ones" (6:4,10), which we interpret as "stars."

As a second step, we turned to other books of the Bible for help. A crucial instance is the word *dodim*, a comprehensive term for lovemaking, including kisses and caresses as well as intercourse. This meaning could not be determined on the basis of the Song alone. However, the word occurs three other times in the Bible, in each case referring to sexual love. In Proverbs 7:18 an adulterous woman invites a young man: "Come, let us drink our fill of *dodim* [*nirveh dodim*], let us make love all night long, for my husband is not at home." This sense of the word is found also in Ezekiel 16:7–8, "Your breasts were well-formed. . . . I saw that you had reached the age of lovemaking [*'et dodim*]," and 23:17, "They came to her into the bed of love [*miškab dodim*] and defiled her with their lust." Given these uses of *dodim*, we can be quite certain that the word also refers to sexual love in the Song—something a reader would not know from most translations, which render it simply as "love."

An example that has a significant bearing on our view of the Shulamite is the word *ṣammah*, which occurs three times in the Song (4:1,3; 6:7); this has been translated either as "hair" or "veil." Some medieval Jewish commentators understood the word as "hair" (the King James Version, accordingly, has "locks"), but the reading "veil," which appeared as early as the Septuagint, made its way into most modern versions. Again, the meaning of *ṣammah* cannot be established on the basis of its occurrences in the Song alone. But the word is found once more in the Bible, in a passage of Isaiah which proves to be decisive. There, in a series of sarcastic imperatives, the prophet tells the Virgin Daughter of Babylon that she will have to bare parts of her body in public, exposing herself to shame:

> Take the millstones, and grind meal:
> uncover thy locks [*galli ṣammatēk*];
> make bare the leg, uncover the thigh [*galli šok*], . . .
> Thy nakedness shall be uncovered,
> yea, thy shame shall be seen.
>
> (Isa. 47:2–3, King James Version)

In this passage, "thigh" and *ṣammah* are both governed by the same verb, *galli* ("lay bare," not "remove"). *Galli šoq* means "lay bare [your] thigh" (obviously not "remove your thigh"!), and therefore *galli ṣammatēk* can only mean "lay bare your *ṣammah*." This verse in Isaiah clearly tilts the scales in favor of the meaning "hair." One can understand why "veil" was adopted by translators in earlier centuries: a Shulamite who hides her seductive charms with a veil, as befits a chaste maiden of Israel, best served the apologetic approach to the Song—what may be called the "pious bias" in biblical exegesis.[1] It is surprising, however, that the Shulamite still remains veiled in most contemporary versions of the Song, which are not governed by that bias. But as so often in the history of translation, a misreading, once established, tends to be perpetuated in version after version.

Only after carefully weighing the internal biblical evidence did we consider that of the surrounding cultures. For example, the straightforward Hebrew meaning of *diglo ʿalay ʾahābah* in 2:4 is "his flag over me is love." We consider this an exuberant metaphoric expression of the Shulamite's delight in the young man's love. There is no need to resort to Akkadian *diglu* "glance, intent," from *dagālu* "to look," and to explain this as "his intent towards me is love," as some scholars have done. It isn't likely that biblical Hebrew would have borrowed such a basic verb as "to look," for which it has its own words (*raʾah, hibbiṭ*). Finding a verbal root in a cognate language is not in itself a solution to a problem in the text; the field of Semitic languages is filled with roots, not every one worth digging up. To our thinking, the traditional Jewish principle of exegesis from within the biblical corpus (*nidrešet torah mi-tok ʿaṣmah*) is often methodologically more sound than the hasty resort to extrabiblical sources.

Readers tend to associate interpretive difficulties primarily with obscure words, but much of the meaning of a text is encoded in the inflections of a language: the moods and tenses of verbs, prefixes and suffixes, definite or indefinite articles, prepositions, and plural forms. Mistranslations occur when their specific functions are overlooked or edited out in unjustified emendations. It is best to proceed from the assumption that every such nuance is motivated and meaningful. For example, the tense of the verbs in 5:1 is crucial to the sense of the passage: "I have come [*baʾti*] into my garden, I have gathered [*ʾariti*] my myrrh, I have eaten [*ʾakalti*], I have drunk [*šatiti*]." The perfect tense here implies a completed action. Translations that resort to a noncommittal present tense ("I come, I gather, I eat, I drink"), or an infinitive construction ("I have come . . . to eat"), downplay the sexual implications of the image, if not by design then at least in effect.

There is no reason to ignore or explain away the possessive suffix of *susati* in 1:9, as exegetes have done for centuries. Although a straight-

---

[1] For another example of the "pious bias" in Bible exegesis, see Ariel Bloch, "Questioning God's Omnipotence in the Bible: A Linguistic Case Study," in *Semitic Studies in Honor of Wolf Leslau*, ed. Alan S. Kaye (Wiesbaden: Otto Harrassowitz, 1991), vol. 1, pp. 174–88.

forward reading of *susati* yields "my mare," the word has usually been translated with the indefinite article ("a mare"), and sometimes even as a collective noun ("my cavalry"). Neither reading is tenable on linguistic grounds. It may be that the erotic connotations of the image prompted the pious translators and exegetes to avoid the possessive suffix—or so at least it seems, since they certainly had no problem translating *yonati* in 2:14, which has the same syntax, as "my dove." Another reading that ought to be taken at face value is the plural *bateynu* ("our houses," 1:17); there is no need to "correct" it to "our house," as the King James and other versions have done. We read this as a metaphorical expression for the places in the countryside where the lovers meet to make love, and we translate the previous line, "Wherever we lie / Our bed is green." Similarly, *har'ini 'et mar'ayik* (literally "let me see your sights," 2:14) is usually rendered "let me see your face." We believe the plural form is intended, and adds a nuance worth preserving: "Let me see all of you, from every side."

In a poetic translation, tone, rhythm, and sound are naturally of crucial importance. Since the Song was almost certainly intended to be recited or sung, we have paid particular attention to the music of the poem, which is rich with assonance and alliteration, as lines like the following may suggest:

> *Nopet tiṭṭopnah śiptotayik kallah,*
> *debaš ve-ḥalab taḥat lešonek,*
> *ve-reaḥ śalmotayik ke-reaḥ lebanon.* (4: 11)

> *Keparim 'im neradim,*
> *nerd ve-karkom, qaneh ve-qinnamon,*
> *'im kol 'aṣey lebonah.* (4:13–14)

Any modern translator of the Song must acknowledge the lofty achievement of the King James Version (1611). With its rich textures and resounding cadences, the King James Version's Song is magnificent English poetry, justly beloved by generations of readers. Nonetheless, significant advances in biblical scholarship during the past four centuries—not to speak of the past four decades—have shown many of its readings to be in error, including some of the best-known verses, such as "Stay me with flagons, comfort me with apples" (2:5) or "terrible as an army with banners" (6:10). And its language is often dated, as in "I am sick of love" (2:5) or "My beloved put in his hand by the hole of the door, and my bowels were moved for him" (5:4).

Taken out of its accustomed liturgical context and read as a work of art, the Song becomes a new poem, just as a painting or statue in a church looks entirely different when displayed in a secular setting. The heightened diction of the King James Version, already somewhat archaic in the seventeenth century, was conceived for liturgical purposes, and would be inappropriate in a contemporary translation. One of the major challenges facing a translator today is to find the proper register in English, neither too formal and stylized nor too breezy and colloquial—language that is fresh and urgent and passionate, and at the same time dignified. Just as earlier interpretations typically erred on the side of prudishness, contemporary translations (perhaps to atone for centuries of exegetical evasiveness) sometimes verge on crudeness, as in a recent translation by a distinguished scholar: "Your vulva [is] a rounded crater; / May it never lack punch!" (7:3) This verse alone, with its three howlers, illustrates how important it is for a translator to be sensitive to levels of style. The word *šorerek* means "navel," not "vulva"—and besides, the anatomical term "vulva" would be out of place in the delicately allusive language of the Song. There is a difference between sex and eros, as the poet of the Song is well aware. A translation of the Song ought to be informed by this distinction.

Translating an ancient text is in some ways analogous to the process of restoring a work of art that has been dulled by time. Not long ago, a team of conservators examined the frescoes on the ceiling of the Sistine Chapel using infrared light to penetrate the surface, and then, with meticulous care, set about removing five centuries of grime, soot, smoke, and old varnish. The work of the conservators revealed unexpectedly brilliant colors, hues of turquoise and orange that seemed quite unlike Michelangelo—that is, unlike the Michelangelo of tradition, who was thought to favor a much darker palette. Readers of this translation will discover that the colors of the Song are brighter, its music more sensuous, than they may have anticipated from other versions. Those charms of the Song are not our invention; they belong to the pleasures of the Hebrew. Our aim has been to restore in English the passion and intensity of the original.

THE
SONG
OF
SONGS
WHICH IS
SOLOMON'S

שִׁיר הַשִּׁירִים אֲשֶׁר לִשְׁלֹמֹה

א

2 יִשָּׁקֵנִי מִנְּשִׁיקוֹת פִּיהוּ
כִּי־טוֹבִים דֹּדֶיךָ מִיָּיִן:

3 לְרֵיחַ שְׁמָנֶיךָ טוֹבִים
שֶׁמֶן תּוּרַק שְׁמֶךָ
עַל־כֵּן עֲלָמוֹת אֲהֵבוּךָ:

4 מָשְׁכֵנִי אַחֲרֶיךָ נָּרוּצָה

הֱבִיאַנִי הַמֶּלֶךְ חֲדָרָיו
נָגִילָה וְנִשְׂמְחָה בָּךְ
נַזְכִּירָה דֹדֶיךָ מִיַּיִן

מֵישָׁרִים אֲהֵבוּךָ:

44

1 2 *Kiss me, make me drunk with your kisses!*
Your sweet loving
is better than wine.

3 *You are fragrant,*
you are myrrh and aloes.
All the young women want you.

4 *Take me by the hand, let us run together!*

My lover, my king, has brought me into his chambers.
We will laugh, you and I, and count
each kiss,
better than wine.

Every one of them wants you.

5   שְׁחוֹרָה אֲנִי וְנָאוָֹה
בְּנוֹת יְרוּשָׁלָ͏ִם
כְּאָהֳלֵי קֵדָר
כִּירִיעוֹת שְׁלֹמֹה:

6   אַל־תִּרְאֻנִי שֶׁאֲנִי שְׁחַרְחֹרֶת
שֶׁשְּׁזָפַתְנִי הַשָּׁמֶשׁ

בְּנֵי אִמִּי נִחֲרוּ־בִי
שָׂמֻנִי נֹטֵרָה אֶת־הַכְּרָמִים
כַּרְמִי שֶׁלִּי לֹא נָטָרְתִּי:

1 5   *I am dark, daughters of Jerusalem,*
and I am beautiful!
Dark as the tents of Kedar, lavish
as Solomon's tapestries.

6   *Do not see me only as dark:*
the sun has stared at me.

My brothers were angry with me,
they made me guard the vineyards.
I have not guarded my own.

א

7 הַגִּידָה לִּי שֶׁאָהֲבָה נַפְשִׁי
אֵיכָה תִרְעֶה
אֵיכָה תַּרְבִּיץ בַּצָּהֳרָיִם
שַׁלָּמָה אֶהְיֶה כְּעֹטְיָה
עַל עֶדְרֵי חֲבֵרֶיךָ׃

8 אִם־לֹא תֵדְעִי לָךְ
הַיָּפָה בַּנָּשִׁים
צְאִי־לָךְ בְּעִקְבֵי הַצֹּאן
וּרְעִי אֶת־גְּדִיֹּתַיִךְ
עַל מִשְׁכְּנוֹת הָרֹעִים׃

1 7 *Tell me, my only love,*
where do you pasture your sheep,
where will you let them rest
in the heat of noon?
Why should I lose my way among the flocks
of your companions?

8 Loveliest of women,
if you lose your way,
follow in the tracks of the sheep,
graze your goats in the shade
of the shepherds' tents.

א

9   לְסֻסָתִי֙ בְּרִכְבֵ֣י פַרְעֹ֔ה
דִּמִּיתִ֖יךְ רַעְיָתִֽי׃

10   נָאו֤וּ לְחָיַ֙יִךְ֙ בַּתֹּרִ֔ים
צַוָּארֵ֖ךְ בַּחֲרוּזִֽים׃

11   תּוֹרֵ֤י זָהָב֙ נַעֲשֶׂה־לָּ֔ךְ
עִ֖ם נְקֻדּ֥וֹת הַכָּֽסֶף׃

1 9   My love, I dreamed of you
as a mare, my very own,
among Pharaoh's chariots.

    10   Your cheekbones,
those looped earrings,
that string of beads at your throat!

    11   I will make you golden earrings
with silver filigree.

א

12 עַד־שֶׁהַמֶּלֶךְ בִּמְסִבּוֹ
נִרְדִּי נָתַן רֵיחוֹ׃

13 צְרוֹר הַמֹּר ׀ דּוֹדִי לִי
בֵּין שָׁדַי יָלִין׃

14 אֶשְׁכֹּל הַכֹּפֶר ׀ דּוֹדִי לִי
בְּכַרְמֵי עֵין גֶּדִי׃

15 הִנָּךְ יָפָה רַעְיָתִי
הִנָּךְ יָפָה
עֵינַיִךְ יוֹנִים׃

16 הִנְּךָ יָפֶה דוֹדִי
אַף נָעִים
אַף־עַרְשֵׂנוּ רַעֲנָנָה׃

17 קֹרוֹת בָּתֵּינוּ אֲרָזִים
רַהִיטֵנוּ בְּרוֹתִים׃

1 12   *My king lay down beside me*
and my fragrance
wakened the night.

13   *All night between my breasts*
my love is a cluster of myrrh,
14   *a sheaf of henna blossoms*
in the vineyards of Ein Gedi.

15   And you, my beloved,
how beautiful you are!
Your eyes are doves.

16   *You are beautiful, my king,*
and gentle. Wherever we lie
our bed is green.
17   *Our roofbeams are cedar,*
our rafters fir.

1   אֲנִי חֲבַצֶּלֶת הַשָּׁרֹון
שֹׁושַׁנַּת הָעֲמָקִים:

2   כְּשֹׁושַׁנָּה בֵּין הַחֹוחִים
כֵּן רַעְיָתִי בֵּין הַבָּנֹות:

3   כְּתַפּוּחַ בַּעֲצֵי הַיַּעַר
כֵּן דֹּודִי בֵּין הַבָּנִים
בְּצִלֹּו חִמַּדְתִּי וְיָשַׁבְתִּי
וּפִרְיֹו מָתֹוק לְחִכִּי:

2 1   *I am the rose of Sharon,*
          the wild lily of the valleys.

    2   Like a lily in a field
          of thistles,
          such is my love
          among the young women.

    3   *And my beloved among the young men*
          is a branching apricot tree in the wood.
          In that shade I have often lingered,
          tasting the fruit.

ב

4 הֱבִיאַ֙נִי֙ אֶל־בֵּ֣ית הַיַּ֔יִן
וְדִגְל֥וֹ עָלַ֖י אַהֲבָֽה׃

5 סַמְּכ֙וּנִי֙ בָּֽאֲשִׁישׁ֔וֹת
רַפְּד֖וּנִי בַּתַּפּוּחִ֑ים
כִּי־חוֹלַ֥ת אַהֲבָ֖ה אָֽנִי׃

6 שְׂמֹאלוֹ֙ תַּ֣חַת לְרֹאשִׁ֔י
וִֽימִינ֖וֹ תְּחַבְּקֵֽנִי׃

7 הִשְׁבַּ֙עְתִּי אֶתְכֶ֜ם בְּנ֤וֹת יְרוּשָׁלַ֙͏ִם֙
בִּצְבָא֔וֹת א֖וֹ בְּאַיְל֣וֹת הַשָּׂדֶ֑ה
אִם־תָּעִ֧ירוּ ׀ וְֽאִם־תְּע֥וֹרְר֛וּ אֶת־הָאַהֲבָ֖ה
עַ֥ד שֶׁתֶּחְפָּֽץ׃

2 4 *Now he has brought me to the house of wine*
and his flag over me is love.

5 *Let me lie among vine blossoms,*
in a bed of apricots!
I am in the fever of love.

6 *His left hand beneath my head,*
his right arm
holding me close.

7 *Daughters of Jerusalem, swear to me*
by the gazelles, by the deer in the field,
that you will never awaken love
until it is ripe.

ב

8 קוֹל דּוֹדִי הִנֵּה־זֶה בָּא
מְדַלֵּג עַל־הֶהָרִים
מְקַפֵּץ עַל־הַגְּבָעוֹת:

9 דּוֹמֶה דוֹדִי לִצְבִי אוֹ לְעֹפֶר הָאַיָּלִים
הִנֵּה־זֶה עוֹמֵד אַחַר כָּתְלֵנוּ
מַשְׁגִּיחַ מִן־הַחַלֹּנוֹת
מֵצִיץ מִן־הַחֲרַכִּים:

10 עָנָה דוֹדִי וְאָמַר לִי
קוּמִי לָךְ רַעְיָתִי יָפָתִי
וּלְכִי־לָךְ:

11 כִּי־הִנֵּה הַסְּתָו עָבָר
הַגֶּשֶׁם חָלַף הָלַךְ לוֹ:

12 הַנִּצָּנִים נִרְאוּ בָאָרֶץ
עֵת הַזָּמִיר הִגִּיעַ
וְקוֹל הַתּוֹר נִשְׁמַע בְּאַרְצֵנוּ:

13 הַתְּאֵנָה חָנְטָה פַגֶּיהָ
וְהַגְּפָנִים | סְמָדַר נָתְנוּ רֵיחַ
קוּמִי לָךְ רַעְיָתִי יָפָתִי
וּלְכִי־לָךְ:

2 8   *The voice of my love: listen!*
bounding over the mountains
toward me, across the hills.

9   *My love is a gazelle, a wild stag.*
There he stands on the other side
of our wall, gazing
between the stones.

10   *And he calls to me:*
Hurry, my love, my friend,
and come away!

11   Look, winter is over,
the rains are done,

12   wildflowers spring up in the fields.
Now is the time of the nightingale.
In every meadow you hear
the song of the turtledove.

13   The fig tree has sweetened
its new green fruit
and the young budded vines smell spicy.
Hurry, my love, my friend
come away.

יוֹנָתִ֞י בְּחַגְוֵ֣י הַסֶּ֗לַע
בְּסֵ֙תֶר֙ הַמַּדְרֵגָ֔ה
הַרְאִ֙ינִי֙ אֶת־מַרְאַ֔יִךְ
הַשְׁמִיעִ֙ינִי֙ אֶת־קוֹלֵ֑ךְ
כִּי־קוֹלֵ֥ךְ עָרֵ֖ב
וּמַרְאֵ֥יךְ נָאוֶֽה׃

2 14   My dove in the clefts of the rock,
in the shadow of the cliff,
let me see you, all of you!
Let me hear your voice,
your delicious song.
I love to look at you.

ב 15 אֶחֱזוּ־לָנוּ שׁוּעָלִים
שׁוּעָלִים קְטַנִּים
מְחַבְּלִים כְּרָמִים
וּכְרָמֵינוּ סְמָדַר:

2 **15** **Catch us the foxes,
the quick little foxes
that raid our vineyards
now, when the vines are in blossom.**

ב 16 דּוֹדִי לִי וַאֲנִי לוֹ
הָרֹעֶה בַּשּׁוֹשַׁנִּים:

17 עַד שֶׁיָּפוּחַ הַיּוֹם
וְנָסוּ הַצְּלָלִים
סֹב דְּמֵה־לְךָ דוֹדִי לִצְבִי
אוֹ לְעֹפֶר הָאַיָּלִים
עַל־הָרֵי בָתֶר:

2 16 *My beloved is mine and I am his.*
He feasts
in a field of lilies.

17 *Before day breathes,*
before the shadows of night are gone,
run away, my love!
Be like a gazelle, a wild stag
on the jagged mountains.

עַל־מִשְׁכָּבִי֙ בַּלֵּיל֔וֹת

ג

1

בִּקַּ֗שְׁתִּי אֵ֚ת שֶׁאָהֲבָ֣ה נַפְשִׁ֔י

בִּקַּשְׁתִּ֖יו וְלֹ֥א מְצָאתִֽיו׃

אָק֨וּמָה נָּ֜א וַאֲסוֹבְבָ֣ה בָעִ֗יר

2

בַּשְּׁוָקִים֙ וּבָ֣רְחֹב֔וֹת

אֲבַקְשָׁ֕ה אֵ֥ת שֶׁאָהֲבָ֖ה נַפְשִׁ֑י

בִּקַּשְׁתִּ֖יו וְלֹ֥א מְצָאתִֽיו׃

מְצָא֙וּנִי֙ הַשֹּׁ֣מְרִ֔ים

3

הַסֹּבְבִ֖ים בָּעִ֑יר

אֵ֛ת שֶׁאָהֲבָ֥ה נַפְשִׁ֖י רְאִיתֶֽם׃

כִּמְעַט֙ שֶׁעָבַ֣רְתִּי מֵהֶ֔ם

4

עַ֣ד שֶֽׁמָּצָ֔אתִי אֵ֥ת שֶׁאָהֲבָ֖ה נַפְשִׁ֑י

אֲחַזְתִּיו֙ וְלֹ֣א אַרְפֶּ֔נּוּ

עַד־שֶׁהֲבֵיאתִיו֙ אֶל־בֵּ֣ית אִמִּ֔י

וְאֶל־חֶ֖דֶר הוֹרָתִֽי׃

הִשְׁבַּ֨עְתִּי אֶתְכֶ֜ם בְּנ֤וֹת יְרוּשָׁלִַ֙ם֙

5

בִּצְבָא֔וֹת א֖וֹ בְּאַיְל֣וֹת הַשָּׂדֶ֑ה

אִם־תָּעִ֧ירוּ ׀ וְאִם־תְּע֥וֹרְר֛וּ אֶת־הָאַהֲבָ֖ה

עַ֥ד שֶׁתֶּחְפָּֽץ׃

3 1   *At night in my bed I longed*
for my only love.
I sought him, but did not find him.

2   *I must rise and go about the city,*
the narrow streets and squares, till I find
my only love.
I sought him everywhere
but I could not find him.

3   *Then the watchmen found me*
as they went about the city.
"Have you seen him? Have you seen
the one I love?"

4   *I had just passed them when I found*
my only love.
I held him, I would not let him go
until I brought him to my mother's house,
into my mother's room.

5   *Daughters of Jerusalem, swear to me*
by the gazelles, by the deer in the field,
that you will never awaken love
until it is ripe.

ג 6 מִי זֹאת עֹלָה֙ מִן־הַמִּדְבָּ֔ר
כְּתִֽימֲר֖וֹת עָשָׁ֑ן
מְקֻטֶּ֤רֶת מוֹר֙ וּלְבוֹנָ֔ה
מִכֹּ֖ל אַבְקַ֥ת רוֹכֵֽל׃

3 6 *Who is that rising from the desert*
like a pillar of smoke,
more fragrant with myrrh and frankincense
than all the spices of the merchant!

ג

7 הִנֵּה מִטָּתוֹ שֶׁלִּשְׁלֹמֹה
שִׁשִּׁים גִּבֹּרִים סָבִיב לָהּ
מִגִּבֹּרֵי יִשְׂרָאֵל:

8 כֻּלָּם אֲחֻזֵי חֶרֶב מְלֻמְּדֵי מִלְחָמָה
אִישׁ חַרְבּוֹ עַל-יְרֵכוֹ
מִפַּחַד בַּלֵּילוֹת:

9 אַפִּרְיוֹן עָשָׂה לוֹ הַמֶּלֶךְ שְׁלֹמֹה
מֵעֲצֵי הַלְּבָנוֹן:

10 עַמּוּדָיו עָשָׂה כֶסֶף
רְפִידָתוֹ זָהָב
מֶרְכָּבוֹ אַרְגָּמָן
תּוֹכוֹ רָצוּף אַהֲבָה
מִבְּנוֹת יְרוּשָׁלָ͏ִם:

11 צְאֶינָה | וּרְאֶינָה בְּנוֹת צִיּוֹן
בַּמֶּלֶךְ שְׁלֹמֹה
בָּעֲטָרָה שֶׁעִטְּרָה-לּוֹ אִמּוֹ
בְּיוֹם חֲתֻנָּתוֹ
וּבְיוֹם שִׂמְחַת לִבּוֹ:

3 7 *Oh the splendors of King Solomon!*
The bravest of Israel surround his bed,
threescore warriors,
8 *each of them skilled in battle,*
each with his sword on his thigh
against the terror of night.

9 *King Solomon built a pavilion*
from the cedars of Lebanon.
10 *Its pillars he made of silver,*
cushions of gold,
couches of purple linen,
and the daughters of Jerusalem
paved it with love.

11 *Come out, O daughters of Zion,*
and gaze at Solomon the King!
See the crown his mother set on his head
on the day of his wedding,
the day of his heart's great joy.

ד

1 הִנָּךְ יָפָה רַעְיָתִי
הִנָּךְ יָפָה
עֵינַיִךְ יוֹנִים מִבַּעַד לְצַמָּתֵךְ

שַׂעְרֵךְ כְּעֵדֶר הָעִזִּים
שֶׁגָּלְשׁוּ מֵהַר גִּלְעָד:

2 שִׁנַּיִךְ כְּעֵדֶר הַקְּצוּבוֹת
שֶׁעָלוּ מִן־הָרַחְצָה
שֶׁכֻּלָּם מַתְאִימוֹת
וְשַׁכֻּלָה אֵין בָּהֶם:

3 כְּחוּט הַשָּׁנִי שִׂפְתוֹתַיִךְ
וּמִדְבָּרֵךְ נָאוֶה

כְּפֶלַח הָרִמּוֹן רַקָּתֵךְ
מִבַּעַד לְצַמָּתֵךְ:

4 כְּמִגְדַּל דָּוִיד צַוָּארֵךְ
בָּנוּי לְתַלְפִּיּוֹת
אֶלֶף הַמָּגֵן תָּלוּי עָלָיו
כֹּל שִׁלְטֵי הַגִּבֹּרִים:

4 1　How beautiful you are, my love,
my friend! The doves of your eyes
looking out
from the thicket of your hair.

Your hair
like a flock of goats
bounding down Mount Gilead.

2　Your teeth white ewes,
all alike,
that come up fresh from the pond.

3　A crimson ribbon your lips—
how I listen for your voice!

The curve of your cheek
a pomegranate
in the thicket of your hair.

4　Your neck is a tower of David
raised in splendor,
a thousand bucklers hang upon it,
all the shields of the warriors.

ד 5 שְׁנֵי שָׁדַיִךְ כִּשְׁנֵי עֳפָרִים
         תְּאוֹמֵי צְבִיָּה
         הָרֹעִים בַּשּׁוֹשַׁנִּים:

    6 עַד שֶׁיָּפוּחַ הַיּוֹם
         וְנָסוּ הַצְּלָלִים
         אֵלֶךְ לִי אֶל־הַר הַמּוֹר
         וְאֶל־גִּבְעַת הַלְּבוֹנָה:

    7 כֻּלָּךְ יָפָה רַעְיָתִי
         וּמוּם אֵין בָּךְ:

4 5   Your breasts are two fawns,
twins of a gazelle,
grazing in a field of lilies.

6   Before day breathes,
before the shadows of night are gone,
I will hurry to the mountain of myrrh,
the hill of frankincense.

7   You are all beautiful, my love,
my perfect one.

8 אִתִּי מִלְּבָנוֹן כַּלָּה
אִתִּי מִלְּבָנוֹן תָּבוֹאִי
תָּשׁוּרִי | מֵרֹאשׁ אֲמָנָה
מֵרֹאשׁ שְׂנִיר וְחֶרְמוֹן
מִמְּעֹנוֹת אֲרָיוֹת
מֵהַרְרֵי נְמֵרִים:

9 לִבַּבְתִּנִי אֲחֹתִי כַלָּה
לִבַּבְתִּנִי בְּאַחַת מֵעֵינַיִךְ
בְּאַחַד עֲנָק מִצַּוְּרֹנָיִךְ:

10 מַה־יָּפוּ דֹדַיִךְ
אֲחֹתִי כַלָּה
מַה־טֹּבוּ דֹדַיִךְ מִיַּיִן
וְרֵיחַ שְׁמָנַיִךְ מִכָּל־בְּשָׂמִים:

11 נֹפֶת תִּטֹּפְנָה שִׂפְתוֹתַיִךְ כַּלָּה
דְּבַשׁ וְחָלָב תַּחַת לְשׁוֹנֵךְ
וְרֵיחַ שַׂלְמֹתַיִךְ כְּרֵיחַ לְבָנוֹן:

4 8   Oh come with me, my bride,
come down with me from Lebanon.
Look down from the peak of Amana,
look down from Senir and Hermon,
from the mountains of the leopards,
the lions' dens.

9   You have ravished my heart,
my sister, my bride,
ravished me with one glance of your eyes,
one link of your necklace.

10   And oh, your sweet loving,
my sister, my bride.
The wine of your kisses, the spice
of your fragrant oils.

11   Your lips are honey, honey and milk
are under your tongue,
your clothes hold the scent of Lebanon.

ד

גַּן ׀ נָעוּל אֲחֹתִי כַלָּה   12
גַּל נָעוּל מַעְיָן חָתוּם:

שְׁלָחַיִךְ פַּרְדֵּס רִמּוֹנִים   13
עִם פְּרִי מְגָדִים
כְּפָרִים עִם־נְרָדִים:
נֵרְדְּ ׀ וְכַרְכֹּם קָנֶה וְקִנָּמוֹן   14
עִם כָּל־עֲצֵי לְבוֹנָה
מֹר וַאֲהָלוֹת
עִם כָּל־רָאשֵׁי בְשָׂמִים:

מַעְיַן גַּנִּים   15
בְּאֵר מַיִם חַיִּים
וְנֹזְלִים מִן־לְבָנוֹן:

4 12   An enclosed garden is my sister, my bride,
a hidden well, a sealed spring.

13   Your branches are an orchard
of pomegranate trees heavy with fruit,
flowering henna and spikenard,

14   spikenard and saffron, cane and cinnamon,
with every tree of frankincense,
myrrh and aloes,
all the rare spices.

15   You are a fountain in the garden,
a well of living waters
that stream from Lebanon.

ד 16 עוּרִי צָפוֹן וּבוֹאִי תֵימָן
הָפִיחִי גַנִּי יִזְּלוּ בְשָׂמָיו
יָבֹא דוֹדִי לְגַנּוֹ
וְיֹאכַל פְּרִי מְגָדָיו׃

ה 1 בָּאתִי לְגַנִּי אֲחֹתִי כַלָּה
אָרִיתִי מוֹרִי עִם־בְּשָׂמִי
אָכַלְתִּי יַעְרִי עִם־דִּבְשִׁי
שָׁתִיתִי יֵינִי עִם־חֲלָבִי

אִכְלוּ רֵעִים
שְׁתוּ וְשִׁכְרוּ דּוֹדִים׃

80

4 16   *Awake, north wind! O south wind, come,*
            breathe upon my garden,
            let its spices stream out.
            Let my lover come into his garden
            and taste its delicious fruit.

5 1   I have come into my garden,
            my sister, my bride,
            I have gathered my myrrh and my spices,
            I have eaten from the honeycomb,
            I have drunk the milk and the wine.

            Feast, friends, and drink
            till you are drunk with love!

ה   2   אֲנִי יְשֵׁנָה וְלִבִּי עֵר
קוֹל | דּוֹדִי דוֹפֵק

פִּתְחִי־לִי אֲחֹתִי רַעְיָתִי
יוֹנָתִי תַמָּתִי
שֶׁרֹאשִׁי נִמְלָא־טָל
קְוֻצּוֹתַי רְסִיסֵי לָיְלָה:

3   פָּשַׁטְתִּי אֶת־כֻּתָּנְתִּי
אֵיכָכָה אֶלְבָּשֶׁנָּה
רָחַצְתִּי אֶת־רַגְלַי
אֵיכָכָה אֲטַנְּפֵם:

4   דּוֹדִי שָׁלַח יָדוֹ מִן־הַחֹר
וּמֵעַי הָמוּ עָלָיו:

5   קַמְתִּי אֲנִי לִפְתֹּחַ לְדוֹדִי
וְיָדַי נָטְפוּ־מוֹר
וְאֶצְבְּעֹתַי מוֹר עֹבֵר
עַל כַּפּוֹת הַמַּנְעוּל:

5 2 *I was asleep but my heart stayed awake.*
      Listen!
      my lover knocking:

   "Open, my sister, my friend,
   my dove, my perfect one!
   My hair is wet, drenched
   with the dew of night."

   3 *"But I have taken off my clothes,*
      how can I dress again?
      I have bathed my feet,
      must I dirty them?"

   4 *My love reached in for the latch*
      and my heart
      beat wild.

   5 *I rose to open to my love,*
      my fingers wet with myrrh,
      sweet flowing myrrh
      on the doorbolt.

6 פָּתַחְתִּי אֲנִי לְדוֹדִי
וְדוֹדִי חָמַק עָבָר
נַפְשִׁי יָצְאָה בְדַבְּרוֹ

בִּקַּשְׁתִּיהוּ וְלֹא מְצָאתִיהוּ
קְרָאתִיו וְלֹא עָנָנִי:

7 מְצָאֻנִי הַשֹּׁמְרִים הַסֹּבְבִים בָּעִיר
הִכּוּנִי פְצָעוּנִי
נָשְׂאוּ אֶת־רְדִידִי מֵעָלַי
שֹׁמְרֵי הַחֹמוֹת:

8 הִשְׁבַּעְתִּי אֶתְכֶם בְּנוֹת יְרוּשָׁלָם
אִם־תִּמְצְאוּ אֶת־דּוֹדִי
מַה־תַּגִּידוּ לוֹ
שֶׁחוֹלַת אַהֲבָה אָנִי:

5 6   *I opened to my love*
but he had slipped away.
How I wanted him when he spoke!

I sought him everywhere
but could not find him.
I called his name
but he did not answer.

7   *Then the watchmen found me*
as they went about the city.
They beat me, they bruised me,
they tore the shawl from my shoulders,
those watchmen of the walls.

8   *Swear to me, daughters of Jerusalem!*
If you find him now
you must tell him
I am in the fever of love.

9 מַה־דּוֹדֵךְ מִדּוֹד
הַיָּפָה בַּנָּשִׁים
מַה־דּוֹדֵךְ מִדּוֹד
שֶׁכָּכָה הִשְׁבַּעְתָּנוּ:

10 דּוֹדִי צַח וְאָדוֹם
דָּגוּל מֵרְבָבָה:

11 רֹאשׁוֹ כֶּתֶם פָּז
קְוֻצּוֹתָיו תַּלְתַּלִּים
שְׁחֹרוֹת כָּעוֹרֵב:

12 עֵינָיו כְּיוֹנִים עַל־אֲפִיקֵי מָיִם
רֹחֲצוֹת בֶּחָלָב
יֹשְׁבוֹת עַל־מִלֵּאת:

13 לְחָיָו כַּעֲרוּגַת הַבֹּשֶׂם
מִגְדְּלוֹת מֶרְקָחִים
שִׂפְתוֹתָיו שׁוֹשַׁנִּים
נֹטְפוֹת מוֹר עֹבֵר:

5 9 *How is your lover different*
       from any other, O beautiful woman?
       Who is your lover
       that we must swear to you?

   10 *My beloved is milk and wine,*
       he towers
       above ten thousand.

   11 *His head is burnished gold,*
       the mane of his hair
       black as the raven.

   12 *His eyes like doves*
       by the rivers
       of milk and plenty.

   13 *His cheeks a bed of spices,*
       a treasure
       of precious scents, his lips
       red lilies wet with myrrh.

14 יָדָיו֙ גְּלִילֵ֣י זָהָ֔ב
מְמֻלָּאִ֖ים בַּתַּרְשִׁ֑ישׁ
מֵעָיו֙ עֶ֣שֶׁת שֵׁ֔ן
מְעֻלֶּ֖פֶת סַפִּירִֽים׃

15 שׁוֹקָיו֙ עַמּ֣וּדֵי שֵׁ֔שׁ
מְיֻסָּדִ֖ים עַל־אַדְנֵי־פָ֑ז

מַרְאֵ֙הוּ֙ כַּלְּבָנ֔וֹן
בָּח֖וּר כָּאֲרָזִֽים׃

16 חִכּוֹ֙ מַֽמְתַקִּ֔ים וְכֻלּ֖וֹ מַחֲמַדִּ֑ים

זֶ֤ה דוֹדִי֙ וְזֶ֣ה רֵעִ֔י
בְּנ֖וֹת יְרוּשָׁלָֽ͏ִם׃

5 14 *His arm a golden scepter with gems of topaz,*
his loins the ivory of thrones
inlaid with sapphire,
15 *his thighs like marble pillars*
on pedestals of gold.

Tall as Mount Lebanon,
a man like a cedar!

16 *His mouth is sweet wine, he is all delight.*

This is my beloved
and this is my friend,
O daughters of Jerusalem.

ו

אָנָה הָלַךְ דּוֹדֵךְ 1
הַיָּפָה בַּנָּשִׁים
אָנָה פָּנָה דּוֹדֵךְ
וּנְבַקְשֶׁנּוּ עִמָּךְ:

דּוֹדִי יָרַד לְגַנּוֹ 2
לַעֲרוּגוֹת הַבֹּשֶׂם
לִרְעוֹת בַּגַּנִּים וְלִלְקֹט שׁוֹשַׁנִּים:

אֲנִי לְדוֹדִי וְדוֹדִי לִי 3
הָרֹעֶה בַּשּׁוֹשַׁנִּים:

6 1   *Where has your lover gone,*
O beautiful one?
Say where he is
and we will seek him with you.

2   *My love has gone down to*
his garden, to the beds of spices,
to graze and to gather lilies.

3   *My beloved is mine and I am his.*
He feasts
in a field of lilies.

ו

4 יָפָה אַתְּ רַעְיָתִי כְּתִרְצָה
נָאוָה כִּירוּשָׁלָ͏ִם
אֲיֻמָּה כַּנִּדְגָּלוֹת:

5 הָסֵבִּי עֵינַיִךְ מִנֶּגְדִּי
שֶׁהֵם הִרְהִיבֻנִי

שַׂעְרֵךְ כְּעֵדֶר הָעִזִּים
שֶׁגָּלְשׁוּ מִן־הַגִּלְעָד:

6 שִׁנַּיִךְ כְּעֵדֶר הָרְחֵלִים
שֶׁעָלוּ מִן־הָרַחְצָה
שֶׁכֻּלָּם מַתְאִימוֹת
וְשַׁכֻּלָה אֵין בָּהֶם:

7 כְּפֶלַח הָרִמּוֹן רַקָּתֵךְ
מִבַּעַד לְצַמָּתֵךְ:

6 4   You are beautiful, my love, as Tirzah,
majestic as Jerusalem,
daunting
as the stars in their courses.

5   Your eyes! Turn them away
for they dazzle me.

Your hair is like a flock of goats
bounding down Mount Gilead.

6   Your teeth white ewes,
all alike,
that come up fresh from the pond.

7   The curve of your cheek
a pomegranate
in your thicket of hair.

8 שִׁשִּׁים הֵמָּה מְלָכוֹת
וּשְׁמֹנִים פִּילַגְשִׁים
וַעֲלָמוֹת אֵין מִסְפָּר:

9 אַחַת הִיא יוֹנָתִי תַמָּתִי
אַחַת הִיא לְאִמָּהּ
בָּרָה הִיא לְיוֹלַדְתָּהּ

רָאוּהָ בָנוֹת וַיְאַשְּׁרוּהָ
מְלָכוֹת וּפִילַגְשִׁים וַיְהַלְלוּהָ:

10 מִי־זֹאת הַנִּשְׁקָפָה כְּמוֹ־שָׁחַר
יָפָה כַלְּבָנָה
בָּרָה כַּחַמָּה
אֲיֻמָּה כַּנִּדְגָּלוֹת:

6 8 Threescore are the queens,
fourscore the king's women,
and maidens, maidens without number.

9 One alone is my dove,
my perfect, my only one,
love of her mother, light
of her mother's eyes.

Every maiden calls her happy,
queens praise her,
and all the king's women:

10 *"Who is that rising like the morning star,
clear as the moon,
bright as the blazing sun,
daunting as the stars in their courses!"*

אֶל־גִּנַּת אֱגוֹז יָרַדְתִּי ‏11
לִרְאוֹת בְּאִבֵּי הַנָּחַל
לִרְאוֹת הֲפָרְחָה הַגֶּפֶן
הֵנֵצוּ הָרִמֹּנִים:

לֹא יָדַעְתִּי נַפְשִׁי ‏12
שָׂמַתְנִי מַרְכְּבוֹת עַמִּי־נָדִיב:

6 11   Then I went down to the walnut grove
to see the new green by the brook,
to see if the vine had budded,
if the pomegranate trees were in flower.

12   And oh! before I was aware,
she sat me in the most lavish of chariots.

ז

1 שׁוּבִי שׁוּבִי הַשּׁוּלַמִּית
שׁוּבִי שׁוּבִי וְנֶחֱזֶה־בָּךְ

מַה־תֶּחֱזוּ בַּשּׁוּלַמִּית
כִּמְחֹלַת הַמַּחֲנָיִם:

2 מַה־יָּפוּ פְעָמַיִךְ בַּנְּעָלִים
בַּת־נָדִיב

חַמּוּקֵי יְרֵכַיִךְ כְּמוֹ חֲלָאִים
מַעֲשֵׂה יְדֵי אָמָּן:

3 שָׁרְרֵךְ אַגַּן הַסַּהַר
אַל־יֶחְסַר הַמָּזֶג

בִּטְנֵךְ עֲרֵמַת חִטִּים
סוּגָה בַּשּׁוֹשַׁנִּים:
4 שְׁנֵי שָׁדַיִךְ כִּשְׁנֵי עֳפָרִים
תָּאֳמֵי צְבִיָּה:

7 1 *Again, O Shulamite,*
dance again,
that we may watch you dancing!

Why do you gaze at the Shulamite
as she whirls
down the rows of dancers?

2 How graceful your steps in those sandals,
O nobleman's daughter.

The gold of your thigh
shaped by a master craftsman.

3 Your navel is the moon's
bright drinking cup.
May it brim with wine!

Your belly is a mound of wheat
edged with lilies.

4 Your breasts are two fawns,
twins of a gazelle.

5 צַוָּארֵךְ כְּמִגְדַּל הַשֵּׁן
עֵינַיִךְ בְּרֵכוֹת בְּחֶשְׁבּוֹן
עַל־שַׁעַר בַּת־רַבִּים
אַפֵּךְ כְּמִגְדַּל הַלְּבָנוֹן
צוֹפֶה פְּנֵי דַמָּשֶׂק:

6 רֹאשֵׁךְ עָלַיִךְ כַּכַּרְמֶל
וְדַלַּת רֹאשֵׁךְ כָּאַרְגָּמָן
מֶלֶךְ אָסוּר בָּרְהָטִים:

7 מַה־יָּפִית וּמַה־נָּעַמְתְּ
אַהֲבָה בַּתַּעֲנוּגִים:

7 5   Your neck is a tower of ivory.
Your eyes are pools in Heshbon, at the gates
of that city of lords.
Your proud nose the tower of Lebanon
that looks toward Damascus.

    6   Your head crowns you like Mount Carmel,
the hair of your head
like royal purple. A king
is caught in the thicket.

    7   How wonderful you are, O Love,
how much sweeter
than all other pleasures!

ז

8 זֹאת קוֹמָתֵךְ דָּמְתָה לְתָמָר
וְשָׁדַיִךְ לְאַשְׁכֹּלוֹת:

9 אָמַרְתִּי אֶעֱלֶה בְתָמָר
אֹחֲזָה בְּסַנְסִנָּיו

וְיִהְיוּ־נָא שָׁדַיִךְ כְּאֶשְׁכְּלוֹת הַגֶּפֶן
וְרֵיחַ אַפֵּךְ כַּתַּפּוּחִים:
10 וְחִכֵּךְ כְּיֵין הַטּוֹב

הוֹלֵךְ לְדוֹדִי לְמֵישָׁרִים
דּוֹבֵב שִׂפְתֵי יְשֵׁנִים:

11 אֲנִי לְדוֹדִי
וְעָלַי תְּשׁוּקָתוֹ:

7 8   That day you seemed to me a tall palm tree
and your breasts
the clusters of its fruit.

9   I said in my heart,
Let me climb into that palm tree
and take hold of its branches.

And oh, may your breasts be like clusters
of grapes on a vine, the scent
of your breath like apricots,
10   your mouth good wine—

*That pleases my lover, rousing him
even from sleep.*

11   *I am my lover's,
he longs for me,
only for me.*

ז

12 לְכָה דוֹדִי נֵצֵא הַשָּׂדֶה
נָלִינָה בַּכְּפָרִים:

13 נַשְׁכִּימָה לַכְּרָמִים
נִרְאֶה אִם־פָּרְחָה הַגֶּפֶן
פִּתַּח הַסְּמָדַר
הֵנֵצוּ הָרִמּוֹנִים

שָׁם אֶתֵּן אֶת־דֹּדַי לָךְ:

14 הַדּוּדָאִים נָתְנוּ־רֵיחַ
וְעַל־פְּתָחֵינוּ כָּל־מְגָדִים
חֲדָשִׁים גַּם־יְשָׁנִים
דּוֹדִי צָפַנְתִּי לָךְ:

7 12 *Come, my beloved,*
let us go out into the fields
and lie all night among the flowering henna.

13 *Let us go early to the vineyards*
to see if the vine has budded,
if the blossoms have opened
and the pomegranate is in flower.

There I will give you my love.

14 *The air is filled with the scent of mandrakes*
and at our doors
rare fruit of every kind, my love,
I have stored away for you.

ח 1 מִי יִתֶּנְךָ כְּאָח לִי
יוֹנֵק שְׁדֵי אִמִּי
אֶמְצָאֲךָ בַחוּץ אֶשָּׁקְךָ
גַּם לֹא־יָבֻזוּ לִי:

2 אֶנְהָגֲךָ אֲבִיאֲךָ אֶל־בֵּית אִמִּי
תְּלַמְּדֵנִי
אַשְׁקְךָ מִיַּיִן הָרֶקַח
מֵעֲסִיס רִמֹּנִי:

3 שְׂמֹאלוֹ תַּחַת רֹאשִׁי
וִימִינוֹ תְּחַבְּקֵנִי:

4 הִשְׁבַּעְתִּי אֶתְכֶם בְּנוֹת יְרוּשָׁלָ͏ִם
מַה־תָּעִירוּ ׀ וּמַה־תְּעֹרְרוּ אֶת־הָאַהֲבָה
עַד־שֶׁתֶּחְפָּץ:

8 1 *If only you were a brother*
who nursed at my mother's breast!
I would kiss you in the streets
and no one would scorn me.

 2 *I would bring you to the house of my mother*
and she would teach me.
I would give you spiced wine to drink,
my pomegranate wine.

 3 *His left hand beneath my head,*
his right arm
holding me close.

 4 *Daughters of Jerusalem, swear to me*
that you will never awaken love
until it is ripe.

מִי זֹאת עֹלָה מִן־הַמִּדְבָּר 5

מִתְרַפֶּקֶת עַל־דּוֹדָהּ

8 ₅ *Who is that
rising from the desert,
her head on her lover's shoulder!*

ח   5   תַּחַת הַתַּפּוּחַ עוֹרַרְתִּיךָ
שָׁמָּה חִבְּלַתְךָ אִמֶּךָ
שָׁמָּה חִבְּלָה יְלָדַתְךָ׃

6   שִׂימֵנִי כַחוֹתָם עַל־לִבֶּךָ
כַּחוֹתָם עַל־זְרוֹעֶךָ

כִּי־עַזָּה כַמָּוֶת אַהֲבָה
קָשָׁה כִשְׁאוֹל קִנְאָה
רְשָׁפֶיהָ רִשְׁפֵּי אֵשׁ
שַׁלְהֶבֶתְיָה׃

7   מַיִם רַבִּים לֹא יוּכְלוּ
לְכַבּוֹת אֶת־הָאַהֲבָה
וּנְהָרוֹת לֹא יִשְׁטְפוּהָ

אִם־יִתֵּן אִישׁ אֶת־כָּל־הוֹן בֵּיתוֹ
בָּאַהֲבָה
בּוֹז יָבוּזוּ לוֹ׃

8 5 *There, beneath the apricot tree,*
your mother conceived you,
there you were born.
In that very place, I awakened you.

6 *Bind me as a seal upon your heart,*
a sign upon your arm,

for love is as fierce as death,
its jealousy bitter as the grave.
Even its sparks are a raging fire,
a devouring flame.

7 *Great seas cannot extinguish love,*
no river can sweep it away.

If a man tried to buy love
with all the wealth of his house,
he would be despised.

אָחוֹת לָנוּ קְטַנָּה
וְשָׁדַיִם אֵין לָהּ
מַה־נַּעֲשֶׂה לַאֲחוֹתֵנוּ
בַּיּוֹם שֶׁיְּדֻבַּר־בָּהּ:

8 ח

אִם־חוֹמָה הִיא
נִבְנֶה עָלֶיהָ טִירַת כָּסֶף
וְאִם־דֶּלֶת הִיא
נָצוּר עָלֶיהָ לוּחַ אָרֶז:

9

אֲנִי חוֹמָה
וְשָׁדַי כַּמִּגְדָּלוֹת
אָז הָיִיתִי בְעֵינָיו
כְּמוֹצְאֵת שָׁלוֹם:

10

8 8   We have a little sister
and she has no breasts.
What shall we do for our sister
when suitors besiege her?

9   If she is a wall, we will build
a silver turret upon her.
If she is a door, we will bolt her
with beams of cedarwood.

10   *I am a wall*
and my breasts are towers.
But for my lover I am
a city of peace.

ח   11   כֶּרֶם הָיָה לִשְׁלֹמֹה
בְּבַעַל הָמוֹן
נָתַן אֶת־הַכֶּרֶם לַנֹּטְרִים
אִישׁ יָבִא בְּפִרְיוֹ אֶלֶף כָּסֶף:

     12   כַּרְמִי שֶׁלִּי לְפָנָי
הָאֶלֶף לְךָ שְׁלֹמֹה
וּמָאתַיִם לְנֹטְרִים אֶת־פִּרְיוֹ:

8 11　King Solomon had a vineyard
on the Hill of Plenty.
He gave that vineyard to watchmen
and each would earn for its fruit
one thousand pieces of silver.

12　My vineyard is all my own.
Keep your thousand, Solomon! And pay
two hundred to those
who must guard the fruit.

הַיוֹשֶׁבֶת בַּגַּנִּים 13
חֲבֵרִים מַקְשִׁיבִים לְקוֹלֵךְ
הַשְׁמִיעִינִי:

בְּרַח | דּוֹדִי 14
וּדְמֵה־לְךָ לִצְבִי אוֹ לְעֹפֶר הָאַיָּלִים
עַל הָרֵי בְשָׂמִים:

8 13 O woman in the garden,
    all our friends listen for your voice.
    Let me hear it now.

  14 *Hurry, my love! Run away,*
    my gazelle, my wild stag
    on the hills of cinnamon.

Afterword

ROBERT ALTER

T HE POETRY of the Song of Songs is an exquisite balance of ripe sensuality and delicacy of expression and feeling. In Chana Bloch's apt phrase in her introductory chapter, "In the Garden of Delights," its language is "at once voluptuous and reticent," and that is precisely the challenge for the translator. The older English renderings, beginning with the King James Version, do have their splendid moments, but they also often fudge the frank sensuality of the original, trading tresses for demure veils, as readers of this translation and commentary will discover. In the proliferation in our own age of new English versions of the Song and of the Bible as a whole, translators have had difficulties negotiating between the extremes of clunky sexual explicitness and the pastels of greeting-card poetry, which are equal if opposite violations of the original. The problem of conveying the Hebrew poet's candid yet beautifully tactful imagination of love is compounded by the sensuous concreteness and the harmonious compactness of the poet's language. The task of unpacking the meaning of the Hebrew into the bulkier syntactic and idiomatic receptacles of a modern Western language can easily lead to ambling paraphrase or shuffling prose approximations of the biblical poem. Chana and Ariel Bloch's translation, a rare conjunction of refined poetic resourcefulness and philological precision, brings us closer to the magical freshness of this ancient Hebrew love poetry than has any other English version.

Let me illustrate with three lines of verse from the first chapter (1:12–14). To indicate the difficulties of getting the Hebrew right and getting it into English poetry, let us first look at the two translations that have exerted the greatest influence in the English-speaking world, the King James Version (completed in 1611) and the Revised Standard Version (a modernization and correction of the KJV undertaken in the 1880's and further revised in 1901 and 1946–52).

> While the king sitteth at his table, my spikenard
> sendeth forth the smell thereof.

> A bundle of myrrh is my well-beloved unto me;
> he shall lie all night betwixt my breasts.
> My beloved is unto me as a cluster of camphire
> in the vineyards of En-gedi.

> While the king was on his couch,
>   my nard gave forth its fragrance.
> My beloved is to me a bag of myrrh
>   that lies between my breasts.
> My beloved is to me a cluster of henna blossoms
>   in the vineyards of En-gedi.

Compare these two time-honored versions to the Bloch translation:

> My king lay down beside me
> and my fragrance
> wakened the night.

> All night between my breasts
> my love is a cluster of myrrh,
> a sheaf of henna blossoms
> in the vineyards of Ein Gedi.

The King James Version evokes a dinner scene in which the female dining companion appears to have doused herself with an excess of perfume. The crucial Hebrew word here, *bi-msibbo,* refers to reclining either at a table or on a bed, and the KJV, in consonance with a certain disposition to dilute the sexuality of the poem, opts with patent improbability for the former meaning. The Revised Standard Version sensibly puts the king back in bed where he belongs, but fails to solve a number of other problems, beginning with the identity of the king and his relation to the female speaker whose body is fragrant with all outdoors. The "is unto me" of the KJV, a literal rendering of the single Hebrew syllable *li,* is pared down to "is to me" by the RSV, but that is still not quite English. The Hebrew idiom for the wafting of odors, *natan reyḥo,* is translated quite literally by the RSV as "gave forth its fragrance" and almost literally by the KJV as "sent forth its fragrance."

One should immediately note that the Bloch translation manages with almost a third fewer words than its two precedessors, thus conveying much of the lovely concision that is one of the hallmarks of biblical poetry. By identifying the male lover as "my king"—the Hebrew does literally say "the king"—this version makes clear that the royal designation is a lover's epithet and that the bed on which he lies is not a divan in a palace but in all likelihood one of those bucolic resting places to which the young couple repair for lovemaking. "Beside me" after "lay down" is not in the Hebrew but is unavoidably implied by the two middle lines. In both the KJV and the RSV, the lover, metaphorically miniaturized as a cluster of myrrh, merely "lies" between the Shulamite's breasts. But as Ariel Bloch rightly observes in his Commentary, the Hebrew *yalin* means "to spend the night." This denotation reinforces the suggestion of a whole night of intimate embraces and provides warrant in the Bloch translation for both the adverbial "all night" (instead of a verb, as in the Hebrew) and the little elaboration, "my fragrance / wakened the night," which solves the problem of English usage in the "sending" or "giving forth" of fragrance. Finally, the compactness and fluency of the Bloch version also owe something to its elimination of an unneeded repetition ("my love" once instead of "my beloved" twice) and its telescoping "nard" and "fragrance" into "my fragrance." The specificity of myrrh and henna is retained, but most of us would in any case not know just what sort of scent nard was. The remarkable compactness of the Hebrew original is largely the result of formal linguistic properties—pronouns and possessives, for example, are not independent words but are indicated merely by the conjugated forms of verbs and the declined form of nouns. Thus an English translation must adopt other strategies of concision, something that the Blochs do with great flair.

THE SONG OF SONGS is the great love poem of commingling—of different realms, different senses, and of the male and female bodies. The lines we have just considered offer a microcosm of this poetics of intertwined realms. The night of lovemaking, as I have suggested, probably takes place in one of the bucolic settings typical of the whole poem. But as the bodies join, inside and outside do as well. In his partner's metaphor, the lover is a sheaf of henna blossoms, but the specification that these henna blossoms are from the lush oasis of Ein Gedi creates an odd spatial displacement, leaving us a little unsure whether the blossoms are merely *from* Ein Gedi (the obviously intended meaning) or whether, metaphor exfoliating into literal landscape, that is where the lovers embrace. Elsewhere, there are abundant cross-overs from the luxuriance of the landscape to the luxuriance of the human body. Perhaps the most famous instance is the sequence from 4:1 through 5:1, which first represents the woman's body as a mountainous landscape teeming with animal life, then evokes the actual mountains of northern Israel and Lebanon from which the lover asks his beloved to come down with him, and finally once again represents the woman's body as landscape: this time, an enclosed bower ripe with fruit, moistened by a fresh-running spring that has its source in Lebanon, the water thus flowing underground from the literal landscape just mentioned to the figurative garden.

What is equally noteworthy in regard to the aim of commingling is the poet's ability to interweave the senses—implicitly in our specimen from the first chapter and quite elaborately throughout the poem. There is a clear hierarchy in the deployment of the five senses in the imagery of the poem. The primary sense for the experience of physical love is, of course, touch, but in keeping with the delicacy of expression of the Song, touch is never mentioned directly (if one excepts a rather general verb like "embrace" in 2:6), never made the explicit object of figurative elaboration. It is, however, constantly and powerfully implied, as in "All night between my breasts / my love is a cluster of myrrh," where the perfume metaphor focuses attention on the attribute of fragrance while the image of a sachet resting between breasts also beautifully suggests the intimate and pleasurable touch of flesh upon flesh. The other four senses are characteristically grouped in two pairs in the poem: sight and sound, taste and smell, although sight also appears by itself. Sight and sound have their place, but it is definitely a secondary place, because they are the senses experienced at a distance, and this is a poem of physical closeness that repeatedly creates an illusion of immediacy of sensory experience. Thus, it is when the young man is playing a game of lovers' hide-and-seek that he invokes sight and sound, weaving the two together in an elegant chiastic (seeing-hearing-hearing-seeing) structure:

> Let me see you, all of you!
> Let me hear your voice,
> your delicious song.
> I love to look at you. (2:14)

The first time sight is mentioned in the poem (1:6), it is in a negative imperative, expressing an impulse to fend off a hostile judgment by the mere—and necessarily distant—ocular observer: "Do not see me only as dark." Elsewhere, sight is prominent in the spectacular set pieces, like the vision of the royal pavilion (3:7–11) or the description of the performing Shulamite: "dance again, / that we may watch you dancing!" (7:1). These two examples, it should be noted, are both eminently public moments, not occasions of intimate union. The one fleeting instance in which sight is a vehicle of intimacy is the exchange of lovers' glances in 4:9: "You have . . . / ravished me with one glance of your eyes, / one link of your necklace."

Again and again, however, it is taste and smell that predominate, almost always implying or associated with the pleasures of touching. The poem begins with an image of taste—"Your sweet loving / is better than wine"—immediately followed by one of smell—"You are fragrant, / you are myrrh and aloes." And whether by conscious design or rightness of poetic intuition, the concluding image of the poem is a little cloud of fragrance: "Run away, / my gazelle, my wild stag / on the hills of cinnamon." In a coordinate movement of symmetry between beginning and end, the young woman's first self-representation is of the body as landscape, the "vineyard" of 1:6, and in the final cross-over between nature and body like those we have noted, she who has just likened herself to a vineyard is last seen by her lover (8:13) sitting in a garden.

The experience of fusion conveyed through the immediate senses of taste and smell is reinforced by an interfusion of sound in the closely clustered alliteration associated with this imagery. Thus, the first half of the first line of the poem ("Kiss me, make me drunk with your kisses!") sounds something like this in the Hebrew: *yiššaQEni minneŠIqot PIhu* (uppercase letters indicate the accented syllable). The *sh* phoneme (transliterated here as *š*) is then picked up three times in the next verse in the words that mean literally "oil" and "your name," *ŠEmen* and *šimKA*. Verse 4:11, a verse that again moves from taste to smell, begins with a tiny explosion of *n*'s and *f*'s (transliterated as *p̄*) and *t*'s: *NOp̄et tiṬṬOp̄nah śip̄toTAYik*—"Your lips are honey, honey and milk / are under your tongue, / your clothes hold the scent of Lebanon."

The predominant order in this pairing of the senses is first taste, then smell. This sequence would appear to run counter to a prevailing pattern of biblical poetry, in which there is a movement of rising intensity from the first half of the line to the second in utterances that are more or less semantically parallel. Perhaps this small reversal of a general pattern reflects an impulse in the language of the poem to plunge into the immediacy of love's pleasures, for which tasting or drinking or eating is a primary metaphor, whereas fragrance is less a metaphor for the thing itself than a pleasurable secondary attribute associated with it. The small sequence of 4:10 is exemplary:

And oh, your sweet loving,
my sister, my bride.
The wine of your kisses, the spice
of your fragrant oils.

The speed of the English version here, achieved by eliminating verbs, is worth noting as a nice equivalent of the always economical Hebrew. The "oh, your sweet loving," instead of the conventional "how fair is your love," at once catches the rapturous excitement of the lover and justifies the omission of verbs. But what is crucial for conveying the sensuous concreteness of the poem is the decision to render the Hebrew *dodim* as "loving"—a decorous term, like the word it translates, but with a clear sexual implication, as it has in blues lyrics—instead of a term of emotional relationship, "love." If *dodim* did not have this physically concrete meaning, it could not be repeatedly associated as it is with delectable wine, with drinking, with the honeyed sweetness of the mouth (as in the verse following the one just cited), and thus by analogy, with the sweetness of the act of love. And if the term did not suggest the gratification of physical love, it would contribute far less effectively to the brilliant pun that joins the very end of 7:13 with the first word of the next verse: "There I will give you my love [*doday*]," a promise immediately followed by the scent of *duda'im,* mandrakes, plants presumed to be aphrodisiac.

The association of taste with the pleasures of love is subtly coordinated with the interweaving of natural landscape and body that we have noted. The triple function in the poem of the pomegranate vividly illustrates this coordination. The pomegranate first appears prominently, and perhaps to modern readers a little puzzlingly, in the head-to-breast description of the young woman in the opening verses of chapter 4: "The curve of your cheek / a pomegranate / in the thicket of your hair" (4:3). (As Ariel Bloch notes in his Commentary, the precise meaning of *raqqah* is uncertain, but the term clearly refers to some part of the face: cheek, temple, or forehead.) The literal meaning of the Hebrew is "a pomegranate slice," so the image evidently suggests the section of a delicately curving contour. The purplish red of the pomegranate's exposed fruit strikes one as the wrong color for any part of the girl's face, unless she were painfully blushing or smeared with rouge, both of which would seem to be out of character. Perhaps the poet is following a procedure evident elsewhere in the poem of concentrating on one aspect of likeness between the metaphor and its referent and excluding the associations of certain other aspects of the object involved in the metaphor. But if the pomegranate is adopted as an image for the cheek chiefly because of the pleasing curve, it has also been chosen because of the gustatory association with luscious, tangy fruit. There is, moreover, a metonymic as well as a metaphoric motivation for the image, since pomegranate trees, among other flora, are within hand's reach in the natural setting through which the young woman moves (again the cross-over between landscape and body is evident). Thus, her invitation in 7:13 to her lover to come out with her to make love in the vernal countryside:

> Let us go early to the vineyards
> to see if the vine has budded,
> if the blossoms have opened
> and the pomegranate is in flower.

> There I will give you my love.

If the pomegranate in this actual landscape is just coming into flower, a few lines later, in an imagined indoor scene ("I would bring you to the house of my mother"), it reappears as fermented nectar in what is obviously a metaphor for the pleasures of love that the young woman proffers to her man: "I would give you spiced wine to drink, / my pomegranate wine" (8:2). The verb for giving drink, *'ašqeka,* as Ariel Bloch observes, puns on the verb for kissing, *yiššaqeni,* which is the very first Hebrew word of the whole poem, and so a circle is drawn between the kissing that is like drinking at the beginning and the drinking which is actually lovemaking here near the end.

To readers who particularly recall the extravagant imagery of artifact and architecture of the Song, the emphasis I have been placing on taste and smell, always ultimately leading back to touch, may seem one-sided, even if the figures based on artifice are less pervasive. But in the poetics of intertwinement manifested in the imagery of the poem, these seemingly opposed semantic fields actually overlap, run into each other. Let us consider a complete poetic unit, one of those public set-pieces to which I referred earlier, the evocation of the dancing Shulamite (7:1–7). Because the speaker invites us to follow with our eyes the rapid steps of the lovely dancer, this vertical description works from the feet upward, the reverse direction from that of the earlier vertical descriptions in the poem.

> Again, O Shulamite,
> dance again,
> that we may watch you dancing!

Why do you gaze at the Shulamite
as she whirls
down the rows of dancers?

How graceful your steps in those sandals,
O nobleman's daughter.

The gold of your thigh
shaped by a master craftsman.

Your navel is the moon's
bright drinking cup.
May it brim with wine!

Your belly is a mound of wheat
edged with lilies.
Your breasts are two fawns,
twins of a gazelle.

Your neck is a tower of ivory.
Your eyes are pools in Heshbon, at the gates
of that city of lords.
Your proud nose the tower of Lebanon
that looks toward Damascus.

Your head crowns you like Mount Carmel,
the hair of your head
like royal purple. A king
is caught in the thicket.

How wonderful you are, O Love,
how much sweeter
than all other pleasures!

In the spectacle of the dance, it is of course the sense of sight that is
invoked by the speaker to take in the beauty of the dancer, and the first-
person plural at the beginning marks that beholding as the activity of a
group, an actual audience. In the first moment of the description, there
is a nice tension between the kinetic image of the graceful steps—the
Bloch translation is quite precise here, for this is not the normal Hebrew
word for "feet" but a term that suggests the rhythmic or pounding
movement of footsteps—and the sculpturesque image of the thighs as
beautifully crafted curves of gold. The immediately following metaphor
for the navel, the moon's drinking cup, carries forward the reference to

the semantic field of exquisite artifacts, but at the same time it associates the object of representation with two other realms of experience. First, it should be noted that the object in question is in all likelihood the navel, and not, as some self-consciously candid modern interpreters have rendered it, the vagina. A phonetically similar word occurring elsewhere in the Bible does mean navel; furthermore, it is utterly implausible to imagine the Shulamite dancing naked, her sex visible to the audience, and the poetic decorum of the Song precludes the direct naming of sexual organs, though the poet may well intimate *correspondences* between navel, or mouth, or door latch, and the woman's hidden parts.

The compact image of the drinking cup has two parts: *'aggan,* cup or bowl, and *sahar,* moon. One is not quite sure whether this is a moon-shaped drinking cup (perhaps a crescent design) or whether the moon itself is imagined as a celestial cup. In either case, the *sahar* component of the Hebrew construction points from art to nature. Even in the elaborate artifice suggested by the image, the natural world is inscribed on the woman's body. If the moon is seen as a cup and not the other way around, then she takes on an attribute of a moon goddess as the speaker looks at her bare midriff in the elastic movement of the dance. The drinking cup, moreover, is not just a pleasing shape but a receptacle brimming with wine. The term used here, *mazeg,* means literally "poured drink." Though it is not the standard word for wine—*yayin,* which occurs repeatedly elsewhere—it surely invites association with that predominant metaphoric usage in which drinking is a figuration of love's pleasures. Here, bodily proximity and the analogy of convexity make the sexual implication of the metaphor more explicit than elsewhere. In any case, through the most economical poetic means, the lovely shape of a glittering artifact is also identified with delectable wine, taste overlapping sight.

The images for belly and breast, wheat-mound and twin fawns, occur several times in previous passages. As metaphors drawn from flora and fauna, they hardly accord with the crafted gold and the drinking cup of the preceding lines. That lack of accord should by no means be thought of as a contradiction because the Song and biblical poetry in general, like many other poetic traditions, in no way assume consistency of imagery as an aesthetic norm. Such an assumption, we must remind ourselves, is a relatively modern Western literary convention. There is surely no universal poetic "logic" that would preclude a poet from speaking in one breath of shining goblets and in the next of fields edged with lilies.

The very recurrence of the image of wheat and fawns reflects another aspect of the figurative language of the Song. The metaphors are by and large drawn from what must have been a traditional stockpile of imagery for love poetry, in a fashion analogous to the inventive recycling of conventional images in the Renaissance sonnet from Petrarch down to the Elizabethans. Graceful orchestration of the traditional materials rather than novelty appears to have been the key aesthetic value, though there is also some pleasing interplay between familiar and novel images— as here, the familiar wheat-heap and gazelles are surrounded by the more unusual moon-goblet for the navel and the tower of ivory for the neck. This counterpoint is coordinated with the contrast between sight and the more intimate senses. That is, innovative imagery in the poem tends to be both literally and figuratively "spectacular": the desired body, beheld from a certain distance, is a splendid apparition, likened, in sometimes surprising comparisons, on a small scale to precious artifacts and on a large scale (or greater imagined distance) to grand architectural structures.

When, on the other hand, the poet evokes the fragrance and tactile beauty of the loved one, there is less of an impulse to strike off new metaphors like bright sparks, more of an inclination to rely on familiar sensuous figures: wine, honey and milk, perfumes, aromatic plants, and gentle animals. In the dance of the Shulamite, as the speaker's ascending gaze pauses on stomach and breasts, sight crosses over into the greater proximity of smell and implied touch in the image of the field surrounded by lilies with its (presumably) sun-warmed mound of wheat. Elsewhere in the Song, fawns as figures for breasts graze among lilies, so the associative path here from lily-edged wheat-mound to the twin gazelles is marked by poetic precedent. The image of fawns for breasts is not quite visual, since no precise similarity of shape could be implied. Rather, the similitude suggested is gracefulness, gentleness, perhaps an invitation to caress. It is as close as the Song will come to a tactile image.

The emphasis on twins, here and elsewhere in the poem, sets up a special resonance in the evocation of love's union. The breasts are of course compared to twin gazelles because they are perfectly matched. But the poem also reaches out toward a gratifying fantasy that the perfectly matched lovers might be twins. That, rather than any conjectured Egyptian precedent, is why he addresses her as "my sister, my bride." The fantasy becomes explicit at 8:1, where the Shulamite says:

> If only you were a brother
> who nursed at my mother's breast!
> I would kiss you in the streets
> and no one would scorn me.

A mere fraternal bond would be sufficient to legitimate the public kisses, but the young woman's imaging of brotherhood as nursing at her mother's breast could suggest twinship: the two infants nursing from the two breasts, and the nursing transmuted into kissing (remember "honey and milk / are under your tongue"), which in turn becomes lovemaking, over which the nurturing or guiding mother actually presides:

> I would bring you to the house of my mother
> and she would teach me.
> I would give you spiced wine to drink,
> my pomegranate wine.

The antithesis of this perfect consummation of union, for which fraternal incest serves as a surprisingly beautiful metaphor—shared life-source, shared nurturance, transmuted into the lovers' shared pleasuring —is the representation of the woman separated from her lover, desperately seeking him through the streets, in Chapters 3 and 5.

In the toe-to-head description of the Shulamite, as the lover's gaze moves up from breasts to neck and head, the figurative language pulls back from such suggestions of intimate closeness to an imposing view as though seen from an overlook. This sense of spacious topographic distance is effectively conveyed by the cluster of place-names: the eyes as "pools in Heshbon," the nose "the tower of Lebanon / that looks toward Damascus" (note how the visual perspective is carried well beyond the Israelite horizon), the head like Mount Carmel. But the inter-cutting we have been following between the spectacular distance of sight and the closeness of the other senses is manifested again in the last image of the sequence. The "royal purple" (*'argaman*) of the hair, no longer part of the complex of landscape and architectural images, suddenly turns into an alluring trap to catch a king. (The crucial Hebrew verb here implies something like "imprisoned" or "fettered.") The king in question is clearly not a hypothetical figure in a hyperbole but the lover himself, who uses the same designation that the woman used for him earlier. The encompassing of beauty from a distance with the eye is suddenly transformed into tactile entanglement. The Shulamite's loveliness, as the expression goes, is captivating, and in the final metaphor the captivation is carried out, the lover happily entangled by her luxuriant hair, presaging other interlacings.

In consonance with this contented captivity, the description of the Shulamite is then rounded off with a verse that stresses delicately but clearly the gratification of the senses: "How wonderful you are, O Love, / how much sweeter / than all other pleasures!" This is a precise counterpart from the male point of view to the summarizing line at the end of the woman's vertical description of her lover: "His mouth is sweet wine [literally 'his palate is sweets'], he is all delight" (5:16). The direct address to the abstract noun "love," *'ahabah,* is unusual, and the Blochs, taking a cue from love poetry of the English Renaissance, capitalize the word, treating it as a personification. (To me it seems plausible that Love here is a tender epithet for the young woman herself; since the noun is feminine in Hebrew, there is no grammatical change from the second person feminine singular that has governed the entire address to the dancing Shulamite. The word, however, is problematic. There is no precedent for using the abstract "love" as a term of endearment, but, in the alternate reading, there is also no precedent for apostrophes to abstract terms.) In any case, the use of the abstract noun at the end of this vividly concrete description conveys a sense that the woman is virtually an embodiment of love's beauty, a beauty that is in turn a kind of visual promise of love's pleasure. *Na'amt*—the verb rendered here adjectivally as "sweeter"—is a term that refers to things that please the ear or palate, and *ta'anugim,* "pleasures," the last word of this unit in the Hebrew as in the English, is a word associated with gratification of the senses.

In all these ways, the figurative language of the Song creates an intricate root system that firmly anchors love in the experience of the body, and Chana and Ariel Bloch's English version faithfully and gracefully registers that essential dimension of the poem. The graceful aspect of the original needs to be stressed, for metaphoric representation, certainly as it is deployed here, is artful mediation: if the poet frankly imagines the body, male and female, as an alluring map of erogenous zones, the figurative language of the poem again and again translates that bodily reality into fresh springs, flowering gardens, highlands over which lithe animals bound, spices and wine, cunningly wrought artifacts, resplendent towers and citadels and gleaming pools. In more explicit erotic literature, the body in the act of love often seems to displace the rest of the world. In the Song, by contrast, the world is constantly embraced in the very process of imagining the body. The natural landscape, the cycle of the seasons, the beauty of the animal and floral realm, the profusion of goods afforded through trade, the inventive skill of the artisan, the grandeur of cities, are all joyfully affirmed as love is affirmed.

The experience of love is enacted through the body, and the Song celebrates the body as few other poems, ancient or modern, have done. But though love manifests itself in bodily impulse, it is also conceived here as an abiding force that transcends the body, a force that cannot be bribed, bought, extorted, deflected by public censure, or prompted to exert its power before it is ripe. In a poem that never mentions God's name, love provides access to a kind of divinity, linking the lovers with each other in a union that ultimately recalls the primal unity of infant and maternal breast and at the same time linking them with the teeming bounty and beauty of the whole world. It is finely appropriate, and perhaps even an indication of architectonic design in this sequence of lyrics, that one of the concluding poetic segments (8:5–7) should be an evocation of the power of love in the larger scheme of human life.

The poet begins here with one of those images of inseparable close-ness, like the bundle of myrrh between the breasts and the nursing brother: "Bind me as a seal upon your heart, / a sign upon your arm." The language of this verse could be a daring adaptation of religious imagery, for it is reminiscent of the injunction in Deuteronomy 11:18 to bind God's words on heart and hand and as a frontlet between the eyes. But from the closeness of heart and arm, the poet's perspective suddenly leaps out to death and the underworld (*She'ol*) and the great seas or water, *mayim rabbim,* which in biblical poetry repeatedly hark back to the primordial waters that God divided and hedged in to create the world. Underlying the physicality of love in the Song is an implicit meta-physics of love, and thus the passage that starts with the simile of a seal to represent intimate, inseparable closeness goes on to imagine love on a cosmic scale, and then the futility of attempting to coerce this cosmic force with anything so paltry as wealth. The poet who revels in the plea-sures of love is also ultimately concerned with its meaning.

> For love is as fierce as death,
> its jealousy bitter as the grave.
> Even its sparks are a raging fire,
> a devouring flame.
>
> Great seas cannot extinguish love,
> no river can sweep it away.
>
> If a man tried to buy love
> with all the wealth of his house,
> he would be despised. (8:6–7)

COMMENTARY

Introductory Note

T HE COMMENTARY is addressed to an audience of both specialists and general readers; thus it has been written insofar as possible without technical jargon. However, a minimum of essential grammatical terms— such as *semikut, pi'el,* and *hip'il*—had to be used; these terms will be familiar to those who know Hebrew grammar.

Because so much of the Song remains open to interpretation, it seemed only right to accord the place of honor in the entries to the Hebrew before offering our own interpretation. Each entry therefore begins with the Hebrew as it appears in the Masoretic Text, followed by a simplified phonetic transliteration and a straightforward prose translation. Our intention is to let the Masoretic Text speak as directly as possible to the reader who has no knowledge of Hebrew, and to facilitate the comparison of our English version of the Song with the biblical text. The literal translations may often seem awkward in English; they have been designed to highlight the stylistic and syntactic features of the Hebrew.

Although the past decades have seen tremendous strides in biblical exegesis, philology, and Semitic linguistics, the earlier commentators still repay study. Even when one is tempted to smile at an interpretation by Rashi or Ibn Ezra, or at a "wrong" translation in the Septuagint, the Vulgate, or the King James Version, one must acknowledge that all these sources offer valuable insights, although—or perhaps precisely because—their point of view is so different from our own.

Among recent studies, no scholar can do without the seminal works by Marvin Pope (the *Anchor Bible* edition of the Song) and Michael Fox (*The Song of Songs and the Ancient Egyptian Love Songs*). With its comprehensive survey of the exegetical literature, Pope's book is indispensable for an overview of interpretations in the course of two millennia. Fox's superb commentary is distinguished by its intellectual rigor and the originality of its solutions to difficult textual problems. We have also benefited from Marcia Falk's and Roland Murphy's books on the Song. Of studies published in Israel, the commentary of Amos Hakham was particularly illuminating. We are indebted to all these scholars, even where we reach substantially different conclusions.

Since commentaries on the Song are arranged by chapter and verse, references to such works are given without page numbers. Scholarly sources are cited by the author's last name; more complete information is found in the Bibliography.

Verse numbers of biblical citations in the Commentary refer to the Hebrew text; the reader should be aware that occasionally the numbering in English translations differs from that in the Hebrew by a verse or two.

All translations from biblical texts in this book are our own, unless otherwise specified.

1:1 שִׁיר הַשִּׁירִים אֲשֶׁר לִשְׁלֹמֹה *šir ha-širim 'ašer li-šelomoh* "The Song of Songs which is Solomon's." Not to be taken to imply authorship by Solomon; it may mean something like "dedicated to" or in some other way "associated with" the biblical king. See pp. 10–11, 22–23.

This, the title of the book, is usually considered a secondary addition. It is not part of the first lyric; compare Ps. 23, which begins "The Lord is my shepherd," not "A Psalm of David."

For the superlative sense of *šir ha-širim*, compare similar constructions such as Exod. 26:33 *qodeš ha-qodašim* "the holiest of the holy places," and Eccles. 1:2 *habel habalim* "vanity of vanities."

אֲשֶׁר *'ašer* here is archaizing usage (for *še-*, see p. 24); this may have been intended to suggest the Hebrew of King Solomon's day.

1:2 יִשָּׁקֵנִי *yiššaqeni* evokes the phonetically similar *yašqeni* "O that he would let me drink," associated with "wine." The association between kissing and wine-drinking is more explicit in *'eššaqeka* "I would kiss you" and *'ašqeka* "I would give you to drink," 8:1–2. "Make me drunk" in the present translation attempts to capture the effect of this wordplay.

יִשָּׁקֵנִי מִנְּשִׁיקוֹת פִּיהוּ כִּי־טוֹבִים דֹּדֶיךָ מִיַּיִן *yiššaqeni mi(n)-nešiqot pihu, ki ṭobim dodeyka mi(n)-yayin,* literally "O that he would kiss me with the kisses of his mouth, for your lovemaking is better than wine." The shift from the third to the second person typically occurs in direct addresses to persons of a higher social standing, as in Gen. 44:7 "Why does my lord speak [third person] such words as these? Far be it from your [second person] servants. . . ." The most plausible explanation is that the courtly, ceremonious tone of the Shulamite's address to her lover belongs to their fantasy world, in which he figures as her "king," her very own "Solomon," as it were; see comment on *ha-melek* in 1:4,12.

דֹּדֶיךָ *dodeyka,* literally "your *dodim.*" The plural *dodim* is a comprehensive term for lovemaking, that is, kisses and caresses as well as intercourse. Compare Prov. 7:18, Ezek. 16:8, 23:17; in the Song see 1:4, 4:10, 5:1, 7:13. The word "love" in most translations is too general and evasive.

1:3 לְרֵיחַ שְׁמָנֶיךָ טוֹבִים *le-reaḥ šemaneyka ṭobim,* literally "as regards scent, your oils are good." Unusual in Hebrew as in English, this syntax may have been deliberately chosen for the sake of chiasmus: (A) *ṭobim* "better," (B) *dodeyka* "your lovemaking," (C) *mi(n)-yayin* "than wine," followed by (C) le-reaḥ "as regards scent," (B) šemaneyka "your oils," (A) ṭobim "good."

שְׁמָן תּוּרַק שְׁמֶךָ *šemen turaq šemeka,* literally "your name is *šemen turaq.*" Enigmatic. The various interpretations proposed—"your name is oil poured out"/"Turaq oil," etc.—are problematic for grammatical or lexical reasons. All that can be said with certainty is that in the Bible a name often reflects a person's characteristic traits (compare 1 Sam. 25:25), and that the "oil" here, whatever its identity, is symbolic of the young man's sensual attractiveness.

The Peshitta has "oil of myrrh." We borrowed "myrrh and aloes" from 4:14 as a concrete referent for scent; compare 1:13 and Ps. 45:9.

עֲלָמוֹת *'alamot* "young women, girls." The word does not imply virginity, contra the interpretation of *'almah* in Isa. 7:14 as "virgin," based on the Septuagint's *parthenos,* which can mean "maiden" or "virgin."

עַל־כֵּן עֲלָמוֹת אֲהֵבוּךָ *'al ken 'alamot 'ahebuka,* literally "therefore young women love you." While *'ahab* "to love" in the Bible has a wide range of meanings, from spiritual to sexual—in the story of Amnon and Tamar it means "lust" (2 Sam. 13:4,15)—in the Song this verb most often refers to erotic love. Since the lover is described in purely sensual terms here (his kisses, the sweet scent of his oils), *'ahab* probably refers to physical attraction.

1:4 מָשְׁכֵנִי אַחֲרֶיךָ נָּרוּצָה *moškeni 'ahareyka naruṣah* "Take me by the hand [literally "pull/draw me after you"], let us run!"

הֱבִיאַנִי הַמֶּלֶךְ *hebi'ani ha-melek,* literally "the king has brought me." Here and in 1:12, "the king" is to be understood as the Shulamite's courtly epithet for her lover. It is by no means a reference to King Solomon as a rival for her love, as some have supposed (see p. 33). The explanatory paraphrase "my lover, my king" here is patterned after the chains of affectionate epithets in the Song, notably "my sister, my bride" in 4:10, or the longer chain in 5:2.

חֲדָרָיו *ḥadarav* "into his chambers." The king's "chambers" are best explained in terms of the lovers' vocabulary of make-believe. Since most of their erotic encounters take place out of doors, this word may designate the sheltered or hidden places in the woods or vineyards where they meet (see below, on the king's "couch," "our bed," and especially "our houses," 1:12,16,17). Note also the expression *ḥeder be-ḥeder*, literally "a chamber within a chamber, an inner chamber," a metaphor for a secret hiding place, 1 Kings 20:30, 22:25; 2 Kings 9:2.

נָגִילָה וְנִשְׂמְחָה בָּךְ *nagilah ve-niśmeḥah baḵ*, literally "let us exult and rejoice in you." This clause with its paired verbs recalls the formulaic expression of festivity and joy in Ps. 118:24 *nagilah ve-niśmeḥah bo* "let us exult and rejoice in it," and similarly Isa. 25:9.

נַזְכִּירָה דֹדֶיךָ מִיַּיִן *nazkirah dodeyḵa mi(n)-yayin*, literally "let us recount/proclaim/extol [compare Ps. 45:18] your lovemaking more than wine." The segment *dodeyḵa mi(n)-yayin* "your lovemaking more than wine" is repeated here verbatim from 1:2 as a kind of refrain. This may explain the interpretively difficult "*your* lovemaking," where one would rather expect something like "our lovemaking" or simply "lovemaking" (as in Prov. 7:18, "Come, let us take our fill of lovemaking till morning").

Similarly, one might have expected "Let us exult and rejoice" rather than "exult and rejoice *in you*" in the preceding phrase. The final word *baḵ* may serve no other purpose than to allude to the formulaic expression of joy just quoted, *nagilah ve-niśmeḥah bo* "Let us exult and rejoice *in it*."

These two difficult clauses have given rise to various explanations. For example, it has been suggested that in using "we" in her address to her lover, the Shulamite is projecting her own love for him onto other young women. This is plausible, given his attractiveness to women (1:3,4), but it is far more likely that *nagilah, niśmeḥah,* and *nazkirah* have as their subject just the two lovers, as in "Take me by the hand, let us run together" earlier in the same verse.

מֵישָׁרִים אֲהֵבוּךָ *meyšarim 'ahebuḵa*, literally "indeed/truly/rightly they love you." The emphatic force of the adverbial *meyšarim* is enhanced by its position before the verb, as also in Ps. 58:2, 75:3.

This refrain echoes the statement at the end of 1:3. Refrains in the Song often occur with some variation in the wording, as here.

1:5 שְׁחוֹרָה *šeḥorah*, literally "dark, black" and the related *šeḥarḥoret* in 1:6 refer to the Shulamite's sunburned skin.

שְׁחוֹרָה אֲנִי וְנָאוָה *šeḥorah 'ani ve-na'vah*. Translations vary between "black am I *and* beautiful" (Septuagint) and "I am very dark, *but* comely" (RSV). This reflects a genuine ambiguity inherent in the Hebrew, where the conjunctive *ve-* may be used either in its common meaning "and" or in an adversative sense, as in Prov. 11:22 "beautiful but [*ve-*] without sense." See also Song 3:1,2 and 5:6. Sunburned skin is associated with a lower social status, a fair complexion being the mark of those who could afford not to work outdoors. In ancient Egyptian and Greek art, the women are shown as having lighter skin than the men, probably because the women worked indoors. The Shulamite's need to account for her dark skin sounds apologetic; on the other hand, since her dark skin may have contributed to her singularity and attractiveness, she may be boasting, not apologizing.

בְּנוֹת יְרוּשָׁלַם *benot yerušalayim* "daughters of Jerusalem." A group of women addressed by the Shulamite throughout the Song, e.g., 2:7, 3:5, 3:11, 8:4, and elsewhere. Except where she engages in a dialogue with them (5:8–9, 6:1–2), the daughters need not be imagined as actually present; they may be a purely rhetorical audience for her declamatory statements.

אָהֳלֵי קֵדָר *'oholey qedar* "the tents of Kedar." Tents of nomadic Bedouins in the Middle East are typically woven from the wool of black goats. The comparison here may have been chosen because Kedar is proverbial in the Bible for opulence (Isa. 21:16, 60:7, Jer. 49:28–29, Ezek. 27:21), and because the name Kedar involves a wordplay on the root *qdr* "to be dark, black."

יְרִיעוֹת שְׁלֹמֹה *yeri'ot šelomoh*. "Solomon's curtains" are mentioned nowhere else in the Bible, and may well belong to the accoutrements of his royal splendor, a memory of which has been preserved in folklore; compare 3:7–11. *Yeri'ot* are specifically mentioned among the booty to be taken from the Kedar in Jer. 49:28–29. The word "tapestries" here is borrowed from Falk's and Jay's translations.

1:6 אַל־תִּרְאֻנִי שֶׁאֲנִי שְׁחַרְחֹרֶת *'al tir'uni še-'ani šeharhoret,* literally "do not see *me* that *I* am dark." For the syntax and semantic nuance of this statement, compare Prov. 23:31 *'al tere' yayin ki yit'addam,* literally "do not see *wine* that *it* sparkles red," an admonition not to consider only one superficial aspect of wine, its color, while ignoring its intoxicating power. Hence "only" in our translation.

שֶׁשֱּׁזָפַתְנִי הַשֶּׁמֶשׁ *še-šezap̄atni ha-šameš.* Outside the Song, the verb *šazap̄* ("look upon, catch sight of") occurs only in Job 20:9 and 28:7, both times with the eye as agent. When the *sun* is considered poetically the "eye" that looks down, the verb acquires the secondary meaning "to tan, sunburn." In the Song we may see the intermediary stage between these two meanings: *šazap̄* is used in the sense of "to sunburn," though the original meaning "to look upon" still reverberates. In Modern Hebrew, the verb no longer means "to look upon," only "to sunburn."

בְּנֵי אִמִּי *beney 'immi,* literally "my mother's sons," a term for full brothers, brothers of the same mother. It sometimes implies a sense of special closeness, as in Judg. 8:19, Gen. 43:29, Ps. 50:20, 69:9. This is also the point of the image in Song 8:1. Brothers of a different mother would have been called "my father's sons," as in 1 Chron. 28:4, a relationship that often implies distance and rivalry, for example, Joseph's half-brothers; see also Judg. 11:2.

כַּרְמִי שֶׁלִּי *karmi šelli,* literally "my vineyard, mine," with the independent possessive added for emphasis. Though the vineyard may be real, the emphatic tone with which the Shulamite speaks of "her own" vineyard suggests an additional metaphorical sense. "Vine" and "vineyard" evoke her sexuality in 6:11 and 7:13 (both Hebrew words, *gep̄en* and *kerem,* are grammatically feminine). "Not having guarded" her vineyard is usually taken to mean either loss of chastity or neglect of her beauty because of work outdoors. For the brothers in the role of guardians of their sister's honor elsewhere, see Gen. 34 and 2 Sam. 13.

1:7 שֶׁאָהֲבָה נַפְשִׁי *še-'ahabah nap̄ši,* literally "the one whom my soul loves," an epithet used also in 3:1–4.

אֵיכָה *'eykah* "where?" is the Aramaic equivalent of older Hebrew *'eyp̄oh.* On the significance of Aramaic and Mishnaic elements for dating the Song, see pp. 23–25.

אֵיכָה תִרְעֶה אֵיכָה תַּרְבִּיץ *'eykah tir'eh 'eykah tarbiṣ* "Where do you/ will you pasture?" Given the imperfect form of the verbs, the question may apply either to the young man's customary place of pasturing, or his whereabouts on that particular day. See also next note.

בַּצָּהֳרָיִם *ba-ṣohorayim.* Meaning "at noon" in a general sense, as in most translations. It may also mean "today at noon" if the definite article is understood in the sense of "this," as in 1 Sam. 24:18 *ha-yom* "this day, today," Gen. 2:23 *ha-paʿam* "this time," Num. 22:8 *ha-laylah* "this night, tonight."

שַׁלָּמָה *šallamah* "lest," i.e., "tell me, . . . lest. . . ." A hapax particle patterned after the Aramaic *di le-mah;* see Ezra 7:23. Also see Dan. 1:10 *ʾašer lamah.* The older Hebrew particle for "lest" is *pen.*

עֹטְיָה *ʿoṭeyah* is obscure. The interpretation offered here follows the Septuagint, Peshitta, Symmachus, Vulgate, and Targum, all of which translate "one who goes astray, loses her way," reflecting a variant reading *ṭoʿiyyah* or *ṭoʿayah.* Compare the Aramaic verb *ṭeʿā,* which is used with this meaning also in the Peshitta of Gen. 37:15, Exod. 23:4, Prov. 21:16.

Verses 1:7–8 may reflect a stock rhetorical theme. Shepherding in the Bible is not infrequently associated with getting lost or losing one's way, as when Joseph loses his way in search of his brothers who are pasturing the flock (Gen. 37:12–17). Conversely, notions of straying from the right path or being led astray are often couched in images of shepherding (as also in the metaphors of the good shepherd and the lost sheep in the New Testament). These associations find expression in the interplay of two phonetically similar verbs, *raʿah* "to tend flocks, to graze," and *taʿah* "to lose one's way, get lost, go astray" (or in the causative hip̄ʿil, "to lead astray"), as in Jer. 50:6 "My people have been lost sheep; their shepherds have led them astray," with the verbs *raʿah* and *taʿah* alternating in close proximity (*roʿeyhem hitʿum*). In Gen. 37:15–16, Joseph, "roaming around, lost" (from *taʿah*) asks a man in the field, "Where are they pasturing?" (from *raʿah*). In 1:7–8 the verb *raʿah* "to shepherd" occurs three times, which confirms the likelihood of the reading *ṭoʿiyyah* "lose my way." This reading reflects both the interplay of the two verbal roots, and the rich literary association of pasturing sheep and losing one's way.

A radically different interpretation, "lest I be like one-who-wraps-herself-up by your companions' flocks" (Fox, Pope), is based on the story of Tamar, who veils her face so that Judah will think her a harlot (Gen. 38:14–15). The verb *ʿaṭah,* though not used in the Tamar story, does indeed mean "wrap/veil/cover oneself." However, verbs with this range of meanings normally do not occur in isolation, without some indication of what is being covered (say, a specific body part, or simply the "self," typically expressed through the reflexive hitpaʿel), or the article of clothing that serves as a covering. Thus Tamar "covered herself with a veil, wrapping herself up, . . . covered her face," and similarly, Rebecca "took the veil and covered herself" (Gen. 24:65). See also 1 Sam. 28:14, Jer. 43:12, Lev. 13:45, Ezek. 24:17,22, Micah 3:7, Ps. 104:2 (where the light is God's "covering"). Lacking any of these specifications or any sign of reflexivity, ʿoṭeyah is not likely to mean "wraps herself up."

1:8 אִם־לֹא תֵדְעִי לָךְ *'im lo' tedeʿi lak* "If you do not know." This *l*-with suffix (the so-called "ethical dative") occurs in the Song more typically with verbs of motion, or in contexts encouraging motion, as in the immediately following *ṣeʾi lak* "go" (here, in the tracks of), and in 2:13, 17; 4:6; 8:14. See also Gen. 12:1.

הַיָּפָה בַּנָּשִׁים *ha-yapah ba-našim*, literally "the beautiful one [feminine] among women," a way of expressing superlativity. The motif of excellence among lesser examples occurs again in 1:9, 2:2–3, 6:8–9.

1:9 לְסֻסָתִי ... דִּמִּיתִיךְ *le-susati . . . dimmitik*. This verse has usually been understood as expressing an act of comparison, as in RSV "I compare you, my love, to a mare," likewise Septuagint, Vulgate, KJV, JPS, NEB, Gordis, Pope, Fox, Murphy, and others. But this particular verb (*dimmah*, piʿel) also has another sense, "to think someone to be, imagine, conjure up a mental image," thus, Ps. 50:21 *dimmita heyot 'eheyeh kamoka* "You imagined me to be like yourself" (God speaking to the self-aggrandizing wicked man); Esther 4:13 *'al tedammi be-napšek le-himmaleṭ* "Do not imagine [literally in your soul] that you could escape." Here the lover is recalling his dreamlike wish or fantasy about the Shulamite; compare the chariot image in 6:12, and see pages 14–15 on *dimmah*.

The verb *dimmitik* should not be rendered in the present tense, as in the RSV and other translations. Indeed, all occurrences of *dimmah* in the perfect tense refer to the past, Judg. 20:5, Num. 33:56, Isa. 14:24, Ps. 48:10.

The placement of *le-* (*le-susati*) follows the pattern "to think X to be *le*-Y." See 1 Sam. 1:13 "Eli took her to be a drunken woman," *le-šikko-rah;* Job 41:19 "He counts iron as straw," *le-teben;* Job 35:2 "Do you think this to be justice?" *le-mišpaṭ;* Gen. 38:15 "He thought her to be a prostitute," *le-zonah.*

סוּסָתִי *susati* "my mare." Traditional Christian and Jewish exegesis devised various evasive strategies to explain away the potentially offensive association of a beloved woman with a mare. Horses are often associated in the Old Testament texts with worldly riches and high living, sinful pagan ways of life, and occasionally with lustfulness. See Deut. 17:16–17, Isa. 2:7–8, Jer. 5:8, Ezek. 23:20. One way to get rid of the troublesome mare was to replace it with a *cavalry* of horses, as in the Vulgate "to my cavalry . . . I likened you," or KJV "I have compared thee, O my love, to a company of horses," or NEB "to Pharaoh's chariot-horses." And thus, purged of all flesh and blood, the mare—now a cavalry—was made fit to enter heaven. But the noun *susah* is neither a collective (contra Rashi, who paraphrases the word with *qebuṣat susim* "a group of horses"), nor a plural.

A different interpretive strategy, likewise going back to the Middle Ages, is to explain the possessive -*i* of *susati* by identifying it with the archaic -*i* in such cases as Isa. 1:21 *mele'ati mišpaṭ* "full of justice," Deut. 33:16 *šokni seneh* "the dweller in the thornbush," or Ps. 114:8 *ha-hopki ha-ṣur* "he who changes the rock." (For this so-called "suffix of connection," see GKC, 252ff. and WO, 127–28). Thus "my mare" became "a mare."

This interpretation, which has found its way into most modern translations (Christian Ginsburg is a notable exception) is based on a false analogy. As the suffix of connection, the -*i* in phrases such as those just mentioned is without semantic value, as is easily recognizable in variant versions of the same text, e.g., Ps. 113:7–8 *meqimi, le-hošibi,* and 1 Sam. 2:8 *meqim, le-hošib.* In contrast, the -*i* of *le-susati* makes perfect sense if read as a fully functional "my" in 1:9. This interpretive strategy was never applied to 2:14 *yonati* "my dove," despite the similar syntax: compare "my dove in the crannies of the rock" with "my mare among the chariots of Pharaoh." But since the dove is a symbol of purity and peace, the possessive "my dove" was no problem for the pious exegetes. Ironically, it was the allegorists who preserved the correct reading, "my mare," by making the people of Israel, the Church, or the faithful soul the object of the comparison, with God as the rider. In our reading, it is the young man who is the potential rider.

The comparison of a beautiful woman to a horse is well known in Greek poetry. Alcman compares Hagesichora to "a sturdy thundering horse, a champion" (Higham and Bowra, poem no. 114), and Theocritus writes of Helen: "As some . . . Thracian steed [adorns] the chariot it draws, so rosy Helen adorns Lacedaemon" (Gow, vol. 1, 143).

In Anacreon the image is given a distinctly erotic turn: "Thracian filly, . . . I could fit you deftly with a bridle / and, holding the reins, could steer you past the end posts of our course, /. . . you lack a rider with a practiced hand at horsemanship" (Bing and Cohen, 92). A similar image is used in our day by the poet Garcia Lorca: "That night I galloped on the best of roads, mounted on a mare all mother-of-pearl, without bridle or stirrups" ("The Faithless Wife," from *Romancero Gitano*).

בְּרִכְבֵי פַּרְעֹה *be-rikḇey par‘oh* "among Pharaoh's chariots." Not referring to chariots in the possession of Pharaoh, but rather to the kind imported by King Solomon *from* Egypt; compare 1 Kings 10:28–29; see Bright, 217. For this type of semikut-construction with the second word denoting point of origin, see 3:9 *‘aṣey ha-lebanon* "cedar wood from Lebanon," 1 Chron. 29:4 *zehab ’opir* "gold from Ophir." For a discussion of the Solomonic images—horse, chariots, Pharaoh (as Solomon's trading partner), gold, and silver—see p. 10–11.

בְּ *be* in the sense of "among, in the midst of," as in 2:3,14,16. The noun *rekeb* (here in the pl., *rikḇey par‘oh*) can denote chariots, but may also be metonymic for chariot horses or simply riding horses (2 Sam. 8:4, 1 Chron. 18:4). In addition to the implied riding imagery, with its erotic overtones, this image may be understood in terms of the motif of excellence among lesser specimens, as in 1:8, 2:2–3, 6:8–9.

Commenting on 1:9, Pope refers to the ancient military stratagem, practiced by Thutmosis III in his campaign against Qadesh, of setting loose a mare in heat to distract the enemy's war horses. But a violent battle image is extremely unlikely in this lyric. The point here is the elegant *beauty* of the mare, not its unbridled ferocity; see 1:10–11. For genuine military imagery associated with the Shulamite, see the metaphors of "siege," "wall," and "towers" in 8:9–10. Compare also the "thousand bucklers" of 4:4.

רַעְיָתִי *ra‘yati* "my friend," the lover's epithet for the Shulamite. She uses the corresponding masculine form *rea‘* for him in 5:16 (*zeh re‘i* "this is my friend"). The use of this term by both lovers highlights the mutuality and reciprocity of their relationship. Compare note on verse 7:11.

1:10 נָאווּ לְחָיַיִךְ *na’vu leḥayayik*, literally "beautiful are your cheeks!" This verse elaborates on the mare image in 1:9. Royal horses in antiquity were often decorated with ornaments. The Shulamite in her jewelry is as lovely as a royal mare with its trappings, tassles, fringes, and bridle.

Both in meaning and word order, this exclamation is the equivalent of the English "How beautiful/good are . . . !" Exclamatory constructions are more typically introduced by the particle *mah* "How!" as in Song 4:10, 7:2,7.

Leḥi "cheek" includes the entire area of the cheek, the side of the face, possibly also the cheekbone; compare Judg. 15:15, "jawbone."

בַּתֹּרִים *ba-torim,* literally "with/between the *torim.*" The word *tor* is unknown, but the root *twr* "to go around" suggests some circular ornament. For the understanding of the definite article in a demonstrative sense (literally "with those *torim*"), compare note 1:7 *ba-ṣohorayim.*

1:11 תּוֹרֵי זָהָב . . . עִם נְקֻדּוֹת הַכָּסֶף *torey zahab . . . ʿim nequddot ha-kasep,* literally "*torim* of gold . . . with dots/points of silver," probably refers to granulation, an ancient technique of jewelry decoration related to filigree. For a reference to the combination of these two metals in ornaments see Prov. 25:11 "apples of gold in a setting of silver." In the Song, gold and silver are emblematic of the splendors of King Solomon's reign; see 3:10, 8:11, and 1 Kings 10:21–22. Notice the intensification of the image: the simple *torim* of 1:10 are followed by golden ones in 1:11 (compare 2:1–2).

נַעֲשֶׂה־לָּךְ *naʿaseh lak,* literally "we will make for you." The young man may be including others in his statement; alternatively, this line may be spoken by a group.

1:12 עַד־שֶׁהַמֶּלֶךְ בִּמְסִבּוֹ *ʿad še-ha-melek bi-msibbo,* literally "while the king is in his reclining. . . ." On the epithet *ha-melek,* literally "the king," see note 1:4. The form *mesab* underlying *bi-msibbo* is understood here as the infinitive "to sit, recline, lie down," rather than as the noun "couch."

ʿAd še- expresses simultaneity; compare the use of *ʿad* in 2 Kings 9:22, 1 Sam. 14:19, Ps. 141:10. Elsewhere, *ʿad še-* means "before/until" as in Song 2:7,17; 3:4; 4:6. Possibly patterned after the Aramaic *ʿad di,* this conjunction is rare in biblical but common in Mishnaic Hebrew.

נִרְדִּי *nirdi* "my spikenard." Spikenard, a costly perfume extracted from the stems and leaves of a plant that grows in the Himalayas, mentioned

again in 4:13–14 (compare Mark 14:3–6). On "night" in this translation see remark under *yalin* in note 1:13.

1:13 הַמֹּר *ha-mor* "myrrh," an aromatic resin from the stems and
branches of a shrub that grows in Arabia, Abyssinia, and Somalia,
which was used to perfume clothing, Ps. 45:9, and bedding, Prov. 7:17.

יָלִין *yalin* means to spend the night (root *lyn / lwn*).

הַכֹּפֶר *ha-koper* "henna." A shrub with clusters of powerfully fragrant
flowers whose scent resembles that of roses.

1:14 עֵין גֶּדִי *'eyn gedi*. Ein Gedi is a fertile oasis on the western shore
of the Dead Sea. The association between the vineyard and female eroticism found throughout the Song (see note 1:6) is evoked here by the
parallelism of "my breasts" and "the vineyards."

1:15 עֵינַיִךְ יוֹנִים *'eynayik yonim* "your eyes are doves." The point of
comparison may be the oval shape, possibly also the gentleness of doves.
The *yonah* is the rock dove (*Columba livia*) which builds its nest "in the
clefts of the rock" (2:14). One of the lover's epithets for the Shulamite
is "my dove" (5:2). Notice that she too compares his eyes to doves in
5:12.

1:16 עַרְשֵׂנוּ רַעֲנָנָה *'arśenu ra'ananah*, literally "our bed is verdant." The
adjective *ra'anan* is typically used in the Bible in reference to flourishing
trees, young plants, fresh leaves, etc. (compare Ps. 92:15). Hence the
statement is best seen as a metaphor for any spot of lush grass where the
lovers lie down.

1:17 קֹרוֹת בָּתֵּינוּ *qorot bateynu*, literally "the beams of our houses."
Since the two young lovers hardly own "houses," commentators taking
the word literally are forced to devise ways of interpreting the plural as
a singular, e.g. "our house," "our bower" (Pope, Fox, Ehrlich). The
problem dissolves if "houses" is seen as a metaphor for places where the
lovers meet. See note on 1:4, "the king's chambers."
   The possessive "our" conveys not ownership but intimacy, something
the two lovers share, as in 1:16 "our bed," 2:9 "our wall," 2:12 "our
land." The same loving "possession" is reflected in the many "my"-
bearing epithets by which they address each other.

אֲרָזִים *'arazim* "cedars" can denote the trees as well as the wood (for the latter, see 2 Sam. 7:7). The same double meaning is found in *'eṣim,* which is "trees" in 2:3, but "wood" in 3:9. Thus the statement could mean that the beams "are cedars" or "are made of cedar wood." Both readings make sense in the fantasy world of the lovers: they are either imagining the trees around their meeting place as "cedars," or imagining themselves in Solomon's luxurious buildings, known for their lavish cedar beams and paneling. See 1 Kings 7:2–3,7.

רַהִיטֵנוּ *rahiṭenu.* Meaning (as well as root and voweling) uncertain. Usually assumed to be related to the Syriac word for "rafter" (*rehṭā*) and taken as a collective noun for rafters, or strips running between ceiling beams.

בְּרוֹתִים *berotim* "fir trees," "pines," "cypresses," or "junipers" (compare Syriac *berūtā* "cypress"). On the divergent opinions about the identity of evergreens in the Bible, see Moldenke, 176.

2:1 חֲבַצֶּלֶת הַשָּׁרוֹן שׁוֹשַׁנַּת הָעֲמָקִים *habaṣṣelet ha-šaron šošannat ha-'amaqim.* "I am the *habaṣṣelet* . . . the *šošannah.* . . ." Neither the experts on Palestinian flora nor the commentators agree about the identity of these flowers. The *habaṣṣelet* is variously translated as "rose" (KJV, RSV), "tulip" (Moldenke), "lily" (Feliks), "crocus" (Pope, Fox), or "wildflower" (Falk), and the *šošannah* as "lily" (KJV, RSV, JPS, Fox), "lotus" (Pope), "hyacinth" (Moldenke), or "narcissus" (Feliks, Falk). Since the identity of these flowers remains unknown, we have kept the familiar "rose" and "lily" because of their resonance in the tradition.

Ultimately, however, the botanical identity of these flowers may be less to the point than their symbolic value in the Bible. The same two flowers are singled out in prophetic visions about the restoration of Zion to her former glory: "The arid desert shall be glad, the wilderness shall rejoice and blossom like the *habaṣṣelet* " (Isa. 35:1–2); "I [God] will be as the dew to Israel, he shall blossom as the *šošannah*" (Hosea 14:6–8). By connecting the *habaṣṣelet* with the Sharon, the fertile coastal plain, Song 2:1 may be alluding to this passage in Isaiah, where the *habaṣṣelet* is associated with "the majesty of Carmel and Sharon." In the Hosea text the *šošannah* is associated with the trees, fragrance, and wine of Lebanon.

Seen in this light, 2:1 is an expression of a young woman's proud awareness of her blossoming beauty. The Shulamite is not presenting herself—either modestly or coyly—as a common, ordinary flower of the field ("I am a mere flower of the plain," as Ginsburg and others would have it). Quite the contrary, she is identifying herself with the *ḥabaṣṣelet* and *šošannah,* two flowers that are the very epitome of blossoming in the symbolism of the Bible.

2:2 כְּשׁוֹשַׁנָּה בֵּין הַחוֹחִים *ke-šošannah beyn ha-ḥoḥim,* literally "like a *šošannah* among thistles." Confirms and reinforces the Shulamite's statement by expanding the *šošannah* image. This verse and the next introduce the motif of comparison: the lovers are unique, distinguished from all others. See 5:9–10, 6:8–9.

2:3 תַּפּוּחַ *tappuaḥ,* has usually been rendered "apple," but many botanists today are inclined to identify the *tappuaḥ* with the apricot (*Prunus armeniaca*), which is abundant in Palestine and most probably has been ever since biblical times. The common apple is not native to Palestine, having been introduced there comparatively recently. Moreover, its fruit in the wild state—before improvement by modern techniques of selection and cultivation—is small and acid, and not likely to be the subject of glowing praise (see Moldenke, 184–88). The apricot, on the other hand, is soft, golden, fleshy, and fragrant.

Notice that the form in the singular in 2:3 and in 8:5 refers to the tree (similarly, *te'enah* "fig tree," 2:13; *tamar* "palm tree" 7:9), but in the plural to the fruit, 2:5, 7:9. For the plural in a generic sense, compare *gannim* 4:15, *šošannim* "lilies" 2:16, 6:2.

בַּעֲצֵי הַיַּעַר *ba-'aṣey ha-ya'ar* "among the trees of the wood." The preposition *b-* alternates with the following *beyn* in the phrase "among the sons." The use of synonymous grammatical forms, prepositions, words, etc., as variants is one of the stylistic hallmarks of the Song. Compare *-hu* alternating with *-v* in 5:6.

חִמַּדְתִּי וְיָשַׁבְתִּי *ḥimmadti ve-yašabti,* literally "I delighted and I sat/lingered on." Meaning and syntax not entirely certain. The form of the verbs suggests a past tense, but the present is also possible; compare Exod. 21:5, "I love ['*ahabti*] my master," Gen. 29:5 *yada'nu* "we know." Normally *ḥamad* "to take delight in something, to covet" is in the qal, but here in the pi'el, possibly to denote continuity or a prolonged experience: "I took delight many times, repeatedly" (the "frequentative" pi'el, WO, 414).

The second verb, *yašabti* "I sat," may relate to the first one as an infinitive, "I delighted to sit," as in Deut. 1:5 "undertook to explain," literally "undertook, explained," and Hosea 5:11 (according to Fox, Ginsburg, Gordis). Or *yašab* may have the meaning "to stay for a long time, linger on, tarry"; see Gen. 22:5, Num. 22:19. Translated freely: "I took delight many times, and stayed on and on."

וּפִרְיוֹ ... בְּצִלּוֹ ... *be-ṣillo . . . u-p̄iryo. . . .* Translating "that shade" and "the fruit" to preserve the delicate ambiguity of the suffix *-o*, which is lost in translations with "its" or "his" (the suffix can mean either in Hebrew). The image of the Shulamite sitting in the shade of the apricot tree savoring the fruit has obvious erotic implications, since her lover is identified with that tree. For the erotic import of the scene under the apricot tree, see also note 8:5.

2:4 בֵּית הַיָּיִן *beyt ha-yayin,* literally "house of wine." This could be a tavern or banquet hall (compare Esther 7:8), but it is more likely to be a metaphor for a place in the fields or orchards where the lovers meet to make love. "He brought me to the house of wine" recalls the scene in 1:4, "He brought me into his chambers," where lovemaking and wine are also associated.

וְדִגְלוֹ עָלַי אַהֲבָה *ve-diglo 'alay 'ahabah,* literally "his banner over me [being] love," a circumstantial clause expressing simultaneity with the main action ("he brought me"). A poetic image of her delight in his exuberant demonstration of love; compare the image in Ps. 20:6, "Let us raise our banner [*nidgol*] in the name of our God," where the verb "to raise a banner" is derived from *degel* "banner, flag."

Scholars who resort to Akkadian *dgl (dagalu)* "to see," and by extension "to intend," have produced translations like "his intention/intent towards me was love" (Pope, Fox). But Hebrew *dgl* does not have this meaning. Nor is it likely that a language would borrow such a basic verb as "to see," or one of its nominal derivates, for which it has its own words (*ra'ah, hibbiṭ, mabbaṭ,* etc.). Rather, the semantic range of the various biblical words of this root follows a clear derivational progression: "banner, flag" → "to raise a banner" (see note on *nidgol,* just above) → "raise high, make conspicuous." The latter meaning is attested in the two passive formations of this root in the Song, *dagul* in 5:10 and probably *nidgalot* in 6:4,10.

2:5 סַמְּכוּנִי בָּאֲשִׁישׁוֹת רַפְּדוּנִי בַּתַּפּוּחִים *sammekuni ba-'ašišot rappe-duni ba-tappuḥim,* approximately "prop me up, make my bed among [or "cover me with"] *'ašišot,* cushion me with/prop me up among apricots" (similarly Fox). The Shulamite dramatically proclaims her erotic hunger for her lover; apricots are "his" fruit, 2:3. *'Ašišot* is often translated as "raisins" and "raisin cakes" (compare 2 Sam. 6:19); according to Fox, one possible meaning is "inflorescence," i.e., blossoms. The word remains enigmatic.

The preposition *b-* may have an instrumental sense "with, by means of," as it is commonly translated. But it may also mean "among," as in 1:8, 2:3,16. For the roots *smk* and *rpd* with the meanings proposed here, see Judg. 4:18 *śemikah* "rug," "cover," or "blanket" (in the older spelling with *ś*); Job 17:13 "I spread [*rippadti*] my bed"; Job 41:22 (in English versions 41:30) "he spreads out [*yirpad*]." Also see Song 3:10, *repidah* "cushions." For the image of spreading a bed as a prelude to an erotic encounter, see Prov. 7:16 "I have decked my couch with coverings."

For the use of the masculine plural in general requests addressing "everybody," compare Isa. 42:10 "sing [*širu,* masc. pl.] to the Lord a new song"; 1 Kings 1:2 "let a young maiden be sought [literally "let them seek," *yebaqqešu*]."

Translations like "sustain me with" and "refresh/comfort me with" (RSV, NEB, Pope) are on shaky ground. The English verbs "sustain," "comfort," and "strengthen" may refer to physical or spiritual support as well as to providing food, but this is not at all true of verbs of the root *smk* "prop up, help to walk straight," as in Ps. 3:6, 51:14, 145:14—and even less so of *rpd*. The semantic range of a linguistic expression in one language does not guarantee the same range in another.

חוֹלַת אַהֲבָה *ḥolat 'ahabah,* literally "sick with love," in this context meaning "faint from the intensity of erotic yearning." For *'ahab* "to desire," see note 1:3.

2:6 שְׂמֹאלוֹ תַּחַת לְרֹאשִׁי וִימִינוֹ תְּחַבְּקֵנִי *semo'lo taḥat le-ro'ši vi-ymino teḥabbeqeni,* literally "his left hand under my head and his right embracing me." A stylized representation of lovemaking. This refrain is repeated in 8:3. Compare a parallel from the Sumerian sacred marriage rite (Kramer, 105): "Your right hand you have placed on my vulva,/ Your left stroked my head." For an ancient Mesopotamian clay plaque showing lovers embracing on a bed in this posture, see Wolkstein and Kramer, 43. For *ḥabbeq* "to embrace" in a sexual sense, see Prov. 5:20. The phrase "holding me close" here is adopted from Jay's translation.

2:7 הִשְׁבַּעְתִּי אֶתְכֶם *hišba'ti 'etkem* "I hereby adjure you." With this oath formula, repeated in 3:5 and 8:4, the Shulamite imparts her own insight to her "audience," the daughters of Jerusalem, warning them against arousing love prematurely, before the time is right. The emphatic tone of this teaching with its repeated "never, never" is reminiscent of Wisdom literature; compare Prov. 31:2, where "do not" appears six times in a row. Underlying this statement is the belief that everything has its proper time of ripening, in human affairs as in nature; compare 2:11–13, 8:8–11.

The typical oath in the Bible is sworn in the name of God, e.g., Deut. 6:13; Josh. 9:18; 2 Chron. 15:14. Here the oath is reconfigured to suit the Song's landscape with its animal imagery of gazelles and deer in the fields. This is not an ironic reference to biblical religion but an artful remaking of a conventional usage.

The use of the perfect tense (here *hišba'ti*) in the sense of a present is common in oaths and other solemn assertions, e.g., Jer. 22:5 "I hereby swear [*nišba'ti*]"; Gen. 14:22 "I hereby lift [*harimoti*] my hand to the Lord in oath." See WO, 488.

Notice the masculine plural form *'etkem,* instead of the expected feminine *'etken* demanded by standard classical Hebrew; or 5:3 *'atannepem,* for expected *'atannepen;* similarly *ta'iru, te'oreru* in this verse; 5:8 *timse'u, taggidu,* etc. The gradual replacement of the feminine plural forms by the corresponding masculine forms is one of the indicators of the lateness of the Song. The special feminine plurals survive only vestigially, in the forms on *-nah,* 3:11.

אִם־תָּעִירוּ וְאִם־תְּעוֹרְרוּ *'im ta'iru ve-'im te'oreru,* literally "not/never to awaken and never to arouse," here applying to erotic arousal; compare 8:5. For *ha'ir* and *'orer* "to arouse, stir up, incite, excite," see Isa. 42:13 "stirs up [*ya'ir*] fury," Jer. 51:11 "stirred up [*he'ir*] the spirit," Job 3:8 "skilled to rouse up [*'orer*] Leviathan," Prov. 10:12 "hatred stirs up [*te'orer*] strife."

While usually meaning "if," the particle *'im* is regularly used with a negative sense in oaths, as in 2 Kings 5:16 *ḥay 'adonay . . . 'im 'eqqaḥ* "as the Lord lives, I will not take a thing," Gen. 14:22–23, 21:23, 2 Sam. 11:11, etc. The semantic shift from a conditional to a negative meaning may have come about as follows: "I swear, *if* I were to commit this crime (may such and such an evil come upon me)" → "I swear *not* to commit . . . ," with the negative consequence left unspoken.

2:8 קוֹל דּוֹדִי הִנֵּה־זֶה בָּא מְדַלֵּג *qol dodi hinneh zeh ba' medalleg,* literally "the voice/sound of my lover, here he/it comes, leaping." The syntax allows a rich variety of analyses. Grammatically, not only the lover, but his voice, or the sound of his footsteps, could be what is "coming near," "bounding," and "leaping." The latter reading is not as farfetched as it may seem. In the imagery of the Bible, a voice or sound—*qol* can mean either—may be treated almost as an independent animate agent, able to "cry out" (Gen. 4:10, Isa. 40:3,6), to "break the cedars of Lebanon" (Ps. 29:5), or "to follow" someone, as in "no doubt the sound of his master's footsteps will follow behind" (2 Kings 6:32). This sort of ambiguity was recognized in the traditional exegesis of Gen. 3:8, "They heard the sound of the Lord God walking in the garden" (*qol 'adonay 'elohim mithallek bagan*), where either God, or his voice, or the sound of his walking, may be what is moving about. Thus the eagerly waiting Shulamite may be referring to either the lover's voice or the sound of his footsteps.

In a different analysis, *qol,* or the phrase *qol dodi,* can be viewed as a self-contained interjection, as in JPS "Hark! My beloved! There he comes. . . ."

The pi'els *medalleg, meqappeṣ* "leaping, bounding" are frequentative; compare 2:3.

2:9 דּוֹמֶה דוֹדִי לִצְבִי אוֹ *domeh dodi li-ṣebi 'o . . . ,* literally "my lover resembles a gazelle, or. . . ." The use of *domeh* "resembles" makes this a more explicit way of comparing than the usual juxtaposition of the two items as metaphor or simile, as in 4:1 "your eyes are doves" or 5:12 "his eyes are like doves." In this formal self-conscious statement of comparison, notice the use of "or" in the Hebrew with which the poet is calling attention to the very *act* of comparing. See also 2:17, 8:14; and compare the "or" in the formula of adjuration in 2:7 and elsewhere.

כָּתְלֵנוּ *kotlenu* "our wall." This and the following *hallonot* "windows" and *harakkim* "gaps, crevices" are probably not to be taken literally, but rather as metaphors for, say, a rough stone wall outdoors with gaps between the stones. For the "house" metaphors and the meaning of "our," see note on "our houses," 1:17.

מַשְׁגִּיחַ מִן *mašgiaḥ min,* literally "peering from." The preposition as used here, in addition to its regular sense of marking the point of origin ("from"), implies a notion of direction, namely toward the speaker. The Shulamite is on one side of the "wall" and her lover on the other, so that his peering "comes" toward her from (*min*) the gaps in the wall. When windows, doors, holes, gaps, etc. are involved, *min* thus acquires a secondary sense of "through"; compare 4:1, 5:4. (Thus regularly in Arabic, "he entered through the window," literally "from").

2:10 עָנָה דוֹדִי וְאָמַר לִי *'anah dodi ve-'amar li,* literally "my lover responded and said to me." A conventionalized formula, occurring often elsewhere in the Bible. Originally used in a meaningful way to introduce the words of a respondent in a dialogue (as in Gen. 18:26–27 "the Lord said, . . . and Abraham responded"), this formula became a rhetorical stereotype used also outside of dialogues to introduce any spoken words, as in Deut. 26:4–5 "the priest shall take the basket from your hands . . . and you shall say before the Lord," literally "you shall answer and say. . . ." See also the beginning of many chapters in Job such as 4, 6, 8, 9, 11, 12, 15, 16, etc., and in the Aramaic of the Book of Daniel, 2:5,7,8,10.

קוּמִי לָךְ *qumi lak.* The lover, looking at the Shulamite from the other side of the "wall" (2:9), invites her to experience nature in its full bloom. Compare 7:11, where she is the initiator. *Qumi,* literally "arise, get up" could be intended in its primary, physical meaning, as in 5:5 *qamti* "I got up," or as an auxiliary to the main verb, "Come on!" as in, e.g., Gen. 27:19 *qum na' šeḇah* "Come on, sit down!" and with other verbs of motion in the imperative, Ps. 95:1 *leku nerannenah* "Come now, let us sing!" (literally "go sing"). See note 1:8 on *lak.*

2:11 הַסְּתָו *ha-setav* "winter, rainy season." Spring begins when the rainy season ends in March or April. Variant consonantal spelling *styw.*

2:12 בָּאָרֶץ *ba-'areṣ,* literally "on the ground," with the preposition *ba-* (for the more common *'al*) denoting "on the surface of," as in Gen. 1:22, 6:17, 9:7, 31:54.

עֵת הַזָּמִיר *'et ha-zamir.* This can mean both "the time of pruning," and "the time of singing" (the root *zmr* has both senses). Some commentators see here a two-directional pun (Pope, Fox), the first meaning pointing backward to the spring (2:11) as the season of pruning, and the second pointing forward to the turtledove. (The second association has left its lexical imprint on Modern Hebrew, where *zamir* assumed the meaning "nightingale.")

תּוֹר *tor* "turtledove," a migratory songbird that returns early in April to Palestine (Jer. 8:7). While other songbirds are heard chiefly in the morning, the turtledove sings from dawn to sunset (Parmalee, 172).

בְּאַרְצֵנוּ *be-'arṣenu*, literally "in our land." The possessive "our" conveys intimacy; the phrase is best understood as referring to the immediate countryside with which the two lovers are familiar (compare 1:17, 2:9). Exegetes who misunderstand the preceding *ba-'areṣ* as "in the land" instead of "on the ground" consider *be-'arṣenu* an "unnecessary repetition," "prosaic and useless" (Pope and others). On the contrary, 2:12 exemplifies the way in which similar word forms may conceal subtle semantic differences.

2:13 חָנְטָה *ḥanetah*. Elsewhere *ḥanaṭ* "to sweeten, embalm, spice" (Ibn Ezra) occurs only in relation to embalming (Gen. 50:2,3,26), which involves the infusion of spices and aromatic plants. The fig tree and the vines are seen as actively involved in the processes of nature: making the figs sweet, giving off scent.

הַגְּפָנִים סְמָדַר נָתְנוּ רֵיחַ *ha-geṗanim semadar natenu reaḥ* "the vines in [the state of] blossom give off scent" (and similarly 2:15). For the syntax, compare other statements denoting seasonal or agricultural phenomena, weather, etc.: Ezra 10:13 *ha-'et gešamim*, "it is the time of heavy rains," literally "the time is heavy rains"; Exod. 9:31 "the barley was in the ear and the flax was in bud," literally "was young ears, was bud." Notice the different syntax in 7:13, where *ha-semadar* functions like any regular definite noun in subject position: "if the blossoms [*semadar*, collective] opened."

Qumi laḵ as in 2:10 is the correct reading for the consonantal spelling *qumi lky*.

2:14 יוֹנָתִי *yonati* "my dove." One of the lover's many affectionate epithets for the Shulamite (2:10,13; 4:1,10,12; 5:2; 6:9), "dove" in this particular instance is truly integral to the scene. In 2:9 the two are separated by a wall and he is attempting to catch a glimpse of her. Here the Shulamite is playfully hiding from him, like a dove in the rocky crevices, as he coaxes her out: "Let me see you, let me hear your voice." Compare 8:13: "All our friends listen for your voice."

בְּסֵתֶר *be-seter* "under the cover of . . . ," compare 1 Sam. 25:20. For the image of the dove hidden among rocks, see Jer. 48:28. For the present translation compare Ps. 91:1, where *be-seter* parallels *be-ṣel* "in the shadow of."

הַרְאִינִי אֶת־מַרְאַיִךְ *har'ini 'et mar'ayik*, literally "let me see your sights, views." The noun *mar'eh* "sight," denoting the image as received by the viewer (as in the German *Anblick*), is in the *plural* form, in the sense of something seen, broken into its constituent parts. Similar to Job 41:1 (41:9 in English versions) *mar'av*, literally "the sights of him," i.e., everything that is visible of him. The plural is meaningful and fully motivated: the lover wants to see the Shulamite from every side.

Standard English translations with "thy countenance," "your face," "your form" take the consonantal sequence of the Hebrew *mr'yk* for a *plene* spelling of the singular *mar'ek* (KJV, NEB, RSV, Pope, Fox, and some modern commentaries). But there is no need to depart from the traditional vocalization *mar'ayik*, which indicates the plural. Compare, for example, the corresponding feminine plural form *mar'ot* for "visions, sights" (in a dream or revelation) in Gen. 46:2, Ezek. 1:1, 8:3, 40:2, 43:3.

כִּי־קוֹלֵךְ עָרֵב *ki qolek 'areb* "for your voice is delicious." Normally used in reference to sweet tastes and smells, *'areb* "delicious" is applied here synesthetically to the voice of the Shulamite.

מַרְאֵיךְ נָאוֶה *mar'eyk na'veh*, literally "your sight is beautiful," meaning "you are lovely to look at." Here the consonantal sequence *mr'yk* can be read only as a singular (*plene* spelling), because of the agreement with the predicate *na'veh*. Translations that render the two words identically—e.g., RSV, "let me see your face . . . , your face is comely"—obliterate the semantic difference between the plural and singular forms.

2:15 אֶחֱזוּ־לָנוּ שׁוּעָלִים *'ehezu lanu šu'alim*, literally "catch/grab us foxes." The concluding words explain the command: the foxes raid the vineyards right at the time when "our vineyards are in bloom" (*u-kera-menu semadar*, a circumstantial clause expressing temporal simultaneity, as in 2:4). The adjective "quick" in the present translation is adopted from Falk.

Though the literal meaning of this verse is unproblematic, everything else about it is enigmatic (speaker? relation to context? figurative meaning?). Since elsewhere the vineyards are symbolic of the Shulamite's blossoming womanhood, and the brothers are her guardians (1:6, 8:8), it seems likely that they are the speakers of 2:15.

This verse, perhaps originally a short folk song, calls to mind Judg. 21:20–22, where the Benjaminites seize wives for themselves from among the daughters of Shiloh, who are dancing in the vineyards. In Judges, as elsewhere in the Bible, the brothers (and fathers) are in a position of responsibility for the girls. Foxes in the vineyard appear in Theocritus' *Idylls*, I.48–50 and V.112.

2:16 הָרֹעֶה בַּשּׁוֹשַׁנִּים *ha-ro'eh ba-šošannim*, literally "the one who pastures among the lilies," the lover's epithet, as in 6:3. Like its English equivalent "to pasture," the Hebrew verb *ra'ah* can mean "to tend flocks," said of a shepherd, as well as "to graze, feed," said of the sheep, see Exod. 34:3. The image of the lover as shepherd (compare 1:7), when amplified by "grazing among the lilies," is an erotic double entendre, especially since lilies are mentioned in connection with the Shulamite's body, 4:5, 7:3, or her lover's lips, 5:13, and he is described as "gathering" lilies, 6:2.

2:17 עַד שֶׁיָּפוּחַ הַיּוֹם וְנָסוּ הַצְּלָלִים *'ad še-yapuah ha-yom ve-nasu ha-selalim*, literally "before the day breathes and the shadows flee," i.e., just before the break of dawn. For *yapuah* (root *pwh*) "to breathe, blow," see discussion in note 4:16. Some commentators have associated the image of the "fleeing shadows" instead with late afternoon, before sunset, when the shadows lengthen. If that were the case, however, different verbs would probably have been used, as Fox convincingly argues. Compare Jer. 6:4 "the day turns away [*panah*], the shadows of the evening are about to decline [*yinnatu*, nip'al *natah*]," Ps. 102:12 "my days are like a declining [*natuy*] shadow," and Ps. 109:23. The last two quotations suggest firmly established collocations that would not be easily departed from.

סֹב דְּמֵה *sob demeh*, literally "turn away, be like. . . ." For *sob* "to turn" in the sense of "to turn away from speaker," see 1 Sam. 22:17,18; 1 Kings 2:15. As daybreak approaches, the Shulamite urges her lover to hurry away, as in the aubade or alba of later tradition, where lovers part at dawn. Given this circumstance, it is unlikely that they are a married couple, as has sometimes been claimed.

עַל־הָרֵי בָתֶר *'al harey bater.* The phrase "mountains of *beter*" is unclear. For a synopsis of interpretations see Fox, 116. If connected with *btr* "to cut, cleave, divide," the mountains could be "cleft" or "jagged."

3:1 בַּלֵּילוֹת *ba-leylot,* literally "in the nights," can mean "at night," as in 3:8, but also, and more likely in this particular context, "night after night," in a frequentative sense. Compare Ps. 16:7, 92:3, 134:1, where the contexts likewise suggest repeated activity.

3:2 בָּעִיר *ba-'ir* "in the city," i.e., Jerusalem, as always when "the city" is mentioned in the Bible; see Micah 6:9, Zeph. 3:1, and elsewhere (compare Latin "urbs" for Rome, "town" for London).

3:3 מְצָאוּנִי *meṣa'uni* "found me," in this case, "crossed my path" by chance. For this sense of the verb see Gen. 44:8, Num. 15:32, Prov. 25:16.

הַסֹּבְבִים בָּעִיר *ha-sobebim ba-'ir,* literally "that make the rounds of the city," i.e., customarily, as the participle indicates. Compare Eccles. 1:6.

אֵת שֶׁאָהֲבָה נַפְשִׁי רְאִיתֶם *'et še'ahabah napši re'item,* literally "the one I love have you seen?" The Shulamite quotes what she said to the watchmen without an introductory phrase such as "I asked them." The effect is a quicker pace, a heightened sense of drama and urgency, as in 5:2. The unusual word order, with the object phrase placed before the verb, serves the same purpose; see note on 1:4 "truly they love you." The repetition here of "Have you seen" is adopted from Wolkstein's translation to convey that urgency.

3:4 אֲחַזְתִּיו וְלֹא אַרְפֶּנּוּ עַד־שֶׁהֲבֵיאתִיו *'aḥaztiv ve-lo' 'arpennu 'ad še-habe'tiv.* This could mean either "I clung to him without letting go, until I [actually] brought him," or alternatively "[next time] I won't let go until I have brought him." For the second alternative, with the perfect tense in the sense of a future perfect, compare 2 Sam. 17:13, Ezek. 34:21. However, the parallelism of the verbs in the perfect, *'aḥaztiv, habe'tiv,* tilts the scales in favor of the first interpretation ("I clung, I brought"). Note a similar parallelism in 8:2, *'enhageka, 'abi'aka* "I would lead you, I would bring you."

בֵּית אִמִּי *beyt 'immi* "my mother's house," also in 8:2. Compare Gen. 24:28 and Ruth 1:8. The mother's house is the place where matters pertaining to marriage may have been discussed. (See Campbell, 64–65; Meyers 1991.)

3:5 The adjuration is repeated verbatim from 2:7.

3:6 מִי זֹאת עֹלָה *mi zo't 'olah.* "Who is that rising" is a stylized formula of dramatization used also in Isa. 60:8, 63:1, Jer. 46:7, Job 38:2, always in the form "Who is that/Who are these." Spoken in the Song three times by the daughters of Jerusalem, the formula presents the Shulamite in terms of a supernatural phenomenon, a fantastic apparition that "rises" from the east; hence the desert (*midbar,* the East par excellence in the Bible, compare Judg. 11:22) and the morning star, 3:6, 6:10, 8:5. None of these three scenes is realistic; all are hyperboles, evoking images of the triumphant appearance of a majestic, numinous, even godlike figure.

It is worth noting in this connection that *'alah* "to rise," 3:6, 8:5, is also the verb commonly used for the rising dawn (Gen. 19:15, 32:25,27; Josh. 6:15; Judg. 19:25; Neh. 4:15). Finally, *nišqap̄* "to look forth," 6:10 (nip̄'al, but also hip̄'il elsewhere) is applied not only to simple mortals "looking forth" but also to towering mountains, abstract forces ominously looming from the sky, and even to God himself looking down onto the earth (Num. 21:20, 23:28; 1 Sam. 13:18; Jer. 6:1; Deut. 26:15; Ps. 14:2, and elsewhere). The astral imagery has been cited as a justification for the cultic theory (the latter is discussed on p. 34). But in the Song this imagery is much more appropriately explained as a poetic way of glorifying the Shulamite.

Contrary to what its words seem to suggest, the formula as used in the Song is purely rhetorical: no question is asked and there is no answer (compare Isa. 60:8). This formula proclaims the Shulamite's dramatic "entrance" onto the scene, as in 3:6 and 8:5.

כְּתִימֲרוֹת עָשָׁן *ke-timarot 'ašan,* literally "like pillars of smoke" (or "a pillar," if the plural is to be understood like that of *gannim* in 6:2). Perhaps in an attempt to make the image more realistic, some critics emend *ke-* "like" to *be-* "in," imagining the Shulamite in a cloud of dust or a sandstorm. But there is no need for an emendation: a Shulamite who appears on the horizon like the dawn or the morning star would surely have no difficulty emanating from the desert *like* (not just *in*) a pillar, even pillars, of smoke. There is no point in explaining the fantasy image of 3:6 in naturalistic terms; as with many other images in the Song, such an interpretation would be reductive.

מְקֻטֶּרֶת מֹר וּלְבוֹנָה *mequṭṭeret mor u-leḇonah*, literally "made fragrant with myrrh and frankincense." *Mequṭṭeret* is a passive participle from *qaṭṭer* "to burn incense"; see also *qiṭor* "thick smoke" and *qeṭoret* "incense." Frankincense is a balsamic resin obtained from the wood of various trees of the genus *Boswellia*, native to India, Somalia, and Southern Arabia.

For the semantics of this construction, compare phrases such as Ps. 104:2 *'oṭeh 'or* "clad in light," Ps. 107:10 *yošeḇey ḥošek ve-ṣalmavet* "dwellers in darkness and gloom," 2 Sam. 6:14 *ḥagur 'eḇod baḏ* "girded with a linen ephod," Exod. 27:17 *meḥuššaqim keseḇ* "banded with silver," expressing a range of meanings united by the basic notion "enveloped/clad in/surrounded by/intimately associated with."

מְקֻטֶּרֶת ... מִכֹּל אַבְקַת רוֹכֵל *mequṭṭeret . . . mi(n)-kol 'aḇkat rokel* is understood here, in a departure from the generally accepted translation, as "more fragrant than," literally "fragrant . . . more than," i.e., as a regular comparative phrase. Compare Judg. 14:18 *matoq mi(n)-deḇaš* "sweeter than honey," Ezek. 28:3 *ḥakam mi(n)-dani'el* "wiser than Daniel," Ps. 45:8, etc. In the combination *mi(n)-kol*, the sense is of an encompassing "more than any/all," as in Gen. 3:1 *'arum mi(n)-kol ḥayyat ha-śadeh* "more cunning than any wild creature," Gen. 34:19 *nikḇaḏ mi(n)-kol* "more honored than all," 2 Kings 5:12 *ṭoḇ mi(n)-kol* "better than all."

The reference to "merchant" is an echo of the far-reaching Solomonic trade, the rich "traffic of the merchants" during his reign; see 1 Kings 10:15 (and pp. 10–11). Verse 3:6 is possibly also an allusion to the Queen of Sheba, who brought the king "a great quantity of spices," 1 Kings 10:10; see also Jer. 6:20, where frankincense is mentioned as coming from the land of Sheba.

3:7 הִנֵּה מִטָּתוֹ שֶׁלִּשְׁלֹמֹה *hinneh miṭṭato šel-li-šelomoh*, loosely "Here is Solomon's bed!" or "Now, look here at Solomon's bed!" When used in its undiminished force, as here, the presentational particle *hinneh* points dramatically to an object or person close at hand. Compare to Gen. 12:19, 31:51; Judg. 8:15, 1 Sam. 9:17, 18:17; 2 Sam. 9:6; 1 Kings 19:5.

The syntax of the phrase "Solomon's bed," literally "his bed which is to Solomon," *miṭṭato šel-li-šelomoh,* with the suffix *-o* "his" pointing forward to *šlomoh,* occurs nowhere else in the Bible, becoming standard only in Mishnaic and Modern Hebrew. Another sign of the Song's late date.

A note on our translation of 3:7 is called for. We have introduced a first line—"Oh the splendors of King Solomon!"—that has no equivalent in the Hebrew text, in order to make explicit what is unclear in most translations: (1) that 3:7 is not an answer to 3:6 but the beginning of a new, thematically self-contained unit, and (2) that 3:7 and 3:9 describe not one but two different items of luxury from Solomon's opulent court.

The allusion to the king's wedding in 3:11 and some of the other narrative tidbits of 3:7–11 have no basis in the biblical texts, and may well be reflexes of ancient orally transmitted Solomonic folklore such as that found in the Midrashic literature (compare Ginzberg, 1909–38, vol. 4, 125ff.). The royal wedding and the role of Solomon's mother in his coronation on that day provide the strongest support for this hypothesis: it is so unmistakably presented as a given, as assumed old information, that the notion of familiar, orally transmitted lore is almost inescapable. Material that is clearly Midrashic in nature certainly could have left its imprint on the Song, even though the Midrash itself was committed to writing only at a much later date.

Although most of the concrete details of 3:7–11 have their roots in extrabiblical folklore, the way they are described clearly calls to mind specific biblical texts. Notice above all the word order, as in literally "his bed, sixty warriors are around it," or "a pavilion Solomon made for himself, its pillars he made of . . . its cushions of . . . . its couches of . . . its interior paved with . . ." This is a word order typical of inventories, with the item that is the focus of attention named first (the "topic," sometimes with a pronominal referent pointing back to it in the body of the sentence). The language of the comparison text in 1 Kings 7:6–8 is characterized by a similar word order, literally "and the Hall of Pillars he made . . . and the Hall of the Throne he made . . . and a house he made for Pharaoh's daughter whom he had married." (See discussion of "its pillars," in note 3:10.) The second comparison text with an inventory of Solomon's possessions to be admired is Eccles. 2:4–8. Although no direct dependency is claimed here between any of these texts, their generic similarity does suggest some kinship.

The Shulamite is the most likely speaker of 3:7–11. This conclusion suggests itself because the unit ends in a direct address to the daughters of Jerusalem (3:11), as do five other units, all spoken by the Shulamite (2:7; 3:5; 5:8,16; 8:4). If the content bears any relation at all to the world of the two lovers, it is in association with their play-acting outdoors: Solomon as the Shulamite's "king," their royal "chambers," their leafy "bed," etc.

Much of the misinterpretation that has befallen 3:7–11 in the history of Song exegesis is rooted in the mistaken assumption that 3:6 and 3:7 are question and answer. This has yielded translations such as "What is that coming up from the wilderness . . . ? Behold, it is the litter of Solomon!" (RSV; compare NEB). Nothing in the text, however, suggests that the bed of 3:7 is moving. But once it was associated with "coming up" (3:6), the bed had to become ambulatory; thus, transformed into a "litter" with Solomon on board in a royal procession, it made its entry into a great many translations. The interpretation of *'appiryon* as "palanquin" or "chariot," etc. (see note 3:9) undoubtedly had a share in fostering this ambulatory image.

The theory of the ambulatory litter must be rejected, if only on linguistic grounds. In all of its occurrences in the Bible, the interrogative particle *mi* is used exclusively with animates, never with inanimates. No amount of linguistic speculation can change the "Who?" of this formula into a "What?" Nor does this particle ever mean anything other than "Who?" outside of the formula.

שִׁשִּׁים גִּבֹּרִים סָבִיב לָהּ *šiššim gibborim sabib lah*, literally "sixty warriors around it." For sixty as a typical number, compare 6:8. These warriors with their swords (3:8) surrounding the king's bed may be imagined inside a spacious royal bedchamber. Another narrative tidbit without a basis in the biblical texts, probably from folklore. For "surrounding" as an image of protection, see Ps. 125:2 "Jerusalem has mountains around it [*sabib lah*], and so the Lord is around [*sabib*] his people."

מִגִּבֹּרֵי יִשְׂרָאֵל *mi(n)-gibborey yiśra'el*. Translations with parallel wording, as in RSV and other versions, "sixty mighty men of the mighty men of Israel," are grammatically unobjectionable, but a superlative reading of the second phrase seems more in line with the admiring tone of this entire section, "the bravest among. . . ." The use of a semikut-construction in a superlative sense is especially common with words denoting an extreme degree or intense quality: Isa. 29:19 *'ebyoney 'adam* "the poorest [literally "the poor ones"] among men"; 2 Chron. 21:17 *qeṭon banav* "the smallest [literally "the small one"] of his sons"; Micah 7:4 *ṭobam* "the best [literally "the good one"] of them."

3:8 אֲחֻזֵי חֶרֶב מְלֻמְּדֵי מִלְחָמָה *'aḥuzey ḥereb melummedey milḥamah,* literally "skilled with a sword, experienced in war." The passive participle *'aḥuz,* a hapax with the meaning "trained in, skilled," is probably modeled after the Aramaic cognate *'aḥid,* used in the Peshitta of 1 Chron. 5:18 "experienced in war," which is synonymous with the present *melummedey milḥamah.* See BDB, 28.

מִפַּחַד בַּלֵּילוֹת *mi(n)-paḥad ba-leylot,* literally "because of the danger of the nights." Commentators who relate this to Solomon's wedding in 3:11 cite the widespread popular fear of supernatural dangers on a wedding night (Pope, Fox). On the other hand, a king, by the very nature of his position, would have to guard himself against usurpation and regicide. For *paḥad* used in the sense of "danger" (rather than the more usual meaning "fear"), see Isa. 24:17,18; Jer. 48:44, 49:5; Ps. 91:5; Prov. 3:25.

3:9 אַפִּרְיוֹן *'appiryon.* Hapax of uncertain meaning; a loan-word, probably from Persian or Greek. The Septuagint's *phoreion* "sedan chair," possibly based on no more than the phonetic similarity to the *'appiryon,* may itself have contributed to interpretation of the word as "litter" or "palanquin." It is thus understood in the Talmud and in many modern translations. However, the description of the *'appiryon* strongly suggests a *stationary* structure; see notes on its pillars and paved interior in 3:10. The *'appiryon* recalls the grandeur of the royal pavilion in Esther 1:6 with its marble pillars, beds (*mittot,* pl. of *mittah*) of gold and silver, and floor paved with precious stones.

A number of commentators have concluded that the context indicates a fixed structure—a palace or a throne room—rather than a portable litter. Ibn Ezra understood *'appiryon* as a "magnificent building," and the Zohar as a palace. Gerleman argued that the structure described in 3:9–10, with its "pillars" and "interior" suggests a building rather than a portable conveyance; other scholars have proposed the emendation *'appeden* ("palace," a biblical Aramaic loan-word from Persian; see Dan. 11:45); see summary in Pope, 441–2. Particularly suggestive in this regard is the reference in 1 Kings 7:8 to the palace that Solomon built for Pharoah's daughter, the most illustrious of his wives; this was constructed, it appears, with a lavish use of cedar and costly stones (7:7–9). If we are indeed dealing with a building rather than a portable structure, this palace would be a likely candidate.

עָשָׂה לוֹ *'asah lo,* literally "he made for himself." The wording is close to Eccles. 2:4–8, with its detailed listing of the houses, vineyards, water pools, gold, silver, singers, etc. that Solomon acquired: "I built, I planted, I collected," with the verbs followed six times by *li-* "for myself" (*baniti li, nata'ti li, kanasti li*).

עֲצֵי הַלְּבָנוֹן *'asey ha-lebanon* "Lebanon wood." The word for "trees," *'esim* (*'asey*), may also refer to the wood, compare Exod. 27:1 *'asey šiṭṭim* "acacia wood." Also see *'arazim* in Song 1:17. The plural form lends a concreteness to the Hebrew, suggesting, as it were, planks of wood in the hands of the craftsman.

3:10 עַמּוּדָיו *'ammudav* "its pillars." Typically the pillars associated with Solomon, described with evident admiration in the two books of Kings, are massive, astounding in height and circumference, supporting impressive buildings. Compare especially the description of the House of the Forest of Lebanon, with its rows of cedar pillars, and the Hall of Pillars, 1 Kings 7:2–6. Some measured twenty-three cubits in height, including their capitals, and twelve cubits in circumference; see 1 Kings 7:15–16. These pillars are mentioned also in 2 Kings 25:13–17 (compare Jer. 52:17–23) among the national treasures destroyed in the Babylonian onslaught of 587 BCE. They loomed large enough in the popular imagination to furnish a topographic metaphor: the rock cliffs near Timna in southern Israel are to this day called "the Pillars of Solomon." Given this association, the pillars admired in 3:10 are likely to be tall and massive, capable of supporting a building, not the slender poles of a traveling litter.

עָשָׂה כָסֶף *'asah kesep,* literally "[its pillars] he made silver," i.e., covered or simply decorated with silver. For a similar ornamentation of pillars see Exod. 27:17. As often in the biblical language for craftsmanship, *'asah* "to make, work" applies here to the surface of the objects; compare the use of the corresponding noun *ma'aseh* in the same sense in *ma'aseh sebakah, ma'aseh šušan* "checker-work" (an ornamental network) and "lily-work," in 1 Kings 7:17,19.

רְפִידָתוֹ *repidato.* For an example of the root *rpd* in the sense of uphol-stery or bedding, compare Song 2:5; see also the related root *rbd* in "couch coverings," Prov. 7:16, 31:22. "Couches of gold and silver," described in Esther 1:6, are among the lavish furnishings in the court of Ahasuerus (Xerxes), another king of legendary wealth.

מֶרְכָּבוֹ *merkabo.* A generic term for anything to sit on, *merkab* is explain-ed as *kol 'ašer yihyeh taḥtav* "whatever is under him" in Lev. 15:9–10.

תּוֹכוֹ רָצוּף אַהֲבָה מִבְּנוֹת יְרוּשָׁלָם *toko raṣup 'ahabah mi(n)-benot yerušalayim,* literally "its interior paved with love from [or "by"] the daughters of Jerusalem." Obscure. For different interpretations involv-ing substantial emendations (from "love" to "stone," "ebony," and the like), see Gordis, Pope, Fox.

רָצוּף *raṣup* "paved." From *rṣp* "to join stones, inlay," which underlies the noun *riṣpah* "paved floor." Compare, for example, the *riṣpah* at King Ahasuerus' court in Esther 1:6, a splendid "mosaic pavement of porphyry, marble, mother-of-pearl, and colored stones" (Moore, *Esther*). For the syntax of *raṣup* "paved with," see the discussion of "perfumed with," 3:6.

מִבְּנוֹת יְרוּשָׁלָם Although problematic grammatically, the preposition *min* may be seen here to introduce the agent; compare Lev. 21:7 *'iššah gerušah me-'išah* "a woman divorced by [literally "from"] her husband."

3:11 **צְאֶינָה וּרְאֶינָה** *ṣe'eynah u-re'eynah* "come out and look!" Notice the archaizing usage with the verbs in the special feminine plural (-*nah*); see discussion under 2:7. The irregular form *ṣe'eynah,* instead of the grammatically expected *ṣe'nah* (with ' unpronounced), is used here to correspond phonetically with *re'eynah.*

עֲטָרָה *'atarah* "a king's crown, or wreath." Also a token of festivity and joy; see Esther 8:15.

שֶׁעִטְּרָה־לוֹ אִמּוֹ *še-'iṭṭerah lo 'immo,* literally "which his mother set on him." Although the biblical account says nothing about Solomon's mother crowning him, she does figure prominently in the events preceding his investiture; see 1 Kings 1:11-31. In the Midrash, Bathsheba awakens Solomon on the day of the consecration of the Temple, when Pharaoh's daughter, his new bride, has kept him asleep (Ginzberg, vol. 4, 128-29). In the present verse, the "crowning" by his mother is part of Solomon's wedding ceremony. This narrative detail, too, may have its roots in the Solomonic legends.

Song 3:11 has a number of possible thematic connections with other parts of the Song: (1) King Solomon as the counterpart of the Shulamite's lover, who is called her "king," see 1:4,12; (2) the king as an object of admiration by the women of Jerusalem ("Come out and look at him!"), like the Shulamite's lover, 1:3; (3) the prominent role given to mother figures: King Solomon's mother at his wedding, and the Shulamite's mother as her teacher in matters of love, 8:2.

4:1 צַמָּתֵךְ *ṣammatek*, literally "your *ṣammah*." Two radically different interpretations for the enigmatic *ṣammah* have been in circulation since the very beginning of Song exegesis: (1) "locks, tresses," "mass of hair," "braided hair," and (2) "veil." Although most English translations and commentaries have opted for the veil—RSV, JPS, NEB, Ginsburg, Gordis, Pope, Fox, Falk, Murphy, and others—there is considerable linguistic and textual evidence against this interpretation.

The word occurs twice more in the Song, 4:3, 6:7, and only once elsewhere in the Bible, in a passage that is crucial to the understanding of the word. In a harshly sarcastic address, the prophet Isaiah gloats over the downfall and humiliation of "the virgin Daughter of Babylon" (symbolizing the Babylonian empire), who will be defeated and forced to perform the most humiliating menial tasks. Here is the passage in the RSV:

> Take the millstone and grind meal, *put off* your veil [*galli ṣammatek*], *strip off* your robe [*ḥespi šobel*], *uncover* your legs [*galli šoq*], pass through the rivers. Your nakedness *shall be uncovered* [*tiggal 'ervatek*], and your shame shall be seen.
>
> (Isa. 47:2-3)

The first two italicized phrases are mistranslations of the Hebrew, while the last two are correct. The two verbs *galleh* and *ḥasap* mean "to reveal, expose, uncover, lay bare, show," *not* "to put off, strip off." For the alternating use of these two verbs in parallel verses, compare Jer. 49:10 "I have exposed [*ḥasapti*] Esau, I have uncovered [*gilliti*] his hiding places," and Jer. 13:22 (*niglu*), and 13:26 (*ḥasapti*). These verbs and others with the same semantic range are used in the Bible for notions of decorum, vulnerability, and inviolability, particularly of the human body. In this case, being forced to bare her thigh (*šoq*), underskirt (?) (*šobel*), and nakedness (*'ervah*) symbolizes the public humiliation of the Daughter of Babylon. For *galleh* compare also texts such as Lev. 20:11 and Deut. 27:20 with their euphemisms for genitals: *gillah 'ervat 'abiv, gillah kenap abiv* "to uncover the nakedness" or "skirt" of one's father. From the domain of the human body these metaphors were extended to exposing the "nakedness" of countries (so Gen. 42:9–12), and "baring" the foundations of walls, fortresses, cities—a typical biblical image of military defeat and conquest (Ezek. 13:14, Micah 1:6). Also see Isa. 22:8 "they exposed the screen of Judah," where "screen" is a metaphor, like "shield, cover," etc., for a specific fortress overtaken by the Assyrians (see note in JPS). Here again, the verb is to "expose" (*galleh*), *not* "take away," as RSV.

In contrast, for taking off articles of clothing, headgear, finery, ornaments, jewelry, and the like, the Bible uses verbs other than those of the Isaiah passage—above all, *hesir*. In fact, this is precisely the verb one would expect for removing a veil; see Gen. 38:19 (*va-tasar ṣe'ipah*), and the long list of items of women's luxury wear that the Lord will strip (*yasir*) from the bodies of the pampered daughters of Israel, Isa. 3:18–23. (Two other verbs of this semantic range, *pašat* and *nasa' me-'al*, actually occur in the Song, 5:3,7.)

In keeping with the tone of the Isaiah passage, the *ṣammah* must refer to something that the Daughter of Babylon would be loath to expose (*galleh*) in public for reasons of decorum, along with her thigh, underskirt, and nakedness. In ancient Mesopotamian society, it was improper for a woman, especially one of the higher classes, to bare her head in public; conversely, a common harlot had to keep her head uncovered, and was not permitted to veil herself like other women (see Lerner, 134). While this information still does not tell us what the *ṣammah* really *is*, the weight of the evidence surely tilts the scales in favor of the traditional understanding of the word (e.g., Ibn Ezra) as relating to hair.

An additional argument in favor of this interpretation is based on the very form of the word. *Ṣammah* exhibits a relatively rare noun pattern: the doubled middle root-consonant preceded and followed by *a*, which is found in only a limited number of words, most relating to parts of the human body: *raqqah*, Judg. 4:21,22, 5:26, Song 4:3 and 6:7 "cheek/temple/forehead"; *dallah*, Isa. 38:12, Song 7:6, "thrums, tufts hanging down" (in a weaver's loom, or said of hair); *'ammah*, Deut. 3:11, "forearm"; *kappah* "palm of hand" (in the expression *kappat šoḥad* "an act of bribery"); and *gabbah* "eyebrow," the latter two being postbiblical back-formations from biblical plural forms in Lev. 14:9, Ezek. 1:18, and Isa. 33:15. This noun pattern appears to be very strongly (though not exclusively) associated with body parts.

In view of the well-known proclivity of the Semitic languages for associating specific formal patterns (*mišqalim*) with specific meanings, this particular association can hardly be accidental. *Raqqah* is associated with the head, and *dallah* (in the Song) with the hair, another factor supporting our identification of the *ṣammah*. Notice, too, the association of this particular noun pattern with paired parts of the body that are symmetrically opposed to each other—the arms, eyebrows, palms—and note further that this pattern is feminine, with *-ah*, just as the Hebrew words for "hand," "foot," "eye," etc., are all (unmarked) feminine. A final argument is that all the other nouns with the possessive "your" (*-ek̲, -ayik̲*) in this descriptive section, 4:1–5, are body parts, which would make "your veil" the sole exception.

There is no way to know how and when the Song's *ṣammah* first came to be understood as "veil," but it is an interpretation with a long history, attested already in the Septuagint and Symmachus. It is easy to understand why the reading "veil" established itself. The veil has long been a symbol of modesty: for example, Rebecca, meeting her future husband, Isaac, "took her veil [*ṣa'ip̲*] and covered herself" (Gen. 24:65). The image of a Shulamite whose face is modestly covered with a veil was in perfect harmony with the apologetic approach that governed much of traditional Jewish and Christian scholarship. Once well established in that tradition, the veil slipped undetected into most translations of the Song, including those that are entirely free of that bias—with the one noteworthy exception of the KJV, which has "thy locks."

מִבַּעַד לְ *mi(n)-ba'ad le-*, literally "from behind." This phrase has the same nuance "from the point of . . ." as expressed by *min-* in 2:9, 5:4. Rather than speaking of her eyes as simply the object of his observation (1:15 "your eyes are doves"), the young man describes them in 4:1 as actively looking out from behind her hair. Also compare the description of the eyes in 6:5.

Notice that the direction here is the reverse of 2:9, where his peering originates outside the wall and comes toward her (the observer/speaker), she being inside. Still, there is a consistency in the Song with a clear symbolic import in Mediterranean culture: *she* (or her eyes, forehead, etc.) is inside, and *he* outside some "barrier," such as her hair (4:1,3, 6:7), the wall (2:9), or the bolted door (5:2); she is concealed behind rock cliffs (2:14); she is *in* the garden (8:13), or is herself the locked garden (4:12).

שֶׁגָּלְשׁוּ *še-galešu*. The verb *galaš*, though a hapax, has been plausibly explained on the basis of its cognate in Ugaritic as relating to the streaming or surging of waters. Compare Greenfield (1969), 99 n. 36. (In Modern Hebrew the verb is commonly applied to gliding, sliding down mountains, also skiing, etc., as well as to spilling down, overflowing of liquids—meanings that most probably derive from the interpretation of this verse). The point of comparison is the movement of a flock of goats coming down the mountainside, suggesting heavy, thick, wavy hair in flowing motion. Contemporary readers remote from the landscape of the poet have sometimes found the similes in 4:1–2 odd or even comic, but sheep and goats were perfectly natural images for a biblical audience. The reference to hair picks up and elaborates *ṣammah* in the previous line, as with lily in 2:1–2, honey (*nopet/debaš*) in 4:11 and spikenard in 4:13–14 (*neradim/nerd*)—another sign of conscious artistry.

4:2 שִׁנַּיִךְ כְּעֵדֶר הַקְּצוּבוֹת *šinnayik ke-'eder ha-qeṣubot* "your teeth are like a flock of ewes." Much of the language and imagery of this verse allows two readings: *qeṣubot*, literally "those that are shorn," is (1) an epithet for *reḥelim* "ewes," as in the otherwise identical verse 6:6, or (2) "those that are similar in size, matching," with obvious relevance to both ewes and teeth. For these two interpretations, compare the root *qṣb* in 2 Kings 6:6, *va-yiqṣob* "he cut, sheared off," and the expression *qeṣeb 'eḥad* "the same form," 1 Kings 6:25, 7:37.

שֶׁעָלוּ מִן־הָרַחְצָה *se-'alu min ha-raḥṣah* "that have come up from the pond" (*raḥṣah*, literally "washing place"), hence the pure white of their wool.

שֶׁכֻּלָּם מַתְאִימוֹת *še-kullam mat'imot*. Here again the text allows two readings: (1) "all of whom bear twins," evoking a notion of fecundity and health of the animals. For *mat'imot* "twin-bearing" (hip̄'il from *te'om* "twin"), see Jer. 4:31 *mabkirah* "one bearing her first child" (hip̄'il from *bekor* "first born"). Or (2) "all of whom are identical in shape," with relevance to both ewes and teeth (root *t'm* "to be identical"); compare *qeṣubot* in the sense "similar in size, matching."

וְשַׁכֻּלָה אֵין בָּהֶם *ve-šakkulah 'eyn bahem,* literally "and among whom there is none bereaved of offspring." A *šakkulah* here is a ewe that has lost its lamb. Normally in a flock the lambs walk beside their mothers, so the place beside a *šakkulah* is empty. Here again, the image applies at the same time to the Shulamite's teeth, none of which is missing. Note the wordplay of *še-kullam* and *šakkulah.*

4:3 וּמִדְבָּרֵךְ נָאוֶה *u-midbarek na'veh,* literally "your *midbar* is lovely." Derived from the verb *dabber* "to speak," the problematical noun *midbar* can be interpreted as either (1) a poetic word for "speaking" (as in Ibn Ezra, Rashi) or even "voice," or (2) "mouth," as in most modern translations. Both interpretations are equally plausible linguistically: the word's pattern can be associated with nouns of place, *miškan* "abode, place of dwelling," *miptan* "doorstep," etc., hence conceivably (literally) "place of speech" → "mouth," as well as with nouns denoting actions, abstract concepts, perceptions, e.g., *mišma'* "that which is heard," *mišpaṭ* "judging, justice," *mibḥar* "the choice, best of," hence "speech, voice." The following consideration favors the reading adopted here. It is hard to ignore the parallel between *u-midbarek na'veh* in this verse and *u-mar'ek na'veh* in 2:14, where the visual and the acoustic aspects are associated, literally "your voice is delicious and the sight of you [German *Anblick*] lovely." This comparison seems to give preference to a reading of 4:3 such as "your lips are like a crimson ribbon [visual], and your voice/speaking [auditory] is . . ." over the somewhat redundant alternative "your lips/your mouth," in which the "mouth" is treated as an object of visual beauty in addition to the lips.

כְּפֶלַח הָרִמּוֹן רַקָּתֵךְ *ke-pelaḥ ha-rimmon raqqatek,* literally "like a slice of pomegranate is your *raqqah.*" The word *raqqah* is uncertain; it is usually understood as referring to a part of the face or head: cheek, temple, or forehead. The point of the comparison is commonly assumed to be the color of the pomegranate; its smoothness to the touch and rounded contour may also be implied.

4:4 כְּמִגְדַּל דָּוִיד צַוָּארֵךְ בָּנוּי לְתַלְפִּיּוֹת *ke-migdal david ṣavva'rek banuy le-talpiyyot,* literally "like the tower of David is your neck built *le-talpiyyot.*" The numerous, widely differing traditional interpretations of the enigmatic hapax *talpiyyot* are mostly based on pure speculation and dubious etymologies. In recent decades, a well-argued reading "built in courses" or "in terraces" has gained wide currency (see Pope,

466–68). The comparison in itself is plausible: a tower of David might have been built in rows, or courses, of stones, and a necklace of the Shulamite (1:10, 4:9) with its rows of beads could evoke the image of such a tower. But this interpretation conflicts with a feature of Hebrew syntax. Verbs of the general meaning to build, make, shape, craft are typically constructed with two objects and no preposition. Significant for the case at hand, this applies also when the resulting "product" consists of separate parts or segments: 1 Kings 6:36, literally "he built [va-yiḇen] the inner court three courses of hewn stones," where English has "with" or "in" three courses. Similarly Deut. 27:6, literally "whole stones you will build [tiḇneh] the altar"; 1 Kings 6:9, literally "he made the ceiling of the house [va-yispon 'et ha-bayit] beams"; Num. 11:8, literally "they made it [ve-'aśu 'oto] cakes," i.e., formed it into cakes; Num. 17:3, literally "they made them [ve-'aśu 'otam] hammered plates," i.e., converted them (the censers) into plates; Exod. 26:14, literally "you shall make [ve-'aśita] a covering for the tent tanned skins," i.e., from skins. The same is true of the corresponding passive construction: Ezek. 41:18, literally "it was made ['aśuy] cherubs and palm trees," i.e., it was composed of cherubs and palm trees (and compare the corresponding active in 1 Kings 6:29). Only exceptionally is a preposition used, and then it is not le- but be-, as in 1 Kings 6:15–16. Thus, it is precisely the preposition le- in le-talpiyyot that speaks against this particular reading and points in a different direction.

Like most of the earlier readings, "in courses" is based on the assumption that talpiyyot is a plural noun. But this approach may be too narrow. Hebrew has a handful of words ending on -ot and -im that are plurals in form only, having become functionally adverbials: Ps. 139:14 "I praise you, for I have been awesomely [nora'ot] made"; 1 Kings 8:13 "a place for you to dwell forever ['olamim]"; Song 1:4 "Truly/rightly [meyšarim] they love you." Now, adverbially used words are so commonly preceded by le- that this preposition can almost be considered a marker of this word class: Isa. 32:1, 42:3 le-ṣedeq, le-mišpaṭ, le-'emet "justly, righteously, faithfully"; Job 36:31, Neh. 5:18, and 2 Chron. 11:12 le-maḵbir, le-harbeh "in abundance, very much"; Joel 2:26 le-hapli' "wondrously"; Job 42:10 le-mišneh "twice as much"; Gen. 3:22 le-'olam "forever." And this applies also to the plural forms, Ps. 77:8, Eccles. 1:10 le-'olamim "forever"; Song 7:10 le-meyšarim "straight, directly, smoothly"; Ps. 140:12 le-madḥepot "in thrusts [?], speedily."

Even when the meaning of some of these words is uncertain, their adverbial function as such is usually not in doubt. This becomes especially evident in a case like 1 Sam. 15:32 "Agag went to him *ma'adan-not.*" This enigmatic word has been correctly understood as an adverb irrespective of the differing interpretations given to it: "with faltering step" (NEB), "cheerfully" (RSV), and "in chains" (Even-Shoshan, Segal). The same is true when a word shows slight fluctuations in meaning in different contexts; for example, the adverbial *meyšarim* in Song 1:4 as compared to 7:10. The approach followed here with respect to the problem phrase "built *le-talpiyyot*" is based on the conviction that its meaning cannot be deciphered via the etymology, root, or pattern of *talpiyyot,* as has been attempted throughout the tradition. But while the meaning of the word itself may forever remain obscure, the analysis adopted here—which focuses exclusively on the morphology (the preposition *le-* and the ending *-ot*) and syntax of this phrase—suggests a semantic range such as that covered by some of the *le-* adverbials listed above, perhaps "built wondrously, magnificently, to perfection," or the like.

In this understanding, the neck itself is the object of admiration, and it alone is compared with the tower, not the neck with its necklace (the necklace is evoked separately in the "bucklers" and "shields"; see next note). A tower of David "built magnificently, to perfection" in 4:4—whether real or imaginary, just as the one made of ivory in 7:5—symbolizes workmanship of the highest order, evoking a master architect. This would closely parallel 7:2, where the Shulamite's thighs are said to be "shaped by a master craftsman." Hence the unnamed early Jewish grammarians (*medaqdeqim,* mentioned by Ibn Ezra) who freely paraphrased *le-talpiyyot* "without equal" may well have been closest to the mark.

אֶלֶף הַמָּגֵן תָּלוּי עָלָיו *'elep̄ ha-magen taluy 'alav* "a thousand bucklers hang upon it." Warriors used to hang their bucklers, helmets, and other items of weaponry on towers and city walls for ornamental display, which "lent splendor" and "made perfect" the city's beauty, so Ezek. 27:10–11. The ornaments on the strands of the Shulamite's necklace evoke the image of the bucklers displayed on David's tower.

The reference to turrets and city walls in relation to the Shulamite (8:10) suggests a daunting, awesome beauty (*'ayummah,* 6:4,10). The "bucklers" around her neck accord with this image.

Literally "the thousand buckler hang," with the enumerated object in the collective singular, as is common especially with large round numbers (see e.g. Song 8:11). But the use of the definite article, as well as the construction with "hang" in the singular (*taluy*), instead of the expected plural (*teluyim*), is less usual and calls attention to itself. It suggests a reference to something well known, as if to say "those famous bucklers of which we have all heard," or perhaps "that group of one thousand strung up together," hence the singular construction. Since there is nothing in the Bible about a tower of David, nor about a thousand bucklers, this may be yet another indication of elements of popular folklore in the Song; see note 3:7 above. The figure "thousand" supports this conjecture.

כֹּל שִׁלְטֵי הַגִּבֹּרִים *kol šilṭey ha-gibborim* "all the shields of the warriors." In the passage just quoted from Ezek. 27:10–11, *šelaṭim* are mentioned among the weaponry displayed on city walls, along with shields and helmets, possibly denoting a special kind of shield, or else quiver, as probably in Jer. 51:11. The *šelaṭim* in 2 Chron. 23:9 are counted among King David's weaponry.

4:5 תְּאוֹמֵי צְבִיָּה *te'omey ṣebiyyah*, "twins of a gazelle," suggesting the identical shape of the breasts. Gazelles evoke grace and youthful liveliness.

הָרֹעִים בַּשּׁוֹשַׁנִּים *ha-ro'im ba-šošannim*, literally "that graze among the lilies." For the rich erotic associations of the image, see note 2:16.

4:6 עַד שֶׁיָּפוּחַ הַיּוֹם *'ad še-yapuaḥ ha-yom*, literally "before the day breathes." See note 2:17 for discussion.

הַר הַמּוֹר ... גִּבְעַת הַלְּבוֹנָה *har ha-mor . . . gib'at ha-lebonah* "the mountain of myrrh . . . the hill of frankincense." For the sensual association of these two spices with the Shulamite, see also Song 3:6, 4:14.

4:7 כֻּלָּךְ יָפָה *kullak yapah*. Hebrew *kullak* is far more concrete than implied in the English "you are wholly/entirely beautiful," and is better rendered freely as "your entirety is beautiful" or colloquially, "every inch of you is beautiful." Coming at the end of the lover's praise song to the Shulamite, this statement is paralleled by her concluding "he is all [*kullo*] delight" in 5:16.

וּמוּם אֵין בָּךְ *u-mum 'eyn bak*, literally "and there is no flaw in you." Our free translation, "my perfect one," is borrowed from Falk.

4:8 תָּבוֹאִי ... אִתִּי מִלְּבָנוֹן *'itti mi(n) lebanon . . . tabo'i* "come with me from Lebanon." This and the other three mountains mentioned in this verse are symbols of inaccessibility and danger, and at the same time of majestic, primeval beauty. Much of the traditional misunderstanding of this verse is rooted in the insistence of many commentators on explaining it literally. But the Shulamite and her lover are *not* in the mountains of Lebanon, close to the dwellings of lions and leopards. This fantasy scene is not unlike the one in 8:5, where the two of them are "coming up" together from the wilderness. The verb *tabo'i,* in the imperfect, seems less a direct invitation (for which an imperative, *bo'i,* would be more appropriate) than a wishful thought, along the line of "Oh that you would come down with me . . ."; see the series of imperfects conjuring up a succession of wished-for, hypothetical events in 8:1–2. Moreover, this is yet another instance of the technique, so pervasive in the Song, of referring to the animal world (the mare, the gazelle, the dove, ewes, goats, the raven, etc.), in order to highlight some characteristic of the lovers, here evoking their freedom and vitality.

There is no compelling reason for the emendation of *'itti* "with me" of the Masoretic text to *'eti* "come!" as in Fox, Pope, and Falk.

כַּלָּה *kallah,* literally "bride," see note 4:9. The word order of the Hebrew, literally "With me from Lebanon, bride, with me from Lebanon come!"—ABAC—reflects a formal pattern that occurs frequently in the Song, 1:15, 4:1, 4:9, 5:9, 6:9, 7:1, sometimes with a variation in the repeating member (A), as in 4:10,12, 5:1, 6:1. For occurrences outside the Song, see Ps. 93:3, literally "the floods have lifted up, O Lord, the floods have lifted up their voice," or Ps. 67:4, literally "shall praise you nations, O Lord, shall praise you nations, all!" Characteristically, one member of the pattern—typically *B*—is an address or an epithet.

אֲמָנָה שְׂנִיר וְחֶרְמוֹן *'amanah senir ve-hermon.* Amana, Senir, and Hermon, along with Mount Lebanon, are the northern mountains that figure prominently in the geography of the imagination of ancient Israel.

4:9 לִבַּבְתִּנִי *libbabtini* "you have ravished my heart," derived from the noun *leb* or *lebab* "heart." One of the functions of the pi'el verbal stem is to express the taking away, removal of something (compare English "to skin," "to bone"); Deut. 25:18 *zanneb* "to cut off at the rear," from *zanab* "tail"; Ps. 52:7 *šareš* "to uproot," from *šoreš* "root," see WO,

412. A different reading could be "you have heartened, encouraged, emboldened me," compare the pi'el *'ammeṣ* "to strengthen," Isa. 35:3. The translation "ravished" comes from the KJV.

אֲחֹתִי כַלָּה *'aḥoti kallah* "my sister, [my] bride." "Sister" suggests intimacy; for a metaphoric use of "brother" and "sister" elsewhere in the Bible, see Gen. 19:7; 2 Sam. 1:26; Job 30:29; and compare Job 17:14 and Prov. 7:4. See also note 8:1 below. In Egyptian love poetry, "sister" (and "brother") are used as terms of endearment (Fox, xii–xiii, 136). "Bride" is not to be taken literally as implying a wedding ceremony, though it may well convey a hope for marriage in the future. The combined epithet occurs again in 4:10,12, 5:1. The two components occur separately in "my sister" 5:2 and "bride" 4:8,11.

Be-*'aḥaṭ* is the correct reading for the spelling *be-'aḥad*.

עֲנָק *'anaq* "link, strand," "chain," or "pendant," or any other segment of a necklace; compare Prov. 1:9.

צַוְּרֹנָיִך *ṣavveronayiḵ*. The meaning "necklace" is suggested by the derivation from the common word for "neck," *ṣavvar* (usually spelled *ṣavva'r*, e.g., 1:10, 4:4). The plural form suggests a necklace with more than a single strand, as is found in ancient Egypt (Fox, 136 and figs. 1–5). Compare the "thousand shields" of 4:4, which likewise suggest a more substantial necklace. The ending -*on*, though of many functions, occurs not infrequently with nouns denoting ornaments and cosmetics, as in Isa. 3:18,23 *śaharon* "crescent," *gilyon* "mirror," and Exod. 28:34 *pa'amon* "decorative bell."

4:10 מַה־יָפוּ ... מַה־טֹּבוּ *mah yapu . . . mah ṭoḇu*, literally, "how beautiful . . . how good are. . . ." A common biblical formula of admiration; see also Song 7:2,7. The young man's praise of the Shulamite as a lover corresponds to her praise of him, including the reference to wine and the fragrance of precious oils, 1:2–3.

4:11 נֹפֶת תִּטֹּפְנָה שִׂפְתוֹתַיִך *nopet tiṭṭopnah śiptotayiḵ*, literally "your lips drip honey," may allude to the Shulamite's sweet words in general or, more likely, specifically to her sweetness in seduction; compare Prov. 5:3, the only other occurrence of this specific phrase, *nopet tiṭṭopnah śiptey*. . . . The wetness of the young man's lips similarly enhances the erotic suggestiveness of the image in Song 5:13.

רֵיחַ לְבָנוֹן *reaḥ lebanon,* the "scent of Lebanon," could refer to the forest, or the wine, of that region, both of which are proverbial for their fragrance; see Hosea 14:7–8.

4:12 גַּן נָעוּל *gan naʿul* "a locked garden" symbolizes the Shulamite's sexuality, like the "hidden well" and "sealed spring": the garden is inaccessible to anyone but her lover, who alone is invited to enter, 4:16–5:1. For a similar use of water, well, cistern, see Prov. 5:15,18.

גַּל נָעוּל *gal naʿul.* Though of uncertain meaning, *gal* has been plausibly linked, via its root (*gll*), with the term "*gullot* of water," which in the context of Josh. 15:19 and Judg. 1:15 must refer to springs, water cisterns, or the like (Pope and others). Water has always been a precious commodity in the Middle East; sealing is one method employed in antiquity to keep a private source of water safe from use by strangers. On the custom of sealing water sources, see 2 Chron. 32: 2–4, and compare 2 Kings 20:20.

Fox opts for the variant reading *gan* (following Septuagint, Vulgate, Peshitta, and some Hebrew manuscripts), against the Masoretic Text's *gal.* But this position may be based on too narrow a view of the pattern involved, *ABAC,* which seems to allow for minor variations in the repeating (A), as in Song 4:10: (A) *mah yapu dodayik,* (B) *'aḥoti kallah,* (A) *mah ṭobu dodayik;* compare 6:1. (See also under note 4:8, above). Indeed, *gan–gal* may well be intended for its play of sound. With its rich water imagery alluding to woman's sexuality and fertility, Song 4:12 in fact calls to mind the language of Prov. 5:15, and also its sound play: "Drink water from your cistern, flowing water from your well," *boreka–be'ereka.*

4:13 שְׁלָחַיִךְ *selaḥayik* "your branches." A hapax of uncertain meaning, though the root *šlḥ* "to send, stretch out, extend" offers a clue. It is found several times in a characteristically biblical image: a richly flourishing tree/vine/cedar that spreads its boughs or roots over a large area, symbolizing a thriving person or nation, e.g., Isa. 16:8 "its branches [*šeluḥoteyha*] spread abroad and passed over the sea"; Ps. 80:12; and the vision of the tree in Dan. 4:7–9. And see also Jer. 17:8 "he is like a tree planted by water that sends out [*yešallaḥ*] its roots to the stream," and Ezek. 17:6.

Given the Song's wide use of tree and plant images in relation to the two lovers—the apricot and fig trees, the cedar and the date palm, the budding vines, the Shulamite's vineyard (1:6, 2:3, 7:6,8–9)—the common understanding of *šelaḥayik* as branches, boughs, or shoots seems more appropriate than the interpretations based on *šelaḥim* (*šelaḥin/ šalḥin*), Mishnaic for "irrigation channels," "irrigated land"; see Fox's "your watered fields," or Pope's "your groove."

שְׁלָחַיִךְ פַּרְדֵּס רִמּוֹנִים *šelaḥayik pardes rimmonim* "your branches are an orchard of pomegranate trees." Apart from pomegranates and other delicious fruits, this fantasy orchard also contains an extravagant assortment of exotic spices. Of those mentioned in 4:13–14, only saffron and henna are known for certain to have grown in Palestine. Myrrh, cinnamon, and cane were probably imported, while spikenard, frankincense, and aloes were certainly luxury imports from distant lands, such as India, Arabia, Somalia, and even China (Feliks, 23–26). On the spices imported "from far away" compare Jer. 6:20 and note 3:6 above, "all the spices of the merchant."

פַּרְדֵּס *pardes* is a loan-word from Persian (and as such another indicator of the Song's lateness) originally meaning "enclosed park" or "pleasure ground," and is still used in that sense in Neh. 2:8. The notion of an enclosure would fit well with the metaphor of the locked garden, 4:12. It is only in the third century BCE that the word is attested with the primary meaning "orchard" in the *paradeisos* of Greek papyri (whence the English word "paradise"). See Ginsberg, 52.

4:15 מַעְיַן גַּנִּים *ma'yan gannim,* literally "a spring of gardens," with the plural in a generic sense, i.e., a spring such as is associated with gardens.

וְנֹזְלִים מִן־לְבָנוֹן *ve-nozelim min lebanon.* The syntax is uncertain. Most translators consider *nozelim* a plural noun, e.g., RSV "[a well of living water, and] flowing streams from Lebanon." This is plausible, since *nozelim* indeed occurs as a common poetic synonym for water, as in Isa. 44:3, Prov. 5:15, Ps. 78:16,44. On the other hand, *nozelim* could conceivably be an active participle with verbal function, "flowing" (*nazal* "to flow" as in Num. 24:7, Jer. 9:17, Job 36:28), paralleling *ḥayyim* "fresh," literally "living." Hence freely, reading against the liturgical accents: "a well of water, fresh and gushing from Lebanon." The word *nozelim* is indeed used in its verbal sense in Jer. 18:14, "waters . . . cold, flowing down," likewise in connection with

Lebanon, to epitomize water at its freshest. The "flowing" waters (4:15) would then parallel the dynamic and sensuous image of "streaming" (*nazal*) spices in 4:16. For a similar use of the participle as a verb in the Song, see 2:8 "bounding," 2:9 "gazing," 3:6 "rising," 5:2 "knocking."

4:16 הָפִיחִי *hapiḥi*. This difficult verb is often translated "to blow, breathe, exhale," on the basis of its use in the simple stem, 2:17, 4:6. But since the form in 4:16 is in the causative stem (root *pwḥ*, hip̄'il), a literal rendition might be closer to the mark: "to cause to breathe," perhaps with a secondary meaning "to bring to life." The association between breathing and bringing to life calls to mind the description of the creation of man in Gen. 2:7, "[God] breathed into his nostrils the breath of life, and the man became a living being." But the text most immediately relevant is Ezek. 37:9—"from the four corners come, O wind, and blow upon these slain that they may live!"—where the connection goes beyond the image to the basic level of phonetic similarity, *peḥi* "blow!" The root used in both the Genesis and Ezekiel texts is *nph* "to blow," phonetically and semantically a close cognate of *pwḥ*. In this interpretation, the Shulamite's garden in Song 4:16 is dormant and magically brought to life by the winds she summons. In its high drama, this verse with the Shulamite "commanding" the elements is also reminiscent of Isa. 5:6, "I will command the clouds."

גַּנּוֹ ... גַּנִּי *ganni* . . . *ganno*. "My garden" becomes "his garden," just as the Shulamite's "my vineyard" in 1:6 becomes the vineyard her lover calls his own in 8:12.

5:1 ... אָרִיתִי ... בָּאתִי *ba'ti* . . . *'ariti* . . . "I have come, . . . I have gathered." The RSV has a present tense: "I come, I gather, I eat, I drink," apparently to imply *intended* actions (see similarly Robert's "je viens" in the sense of an imminent future, quoted in Pope). This interpretation must be rejected out of hand, if only on linguistic grounds. While the Hebrew "perfect" verb is indeed able to express a variety of temporal and aspectual nuances, its most typical role—especially in the Song—is to denote a narrative past, and a completed action (except for a limited number of well-definable uses, such as stative verbs, as in 4:10 *yapu,* or where the perfect is demanded by the syntactic structure, e.g., 2:17 *ve-nasu*). In this case, the perfect implies consummation.

מֹורִי עִם־בְּשָׂמִי ... יַעְרִי עִם־דִּבְשִׁי *mori ʿim beśami . . . yaʿri ʿim dibši,* literally "my myrrh with my spice, . . . my honeycomb with my honey." The preposition "with" (*ʿim*) implies a special semantic nuance that the regular connective "and" (*ve-*) cannot express: "Not only *a*, but *b*, too," or "*a* and, on top of it, *b*!" The same repeated *ʿim* occurs in the long list of rare spices that the lover finds in his magical garden, 4:13–14, where the tone is as exuberant: "henna, and spikenard too!" The same use of *ʿim* occurs in Josh. 11:21, "he wiped them out, as well as their cities" (*ʿim ʿareyhem*).

For *yaʿar* meaning "honeycomb" compare 1 Sam. 14:27 (*yaʿrat ha-debaš*). *Beśami* is irregularly voweled, for the expected *bośmi*.

שִׁכְרוּ דֹודִים *šikru dodim,* literally "get drunk on love." For *ravah dodim* "to drink one's fill of love," see Prov. 7:18. For the syntax *šakar* + direct object, "to imbibe, get drunk on," see Isa. 29:9, 49:26.

In this reading, the sentence shows the favored address pattern of the Song: (A) "eat, (B) friends, (A) drink and get drunk (C) on love!," with the address form in the expected (B) slot. See note 4:8.

Interpreting rather differently, the Septuagint, Peshitta, Vulgate, Rashi, KJV, and others render *dodim* as a concrete plural noun in synonymous parallelism with "friends": "Eat, O friends, and drink: drink deeply, O lovers!" (RSV). One can see why this reading was preferred by those to whom the notion of getting drunk on love may have been too blatantly erotic. But it is an interpretation with a very low degree of plausibility. The word *dodim,* so well attested throughout the Bible in reference to lovemaking (see note 1:2)—including the expression just quoted, "to drink one's fill of *dodim*"—is not likely to have been used just this one time in a different meaning, especially in a text like the Song, which consistently associates erotic love with wine. If indeed there is an allusion to *dodim* as "lovers" here, it is only secondarily, in a delightful wordplay.

A self-contained epigram, this boisterous call to enjoy life's earthly pleasures may have been taken from a popular wine song (Segal, 1967). The words serve as an exuberant finale to this entire unit. They are thematically integral to the rest of the verse, and there is no compelling reason to assume that they are spoken by a different voice (Fox, Gerleman). Nor are the "friends" (*reʿim*) necessarily to be taken as referring to identifiable persons (say, the young man's companions of 1:7, 8:13). They may well be the proverbial friends or "comrades" rhetorically addressed in a wine song. Compare the analogous use of "young man!" in Eccles. 11:9, or the ubiquitous "my son!" in Proverbs.

5:2　אֲנִי יְשֵׁנָה וְלִבִּי עֵר 'ani yešenah ve-libbi 'er "I was asleep but my heart was awake" fits the condition of the Shulamite who yearns for her lover at night; compare 3:1. The words suggest the kind of restless sleep in which the mind is not totally unconscious but stays alert in anxiety or expectation.

Many readers have taken this to be a dream. This is a possible interpretation, though 5:2–7 exhibits none of the typical features of dream narratives in the Bible, and the events narrated here seem realistic enough. The lyric may be read as a dream, a fantasy, or an actual event; the Song, characteristically, doesn't distinguish sharply between any of these.

קוֹל דּוֹדִי דוֹפֵק qol dodi dopeq, literally "the voice/sound of my lover, knocking." For a discussion of the multiple meanings and different syntactic ways to analyze this construction, see note 2:8.

פִּתְחִי־לִי pithi li, literally "Open to me." It is not uncommon for the verb "to open" to be used without a word for door, gate, etc. in unambiguous contexts, for example, in 2 Kings 15:16, literally "because they did not open to him," i.e., the gates of the city. Similarly Deut. 20:11, Isa. 22:22, and compare Isa. 45:8, Ps. 106:17. The erotic implications are therefore probably in the scene itself, not in the absence of the expected object noun "door," as is sometimes assumed (Pope, Fox).

Notice that the Shulamite quotes her lover's words without an introductory phrase, such as "he said to me," and does the same with her own words in the next verse. The effect is a quicker pace, a heightened sense of drama and urgency, as in 3:3. Contrast the more leisurely pace of 2:10.

קְוֻצּוֹתַי qevuṣṣotay. Occurring in the Bible only here and in 5:11 and usually translated "my locks." The word probably refers to thick, heavy hair; compare the related Midrashic qavvaṣ "bushy haired" (Pope).

רְסִיסֵי לָיְלָה resisey laylah, approximately "drops of night." Though resis is found nowhere else in this precise meaning, the word's connection with drops is plausibly suggested by its root rss "to moisten, sprinkle," Ezek. 46:14 (compare Arabic ršš "to spray, rain lightly"), as well as by the use of *resisim* for fragments, tiny bits, splinters, Amos 6:11. The word is likely a poetic synonym of "dew," *ṭal,* which is its parallel in this sentence. The dew falls copiously in the Near East during certain months; compare Judg. 6:38.

The motif of the frustrated lover begging admittance at the door of the beloved is a topos also of ancient Egyptian and Greek poetry. See Fox, 282–83, and the examples cited there.

5:4 שָׁלַח יָדוֹ מִן־הַחֹר *šalaḥ yado min ha-ḥor,* literally "stretched his hand through the hole," most likely the keyhole. A traditional door key in Near Eastern villages, commonly made of wood, was of considerable size, and the keyhole large enough for a man to put his hand through it and open an (unlocked) door from the outside by slipping the inside bolt (Pope). The word "latch" here is borrowed from the JPS and Falk's translation.

שָׁלַח יָד *šalaḥ yad* "to stretch out one's hand" is a standard biblical idiom; see Gen. 22:10, 1 Kings 13:4, Ezek. 10:7, Ps. 144:7. For a discussion of *min* "through" see notes 2:9, 4:1.

מֵעַי הָמוּ עָלָיו *me'ay hamu 'alav,* literally "my innards stirred for him." The inner organs, specifically the bowels, the heart, the "walls" of the heart, as well as the soul, are used metaphorically in poetic idioms, often with the verb *hamah* "to stir," to express emotions, intense excitement, love, desire, yearning, but also sorrow, regret, anxiety, as in Jer. 4:19, 31:19, Ps. 42:6; see also Ps. 40:9, Gen. 42:28. Our translation with the heart beating "wildly" borrows from Carmi, 175.

Notice the preposition *'al* (in *'alav*) to mark the object of the yearning, in contrast with *l-* in the same idiom in Jer. 31:19, *hamu me'ay lo* "my innards stirred for him." The preference for *'al* may be a peculiarity of the language of the Song; see also 7:11.

Some commentators have attempted to understand this verse as a euphemistic account of sexual intercourse. This is implausible in the context, since the Shulamite has yet to open the door (see Fox). Moreover, this approach is faulty, since it disregards the idiomatic nature—and hence inviolability—of these two phrases; since they are idioms, they cannot be understood by an analysis of their individual components.

5:5 מוֹר עֹבֵר *mor 'ober,* "liquid myrrh" (also 5:13) is probably the same as the oil of myrrh of Esther 2:12. If the Shulamite perfumed herself in anticipation of the young man's visit (see Ruth 3:3 and also Prov. 7:17, where the bed is perfumed), her speech in 5:3 is clearly a form of coquetry.

5:6 וְדוֹדִי *ve-dodi* "but my lover," with the adversative meaning of the conjunction *ve-* as in Song 3:1,2, and later in 5:6. See discussion in note 1:5.

חָמַק עָבָר *ḥamaq ʿabar*, approximately "had slipped away, was gone." (Elsewhere *ḥamaq* occurs only in Jer. 31:21, in the hitpaʿel "turn oneself, turn away"). Verbs of the general meaning "to pass, go away" in close sequence mark quick departure and total disappearance, as in Song 2:11, literally "has passed and is gone." See also Isa. 8:8, Dan. 11:10,40. The lover may have left abruptly because he was concerned about the watchmen making their rounds.

נַפְשִׁי יָצְאָה *napši yaṣeʾah*, literally "my soul went forth." Elsewhere an expression for dying; see Gen. 35:18, Ps. 146:4. Here it is a hyperbolical "I nearly died," expressing a deep emotional upsurge; compare 5:4.

בְדַבְּרוֹ *be-dabbero*, literally "as he spoke." The difficulty here is that the lover's speech occurs earlier, in 5:2. Various alternative readings and emendations have been proposed (Rashi, Ginsburg, Pope, Fox), but this appears to be the Shulamite's recollection of her feelings, an expression of regret about her delay (similarly Zakovitch, 1992).

5:7 הִכּוּנִי פְצָעוּנִי *hikkuni peṣaʿuni* "they beat me, they wounded me." Whether this verse recounts an actual situation, a fantasy, or a dream, it reveals a tension between the conventional social mores and the behavior of the young lovers.

נָשְׂאוּ ... מֵעָלַי *naśeʾu . . . me-ʿalay* "they took . . . from me," literally "they lifted from on top of me." For this less common use of the verb *naśaʾ*, usually meaning "to lift, carry," compare Num. 16:15 "not even one ass have I taken [*naśaʾti*] from them."

The *redid*, a veil (Syriac *redidā*) or shawl, or any other light article of clothing, is mentioned only once more, by Isaiah (3:23), in his list of the fashionable apparel worn by the wanton women of Jerusalem as they saunter about the city. Hence this would seem to suggest a stylish bit of finery rather than a basic article of clothing.

The translation offered here assumes a break after *me'alay* (in accord with the liturgical accents), with the words "the watchmen of the walls" following as an independent phrase. Far from being a superfluous addition, "tacked on" at the end of the utterance, this wording is a favored dramatizing device in many languages, often used in writing to imitate everyday spoken usage, as in English, "They haven't done a thing for the environment, those scientists!" A mark of excited speech, this syntax in 5:7 artfully captures the tone of exasperation in the words of the Shulamite as she relates the violent encounter. The nuance is lost in translations such as NEB: "The watchmen . . . struck me and wounded me; the watchmen on the walls took away my cloak." It is a sign of the subtly differentiated verbal artistry of the Song that this syntax is not used in the corresponding peaceful scene in 3:3.

5:8 הִשְׁבַּעְתִּי אֶתְכֶם *hišba'ti 'etkem,* literally "I hereby adjure you." Notice that the characteristic oath "never to awaken, never to arouse love" in the other three uses of the adjuration formula, 2:7, 3:5, 8:4, is conspicuously absent in 5:8; here the adjuration phrase is followed instead by a "real" request to the daughters of Jerusalem about what they should say to the lover if they find him. Song 5:8–9 involves an actual dialogue, with the Shulamite's "Swear to me" picked up by the daughters in their response, ". . . that we must swear to you?" The verb of adjuration loses much of its literal meaning here, and amounts to little more than an urgently solemn "I entreat you, please promise me!" We are dealing with a well-known phenomenon in language: the semantic "depletion" of originally emphatic expressions, specifically when used in a new context.

שֶׁ לוֹ תַּגִּידוּ־מַה דּוֹדִי־אֶת תִּמְצְאוּ־אִם *'im timṣe'u 'et dodi mah tag-gidu lo še.* . . . Literally, "If you find my lover, what will you tell him? That . . ." The question-answer format is purposeful, serving to emphasize the message "You must tell him, tell him nothing other than . . . !" and is similarly used in Hosea 9:14, "Give them, O Lord—What will you give them? Give them an aborting womb and dry breasts!" (Pope). The Song may in fact attempt to recapture here the actual broken speech of the exasperated Shulamite.

Notice that all four versions of the adjuration formula use the same particles, *'im* and *mah.* In 2:7, 3:5 and 8:4 they function as negations, while 5:8 uses them in their ordinary conditional and interrogative function.

5:9 מַה־דּוֹדֵךְ מִדּוֹד *mah dodek mi(n)-dod,* literally "What is your lover from a lover?" A loose paraphrase would be something like "What's so special about your lover, what makes him different from others?" The positioning of this question suggests that it serves at least in part as a rhetorical invitation for the praise song to begin, 5:10–16. Compare the question in 7:1.

Though found nowhere else in the Bible, this specific question pattern—*mah* X *mi(n)* Y "How is this different from that?"—is a staple of talmudic and rabbinic usage, e.g., *mah yom mi(n)-yomayim* "How is this particular day different from others?" or *mah 'eloheykem mi(n)-kol ha-'elohim* "How is your God different from all other gods?" (Rashi paraphrasing Song 5:9). For use of the preposition *mi(n)-* in the same sense but with the verb *šanah,* see *mah ništannah ha-laylah ha-zeh mi(n)-kol ha-leylot* "How is this night different from all other nights?," the well-known question in the Passover Haggadah. And see Esther 3:8 *dateyhem šonot mi(n)-kol ʿam* "their laws are different from those of other nations."

Since the question of Song 5:9 is in the format *mah* X *mi(n)* Y? known from postbiblical Hebrew, this question is likely to have the "differentiating" meaning characteristic of that pattern rather than the comparative meaning commonly ascribed to it: "What/how is your lover better/above/more than any lover?" (KJV, RSV, NEB, Ginsburg, Gordis, Pope, Fox). In the latter reading, one would have expected an explicit predicate word (verb or adjective), as in the standard comparative structure of biblical Hebrew, e.g., Song 1:2 *tobim mi(n)-yayin* "better than wine," 4:10 *mah yapu . . . mah tobu mi(n)-yayin* "how much sweeter than wine," 5:10 *dagul me-rebabah* "more elevated than ten thousand." Since the question pattern under discussion is a syntactic hapax in the Bible, but a stylistic hallmark of postbiblical phraseology, its use in the Song is another indicator of late composition. Analyzed in this way, the Masoretic Text is surely not in need of an emendation because it makes no "grammatical sense," as claimed by Albright (quoted in Pope, 530).

שֶׁכָּכָה הִשְׁבַּעְתָּנוּ *še-kakah hišbaʿtanu,* literally "that you make us swear in this way," more likely means simply "that you entreat us like that?" See note 5:8.

5:10 צַח וְאָדוֹם *ṣaḥ ve-ʾadom,* literally "white and red," but covering a broader spectrum, such as "radiant, shining," and "earth-colored, ruddy." Compare the idealized image of Jerusalem's princes in Lam. 4:7, "more radiant than milk, their bodies more ruddy than coral" (ṣaḥḥu, 'ademu). Since the image refers not only to the outward appearance of the lover, its broader symbolism is here suggested by a free rendition with "milk" and "wine," the pair of substances epitomizing "white" and "red" in the Bible. Milk and wine are associated with health, youthful strength, earthiness, and marvelous fertility, Gen. 49:11–12, Joel 4:18. In the Song, in addition, they evoke sweetness and intoxicating sensuality, in reference to both the young man and the Shulamite, 1:2; 4:10,11; 5:1,12; 7:10. Also compare Prov. 23:31, where the red sparkle of the wine is considered seductively attractive.

In the following passage the lover is presented in a mixture of images denoting, on the one hand, a sculptural or architectural solidity, and on the other, tenderness and sweetness. His statue-like image, the comparisons with precious metals, the movement from the "head of gold" down to the legs (5:15), call to mind the description of the idol in Dan. 2:31–33. The similarity extends to the very choice of terms; see note on me'av, 5:14. Both descriptions may owe something to the knowledge of Greek sculpture in Palestine (see p. 26). Also, the "rods of gold" and "marble pillars," 5:14,15, are reminiscent of Esther 1:6, where specific objects of accomplished craftsmanship at the court of King Ahasuerus are similarly described.

5:11 כֶּתֶם פָּז ketem paz. Two different types of gold, or poetic synonyms for the metal. The pairing of the two nouns means "pure gold," compare 2 Chron. 9:17, interpreting 1 Kings 10:18.

תַּלְתַּלִּים taltallim is a hapax. Whether meaning "fronds of a date palm" (Fox, based on Akkadian taltallu), or "hill upon hill," as in the Mishnaic interpretation of this verse, the word amplifies the notion of the young man's thick hair implied in the word qevuṣṣot, 5:2.

5:12 ... עֵינָיו כְּיוֹנִים 'eynav ke-yonim . . . , literally "his eyes are like doves by streams of water, bathed in milk." A poetic fantasy. Doves indeed choose regions with abundant water, and "milk" may allude to the color of doves, or the whites of the lover's eyes, as has been suggested. But here again it is pointless to approach the images with a dogged literalism. Rather, the images of abundant waters and sensuous bathing in milk suggest lushness and a tranquil sensuality. In this understanding, the core of the image is the phrase *roḥaṣot be-ḥalaḇ* "bathed/immersed/ awash in milk," a hyperbole of abundance similar to that of Job 29:6 "when my feet were bathed in butter," with the same verb *raḥaṣ be-*. For "milk" and "streams of water" in similar symbolic contexts elsewhere, compare Ps. 126:4, Joel 4:18, Judg. 5:25.

The enigmatic *mille't* occurs nowhere else, but the root suggests "plenty, fullness"; in this respect the image may be similar to that of the pools in 7:5.

5:13 כַּעֲרוּגַת הַבֹּשֶׂם *ka-'arugat ha-bośem* "like a bed of spices." The point of the simile is that the *scent* of the cheeks is like a bed of spices. There is no need to read "beds" (plural *ka-'arugot*) against the Masoretic Text, as do the Septuagint and most modern commentators. On the other hand, the plural form is fully justified in 6:2, which refers to "actual" spice beds in the lover's garden.

מִגְדְּלוֹת מֶרְקָחִים *migdelot merqaḥim,* literally "towers of perfumes, mixed spices, or ointments." A hyperbole for exquisite scent, bettering the preceding comparison—"a bed of . . . no, towers of!"—with the intensification expressed both in the shift from the singular to the plural and from the smaller to the larger. *Migdalot* "towers" are hyperbolic also for the Shulamite's breasts, 8:10. Again, there is no justification for revoweling the Masoretic Text to *megaddelot* (agentive pi'el) "that make grow," as correctly argued by Fox.

Spices were considered so precious that they were kept in storehouses along with other valuables; compare Hezekiah's "treasuries" (*'oṣarot*) for silver and gold, precious stones, spices, etc. in 2 Chron. 32:27.

שׁוֹשַׁנִּים *šošannim.* According to Ibn Ezra, the lilies are mentioned "for the smell, not the sight."

5:14 יָדָיו גְּלִילֵי זָהָב מְמֻלָּאִים בַּתַּרְשִׁישׁ *yadav geliley zahaḇ memulla'im ba-taršiš,* literally "his arms are rods of gold filled [i.e., studded, inlaid] with *taršiš*," a precious stone of unknown nature, mentioned also Exod. 28:20, Dan. 10:6, and elsewhere. Normally *yad* "hand" can also be used in a broader sense for the upper as well as the lower arm.

מֵעָיו עֶשֶׁת שֵׁן *me'av 'ešet šen,* literally "his belly a polished block of ivory." Unique use of *me'ayim,* elsewhere in the Bible exclusively denoting the inner organs, bowels, intestines, womb; see Gen. 15:4, Num.

5:22, Ezek. 3:3, Isa. 49:1, Jonah 2:1–2 (see note 5:4 above). The use of *me'ayim* in the sense of "belly" strongly points to the word's Aramaic cognate as the source for this meaning, especially since the present verse recalls the statue of the idol in Dan. 2:32, with "its belly [*me'ōhî*] made of bronze." The Song may have resorted to this term for the purpose of differentiation: the Shulamite's belly (7:2) is simply a *beṭen,* the common Hebrew word for this body part in humans and animals, with the comparison to a mound of wheat further suggesting softness. The youth's hard muscular belly, on the other hand, is referred to as *me'ayim,* a term that may have been borrowed from the technical vocabulary of sculpture.

עֶשֶׁת *'ešet,* a biblical hapax, but used in Mishnaic Hebrew in reference to a work of artistic craftsmanship, specifically a polished block or bar.

שֵׁן *šen* "ivory," not just stark white but also in rosy flesh tones, was treasured in ancient Israel as a rare and beautiful material. It was carved, covered with gold leaf, inlaid with semiprecious stones, and used for furniture, beds, and panels of palace walls, as in Amos 3:15, 6:4, 1 Kings 22:39, Ps. 45:9. Some of these decorative inlays have been found in an archaeological excavation at Samaria, the capital of the ancient northern kingdom of Israel. Solomon's luxury imports included ivory, and 1 Kings 10:18–22 singles out his "majestic ivory throne . . . overlaid with the finest gold." In Midrashic folklore, that throne in addition was "studded with beryls, inlaid with marble, and jeweled with emeralds, and rubies, and pearls, and all manner of gems" (Ginzberg, vol. 4, 157).

מְעֻלֶּפֶת סַפִּירִים *me'ullepet sappirim,* literally "covered with sapphires/ lapis lazuli," i.e., adorned, inlaid with; see preceding note. For the root *'lp* see Gen. 38:14 *va-tit'allap* (hitpa'el) "she wrapped herself up," and compare the cognate Arabic root *ġlf* "to cover, wrap, envelop."

5:15 מְיֻסָּדִים עַל־אַדְנֵי־פָז *meyussadim 'al 'adney paz,* literally "set upon foundations of gold," i.e., the young man's feet/lower legs upon which his marble legs/thighs rest. Apart from providing a suitable closure to this account of the body parts which began with the head of gold (5:11), golden feet may also have been deliberately conceived as a contrast to feet of a baser material, such as those of iron and clay that spell the doom of the idol in Dan. 2:33–34. (This does not presuppose a connection between the accounts in Daniel and the Song, both of which may well go back to similar, yet independent, earlier sources).

מַרְאֵהוּ כַּלְּבָנוֹן *mar'ehu ka-lebanon,* literally "the sight of him is like Lebanon." A hyperbole with Lebanon as the typical symbol of majesty evokes not just the mountain (Judg. 3:3), but also the towering cedar trees, lush vegetation, wine, and sweet fragrance associated with that region; see Isa. 35:2, 40:16, 60:13, Hos. 14:6, Nahum 1:4. Also see notes 2:3, 5:10.

בָּחוּר כָּאֲרָזִים *bahur ka-'arazim,* literally "a young man like cedars," continues the preceding comparison. For the use of the plural in a generic sense to denote the species, compare Song 2:9, 4:15, 7:9. This translation understands *bahur* as a noun (as in Deut. 32:25, Amos 2:11, Eccles. 11:9), but the interpretation as a passive participle "distinguished" is equally possible.

5:16 חִכּוֹ מַמְתַקִּים *hikko mamtaqqim,* literally "his palate is sweet wine," an allusion to his kisses (compare 7:10) or also sweet words, with the palate, *hek,* as the organ of speech (compare Prov. 8:7, Job 31:30). For *mamtaqqim* "sweet wine," see Neh. 8:10. Here again, an image— "the palate as wine"—is applied to both lovers (5:16 and 7:10). Compare the image of the eyes as doves, 1:15, 4:1 and 5:12.

כֻּלּוֹ מַחֲמַדִּים *kullo mahmaddim,* literally "his entirety is delight," a generalizing statement summing up the details of the praise song, paralleling the young man's words to the Shulamite at the end of his praise song, 4:7.

6:2 לִרְעוֹת בַּגַּנִּים *lir'ot ba-gannim,* literally "to pasture/graze in the gardens." For the garden metaphor and "pasturing," compare 2:16, 4:16, 6:3. For "gathering lilies," compare 5:1 "gathering myrrh and spices," with the same erotic meaning. The plural *gannim* probably does not refer to gardens but to a single garden or garden area, as the so-called plural of local extension; compare *panim* "face," *savva'rim* "neck," *ma'amaqqim* "depth," *margelot* "area close to the feet," *miškanot* "dwelling place." See WO, 120.

6:4 יָפָה ... כְּתִרְצָה *yapah . . . ke-tirsah* "beautiful as Tirzah." The purpose of the comparison with a renowned metropolis is to evoke the Shulamite's regal appearance and proud beauty. That the name Tirzah is associated via its root (*rasah*) with notions such as "pleasant," "to please, favor" may have also been a factor.

Tirzah is yet another element in the rich allusive web that links the Song with the long bygone era when this ancient royal city, like Heshbon (7:5), was part of Solomon's vast empire. Its mention alongside Jerusalem—indeed, on a par with the revered city that is the "joy of all the earth," the "perfection of beauty" (Ps. 48:3, 50:2)—points to the glorious times before the breakup of that empire into a northern and southern kingdom in the tenth century BCE. Tirzah was the capital of the northern kingdom for a brief period, but by the time of the composition of the Song it was hardly more than a memory of a legendary royal city. Like all the references to Solomon and his glorious age, the reference to Tirzah should not be taken as an indicator of an early date of composition, as is sometimes done.

אֲיֻמָּה *'ayummah,* literally "terrifying," "awe-inspiring." The Shulamite's beauty is so intense, her appearance so majestic, as to strike awe in those who see her. This interpretation accords well with her cosmic attributes in 6:10. Alternatively, one may be dealing here with a semantic transition, such as found in many languages, from the literal sense, "frightful, horrible," to "extraordinary," "of unusual, exquisite quality"; compare English *terrific,* French *terrible.*

כַּנִּדְגָּלוֹת *ka-nidgalot,* see 6:10.

הָסֵבִּי עֵינַיִךְ מִנֶּגְדִּי שֶׁהֵם הִרְהִיבֻנִי 6:5 *hasebbi 'eynayik mi(n)-negdi še-hem hirhibuni,* literally "turn your eyes away from me, for they frighten me!" The free translation with "dazzle" is adopted here from the NEB. There is a gradual intensification in the way the Song speaks of the Shulamite's eyes: first simply "like doves," 1:15, 4:1, then as powerful enough to ravish the heart of her lover, 4:9, and finally even to elicit his fear, 6:5. Verse 6:5 breaks away from the conventional list, in which the eyes are merely described, or compared, and speaks of their effect on the young man. This breach of the convention is especially meaningful in chapter 6 with its hyperboles about the Shulamite's intimidating beauty.

וּשְׁמֹנִים פִּילַגְשִׁים 6:8 *u-šemonim pilagšim,* literally "and eighty the concubines." Sixty and eighty are conventional round figures; see 3:7. Their juxtaposition is here possibly intended as a variation on the biblical "three-and-four" formula (e.g., Amos 1:3,6,9, 2:1), with the two figures representing multiples of three and four. Compare Greenfield (1965), 257.

Though the figures are far more modest than Solomon's "seven hundred royal wives" and "three hundred concubines" (1 Kings 11:3), the very mention of queens and concubines, and the court setting in 6:9, suggest another bit of extrabiblical Solomonic folklore, as in 3:7–11.

עֲלָמוֹת *'alamot,* "maidens," the same word as in 1:3. Simply young women, paralleling *banot* in 6:9, in contrast to the preceding two classes of women, which are associated with royalty.

6:9 אַחַת הִיא יוֹנָתִי *'aḥat hi' yonati,* literally "one she is, my dove," i.e., one of a kind, without equal. The Shulamite would stand out in any crowd, even among royalty. Compare the corresponding affirmation of the young man's uniqueness in 5:10.

אַחַת הִיא לְאִמָּה *'aḥat hi' le-'immah,* literally "one she is to her mother." A biblical idiomatic expression, involving a father or mother, to indicate a child's unique belovedness or preciousness; see Gen. 22:2, Prov. 4:3. For the use of the cardinal numeral "one" in the sense of "unique, one of a kind" (*yaḥid* elsewhere), compare 2 Sam. 7:23 *goy 'eḥad* "a unique nation on earth" (JPS).

This "listing" style, with the numeral characteristically in frontal position, followed by the subject, literally "Sixty they are, the queens, and eighty the concubines . . . One she is, my dove," is found in Prov. 30:24,29 "Four are the small of the earth" and later in the counting games of the Passover Haggadah, where various numerals are associated with specific entities.

בָּרָה הִיא לְיוֹלַדְתָּה *barah hi' le-yoladtah,* literally "clear/pure/without blemish she is to the one who bore her." Secondarily, the adjective evokes the notions "bright," "luminous," "full of light"; see its use with the sun in 6:10. For a similar association see Ps. 19:9, where *barah* is followed by "making the eyes light up" (*me'irat 'eynayim*).

רָאוּהָ בָנוֹת וַיְאַשְּׁרוּהָ . . . וַיְהַלְלוּהָ *ra'uha banot va-ye'ašševuha . . . va-yehalleluha,* literally "women saw her and called her fortunate/happy/blessed . . . and praised her," compare to Gen. 30:13 *'išševuni banot* "the daughters will call me happy." These two "speech act" verbs (see WO, 403) are used specifically to introduce a quotation of praise, see 6:10, and occur in the same order, and for the same purpose, in Prov. 31:28.

These are the only two occurrences of verbs with the *waw*-conversive in the Song. This deliberately archaizing usage is in keeping with the lofty tone of the passage. Compare *'ašer* in 1:1.

6:10 מִי־זֹאת הַנִּשְׁקָפָה *mi zo't ha-nišqapah*, literally "who is that looking forth . . . ," a stylized formula; see note 3:6.

שַׁחַר *šaḥar* "dawn" or "morning star." Here most likely the latter, in parallelism with the astral bodies mentioned in the following. A beloved woman is compared to a star in the ancient Egyptian poem quoted on p. 15: "Behold her, like Sothis rising." Sothis is the star Sirius (Fox, pp. 52, 56).

כַּנִּדְגָּלוֹת *ka-nidgalot* "like the *nidgalot*." Though *nidgalot* itself remains obscure, the word's morphology and its root (*dgl*) offer a clue. A passive participle (of the nip̄'al), the word has its closest formal parallel in the passive participle (qal) *dagul* in 5:10, "prominent, conspicuous, outstanding" ("towering above" in our free translation). Since it has the definite article, *nidgalot* is a nominalized plural adjective, literally "those who are prominent, conspicuous."

Examining the word in its context yields a further insight. Whenever "sun" and "moon" in the Bible are followed by a third term, that term is typically "stars," "the hosts of the heavens," or the like; see Gen. 37:9; Deut. 4:19, 17:3; 2 Kings 23:5; Jer. 8:2, 31:34; Ps. 148:3. Hence the word is best understood as an epithet for stars, or for a specific group of stars. This fits well with the two preceding words for the moon and the sun, which are epithets, *lebanah* "the white one" and *ḥammah* "the hot one." Analyzed in this way, the verse reveals a recognizable organizing principle: day-night-day-night (parallelism) or star-moon-sun-stars (chiasmus).

No similar argument based on contextual plausibility could be made in 6:4 for *nidgalot* as an epithet, say, for a group of cities distinguished by their elevated locations, as a parallel to Tirzah and Jerusalem. Observing that 6:4 lacks a fourth member, Goitein (1965) suggested that the phrase *ka-nidgalot* is integral only to 6:10, and secondary in 6:4. Though his approach differs from the one presented here, Goitein arrived at a similar conclusion concerning the meaning of *nidgalot*, proposing that this was a term of popular astronomy for especially brilliant stars of the first order of magnitude, for which the less technical term was *kokebey 'or* "stars of light," Ps. 148:3. The expression "daunting as the stars" reflects the awe the ancient Hebrews felt for these heavenly bodies, see Job 9:9, 38:31–33, Amos 5:8. The astral references in Song 6:10 must be understood as hyperboles of adulation, like the image of the Shulamite "rising" from the desert, 3:6. The free translation offered here ("the stars in their courses") borrows from Judg. 5:20.

Much of the fame of this enigmatic phrase, which occurs in the Bible only here and in 6:4, rests on fanciful translations of the type "like ranked phalanxes," "like bannered hosts," or "as an army with banners" (compare Septuagint, Ibn Ezra, KJV, RSV). But these readings cannot be upheld. Though they have the same root as *degel* "banner," the words *nidgalot* and *dagul* attest to the fact that by the time of the Song this root had developed new metaphorical meanings no longer associable with the literal "banner." See discussion in note 2:4.

6:11 At least some of the interpretive difficulties of 6:11–12 dissolve if the young man is understood as the speaker of both verses, rather than the Shulamite, as has generally been assumed (KJV, RSV, Pope, Fox, Murphy, and others). Although there is no grammatical way to tell the gender of the speaker in 6:11, the garden and fruit symbolism offers an important clue. Throughout the Song the garden is a symbol of the Shulamite and her sexuality: she is the "locked garden" (4:12), inaccessible to anyone but her lover; he alone is invited to the garden (4:16), and he alone enters it (5:1). He describes her as a "garden spring" (4:15) and addresses her as "the one who dwells in the gardens" (8:13). Only she is associated with both vines and pomegranates in erotic contexts (1:6, 4:13, 7:9,13, 8:2); the only fruit associated with him is the apricot. For all these reasons, it makes better sense to see the young man as the one "going down" to the garden in 6:11. This verse parallels 6:2, where the lover "has gone down to his garden."

The preceding argumentation is supported by a more general consideration. In the customary expression for sexual intercourse in the Bible, the male is the agent: "he came to her," never "she came to him." Correspondingly, in the Song it is always the man who comes to visit the woman, not the other way around: compare the two visits to the Shulamite, 2:8–14, 5:2–6, and the visits to the garden, 5:1, 6:2. Similarly, in the two parting scenes, 2:17 and 8:14, her request that he "run away" presupposes that he has come to visit her.

גִּנַּת אֱגוֹז *ginnat 'egoz*, literally "nut garden." For *ginnah* "garden" see Esther 1:5; 7:7,8. A biblical hapax, *'egoz* is the common term in postbiblical Hebrew for nuts, specifically walnuts (its close phonetic cognates suggest an old shared Mediterranean word; compare Arabic *jawz;* Ethiopic, Syriac, Persian *gawz;* Aramaic *goza, 'egoza;* Armenian *engoiz*). Here likely used as a collective noun for the trees rather than the fruit, paralleling the vine and the pomegranates in the following. Compare 2:3, *tappuaḥ.*

אִבֵּי הַנָּחַל *'ibbey ha-naḥal.* Based on Job 8:12 *be-'ibbo* "in its prime," the phrase is usually taken to refer to fresh young vegetation. *Naḥal* "valley, wadi," but also commonly "stream, torrent, brook," which would fit the water imagery associated with the Shulamite, 4:12,15.

6:12   Generally conceded to be the most difficult verse in the Song, 6:12 has received the widest range of interpretations imaginable and countless suggested emendations, and has at times been omitted as untranslatable (Segal, Falk). See Pope, 548ff. for an overview. The translation proposed here is based on the Masoretic Text, with a single crucial emendation at the end of the verse.

לֹא יָדַעְתִּי נַפְשִׁי *lo' yada'ti napši,* literally "I did not know myself." A fixed idiom denoting the unexpectedness of the event described in the next clause, approximately meaning: "Before I knew myself [such and such happened]." For the connection between "not knowing" and the perception of suddenness, see also uses such as Isa. 47:11 "ruin shall come to you suddenly, and you will not know," Jer. 50:24 "I set a snare for you, and you were trapped unawares," literally "and you did not know" (Ginsburg).

But *lo' yada'ti napši* may be understood in a different way, namely as an expression of deep emotional agitation. Just as in the corresponding English phrase "I was beside myself with . . . ," the Hebrew expression marks only the intensity, not the nature, of the emotion; the latter is revealed by the context. (In Modern Hebrew literature, *lo' yada'ti napši* can indeed be followed by phrases such as "with grief/despair" as well as "with joy/delight." Compare also "my innards stirred for him," discussed in note 5:4.) In the one other occurrence of *lo' yada'ti napši* in the Bible, Job 9:21 "I do not know myself, I loathe my life," the context is one of despair. In 6:12, on the other hand, the context is clearly one of great joy, excitement, or amazement.

In either interpretation, *nepeš* "self," literally "soul," functions as an integral component of the idiom (marking reflexivity, as it does occasionally also in other contexts, e.g., Isa. 44:20, Prov. 22:5). Hence *nepeš* is not the subject of the following verb, as implied in translations of the type "my soul/fancy/desire has made/set/hurled me" (KJV and others).

שָׂמַתְנִי מַרְכְּבוֹת עַמִּי־נָדִיב *śamatni markebot 'ammi-nadib,* literally "she put/placed me in the chariots of *'ammi-nadib.*" We understand this as the young man's metaphorical description of his erotic encounter with the Shulamite.

A key to the enigma of *'ammi-nadib* may be found in a poetic expression that occurs in some of the most ancient texts in the Bible, "the nobles of the people." It manifests itself in this form, or with minor variations, in Num. 21:18 *nedibey ha-'am,* Ps. 47:10 *nedibey 'ammim* (with "people" in the plural), and Judg. 5:2,9, *be-hitnaddeb 'am, ha-mitnaddebim ba-'am,* referring to those who "behaved nobly among the people" (two forms of the root *ndb* followed by *'am* "people"). But most illuminating to the language and imagery of Song 6:12 are two parallel texts, Ps. 113:7–8, "He raises the poor from the dust, lifts up the needy from the ash heap, to seat them with nobles, with the nobles of His people" (*le-hošibi 'im nedibim, 'im nedibey 'ammo*), and 1 Sam. 2:8, with identical wording but a modified ending, "He raises the poor . . . , lifts up the needy . . . , to seat them with nobles [*'im nedibim*], granting them a seat of honor."

The expression "the nobles of the people" contains the same two components that make up *'ammi-nadib,* though in reverse order. Hence, an emendation restoring the order would yield *nedib 'ammi,* literally "the nobleman of my people," or in a superlative sense "the most noble of my people." Such an emendation would not be unique in the Bible. As Gordis (1933) has shown, the enigmatic Deut. 33:21 *spwn vyt'* defies all interpretation, until the order is reversed to *vyt'spwn* (a single word), which reads *va-yit'assepun* "and they gathered." This emendation, too, is supported by the context: thus restored, Deut. 33:21 reveals itself as semantically identical with Deut. 33:5 *be-hit'assep* "when (they) gathered." Two other cases of erroneous inversions are Jer. 17:3 and Ezek. 24:17 (Zakovitch, 117). The fact that *'m* stands orthographically for both "with" and "people" may have contributed to the error in Song 6:12. And so probably did the clause-final position of *nadib* "nobleman" in 7:2.

To "seat with the nobles" means, in a physical sense, to raise from the ground, to elevate someone to a higher location. But the image must also be understood in terms of its symbolism: to grace an individual by the gesture of letting him sit among the powerful. In Song 6:12 both associations come together: to be placed "in the chariot of the most noble of my people" evokes the notion of an "elevation," a grace granted by the Shulamite to her lover, in this case serving as a metaphor for the erotic act. The metaphor of the chariot performs a double role here: (1) a royal chariot is a place of great honor, as in the case of Joseph the viceroy, Gen. 41:43, and compare the expression in Isa. 22:18, "the chariots of your pride." Similarly, letting someone ride a horse, Esther 6:9,11, 1 Kings 1:33–38, or ride "the high places of the earth," Deut. 32:13, Isa. 58:14, Hab. 3:19. (2) In addition, in the context of Song 6:12, the "chariot" has a sexual connotation, evoking an image of riding, as in "my mare," 1:9. The Song in 6:12 thus uses for an erotic purpose a specific topos that is used elsewhere in the Bible in a nonerotic sense.

In this analysis, there is a thematic connection between two sets of verses: the anticipation of the erotic encounter in 4:16 "let my lover come into his garden" is followed by the fulfillment in 5:1 "I have come into my garden." Similarly, the anticipation of 6:11 "I went down to the walnut grove to see if . . ." is followed by the fulfillment in 6:12 "she sat me. . . ."

Finally, a few grammatical clarifications:

The plural "chariots" is the so-called plural of local extension; compare note 6:2 on *gannim*.

For the superlative sense of *nedib 'ammi* "the most noble of my people" (instead of the literal "the nobleman of my people"), compare to similar semikut-constructions listed in note 3:7, under *mi(n)-gibborey yiśra'el*. Taken in the superlative sense, the "chariot of the most noble of my people" implies something like "the most wonderful, most noble of chariots." The association of the Shulamite with nobility is all the more meaningful in the context of her epithet in 7:2.

The use of *śam* "to place something" without a preposition "in/on/at" is common in Hebrew: Gen. 28:11, Exod. 40:29, 1 Sam. 19:13. (The same applies to other verbs, as in Gen. 18:1 "to sit at" and elsewhere.)

7:1   Apart from the widespread assumption, accepted here, that verse 7:1 begins a scene involving a dance by the Shulamite, there is no consensus as to the identity of the other participants, the speakers involved in the verbal exchange, the physical setting, or indeed the meaning of the verse. The following is only one of several possible interpretations: two groups facing each other, possibly of the daughters of Jerusalem, are engaged in a dance (*meholat ha-mahanayim*, see pp. 199-200), with the Shulamite, the object of everybody's attention, dancing between them. One group urges her on enthusiastically, while the other responds with a rhetorical question ("Why do you gaze at the Shulamite?"). This "elicits" the young man's praise of her in the next verse, just as the daughters' question in 5:9 "How is your lover different from any other?" elicits the Shulamite's praise of him in 5:10–16.

שׁוּבִי שׁוּבִי הַשּׁוּלַמִּית *šubi šubi ha-šulammit*. The wide variety of interpretations offered for the imperative *šubi* attest to the inherent difficulty of this usage. The translation offered here assumes that the verb *šub* is not used in its primary meaning, as reflected in translations of the type "Return, return, O Shulamite!" (KJV, RSV, JPS, Fox, and others), but in the special sense of "do again, do once more," or "go on doing!" When used with this meaning, the verb *šub* typically modifies another verb, as in Gen. 30:31 *'ašubah 'er'eh so'nka* "I will again pasture your flock," literally "I will do again, I will pasture . . ."; Zech. 6:1 *va-'ašub va-'eśśa' 'eynay* "and once again I lifted my eyes," literally "and I did again, I lifted . . ."; Jer. 18:4 *ve-šab va-ya'aśehu* "[and the vessel he was making of clay was spoiled] and he reworked it [into another vessel]," literally "did again and made it into . . ." (also Jer. 36:28). Verbs other than *šub* are also used similarly, e.g., *yasap*: Gen. 25:1 *va-yosep va-yiqqah 'iššah* "and took another wife," literally "did again, took a wife"; Job 20:9 *'ayin šezapattu ve-lo' tosip* "the eye glimpses him only once," literally "glimpses, and does not do again." (For more examples of this usage see WO, 656.)

Now, in situations where the activity referred to is evident from the context (the "scene"), a modifying verb of this class may be used *without* an accompanying content verb. Compare 1 Kings 18:33–34, where Elijah the prophet instructs his Baal-worshiping colleagues: "And he said, 'Fill four buckets with water, and pour it on the burnt offering, and on the wood.' And then he said [*šenu, va-yišnu . . . šallešu, va-yešallešu*] 'Do a second time'; and they did a second time. And he said 'Do a third time'; and they did a third time." In a context like this, there is no doubt as to the activity referred to by the verbs. Similarly, the spectators' urgently repeated *šubi, šubi* addressed to the dancing Shulamite can only be understood as a request such as "Go on, dance some more!" or simply "Encore, encore!" In both instances, the concrete situation obviates the need to spell out the request: it clearly refers to the activity being performed right there on the scene.

The same address pattern, *ABAC,* with a quadruple imperative and a strong dynamic rhythm, occurs in Judg. 5:12, where, similarly, it serves to "cheer on" the person addressed: *'uri, 'uri, deborah, 'uri, 'uri, dabberi šir,* literally "Awake, awake, Deborah, awake, awake, utter a song!" Here too, as in Song 7:1, the verb must not be understood in its primary literal meaning but as a call to action: "Come on, Deborah! Sing!" Compare note 2:10 on *qumi.*

Interpretations of *šubi* along the line of "Turn!" (Gordis, Murphy), "Leap!" (Pope), "Halt!" (Ehrlich), "Twist, whirl!" (Budde) are untenable, either requiring emendations, such as to *sobbi* to achieve "turn,"or to *šebi* to achieve a cognate of Arabic *wtb* "to leap," or ascribing meanings to the Hebrew verb that it does not have.

The difficulty for commentators taking the imperative *šub* to mean "Return!" is that they must explain why the Shulamite is being asked to come back, and from where. Despite differences in detail, the various explanations provided to account for her alleged departure (e.g., Ginsburg), or intention to leave (Hakham), are narrative "fillers" that have no basis in the text.

הַשּׁוּלַמִּית *ha-šulammit* "the Shulamite." Of uncertain meaning. Found in the Bible only in this verse, this word has been variously explained as (1) "the Shunammite," i.e., from the village Shunem in the Jezreel plain, Josh. 19:18; 2 Kings 4:8,12; and compare 1 Kings 1:3,15 (Septuagint, Budde, and others); (2) "the peaceable one," or "complete, perfect one," on the basis of different formations of the root *šlm* (Fox); (3) a formal blend of the name of the Mesopotamian war goddess Shulmānītu (Ishtar) and "Shunammite" (Albright); (4) a feminine name corresponding to the name Solomon (Rowley, Goodspeed). For surveys of the arguments, see Fox, 157; Pope, 596–600; Murphy, 181.

Despite their substantial differences, these four views agree that the word is derived from some base form by means of the ending *-i/-it* (masc./fem.), but disagree as to the identity of that base form. Now, one of the most common uses of *-i/-it* in the Semitic languages is to form adjectives from the names of places, tribes, cities, peoples, nations, etc., the so-called *nisbe*-formations, or "gentilics" (English words borrowed from Arabic and Hebrew ending on *-i,* like "Iraqi," "Israeli," and "Saudi" are of this origin). Such a formation indeed underlies "the Shunammite," though this is not likely to be the epithet intended in the Song. Apart from the formal discrepancy between "Shulamite" and "Shunammite," the association of the heroine of the Song with Shunem has little to recommend it. The Shulamite lives in "the city," as Jerusalem is called, a walled metropolis with streets and squares (3:2–3, 5:7), not in a distant village, as Fox has rightly observed.

This reasoning points in the direction of another view, one not discussed above. Medieval Jewish exegetes like Ibn Ezra understood the word as an epithet "the Jerusalemite [fem.]" derived from *šalem*, a poetic term for Jerusalem, and one of the city's ancient names. See Ps. 76:3, where *šalem* is in parallelism with Zion—"His tent is in Salem, His dwelling in Zion"—and probably also Gen. 14:18. (In both instances *šalem* is rendered "Salem," which became the name of a Puritan settlement in the United States). In this derivation, the *šulammit* retains the root of *šalem* (*šlm*), but adopts the vocalic sequence *u - a* contained in the fuller name *yerušalayim* "Jerusalem" (the *u* is long in both *šulammit* and *yerušalayim*, as reflected in the consonantal spellings with *waw*, that is, *šwlmyt* and *yrwšlm*). Such condensed morphology is not atypical in the formation of gentilics. For example, in Num. 26:39 *ha-šupami* "the Shuphamite," a clan name, derives from *šepupam*. Here, too, the characteristic vowel sequence is maintained (it happens also to be *u - a*) despite the change in the consonantal makeup, *šppm* → *špm*.

In this interpretation, the woman in Song 7:1 is addressed by her epithet, "the Jerusalemite [fem.]." It is not uncommon in the Semitic languages for a person to be known not just by his or her name, but also by some gentilic term (of the type "Laban the Aramean"). Such a term may in fact become the major component of the form of address, as in the case of Mary Magdalene, who in Luke 8:2 is introduced as "Mary, called Magdalene" (from the town of Magdala; see Matt. 15:39).

This is not to rule out that *šulammit*, via its root *šlm*, may also allude to notions of peace, see Song 8:10 (*šalom*), or perfection, or to the name of Solomon (*šelomoh*), as assumed in views (2) and (4). Indeed this specific local epithet may have been chosen by the poet precisely for its echoes of *šalom* and *šelomoh*.

The article *ha-* of *ha-šulammit* fulfills the role of a vocative, hence literally "O Jerusalemite," or "O woman from Jerusalem," or the like. Compare 2 Sam. 14:4 *hoši'ah ha-melek* "help, O king!" and 2 Kings 6:26. It is only in Modern Hebrew that the word came to be a proper noun, Shulamit, in which status it no longer takes the article.

וְנֶחֱזֶה־בָּךְ *ve-neḥezeh bak*, literally "and we will watch you," with *ḥazah* perhaps implying specifically watching a scene, or even a "performance," to use a modern term. This may explain the choice of *ḥazah* here over the more common *ra'ah* in 3:11, 6:11 (in all three instances with *b-* introducing the object). Though both are verbs of seeing, *ḥazah* has a more specialized sense than *ra'ah*, as in *maḥazeh/ḥizzayon/ḥazut/ḥazon* "vision, theophany"; see Gen. 15:1, 2 Sam. 7:17, Isa. 21:2. (In Modern Hebrew, *ḥazah* underlies *maḥazeh* "theatrical performance," and its use in Song 7:1 may well have contributed to this noun's "secularization.")

מַה־תֶּחֱזוּ *mah teḥezu,* "Why do you [pl.] watch?" The plural may address the other group in this antiphonic exchange; alternatively, it may be the general, encompassing plural addressing "everybody," as in 2:5.

Though more typical in other interrogative functions, *mah* can be used in the sense of "why?" as in Exod. 14:15 *mah tiṣʿaq 'elay* "Why are you crying out to me?"; 2 Kings 7:3 *mah 'anaḥnu yošebim* "Why should we stay?"; 2 Kings 6:33 *mah 'oḥil* "Why should I wait?"

כִּמְחֹלַת הַמַּחֲנָיִם *ki-meḥolat ha-maḥanayim,* literally "as the dance of the two camps." Outside of Song 7:1, *maḥanayim* occurs only as the name of a specific location, in Gen. 32:3, 2 Sam. 2:8, and elsewhere. But an association of the dance with that place, say, a dance "à la Mahanayim," is out of the question because of the definite article (contra Murphy, 181). Rather, the dual form *maḥanayim* suggests a specific dance, such as one performed by two groups, or circles, or rows of dancers, as has been assumed by many commentators. The phrase itelf may well be a technical term for any dance characterized by two such formations.

Some translations assume the "camps" to be military, as in the RSV "a dance before two armies," and similarly KJV and Septuagint. But while a *maḥaneh* is often a military camp, it can also be simply a dwelling place a tribe temporarily "settling down," or any group of people in a place at a given time, not necessarily soldiers; see Gen. 33:8, 50:9; Exod. 14:19,20; Lev. 17:3. Indeed, the "armies" of the Septuagint and the KJV have as little cause to appear in 7:1 as in 6:4 and 6:10.

Meḥolah is a variant of *maḥol* "dance." Similar doublets in nonanimate nouns are *magor/megorah* "terror," *ḥeleq/ḥelqah,* "portion, allotted territory," *ḥagor/ḥagorah* "loin covering, belt," *gil/gilah* "joy," *gan/gannah* (also *ginnah,* 6:11) "garden," *yaʿar/yaʿrah* "honeycomb" (in 5:1 and 1 Sam. 14:27, respectively). These are far more common than is generally realized. For more examples, see WO, 106.

The interpretation adopted here is based on a widely accepted variant reading of Symmachus and various manuscripts, reflecting *bi-meḥolat ha-maḥanayim* "*in* the dance of the two camps." Attempts to make sense of the Masoretic Text's *ki-meḥolat* have yielded renditions such as "Why do you gaze upon the Shulamite as upon the dance of the two camps?" (Murphy), and "Why would you gaze . . . as if she were a camp-dancer?" (Fox). The second view requires either the acceptance of an exceptional "abbreviated form" *meḥolat* for the required *meḥolelet* (Hakham), or emendation of both the consonantal text and the vocalization, *ki-meḥolat ha-maḥanayim → ki-meḥolelet ha-maḥanim*. However, neither of these alternative interpretations can be entirely ruled out.

7:2   The dynamism of the scene, with the Shulamite described while she is dancing, as well as the order of the details, from feet to head, contrast with the order in the preceding three praise songs (4:1–5, 5:11–15, 6:5–7).

מַה־יָּפוּ פְעָמַיִךְ *mah yapu p̄eʿamayik̄.* Commonly rendered "how graceful are your feet," KJV, RSV, NEB, JPS, Pope, Fox, Murphy, and others. But the plural of *paʿam* refers less typically to the feet as such (Ps. 58:11) than to their activity, as in the Septuagint and Vulgate, "your steps." The words *mah yapu*—literally "how beautiful!"—cover a range far beyond that of mere physical appearance, for instance, in 4:10, where they apply to the Shulamite's lovemaking. Moreover, the plural of *paʿam,* as well as of *regel* "foot," may pertain not just to the visual, but also the acoustic effect: Judg. 5:28 *maddua̅ʿ ʾeḥeru paʿamey markebotav* "Why tarries the clatter of his chariots?" and Isa. 52:7 *mah naʾvu ʿal he-harim ragley mebasser* "How welcome on the mountain are the footsteps of the herald!" (JPS). Here in 7:2 the reference is to the graceful tapping sound of sandaled feet.

חַמּוּקֵי יְרֵכַיִךְ *ḥammuqey yerek̄ayik̄,* approximately "the turns/curves/rounds of your thighs." The root *ḥmq* (see 5:6) evokes notions of slippery smoothness.

כְּמוֹ חֲלָאִים מַעֲשֵׂה יְדֵי אָמָּן *kemo ḥalaʾim maʿasey yedey ʾomman,* literally "like ornaments, the work of a craftsman's hands." The *ḥalaʾim* are ornaments of unknown identity. The singular *ḥali* parallels *nezem* "[ornamental] ring" in Prov. 25:12 and Hosea 2:15. For *ʿasah* "to make, work" (here the noun *maʿaseh*) specifically in relation to artistic craftsmanship, see 1:11, 3:9,10.

7:3   שָׁרְרֵךְ אַגַּן הַסַּהַר *šorerek̄ ʾaggan ha-sahar,* literally "your navel is the bowl/basin/cup of the moon." Most commentators take the moon here as a metaphor for an idealized roundness, i.e., "Your navel is a rounded [i.e., moonlike] bowl" (RSV). Alternatively, the phrase "cup of the moon" may be understood in a possessive sense, as reflected in the present translation. The nature of the vessel called 'aggan is uncertain. In Isa. 22:24, the 'aggan is named along with other small vessels, indicating a cup or a bowl (rather than "basin," as elsewhere); the mention of wine in the following phrase also suggests a drinking vessel. In Akkadian agannu is a bowl.

The interpretation of sahar, a biblical hapax, as "moon" is supported by the cognates, Syriac sahrā "the moon" and Arabic šahr "month." The spelling with s (another indicator of lateness) replaces the earlier spelling with ś underlying Isa. 3:18 śaharonim "crescents." See the discussion in note 2:5 of sammekuni. The reference in Song 7:3 is most likely to the full moon, not a crescent or three-quarter moon, but see discussion in Pope, 618.

There is no compelling reason to support the assumption (Pope, Murphy) that the word šorerek is used here as a euphemism for the vulva. The related meaning "umbilical cord" occurs in Ezek. 16:4 and Prov. 3:8. And see the Arabic cognate surr, surrah "umbilical cord, navel." See pp. 41, 127.

אַל־יֶחְסַר הַמָּזֶג 'al yeḥsar ha-mazeg, literally "may it never lack mixed wine." Wine was mixed with water and with other wines or spices; the Midrash relates the custom of mixing strong and weak wines so as to increase their intoxicating effect (Pope). For the underlying spirit of this verse, see Eccles. 9:8 ve-šemen 'al ro'šeka 'al yeḥsar "and may you never lack oil to anoint your head," quoted in its context on p. 12.

The root mzg is a biblical hapax, but see Aramaic mezag "to mix wine," mizgā "mixed wine, mixture," Arabic mizāj "mixture of liquids." The related Hebrew root is msk "to mix, pour," as in Ps. 75:9 mesek "wine mixed with spices [?]," similarly Prov. 23:30 and Isa. 65:11 mimsak.

בִּטְנֵךְ עֲרֵמַת חִטִּים biṭnek 'aremat ḥiṭṭim "your belly is a mound of wheat." Insofar as 'aremah applies to threshed and winnowed wheat (compare Ruth 3:2 and 3:7), the image suggests the softness of her belly, in contrast to the young man's belly which is literally "a polished block of ivory," see 5:14.

7:4 Compare 4:5.

7:5 צַוָּארֵךְ כְּמִגְדַּל הַשֵּׁן *ṣavva'rek ke-migdal ha-šen* "your neck is like a tower of ivory." The comparison with a tower suggests a long neck, a quality praised in a woman also in Egyptian love poetry (Fox); compare 4:4. For a discussion of ivory as a precious material in the Bible, see note 5:14. The image suggests a tall, proudly erect Shulamite, who carries her head high. The reference to Mount Carmel (7:6) serves the same purpose. Compare also 7:8.

עֵינַיִךְ בְּרֵכוֹת בְּחֶשְׁבּוֹן *'eynayik berekot be-ḥešbon* "your eyes are pools in Heshbon." Heshbon figures prominently in the early history of Israel as the thriving capital of a once-powerful neighboring state (Num. 21:25–34). In the days of King Solomon, the city was part of the Israelite empire, together with Mahanayim, Gilead, and the "land of Sihon" between the Arnon and Jabbok rivers (May et al., 64). Heshbon was famous for its great fertility and rich vineyards; see Isa. 16:8–9. It was well supplied with water, and remains of a huge reservoir of excellent masonry have recently been excavated on the site (Pope). As an illustrious city of a glorious bygone era, Heshbon fulfills a role in the Song like that of Tirzah, evoking the Shulamite's great beauty and regal appearance; see note 6:4.

The association of eyes with abundant waters suggests a tranquil and lush sensuality; compare 5:12. It may furthermore have a basis in the fact that *'ayin* means both "eye" and "spring, water source."

עַל־שַׁעַר בַּת־רַבִּים *'al ša'ar bat rabbim* "at the gate of *bat rabbim*." The enigmatic *bat rabbim* is understood here as a personifying epithet of the city of Heshbon.

The word *bat* "daughter" figures prominently in poetic epithets that personify cities and nations, as in Isa. 62:11 "Say to the Daughter of Zion: Behold, your salvation comes," where "Daughter of Zion" (*bat ṣiyyon*) symbolizes the nation of Israel. In Zech. 9:9, Micah 4:8, and Isa. 37:22, "Daughter of Zion," in poetic parallelism with its synonym "Daughter of Jerusalem" (*bat yerušalayim*), stands for the city of Jerusalem and, by extension, the people of Israel. In Jer. 8:20–23, 14:17, the epithet "Daughter of my people" (*bat 'ammi*) is used with the same meaning. In Isa. 47:1, "Daughter of Babylon" (*bat babel*) and "Daughter of the Chaldeans" (*bat kaśdim*) personify the Babylonian empire; compare Ps. 137:8. The place called *gallim* (1 Sam. 25:44) is personified in the poetic address of the prophet, Isa. 10:30, "Cry out aloud, O Daughter of Gallim" (*bat gallim*).

In this reading, the phrase *bat rabbim* is taken to be in apposition with the name Heshbon, "in Heshbon, at the gate of *bat rabbim*." For a similar apposition of name and epithet see Isa 10:32 (where the order is reversed): "He will shake his hand at the mount of the Daughter of Zion, the hill of Jerusalem." The plural *rabbim* functions here as a noun, meaning "important people," "the great and mighty," "the nobles." See Jer. 39:13 *rabbey melek babel* "the officials of the king of Babylon" (similarly Jer. 41:1); Isa. 53:12 *'aḥalleq lo ba-rabbim ve-'et 'aṣumim yeḥalleq šalal* "I will divide him a portion among the great, and he will share the spoil with the strong." For the corresponding singulars in the same meaning, see *rab* in Esther 1:8 *'al kol rab beyto* "to every official of his household," and *rabbah* in Lam. 1:1 *rabbati ba-goyim* "the mighty one [fem.] among the nations."

Heshbon as a "daughter of nobles" would fit well with the dignified status which that legendary city held in national memory. Moreover, this epithet would be especially meaningful in view of the association the Song makes between Heshbon and the Shulamite, who is herself given the epithet "nobleman's daughter" (7:2). Since the epithet *bat rabbim* occurs only here in the Bible, it may be the poet's own creation, perhaps on the analogy of the many other city epithets where *bat* means "daughter of." For another likely poetic invention (Hill of Plenty) involving a place name in the Song, see 8:11.

אַפֵּךְ *'appek* "your nose." The comparison to a tower probably refers to the elegant straightness of the nose. The same idealization may have been a factor also in the reference to towers in the two descriptions of the neck, 4:4, 7:5. "Tower of Lebanon" may be a designation of the mountain itself, or of one of its peaks, or of an actual tower.

7:6 כַּכַּרְמֶל *ka-karmel* "like Mount Carmel." This mountain with its densely wooded summit is a common symbol of lush vegetation and majestic beauty in the Bible; see Jer. 50:19, Amos 1:2, Nahum 1:4, Isa. 33:9 and 35:2 (where it is mentioned together with the Sharon plain and Lebanon; see note 2:1).

וְדַלַּת רֹאשֵׁךְ *ve-dallat ro'šek*. Occurring elsewhere only in Isa. 38:12, in relation to threads, or thrums, hanging down in a weaver's loom, *dallah* in 7:6 is usually understood as referring to the Shulamite's long wavy hair.

אַרְגָּמָן *'argaman* "purple," as well as "purple thread and cloth" (see 3:10). Very dark hair has a sheen that may resemble blue-black or purple. The term "purple" is applied to hair in Anacreon and Lucian. The dye was derived from the murex shellfish and varied in color, including blue-black (Pope).

Fox observes here a two-directional ("Janus") pun: "Carmel" is the name of a mountain, and as such points back to Mount Lebanon in 7:5; at the same time it is phonetically close to the word *karmil* "crimson cloth," which evokes the following *'argaman* "purple cloth." *Karmil* occurs three times in the Bible (2 Chron. 2:6,13, 3:14), always alongside *'argaman* (or its variant *'argevan*), which supports the close association of these two words.

מֶלֶךְ אָסוּר בָּרְהָטִים *melek̄ 'asur ba-rehaṭim* "a king is bound/held captive/trapped in the *rehaṭim*." The enigmatic *rehaṭim* is generally viewed as a metaphor for hair. He is her "king" (1:4), and is "held captive" by her long hair. For images of entrapment in Egyptian love poetry, see Fox, 160.

In Gen. 30:38,41 and Exod. 2:16, *rehaṭim* are "water troughs, conduits"; compare the Aramaic *rāhṭā* "watercourse, stream." The basic meaning seems to be something like "runners" (see also "rafter" 1:17), hence the possible metaphoric extension to long streaming hair. But this interpretation is highly uncertain.

7:7 מַה־יָּפִית וּמַה־נָּעַמְתְּ אַהֲבָה בַּתַּעֲנוּגִים *mah yap̄it u-mah na'amt 'ahabah ba-ta'anugim,* literally "How splendid and how sweet you are, O Love, among [all] the delights!" This is another example of a type of statement frequent in the Song: "X is unique, better than all other specimens of its kind"; see 2:2–3, 4:10, 5:9–10, 6:8–9. The preposition *b-* in the sense of "among" marks the domain in which the statement applies; compare 1:8 *ha-yap̄ah ba-našim,* literally "the [most] beautiful among women," 2:3 *ke-tappuaḥ ba-'aṣey ha-ya'ar,* literally "like an apricot tree among the trees of the wood."

Having singled out for praise each of the Shulamite's body parts, the young man concludes this section with an enthusiastic paean addressed to Love itself. The shift from the specific and detailed (7:2–6) to the abstract and general (7:7) has its parallels in the two earlier praise songs, which likewise end with generalizing statements in 4:7 and 5:16. For the personification of another abstract concept, see Prov. 7:4 "Say to Wisdom, 'You are my sister,' and call Understanding your friend," Prov. 8:1 "Does not Wisdom call, does not Understanding raise her voice?" or Prov. 9:1 "Wisdom has built her house, has hewn her seven pillars."

Some commentators propose an alternative translation, "How beautiful you are, how pleasant, O love, delightful girl!" emending *bata'anugim* to *bat ta'anugim,* "daughter of delights," and postulating *'ahabah* "love" as a vocative addressed to the Shulamite. But an emendation is not necessary here. Nor is it at all likely that *'ahabah* "love" was ever used in biblical Hebrew to address a beloved person as it is in contemporary English, for example, in "Kiss me, love."

7:8 זֹאת קוֹמָתֵךְ דָּמְתָה לְתָמָר *zo't qomatek dametah le-tamar,* literally "this stature/height of yours was like/resembled a palm tree." The interpretive translation offered here for this verse is based on the conviction that the perfect form of the verb denotes a past tense, as it typically does in the Song (see note 5:1), not the present, as in most translations: "is like/resembles." If the present were intended, one would have expected a participle, the form most consistently used for this tense in the Song. Indeed, the participle of *damah* is used in 2:9, *domeh dodi* "my lover resembles." With the past tense the young man may be referring to an earlier point in time: when he saw the Shulamite—at a particular moment in the past—she seemed to him like a date palm bearing delectable fruit. This erotic fantasy about the Shulamite calls to mind the one about the mare in 1:9.

As Fox notes, the image of the palm tree suggests her initial inaccessibility. In this sense it resembles an image in Sappho: "Like the sweet-apple ripening to red on the topmost branch, /on the very tip of the topmost branch, and the apple-pickers have overlooked it— / no, they haven't overlooked it but they could not reach it" (Winkler, 183).

אַשְׁכֹּלוֹת *'aškolot* "clusters." The *'eškol* usually refers to a cluster of grapes, but its association with henna blossoms in the Hebrew of 1:14 indicates that the term could be used in a broader sense. Here it applies to clusters of dates.

7:9 אָמַרְתִּי *'amarti,* literally "I said," in the sense of "I thought," as in Gen. 20:11, 44:28. A rhetorical device used often in the Bible to indicate the inner process of thought. Note also the related expressions of the type "I said in my heart," Eccles. 1:16, 2:1, 3:17,18, Isa. 14:13, 49:21.

בְּתָמָר *be-tamar.* One would expect *ba-tamar;* the sense requires that "palm" here have the definite article.

אֹחֲזָה בְּסַנְסִנָּיו 'oḥazah be-sansinnav "let me hold on to its *sansinnim*." The exact meaning of *sansinnim* is uncertain. Possibly referring to the stringlike stalks of the palm tree that hold the fruit. One grasps these stalks to pick the fruit.

וְרֵיחַ אַפֵּךְ ve-reaḥ 'appek, literally "the scent of your nose." Since the nose is the organ associated with breathing and breath, as in the common expressions *nišmat 'appo, nišmat ruaḥ 'appo* "breath of his nose" (Gen. 2:7, 7:22; Isa. 2:22; 2 Sam. 22:16; Ps. 18:16), "nose" may be explained as a metonymy for "breath" here. See Isa. 52:7, where the literal "feet" is used in the sense of "steps."

7:10 **וְחִכֵּךְ כְּיֵין הַטּוֹב** ve-ḥikkek ke-yeyn ha-ṭob, literally "and your palate like good wine." For the association of the lovers' palates with wine, see 5:16, and also 4:11, where the Shulamite's mouth is associated with sweetness.

הוֹלֵךְ לְדוֹדִי לְמֵישָׁרִים holek le-dodi le-meyšarim, literally "going to my lover smoothly." Here the Shulamite playfully interrupts her lover, completing his sentence (see pp. 16–17). For *hlk* "go" in the sense of "flow" see Eccles. 1:7 and Joel 4:18 (3:18 in English versions), and especially Prov. 23:31, where the expression *yithallek be-meyšarim* "flows smoothly" is said specifically of wine and its effect.

דּוֹבֵב שִׂפְתֵי יְשֵׁנִים dobeb šiptey yešenim. Rashi, Ibn Ezra, and some modern commentators translate this enigmatic phrase along the lines of "[wine] that causes the lips of those that are asleep to speak or move." One possible way to understand this image is as a hyperbole: the wine is so powerful, and so irresistible, that it is capable even of arousing one from sleep. But the association of the root *dbb* with either "to speak" or "to move" is highly problematic, making the interpretation adopted here as conjectural as all others offered for this phrase.

7:11 **אֲנִי לְדוֹדִי וְעָלַי תְּשׁוּקָתוֹ** 'ani le-dodi ve-'alay tešuqato, literally "I am my lover's and his desire is for me." The use of *tešuqah* "desire" calls attention to itself, since this particular word occurs at only two other points in the Bible—in decidedly negative contexts: Gen. 3:16 "your desire shall be for your husband [*'el 'išek tešuqatek*] and he shall rule over you," and Gen. 4:7 "its [Sin's] desire is for you [*'eleyka tešuqato*] yet you must master [literally, rule over] it." The resemblance between these three verses extends beyond the use of this particular word to a specific detail of syntax, namely that the prepositional phrase marking the object of desire occurs before *tešuqah* for emphasis; compare 1:4, 3:3.

In Genesis, man is expected to rule over woman, as well as over Sin (the use of the same verb—*mašal* "to rule"—in both verses makes the parallelism painfully obvious). Moreover, sexual desire is presented as entirely one-directional: woman desires man, and he has dominion over her.

In light of this patently similar wording, Song 7:11 reads almost like a deliberate reversal of Gen. 3:16, turning it upside down by making the *woman* the object of desire. And instead of the dominion of man over woman, the present verse speaks of a relationship of mutuality, expressed in a formula of reciprocal love like that in 2:16, 6:3. In the Song, sex is free of notions of control, dominion, hierarchy.

7:12 נָלִינָה בַּכְּפָרִים *nalinah ba-keparim,* literally "let us pass the night among the henna bushes." Song 7:12–13 and 1:13–14 are similar in their sequence of associations: compare the sequence in 7:12–13 *nalinah* "to pass the night," *keparim* "henna bushes" and *keramim* "vineyards" with that in 1:13–14 *yalin* "passing the night," *'eškol ha-koper* "henna cluster" and *karmey 'eyn gedi* "vineyards of Ein Gedi" (Fox).

It has been suggested that the invitation in 7:12 allows two readings, "among the henna bushes" or "in the villages" (Fox, Murphy). For *keparim* "villages" see 1 Chron. 27:25. But the tightly woven web of associated images in 7:12–13 and 1:13–14 supports only the reading "henna bushes."

7:13 נִרְאֶה אִם־פָּרְחָה הַגֶּפֶן ... הֵנֵצוּ הָרִמּוֹנִים *nir'eh 'im parehah ha-gepen . . . henesu ha-rimmonim,* literally "we will see if the vine is in bloom, . . . if the pomegranates have budded." Vines and pomegranates are associated with the Shulamite's sexuality throughout the Song, as in 1:6, 4:13, 7:9, 8:2. In the present verse this association is even more narrowly focused, and relates specifically to her readiness for a sexual encounter: in the place where the vines and pomegranates are in bloom, she promises, "There I will give you my love [*dodim*]." The wording, the scene, and the erotic association is much the same as in 6:11. In that case, it is the young man who goes down to the walnut grove in order to find out whether the vines and pomegranates are blooming, a visit that culminates in the sexual encounter of 6:12. In both instances erotic readiness is reflected in nature.

פִּתַּח הַסְּמָדַר *pittaḥ ha-semadar* "[if] the blossoms have opened." *Semadar,* occurring only in the Song, is a collective noun for buds or blossoms of the vine; compare 2:13,15. *Pittaḥ* (pi'el) is used here in an intransitive sense; compare Isa. 48:8 *lo' pitteḥah 'ozneka* "your ear has never opened up," Isa. 60:11 *pitteḥu še'arayik tamid* "your gates shall be open continually."

דֹּדַי *doday,* literally "my lovemaking." The preceding verb "give" underlines the physical concreteness of *dodim;* compare note 1:2.

7:14 דּוּדָאִים *duda'im* "mandrakes." A native of the Mediterranean area, the mandrake plant, or mandragora (*Mandragora officinarum*) is found in most parts of Israel. It has large leaves, beautiful purple flowers, and juicy, golden fruits. Its odor is reportedly pungent and distinctive, and may have been considered pleasant or exciting (Pope). For the ancient belief in its aphrodisiac properties, see Gen. 30:14–16. The association of mandrakes with sex may rest in part on the fact that the sound of the word *duda'im* is similar to *dodim* "lovemaking." The poet plays with these sound associations in the present text, hence *doday* and *duda'im* in proximity (7:13–14), and *dodi* "my lover" in nearly every verse of this section (7:10,11,12,14).

נָתְנוּ־רֵיחַ *natenu reaḥ,* literally "have given off fragrance"; see 1:12, 2:13. Again, erotic readiness is mirrored by nature: "I will give you my love" (7:13) resembles "the mandrakes have given [their] fragrance" (7:14), with the use of the identical verb *natan* emphasizing the association.

עַל־פְּתָחֵינוּ *'al petaḥeynu* "at our doors." The "doors" belong to the "houses," or "chambers" in the outdoors where the two lovers meet; compare notes 1:4,17. The possessive "our" conveys loving intimacy, not ownership, as in 1:16 "our bed," 1:17 "our houses," "our rafters," 2:9 "our wall," 2:12 "our land." The phrase itself carries a special symbolism: in Hebrew, as in other languages, being "at the door" conveys immediate availability, closeness at hand, easy reach.

כָּל־מְגָדִים *kol megadim,* literally "all kinds of delicious things, delicacies." Outside the Song, this word occurs only in Deut. 33:13–16 (in the singular *meged*) with reference to the choicest bounties bestowed on mankind by nature. Since *megadim* was mentioned in 4:13,16 in association with fruit (*peri megadim*) and in the context of exotic spices, the reference in the present verse is probably to delicious rare fruit.

Kol, commonly just "all," may also mean "all kinds of," as in Gen. 2:9 *kol 'eṣ neḥmad le-mar'eh,* implying "every kind of tree pleasant to look at."

חֲדָשִׁים גַּם־יְשָׁנִים *ḥadašim gam yešanim,* literally "both new and old." This particular expression, also used in relation to something valuable that is hidden, occurs in Matt. 13:52 in the parable of the householder who "brings out of his treasure things new and old." Such similarities of language and imagery may belong to a common stock of idiomatic expressions underlying the Old and New testaments.

The translation offered here presupposes this syntactic analysis (in simplified paraphrase, reflecting the Hebrew word order): "at our doors delicacies new and old I hid for you." This parsing of 8:14 seems more straightforward than the one suggested by the liturgical accents, which is syntactically rather problematical.

8:1 מִי יִתֶּנְךָ כְּאָח לִי יוֹנֵק שְׁדֵי אִמִּי *mi yittenḵa ke-'aḥ li yoneq šedey 'immi,* literally "if only you were like a brother to me, one who nursed at my mother's breasts." If the young man were her brother, she could kiss him freely in the street without being exposed to contempt or reprimand—or possibly even being taken for a harlot, like the woman in Prov. 7:13, who "caught hold of [a young man] and kissed him" in the street. These words should not be taken to imply that the Shulamite wishes for a brother-sister relation with her lover; rather, as Fox notes, a brother is someone to whom she could legitimately show her affection in public.

Mi yitten is commonly used to introduce a fervent wish, as in Jer. 9:1 "Oh that I were [*mi yitteneni*] in the desert at an encampment for wayfarers," or 2 Sam. 19:1 (18:33 in English versions) "Would that I had died instead of you!" (*mi yitten muti 'ani taḥteyḵa*).

The second phrase, *yoneq šedey 'immi,* is an expression of tenderness and intimacy: the Shulamite wants to be as close to her lover as if they were nursing together at their mother's breasts.

Ke- generally means "as, like," but in hypothetical, contrary-to-fact statements like this one, the particle may mean "as if," as in Gen. 27:12 "I shall seem to him as if I were someone who is mocking," *ki-meta'tea'*; Ps. 126:1 "we were like those who dream," *ke-ḥolemim,* i.e., as if in a dream.

אֶשָּׁקְךָ ... אֶמְצָאֲךָ *'emṣa'aka . . . 'eššaqeka*, literally "I would find/ meet you . . . I would kiss you." The logical relation is conditional-temporal: "If I were to meet you, or, when I met you, I would. . . ." For *maṣa'* used in the sense of incidentally crossing someone's path, see also 3:3, 5:8.

גַּם לֹא־יָבֻזוּ לִי *gam lo' yabuzu li* "yet no one would scorn/despise me," literally "they would not," with the masculine plural in the generalizing sense of "everybody." For *gam* in the adversative sense "yet," see Ps. 129:2 "Sorely have they afflicted me from my youth, yet they have not prevailed against me," *gam lo' yakelu li.*

8:2 אֶנְהָגְךָ אֲבִיאֲךָ *'enhageka 'abi'aka*, literally "I would guide you, I would bring you." Here and in 3:4 one may note a departure from the tradition, at least as reflected in Gen. 24:67, where it is the man (Isaac) who brings the woman (Rebecca) into his mother's tent. Compare note on 7:11.

For examples of the joining of verbs without an expected conjunction (called "asyndeton"), compare 2:11 *halap halak*, literally "passed, was gone," 5:6 *hamaq 'abar*, literally "slipped away, was gone."

תְּלַמְּדֵנִי *telammedeni* can mean either "she will teach me," or "you [masc. sing.] will teach me"; either way the actual meaning remains uncertain. Since the word *telammedeni* does not itself constitute a complete line of verse, some commentators consider the Masoretic Text here corrupt, emending it to "and to the room of her who bore me," following the parallel in 3:4; this is supported by the variant readings in the Septuagint and Peshitta.

On the other hand, the unemended Masoretic Text in the reading "she will teach me" makes sense if the Shulamite were expecting her mother to instruct her in the art of love. Commenting on this verse, Landy (1983), 100, 250, sees the mother as participating in "the lovers' amorous education." Compare Ruth 3:1–5, where Naomi instructs her daughter-in-law to wash and anoint herself, and put on her best clothes, in preparation for her expected encounter with Boaz. This custom has ancient antecedents: the Sumerian goddess Inanna, at her mother's command, "bathed herself, anointed herself with goodly oil," before her meeting with Dumuzi; see Kramer (1969), 77.

אַשְׁקְךָ *'asqeka* "I will give you to drink," compare *'eššaqeka* "I would kiss you," 8:1. The phonetic similarity between these two verbs points to the associative link between kissing and wine so prevalent in the Song; see also 1:2.

עָסִיס רִמֹּנִי *'asis rimmoni,* literally "the juice of my pomegranate." *'Asis* is consistently used as a poetic term for wine and intoxicating juices in general, Isa. 49:26, Joel 1:5, 4:18 (3:18 in English versions), Amos 9:13.

8:3 See 2:6.

8:4 מַה־תָּעִירוּ וּמַה־תְּעֹרְרוּ *mah ta'iru u-mah te'oreru,* literally "never to . . . , and never to," as in 2:7 and 3:5, but here with *mah* instead of *'im* of the earlier adjurations. For *mah* as a negation see 1 Kings 12:16, Job 31:1, Prov. 31:2.

8:5 מִי זֹאת עֹלָה מִן־הַמִּדְבָּר *mi zo't 'olah . . .* "Who is that rising. . . ." See remarks in note 3:6.

מִתְרַפֶּקֶת עַל־דּוֹדָהּ *mitrappeqet 'al dodah,* literally "leaning on her lover." Though a biblical hapax, the root *rpq* occurs in a number of Semitic languages in words with meanings ranging from the noun "elbow" to the verb "to rest one's arm, lean on something."

תַּחַת הַתַּפּוּחַ עוֹרַרְתִּיךָ *taḥat ha-tappuaḥ 'orartika,* literally "under the apricot tree I awakened you," with "awaken" in the erotic sense, as in the adjurations 2:7, 3:5, 8:4. The erotic import is manifest in view of the implications of 2:3, where the Shulamite tells of sitting in the shade of the apricot tree and tasting its fruit. In the symbolism of 2:3, the apricot is of course *his* fruit. The speaker here is the young woman, as the Masoretic Text voweling clearly indicates.

שָׁמָּה חִבְּלַתְךָ אִמֶּךָ *šammah ḥibbelatka 'immeka,* literally "there your mother conceived you." *Ḥibbel* (pi'el) "conceive, get pregnant," as in Ps. 7:15 "He conceives evil [*yeḥabbel 'aven*], is pregnant with mischief, and gives birth to a lie."

שָׁמָּה חִבְּלָה יְלָדַתְךָ *šammah ḥibbelah yeladatka,* literally "there she conceived, gave birth to you," i.e., "conceived and gave birth," with the coordinate verbs joined asyndetically, as in 8:2, "I will lead you, bring you."

There can be little doubt that the conception and birth under the apricot tree must not be taken as realistic reportage, as in some commentaries. These details add a mythic dimension to the figure of the young man; the motif of a birth under a tree is found in many myths in antiquity (Pope, 663). But the association of birth and tree may have an additional explanation. In order to give birth to their fawns, hinds often return to their own birthplace under a tree (Feliks, quoted in Hakham, 16). Since the young lover in the Song is repeatedly compared to a gazelle (2:9,17, 8:14) this association would be especially evocative.

Many versions translate along the lines of "there your mother conceived you, there the one who bore you conceived," treating the last word of the sentence as if it were an epithet, "the one who gave birth to you," parallel to the preceding "your mother." In this understanding, only the conception takes place under the apricot tree, not the birth. But a reading with "the one who" would require a participial form *yoladteka*, a word that is typically spelled with a *waw* (*ywldtk*), as in Song 6:9, Jer. 50:12, Prov. 17:25, 23:25, whereas the word in the present verse unmistakably indicates a verb in the perfect, *yeladatka*. In an alternative approach, Fox (compare Grossberg, 488) suggests that the verb be understood as nominalized, literally "conceived [the] she-bore-you." But this admittedly attractive proposal is not without its own problems. Nominalizations of verbs do of course occur but, significant to the case at hand, they typically function attributively, as genitives or as relative clauses, and not as the subject of a verb. See also WO, 87, n. 13.

8:6 עַל־זְרוֹעֶךָ ... עַל־לִבֶּךָ כַחוֹתָם שִׂימֵנִי *śimeni ka-ḥotam 'al libbeka . . . 'al zero'eka*, literally "Set me as a seal upon your heart, . . . your arm." A seal on the heart and arm implies belonging, physical closeness, and intimacy. Seals or signets, made of metal or stone and often exquisitely engraved, were worn on the hand as a ring, higher up on the arm as an amulet, or on a cord around the neck, resting on the chest (Pope). A seal served as a form of identification, as in the story of Tamar and Judah (Gen. 38:18–26), and was numbered among a person's most precious possessions. Of deep symbolic significance, a seal stands for the owner's identity, honor, and fate; see Jer. 22:24, Hag. 2:23. For the weighty significance implied in placing an object of symbolic import on one's hand or heart, see Prov. 3:3, 6:21, 7:3, and Deut. 6:8, 11:18. (The verses in Deuteronomy furnish the biblical basis for the wearing of phylacteries.)

עַזָּה כַמָּוֶת ‘azzah ka-mavet "as strong/fierce as death." For ‘az used specifically in the sense of "fierce," see Deut. 28:50 ‘az panim "fierce of countenance," Judg. 14:18 ‘az me-’ari "more fierce than the lion" (rather than "more strong"; compare Prov. 30:30, where the lion is proverbial for ferocity, not strength).

קָשָׁה כִשְׁאוֹל qašah ki-š’ol, literally "hard/cruel as Sheol." Although Sheol is the personified netherworld in the biblical worldview (see Isa. 28:15,18, Ps. 89:49, Hab. 2:5), the word is often used simply as a synonym for "death."

קִנְאָה qin’ah "jealousy," as correctly noted by Fox (not "passion," as in many modern translators and commentators). What is meant here is not jealousy as an independent force, but the jealousy that is a by-product of love, the jealousy ignited by love. The real focus of this line, as of the ones that follow, is love. We have added the "its" in "its jealousy" to clarify the point.

רְשָׁפֶיהָ רִשְׁפֵּי אֵשׁ שַׁלְהֶבֶתְיָה rešapeyha rišpey ’eš, šalhebetyah, literally "its sparks are sparks of fire, an enormous flame." The exact meaning of rešep is uncertain; in Job 5:7 the word has been widely understood as referring to sparks rising from a fire. Taking "spark" as a metaphor for something very small, we see in Song 8:6 an intensification by way of contrast. The image moves from the sparks to the flame: love is so powerful that even its tiny sparks burn like great fires.

It has long been debated whether or not šalhebetyah contains the name of the God of Israel. While it is likely that -yah derives from "Yah," the short form of "Yahweh," this ending long ago lost its association with God's name, and became simply a suffix denoting intensity, as in Jer. 2:31 ma’pelyah "thick darkness," Ps. 118:5 merhabyah "great relief." (For the semantic change involved, compare the expression 1 Sam. 14:15 herdat ’elohim "a great terror," literally "God's terror," and similarly Gen. 35:5, 1 Sam. 11:7, and others.) The very spelling of šalhebetyah as a single word supports this assessment, since the name "Yah" (God) is always spelled as a separate word, as in Ps. 115:18 va-’anahnu nebarek yah "but we will bless the Lord," Exod. 15:2, 17:16, Ps. 68:19.

8:7 בְּאַהֲבָה ... אִם־יִתֵּן אִישׁ ’im yitten ’iš . . . ba-’ahabah, literally "if a man gave [all the wealth of his house] for love," i.e., traded it, or tried/offered/intended to trade it, in exchange for love. The point of this aphorism is that love is beyond all material value, and cannot be bought for any price. Hence anyone attempting to buy love would be considered a fool. An alternate reading—the man who gives up everything for love is mocked by an uncomprehending world—seems less fitting in this context: the poet is praising the greatness of love, a cosmic force, not bemoaning the small-mindedness of human beings. The topos of comparison with mere earthly wealth continues in 8:11–12.

For the idiomatic expression "to give all the wealth of one's house" or "half of one's house" see 1 Kings 13:8 and Prov. 6:31. For the special sense of the preposition *b-* as used here, compare Gen. 29:18 *'e'ĕbodĕkā . . . bĕ-raḥel* "I will serve you for [i.e., in order to obtain] Rachel."

בּוֹז יָבוּזוּ לוֹ *boz yābuzu lo* "he would be utterly scorned / despised" (the so-called absolute infinitive preceding the verb for strong affirmation; see WO, 586). One may perceive a closure here, formally echoing 8:1: "If only you were like . . . , no one would scorn me," "If a man gave . . . , he would be scorned." The formal similarity is more sharply profiled in Hebrew because of the presence of the verbs *yitten* and *būz* in both verses.

Despite the obvious differences in purpose and tone, this aphorism recalls the sayings in Matt. 13:44–46 and 16:26. In each case, something of material worth is weighed against a spiritual value such as love, the soul, the Kingdom of Heaven.

8:8–10   The great difficulty of this section is reflected in the widely differing interpretations given in the commentaries. There is hardly any consensus even on essential questions such as (1) the identity of the "little sister" (some commentators postulate a younger sister of the Shulamite); (2) the identity of the speakers in 8:8–9 (proposals include the brothers; a group of suitors; the brothers in 8:8, and the suitors in 8:9; the girls of Jerusalem; the young man; the Shulamite, quoting an earlier speech by her brothers); and, most crucially, (3) the meaning of the "wall" and "door" metaphors. For overviews of the various possibilities, see Pope and Fox.

8:8   The brothers are the most likely speakers in 8:8–9 (compare Pope, Fox, Falk). Responsibility of brothers for a sister is well established in the Bible, especially in matters pertaining to sexuality and marriage, as in the case of Rebecca, Gen. 24:29–60; Dinah, Gen. 34:6–17; and the daughters of Shiloh, Judg. 21:22. Song 1:6 clearly reflects the fraternal authority of the brothers over the Shulamite.

קְטַנָּה *qeṭannah* "little" does not refer to the Shulamite's size but to her sexual immaturity in her brothers' eyes. (In the language of the Mishnah, *qeṭannah* and *qaṭan* become the legal terms for minors, defined as "a girl up till twelve years and one day," and "a boy till thirteen and one day.")

וְשָׁדַיִם אֵין לָהּ *ve-šadayim 'eyn lah* "and she has no breasts." Well-formed breasts and pubic hair are indicators that a girl has reached sexual readiness, Ezek. 16:7–8 *'et dodim* "the age for lovemaking." (The same criteria apply in the Mishnah, see R. Biale, 206.) The brothers' statement about the Shulamite's having "no breasts" is as much a poetic hyperbole as her defiant counterassertion of having breasts "like towers."

בַּיּוֹם שֶׁיְּדֻבַּר־בָּהּ *ba-yom še-yedubbar bah,* literally "on the day when she will be spoken for/wooed," i.e., by prospective suitors. For an example of *dabber b-* used in this sense see 1 Sam. 25:39. Our free translation with the verb "besiege" borrows from the language and imagery of 8:9–10.

8:9 ... וְאִם־דֶּלֶת הִיא ... אִם־חוֹמָה הִיא *'im ḥomah hi'* . . . *ve-'im delet hi'* . . . , literally "if she is a wall . . . and if she is a door. . . ." The question here is whether the "wall"/"door" metaphors are synonymous or antithetical. To commentators who see them as antithetical, the dualism has a sexual connotation—inaccessibility/accessibility—with the clear implication of a warning. Commentators who see the metaphors as synonymous, on the other hand, argue that no such contrast is intended, citing specific contexts in which *delet* unmistakably denotes the door as a structure rather than an opening.

The case for the antithetical reading is substantially stronger. In a familiar biblical pattern, *'im . . . ve-'im . . .* , the second of the two coordinated conditional sentences spells out the negative consequence if the first condition is not fulfilled, as in Isa. 1:19–20, "If you are willing . . . you shall eat the good of the land; but if you refuse and rebel, you shall be devoured by the sword"; see also Deut. 20:11–1, etc. In this antithetical reading, the conjunctive *ve-* is the semantic equivalent of "but" (the adversative *ve-*, WO, 677); compare above 3:1,2, 5:6, and discussion in note 1:5. On the other hand, if these metaphors were indeed synonymous, one would have expected the two conditional sentences to be arranged in the opposite order, so that the verse would end on "turret of silver"—surely the more dramatic image—rather than on "panel of cedarwood." As Alter has shown (1985) 18ff., when parallelism occurs in biblical poetry, "the characteristic movement of meaning is one of heightening or intensification."

נִבְנֶה עָלֶיהָ טִירַת כָּסֶף *nibneh 'aleyha ṭirat kasep̄* "we will build a silver turret upon her." The meaning of *ṭirah* is uncertain, but the use in Ezek. 46:23 suggests some round formation of masonry. In a verse such as this, in which everything has a symbolic import, a *ṭirah* made of silver instead of stone surely adds a note of grandeur.

נָצוּר עָלֶיהָ לוּחַ אָרֶז *naṣur 'aleyha luaḥ 'arez,* literally "we will besiege her with a plank/panel of cedar," i.e., bolt her, or enclose her with it. Commentators trying to play down the harshness implied in this image tend to explain the board of cedar as primarily ornamental, like the silver turret. In a similar vein, others consider "silver" and "cedar" to be allusions to conciliatory gifts by the brothers (Hakham), or by suitors hoping to overcome the Shulamite's resistance (Gordis). But it is hard to ignore the contrast between these two materials. For although cedar wood was greatly prized for its strength and durability, silver was a far more precious material. It is therefore more plausible that these materials are named here for their difference, not for any possible similarity. Indeed, the contrast in value between silver and cedar is most likely intended to underline and enhance the "wall"/"door" antithesis.

A word on the language is called for. The most frequent use of the verb *ṣar* followed by the preposition *'al* occurs in contexts in which a siege is laid against a city, e.g., Jer. 37:5 *ha-ṣarim 'al yerušalayim* "those who were besieging Jerusalem," and 2 Kings 18:9 *va-yaṣar 'aleyha* "and he besieged it." If indeed a siege metaphor is implied in this verse, then the plank of cedar functions as the instrument with which the "siege" is carried out. In this regard, Isa. 29:3 provides a close analogue: *ve-ṣarti 'alayik̄ muṣṣab̄ va-haqimoti 'alayik̄ meṣurot* "I will besiege you [Jerusalem] with a *muṣṣab̄,* and I will raise siegeworks [*meṣurot*] against you," with the siege instrument as the direct object of the verb *ṣar,* as in the phrase at hand. (The identity of the term *muṣṣab̄* is unknown, but its syntactic parallelism with *meṣurot* "siegeworks" suggests a specific structure or instrument used in a siege.)

It is hard to ignore the antithesis between "building a silver turret" upon the Shulamite, which evokes notions of crowning, and the threatening siege metaphor in the second half of the verse. Notice in this connection the difference in the use of the preposition *'al*. With the verb *ṣar*, it has an adversarial sense, "laying a siege against" (*'al* with the meaning "against" occurs also with other verbs). But with *banah* "to build," *'al* has a simple locative sense, "we will build upon her" (as in 8:6 *'al libbeka, 'al zero'eka* "upon your heart, upon your arm").

8:10 אֲנִי חוֹמָה *'ani ḥomah* "I am a wall." Contrary to the common view (Pope, Ginsburg, and others), it is very unlikely that the Shulamite uses "wall" as a metaphor for chastity—no matter how her brothers intended that metaphor in the first place. A claim of chastity by the Shulamite would make little sense since the two lovers have spent the night together (1:13–14, and probably also 7:12–13), and have made love (5:1, 6:12, etc.); similarly Fox. A more plausible interpretation is to see the "wall" as related to another metaphor of the Song, the "locked garden," which symbolizes the Shulamite's sexuality: she is inaccessible to anyone but her lover. The common element of a wall and a locked garden is the sense of enclosure, of a concealed space behind a barrier. It evokes a sexuality that is hidden, even mysterious, and therefore all the more inviting. The lover has the key to the garden, as well as to the "door" in the wall. Viewed in this way, the "wall" activates a whole set of related images, such as the Shulamite as a dove concealed in the shadow of rocks (2:14), as a "hidden well" and "sealed spring" (4:12), as waiting behind the door at night (5:2–5), and as the mysterious "dweller in the gardens" (8:13).

כַּמִּגְדָּלוֹת *ka-migdalot*, literally "like towers," alludes both to the breasts and to towers or battlements on a wall. With this image the Shulamite sharply opposes her brothers' claim about her lack of physical maturity.

אָז הָיִיתִי בְעֵינָיו כְּמוֹצְאֵת שָׁלוֹם *'az hayiti be-'eynav ke-moṣ'et šalom*, literally "so then I became in his eyes as one who finds peace." The phrase is so obscure that any interpretation is necessarily tentative. We presume an associative link between two images: the Shulamite under "siege" (8:9) and the besieged city that achieves peace, see Deut. 20:10–11. At the root of this association is the well-known symbolic connection between "city" and "woman" which manifests itself in various ways, such as in the typical feminine gender of the words for "city" in Hebrew and many other languages; the use of city epithets with "daughter" (see note 7:5); the obvious sexual connotations of conquering and entering a city. These associations may be combined in a hypothetical scenario: the victorious lover enters the gate of the city, which then becomes a city "that finds peace." (We owe this final image in our free translation to Robert Alter.)

In a different approach, several commentators understand the difficult idiom *moṣ'et šalom* as synonymous with *moṣ'et ḥen* "one who finds favor." However, because antithetical images dominate in 8:9, it seems more plausible to understand *šalom* in its regular meaning, "peace," and to see this concept as a deliberate contrast to the preceding expressions of war and siege, "we will besiege her," "breasts like towers/battlements" (see also Falk, 195).

The possessive pronoun "his" of "his eyes" has no explicit antecedent in the preceding verses. But since this is an exchange between the Shulamite and her brothers, who have just been discussing in her presence what to do when suitors ask for her hand (8:8), one can safely assume that her lover is uppermost in her mind, and that he is the one she refers to.

8:11–12   This Parable of the Vineyard implies that love outweighs the riches of this world; in this respect it resembles the spirit of 8:7. The young man, who is the speaker (as conclusively argued by Falk, and see also Fox), compares his lot to that of King Solomon and finds that he has the better deal—never mind the king's enormous wealth. Solomon owns a marvelously lucrative vineyard, but must share its profits with keepers who guard it and market its fruit. In contrast, the young man's "vineyard" is entirely his own, and that makes all the difference. The tone is sprightly with a touch of humor, a pleasant contrast to the weightiness of the preceding verses.

8:11   כֶּרֶם הָיָה לִשְׁלֹמֹה *kerem hayah li-šelomoh* "Solomon had a vineyard." The style is narrative, and the word order, beginning with an indefinite noun (literally "a vineyard was to Solomon") is like that in two other stories involving vineyards, the parable in Isa. 5:1 *kerem hayah li-ydidi* "my beloved had a vineyard," and the story of Naboth's vineyard in 1 Kings 21:1. Compare also the beginning of Job, *'iš hayah* "There was a man. . . ."

בְּבַעַל הָמוֹן **be-ba'al hamon** "in Baal Hamon." Even if Solomon did own a vineyard in a location called Baal Hamon (for possible identifications see Pope, 687), the historical existence of either the place or the vineyard is not relevant to the purpose of the parable. Read literally, *ba'al hamon* means "owner of great wealth" and thus may well be a playfully invented place name alluding to the king himself (compare *bat rabbim*, note 7:5), formed on the model of the many actual place names with *ba'al* as the first term, e.g., Josh. 11:17 *ba'al gad*, Num. 33:7 *ba'al ṣepon*, 2 Sam. 13:23 *ba'al ḥaṣor*, etc. For a similarly symbolic place name see Gen. 4:16 *'ereṣ nod*, literally "the Land of Wandering," the area of Cain's banishment; see Speiser, 31.

The meaning of *hamon* evokes the earlier *hon* "wealth" (8:7), and the phonetic similarity of the two words further enhances the association. A parallel is thus suggested between the wealthy king (*ba'al hamon*) who cannot fully enjoy his possessions but must keep a watchful eye over them, and the foolish man who thinks he can use his wealth (*hon*) to buy love.

נֹטְרִים **noṭerim** "watchmen/keepers," specifically of a vineyard (root *nṭr*, used also in 1:6, replacing earlier *nṣr*). The keepers and their specified wages are the one element that ties this parable to the reality of everyday life. In this regard, the keepers are the counterpart of the laborers in the New Testament parable of the vineyard in Matt. 20:1–16.

אִישׁ יָבִא בְּפִרְיוֹ אֶלֶף כָּסֶף **'iš yabi' be-piryo 'elep kasep,** literally "each would obtain/procure/bring for its fruit a thousand pieces of silver." Each keeper would sell the fruit of the plot in his charge and get a thousand pieces of silver for it, of which he would keep two hundred for his labor (8:12). A vineyard that brought in one thousand pieces of silver was proverbial for a rich vineyard, see Isa. 7:23; thus the one owned by Solomon must have been especially lucrative, since each of the keepers procured that sum.

8:12 כַּרְמִי שֶׁלִּי לְפָנָי **karmi šelli lepanay,** literally "my vineyard, mine, is before me." The independent emphatic possessive (*šelli* "my very own") is added to underline the contrast: Solomon must share his vineyard with others, whereas the young man has his vineyard all to himself. For the idiomatic use of "before me" in the sense of "right at hand, close by, within reach," sometimes also "in someone's care," see Gen. 47:6.

On the level of the metaphor, the "vineyard" represents the Shulamite's womanhood and, more specifically, her sexuality. This image provides a sense of closure: the vineyard she says she failed to guard earlier (1:6) is now in the care of her lover (8:12). Both lovers refer to the vineyard as theirs, *karmi šelli*—just as the "garden" she calls hers (4:16) is the one he calls "my garden" (5:1).

הָאֶלֶף לְךָ שְׁלֹמֹה *ha-'elep̄ leka, šelomoh*, literally "the thousand be yours, Solomon!" i.e., the thousand pieces of silver you get from each keeper. Apart from the money, the statement may also allude to Solomon's thousand wives; see 1 Kings 11:3. This adds another implication to the phrase *ba'al hamon* (8:11), namely "husband of a multitude," since *ba'al* can mean both "owner" and "husband." The tone here is mocking: Have your thousand, great king, whatever they be!

לְנֹטְרִים *le-noṭerim*, but one variant reading has *la-noṭerim*, the voweling one would expect, to indicate the definite article ("those who guard").

8:13 הַיוֹשֶׁבֶת בַּגַּנִּים *ha-yošebet ba-gannim*, literally "O the one who dwells [fem.] in the gardens." Probably meaning a woman associated with a garden, or gardens, with the plural *gannim* as in 4:15.

חֲבֵרִים מַקְשִׁיבִים לְקוֹלֵךְ הַשְׁמִיעִינִי *ḥaberim maqšibim le-qolek, hašmi-'ini*, literally "companions/friends listen for your voice, let me hear [it]!" In the absence of any further identification, the indefiniteness of the noun "friends" is difficult; commentators have suggested various emendations of the Masoretic Text. In the present reading, the words are understood as one of the many hyperboles the lovers use in their enthusiasm for each other. Earlier, the Shulamite uses an indefinite *'alamot* "young women" in her emphatic assertion (1:3) "young women love you." In the same spirit, the young man is saying here in effect that *all* friends—his, hers, always!—listen for her voice. Interpreted in this light, *ḥaberim maqšibim* does not presuppose the actual presence of the friends at the scene, contrary to the many translations with "are listening."

The liturgical accents mark a break after *le-qolek* "your voice." An alternative though somewhat less natural parsing is to view this phrase as a fronted direct object of "let me hear," i.e., *le-qolek hašmi'ini* (introduced by *le-*, as in Job 5:2). The meaning is the same in either case.

8:14 עַל הָרֵי בְשָׂמִים ... בְּרַח דּוֹדִי וּדְמֵה־לְךָ לִצְבִי *beraḥ dodi u-demeh le-ka li-ṣebi . . . 'al harey beśamim.* Literally "Run away, my love, and be like a gazelle . . . on the mountains of spices." Our free translation with "cinnamon" borrows from the NEB of 2:17, "the hills where cinnamon grows."

Coming at the end of the Song, this request by the Shulamite—"Run away"—has caused difficulties for many translators, who prefer to read "flee with me," or "flee to me," or "return," or "come into the open," or the like. All these readings are unacceptable, since *baraḥ* can only mean "to flee *away from*" someone, or something; nor is there any textual support for the suggestion that she asks him to run away with her. Rather, this final exchange between the two lovers, 8:13–14, evokes a familiar setting: the young man asking the Shulamite to let him hear her voice, as in 2:14, and she urging him to run away before sunrise so that he will not be caught, as in 2:17 (where *sob* "to turn" is likewise meant in the sense of "to turn away from speaker"). The Song thus ends with the motif of the lovers parting at dawn, as in the aubade of later traditions—an ending that looks forward in anticipation to another meeting.

Transliteration Table

THE TRANSCRIPTION represents the sounds as they are pronounced in Modern Hebrew, not the presumed original pronunciation. In specific cases, however, we depart from a purely phonetic representation in order to facilitate the recognition of the Hebrew forms and to enhance their grammatical transparency. For example, the transcription differentiates between ' and ', $\bar{b}$ and v, $\bar{k}$ and $ḥ$, $ṭ$ and t, k and q, s and $ś$, even though these sounds are no longer phonetically distinguished in Modern Hebrew. For the same reason, we reproduce the feminine ending *-ah,* even though the *h* is not pronounced. For the sake of simplicity, the doubling of consonants after the definite article and after the *waw-conversive* is not reproduced.

HEBREW LETTER	TRANSCRIPTION	PRONUNCIATION
א	'	glottal stop
ב	b	b
ב	$\bar{b}$	v
ג	g	g as in *garden*
ד	d	d
ה	h	h
ו	v	v
ז	z	z
ח	ḥ	German *ch* as in *doch*
ט	ṭ	t
י	y	y as in *young*
כ	k	k as in *king*
כ	$\bar{k}$	German *ch* as in *doch*
ל	l	l as in French, German, or Spanish

HEBREW LETTER	TRANSCRIPTION	PRONUNCIATION
מ/ם	m	m
נ/ן	n	n
ס	s	s as in *song*
ע	'	glottal stop
פ	p	p
פ/ף	p̄	f
צ/ץ	ṣ	ts as in *goats*
ק	q	k as in *king*
ר	r	French *r* as in *grand* (or rolled as in Spanish *oro*)
שׁ	š	sh
שׂ	ś	s as in *song*
ת	t	t

Abbreviations

AJSL	*American Journal of Semitic Languages and Literatures*
BA	*Biblical Archaeologist*
BDB	Brown, Driver, and Briggs, *Hebrew and English Lexicon of the Old Testament*
BCE	before the common era (B.C.)
BHK	*Biblia Hebraica* (Kittel et al., eds.)
BHS	*Biblia Hebraica Stuttgartensia* (Elliger and Rudolph, eds.)
BR	*Bible Review*
CBQ	*Catholic Bible Quarterly*
CE	common era (A.D.)
1 Chron.	First Book of Chronicles
2 Chron.	Second Book of Chronicles
Dan.	Daniel
Deut.	Deuteronomy
Eccles.	Ecclesiastes
Exod.	Exodus
Ezek.	Ezekiel
Gen.	Genesis
GKC	Gesenius' *Hebrew Grammar* (Kautzsch and Cowley, eds.)
Hab.	Habakkuk
Hag.	Haggai
HAR	*Hebrew Annual Review*
Isa.	Isaiah
JAOS	*Journal of the American Oriental Society*
JBL	*Journal of Biblical Literature*
Jer.	Jeremiah
Josh.	Joshua
JPS	Jewish Publication Society translation of the Old Testament
JSOT	*Journal for the Study of the Old Testament*
JSS	*Journal of Semitic Studies*

JTS	*Journal of Theological Studies*
Judg.	Judges
1 Kings	First Book of Kings
2 Kings	Second Book of Kings
KJV	King James Version (Authorized Version)
Lam.	Lamentations
Lev.	Leviticus
Matt.	Matthew
MT	Masoretic Text
NEB	New English Bible
Neh.	Nehemiah
NT	New Testament
Num.	Numbers
OT	Old Testament
Peshitta	Syriac version of the Bible
PMLA	*Proceedings of the Modern Language Association*
Prov.	Book of Proverbs
Ps.	Book of Psalms
RSV	Revised Standard Version of the Bible
1 Sam.	First Book of Samuel
2 Sam.	Second Book of Samuel
Septuagint	Greek version of the Old Testament
Song	Song of Songs
VT	*Vetus Testamentum*
Vulgate	Latin version of the Bible
WO	Waltke and O'Connor, *Introduction to Biblical Hebrew Syntax*
ZAW	*Zeitschrift für die alttestamentliche Wissenschaft*
Zech.	Zechariah
Zeph.	Zephaniah

Bibliography

I. Versions of the Bible

Biblia Hebraica. Ed. Rudolf Kittel et al. 7th ed. Stuttgart: Württembergische Bibelanstalt, 1951.

Biblia Hebraica Stuttgartensia. Ed. K. Elliger and W. Rudolph. 3rd rev. ed. Stuttgart: Deutsche Bibelgesellschaft, 1987.

Biblia Sacra Iuxta Latinam Vulgatam Versionem. Vol. 11. Rome: Typis Polyglottis Vaticanis, 1957.

The Holy Bible: Authorized King James Version. 1611. Reprint. New York: Oxford University Press, 1967.

The Holy Bible: Revised Standard Version. 1946–52. Reprint. New York: Oxford University Press, 1973.

The Holy Scriptures According to the Masoretic Text. 3 vols. Philadelphia: Jewish Publication Society, 1962–82.

The Jerusalem Bible. Garden City, N.Y.: Doubleday, 1966.

The New English Bible with the Apocrypha. New York: Oxford University Press, 1971.

Peshitta. The Old Testament in Syriac. Damascus: United Bible Societies, 1979.

The Revised English Bible. Oxford: Oxford University Press, 1992.

Septuaginta. Ed. Alfred Rahlfs. 1935. Reprint. 3rd ed. Stuttgart: Deutsche Bibelgesellschaft, 1979.

II. General Bibliography

Aharoni, Yohanan, and Michael Avi-Yonah. *The Macmillan Bible Atlas.* New York: Macmillan, 1968.

Albright, William Foxwell. "Archaic Survivals in the Text of Canticles." In *Hebrew and Semitic Studies Presented to Godfrey Rolles Driver.* Ed. D. Winton Thomas and W. D. McHardy. Pp. 1–7. Oxford: Clarendon Press, 1963.

———. *From the Stone Age to Christianity: Monotheism and the Historical Process.* Baltimore: The Johns Hopkins Press, 1940.

Alter, Robert. *The Art of Biblical Narrative.* New York: Basic Books, 1981.

———. *The Art of Biblical Poetry.* New York: Basic Books, 1985.

——. *The World of Biblical Literature.* New York: Basic Books, 1992.

Alter, Robert, and Frank Kermode, eds. *The Literary Guide to the Bible.* Cambridge: Harvard University Press, 1987.

Andersen, Francis I., and David Noel Freedman. *Hosea: A New Translation, with Introduction and Commentary.* Vol. 24 of *The Anchor Bible.* Garden City, N.Y.: Doubleday, 1980.

Aschkenasy, Nehama. *Eve's Journey: Feminine Images in Hebraic Literary Tradition.* Philadelphia: University of Pennsylvania Press, 1986.

Astell, Ann W. *The Song of Songs in the Middle Ages.* Ithaca, N.Y.: Cornell University Press, 1990.

Avi-Yonah, Michael. *The Holy Land from the Persian to the Arab Conquest (536 B.C.–A.D. 640): A Historical Geography.* Rev. ed. Grand Rapids: Baker Book House, 1977.

Baillet, M., J. T. Milik, and R. de Vaux. *Les 'Petites Grottes' de Qumran.* Oxford: Clarendon Press, 1962.

Bainton, Roland H. "The Bible in the Reformation." In *The Cambridge History of the Bible: The West from the Reformation to the Present Day.* Ed. S. L. Greenslade. Pp. 1–37. Cambridge: Cambridge University Press, 1963.

Bal, Mieke. *Death and Dissymmetry: The Politics of Coherence in the Book of Judges.* Chicago: University of Chicago Press, 1988.

——. *Lethal Love: Feminist Literary Readings of Biblical Love Stories.* Bloomington: Indiana University Press, 1987.

Barnard, Mary, trans. *Sappho: A New Translation.* Berkeley: University of California Press, 1958.

Barnstone, Willis. *The Poetics of Translation: History, Theory, Practice.* New Haven: Yale University Press, 1993.

——, trans. *The Song of Songs.* Athens: Kedros, 1970.

Barr, James. "Hebrew, Aramaic and Greek in the Hellenistic Age." In *The Hellenistic Age.* Vol. 2 of *The Cambridge History of Judaism.* Ed. W. D. Davies and Louis Finkelstein. Pp. 79–114. Cambridge: Cambridge University Press, 1989.

——. *Holy Scripture: Canon, Authority, Criticism.* Philadelphia: Westminster Press, 1983.

Bauer, Hans, and Pontus Leander. *Historische Grammatik der hebräischen Sprache.* Hildesheim: Georg Olms, 1965.

Bendavid, Abba. *Leshon Miqra u-Leshon Hakhamim* (Biblical Hebrew and Mishnaic Hebrew). Vol. 1. Tel Aviv: Dvir, 1967.

Bentzen, Aage. "Remarks on the Canonisation of the Song of Solomon." In *Studia Orientalia Ioanni Pedersen.* Pp. 41–47. Copenhagen: Munksgaard, 1953.

Bernard of Clairvaux. *On the Song of Songs.* 4 vols. Trans. Kilian Walsh and Irene Edmonds. In *The Works of Bernard of Clairvaux.* Cistercian

Fathers Series, nos. 4, 7, 31, 40. Spencer, Mass. / Kalamazoo, Mich.: Cistercian Publications, 1971–80.

Biale, David. *Eros and the Jews: From Biblical Israel to Contemporary America.* New York: Basic Books, 1992.

Biale, Rachel. *Women and Jewish Law: An Exploration of Women's Issues in Halakhic Sources.* New York: Schocken Books, 1984.

Bickerman, Elias J. "The Historical Foundations of Postbiblical Judaism." In vol. 1 of *The Jews: Their History, Culture, and Religion.* Ed. Louis Finkelstein. Pp. 70–114. 3rd ed. New York: Jewish Publication Society, 1960.

Bing, Peter, and Rip Cohen, trans. and eds. *Games of Venus: An Anthology of Greek and Roman Erotic Verse from Sappho to Ovid.* New York: Routledge, 1991.

Bird, Phyllis. "Images of Women in the Old Testament." In *Religion and Sexism: Images of Woman in the Jewish and Christian Traditions.* Ed. Rosemary Radford Ruether. Pp. 41–88. New York: Simon and Schuster, 1974.

Bloch, Ariel. "Questioning God's Omnipotence in the Bible: A Linguistic Case Study." In vol. 1 of *Semitic Studies in Honor of Wolf Leslau.* Ed. Alan S. Kaye. Pp. 174–88. Wiesbaden: Otto Harrassowitz, 1991.

Bloch, Chana. "Shakespeare's Sister." Review of *The Book of J*, by Harold Bloom and David Rosenberg. *Iowa Review* 21 (1991): 66–77.

Bloch, Joshua. "A Critical Examination of the Text of the Syriac Version of the Song of Songs." *AJSL* 38 (1921–22): 103–39.

Bloom, Harold, and David Rosenberg. *The Book of J.* New York: Grove Weidenfeld, 1990.

Bloom, Harold, ed. *The Song of Songs.* Modern Critical Interpretations. New York: Chelsea House, 1988.

Boyarin, Daniel. *Carnal Israel: Reading Sex in Talmudic Culture.* The New Historicism: Studies in Cultural Politics, no. 25. Berkeley: University of California Press, 1993.

Brenner, Athalya. "Aromatics and Perfumes in the Song of Songs." *JSOT* 25 (1983): 75–81.

———. *The Israelite Woman: Social Role and Literary Type in Biblical Narrative.* Sheffield: JSOT Press, 1985.

———. *The Song of Songs.* Old Testament Guides. Sheffield: JSOT Press, 1989.

———, ed. *The Song of Songs: A Feminist Reader.* Sheffield: Sheffield Academic Press, 1992.

Bright, John. *A History of Israel.* Philadelphia: Westminster Press, 1959.

Brockelmann, Carl. *Lexicon Syriacum.* 2nd ed. Halle: Max Niemeyer, 1928.

Brown, Francis, S. R. Driver, and Charles A. Briggs. *A Hebrew and English*

Lexicon of the Old Testament. 1907. Reprint. Oxford: Clarendon Press, 1952.

Brown, Peter. "Bodies and Minds: Sexuality and Renunciation in Early Christianity." In *Before Sexuality: The Construction of Erotic Experience in the Ancient Greek World.* Ed. David M. Halperin, John J. Winkler, and Froma Zeitlin. Princeton: Princeton University Press, 1990.

Bruns, Gerald L. "Midrash and Allegory: The Beginnings of Scriptural Interpretation." In *The Literary Guide to the Bible.* Ed. Robert Alter and Frank Kermode. Pp. 625–46. Cambridge: Harvard University Press, 1987.

Budde, Karl F. R. "Das Hohelied." In *Die fünf Megillot.* Ed. Karl Budde, Alfred Bertholet, and D. G. Wildeboer. Pp. 1–48. Kurzer Hand-Commentar zum Alten Testament. Freiburg: J. C. B. Mohr, 1898.

Campbell, Edward F. *Ruth: A New Translation, with Introduction, Notes, and Commentary.* Vol. 7 of The Anchor Bible. Garden City, N. Y.: Doubleday, 1975.

Carmi, T., ed. and trans. *The Penguin Book of Hebrew Verse.* Harmondsworth: Penguin Books, 1981.

Childs, Brevard S. *Biblical Theology in Crisis.* Pp. 186–99. Philadelphia: Westminster Press, 1970.

Cohen, Gerson D. "The Song of Songs and the Jewish Religious Mentality." Reprint. In *The Canon and Masorah of the Hebrew Bible: An Introductory Reader.* Ed. Sid Z. Leiman. New York: Ktav, 1974.

Cook, Albert. *The Root of The Thing: A Study of Job and the Song of Songs.* Bloomington: Indiana University Press, 1968.

Cooper, Jerrold S. "New Cuneiform Parallels to the Song of Songs." *JBL* 90 (1971): 157–62.

Daiches, David. *The King James Version of the English Bible.* Chicago: Chicago University Press, 1941.

Danby, Herbert, trans. *The Mishnah.* Oxford: Clarendon Press, 1933.

De Rougement, Denis. *Love in the Western World.* Trans. Montgomery Belgion. 1940. Rev. ed. New York: Pantheon Books, 1956.

Driver, Samuel R. *An Introduction to the Literature of the Old Testament.* 1913. Reprint. Cleveland: Meridian Books, 1956.

Ehrlich, Arnold B. *Randglossen zur hebräischen Bibel.* Vol. 7. 1914. Reprint. Hildesheim: Georg Olms, 1968.

Eilberg-Schwartz, Howard, ed. *People of the Body: Jews and Judaism from an Embodied Perspective.* Albany: State University of New York Press, 1992.

Eissfeldt, Otto. *The Old Testament: An Introduction.* Trans. Peter R. Ackroyd. New York: Harper and Row, 1965.

Epstein, Louis M. *Sex Laws and Customs in Judaism.* 1948. Reprint. New York: Ktav, 1967.

Even-Shoshan, Avraham. *Ha-Millon he-Hadash* (The New Lexicon). 3 vols. Jerusalem: Kiryat Sefer, 1982.

Exum, J. Cheryl. "A Literary and Structural Analysis of the Song of Songs." *ZAW* 85 (1973): 47–79.

Falk, Marcia. *The Song of Songs: A New Translation and Interpretation.* San Francisco: HarperCollins, 1990.

Fauna and Flora of the Bible. 2nd ed. New York: United Bible Societies, 1980.

Feliks, Yehuda. *Song of Songs: Nature, Epic and Allegory.* Jerusalem: Israel Society for Biblical Research, 1983.

Fisch, Harold. *Poetry with a Purpose: Biblical Poetics and Interpretation.* Bloomington: Indiana University Press, 1988.

Fishbane, Michael. *Text and Texture.* New York: Schocken Books, 1979.

Fishelov, David. "The Song of Songs: Hard and Soft, Dynamic and Static" (in Hebrew). In *'Iyyunim ba-Dimmuy ha-Po'eti* (Studies in Poetic Simile). Unpublished manuscript.

Fohrer, Georg. *Introduction to the Old Testament.* Trans. David Green. Nashville: Abingdon Press, 1968.

Fox, Michael V. *The Song of Songs and the Ancient Egyptian Love Songs.* Madison: University of Wisconsin Press, 1985.

Freedman, David Noel. "Psalm 113 and the Song of Hannah." *Eretz Israel* 14 (1978): 56–69.

Friedman, Richard Elliott. *Who Wrote the Bible?* New York: Harper and Row, 1987.

Frye, Northrop. *The Great Code: The Bible and Literature.* New York: Harcourt Brace Jovanovich, 1981.

———. *Words with Power.* New York: Harcourt Brace Jovanovich, 1990.

Fuchs, Esther. "The Literary Characterization of Mothers and Sexual Politics in the Hebrew Bible." In *Feminist Perspectives on Biblical Scholarship.* Ed. Adela Yarbro Collins. Pp. 117–36. Chico, Calif.: Scholars Press, 1985.

Gerleman, Gillis. "Die Wurzel *šlm.*" *ZAW* 85 (1973): 1–14.

———. *Ruth, Das Hohelied.* Vol. 18 of Biblischer Kommentar: Altes Testament. Neukirchen-Vluyn: Neukirchener Verlag, 1965.

Gesenius, Friedrich H. W. *Hebrew Grammar.* Ed. E. Kautzsch. Trans. and rev. A. E. Cowley. 2nd English ed., 1910. Reprint. Oxford: Clarendon Press, 1966.

Ginsberg, H. L. "Introduction to the Song of Songs" and "Introduction to Ecclesiastes." In *The Five Megilloth and Jonah.* Pp. 3–4, 52–56. Philadelphia: Jewish Publication Society, 1969.

Ginsburg, Christian D. *The Song of Songs and Coheleth: Translation and Commentary.* 1857. Reprint. New York: Ktav, 1970.

Ginzberg, Louis. "Allegorical Interpretation of Scripture." In his *On Jewish Law and Lore.* Pp. 127–50. Philadelphia: Jewish Publication Society, 1955.

———. *The Legends of the Jews.* 7 vols. Philadelphia: Jewish Publication Society, 1909–38.

Givón, Talmy. "The Drift from VSO to SVO in Biblical Hebrew: The Pragmatics of Tense-Aspect." In *Mechanisms of Syntactic Change.* Ed. Charles N. Li. Pp. 181–254. Austin: University of Texas Press, 1977.

Goitein, S. D. "*Ayumma Kannidgalot* (Song of Songs 6:10)." *JSS* 10 (1965): 220–21.

———. "Women as Creators of Biblical Genres." Trans. Michael Carasik. *Prooftexts* 8 (1988): 1–33.

Gollancz, Herman, trans. *The Targum to "The Song of Songs."* 1908. Reprint in *The Targum to the Five Megilloth.* Ed. Bernard Grossfeld. New York: Hermon Press, 1973.

Gollwitzer, Helmut. *Song of Love: A Biblical Understanding of Sex.* Trans. Keith Crim. Philadelphia: Fortress Press, 1979.

Good, Edwin. "Ezekiel's Ship: Some Extended Metaphors in the Old Testament." *Semitics* 1 (1970): 79–103.

Goodspeed, E. J. "The Shulammite." *AJSL* 50 (1933): 102–4.

Gordis, Robert. "Critical Notes on the Blessing of Moses (Deut. 33)." *JTS* 34 (1933): 390–91.

———. *Koheleth, The Man and His World: A Study of Ecclesiastes.* 1951. Reprint. New York: Schocken Books, 1968.

———. "The Root *dgl* in the Song of Songs." *JBL* 88 (1969): 203–4.

———. *The Song of Songs and Lamentations: A Study, Modern Translation and Commentary.* New York: Jewish Theological Seminary, 1954.

Gottwald, N. K. "Song of Songs." In vol. 4 of *The Interpreter's Dictionary of the Bible.* Pp. 420–26. Nashville: Abingdon Press, 1962.

Goulder, Michael D. *The Song of Fourteen Songs. Journal for the Study of the Old Testament.* Supplement Series no. 36. Sheffield: JSOT Press, 1986.

Gow, A. S. F., ed. and trans. *Theocritus.* 2 vols. Cambridge: Cambridge University Press, 1950.

Graves, Robert, trans. *The Song of Songs: Text and Commentary.* New York: Clarkson N. Potter, 1973.

Green, Arthur. "The Song of Songs in Early Jewish Mysticism." *Orim* 2 (1987): 49–63.

Green, Peter. *Alexander to Actium: The Historical Evolution of the Hellenistic Age.* Berkeley: University of California Press, 1990.

Greenberg, Moshe. *Ezekiel, 1–20: A New Translation, with Introduction and Commentary.* Vol. 22 of *The Anchor Bible.* Garden City, N.Y.: Doubleday, 1983.

————. "The Stabilization of the Text of the Hebrew Bible, Reviewed in the Light of the Biblical Materials from the Judean Desert." *JAOS* 76 (1956), 157–67.

Greenfield, Jonas C. "Amurrite, Ugaritic and Canaanite." In *Proceedings of the International Conference on Semitic Studies, 1965.* Pp. 92–101. Jerusalem: Israel Academy of Sciences and Humanities, 1969.

————. Review of *Hebrew and Semitic Studies presented to Godfrey Rolles Driver,* ed. D. Winton Thomas and W. D. McHardy. *JAOS* 85 (1965): 256–58.

Greenspahn, Frederick E. "Words that Occur in the Bible Only Once: How Hard Are They to Translate?" *BR* 1 (Feb. 1985): 28–30.

Greenstein, Edward L. "Theories of Modern Bible Translation." *Prooftexts* 3 (1983): 9–39.

Grossberg, Daniel. "Noun/Verb Parallelism: Syntactic or Asyntactic." *JBL* 99 (1980): 481–88.

Hadas, Moses. *Hellenistic Culture: Fusion and Diffusion.* New York: Columbia University Press, 1959.

Hakham, Amos. "Commentary on the Song of Songs" (in Hebrew). In *Hamesh Megillot* (The Five Scrolls). Ed. Aharon Mirsky, Feibel Meltzer, and Yehuda Kiel. Pp. 1–76. Jerusalem: Mossad Harav Kook, 1990.

Halperin, David M. *Before Pastoral: Theocritus and the Ancient Tradition of Bucolic Poetry.* New Haven: Yale University Press, 1983.

Hartman, Louis F., and Alexander A. Di Lella. *The Book of Daniel: A New Translation, with Introduction, Notes, and Commentary.* Vol. 23 of *The Anchor Bible.* Garden City, N.Y.: Doubleday, 1978.

Havelock, Christine M. *Hellenistic Art.* Greenwich, Conn.: New York Graphic Society, 1971.

Held, Moshe. "A Faithful Lover in an Old Babylonian Dialogue." *Journal of Cuneiform Studies* 15 (1961): 1–26.

Hengel, Martin. *Judaism and Hellenism: Studies in their Encounter in Palestine During the Early Hellenistic Period.* Trans. John Bowden. 2 vols. Philadelphia: Fortress Press, 1974.

————. *Jews, Greeks and Barbarians: Aspects of the Hellenization of Judaism in the Pre-Christian Period.* Trans. John Bowden. Philadelphia: Fortress Press, 1980.

Higham, T. F., and C. M. Bowra, eds. *The Oxford Book of Greek Verse in Translation.* Oxford: Clarendon Press, 1938.

Hirst, Michael, et el. *The Sistine Chapel: A Glorious Restoration.* New York: Harry N. Abrams, 1994.

Honeyman, A. M. "Two Contributions to Canaanite Toponymy." *JTS* 50 (1949): 50–52.

Hrushovsky, Benjamin. "Prosody, Hebrew." *Encyclopedia Judaica*. 1971 ed.

Hunt, Morton M. *The Natural History of Love*. New York: Knopf, 1959.

Hurvitz, A. "The Chronological Significance of 'Aramaisms' in Biblical Hebrew." *Israel Exploration Journal* 18 (1968): 234–40.

———. "Linguistic Criteria for Dating Problematic Biblical Texts." *Hebrew Abstracts* 14 (1973): 74–79.

Hyde, Walter Woodburn. "Greek Analogies to the Song of Songs." In *The Song of Songs: A Symposium*. Ed. W. H. Schoff. Pp. 31–42. Philadelphia: Commercial Museum, 1924.

Ibn Ezra, Abraham. "Commentary on the Song of Songs" (in Hebrew). In *Hamesh Megillot* (The Five Scrolls). The *Miqra'ot Gedolot* Commentary. Pp. 415–72. New York: Abraham Y. Friedman, n.d.

Jastrow, Morris. *The Song of Songs: A Collection of Love Lyrics of Ancient Palestine*. Philadelphia: J. B. Lippincott, 1921.

Jay, Peter, trans. *The Song of Songs*. Introduction by David Goldstein. London: Anvil Press Poetry, 1975.

John of the Cross. *The Poems of St. John of the Cross*. Trans. John Frederick Nims. 3rd ed. Chicago: University of Chicago Press, 1979.

John of the Cross. "The Spiritual Canticle." In *The Collected Works of St. John of the Cross*. Trans. Kieran Kavanaugh and Otilio Rodriguez. Pp. 393–565. New York: Doubleday, 1964.

Josipovici, Gabriel. *The Book of God: A Response to the Bible*. New Haven: Yale University Press, 1988.

Koehler, Ludwig, and Walter Baumgartner. *Hebräisches und aramäisches Lexikon zum Alten Testament*. 3rd ed. Leiden: E. J. Brill, 1967.

Kramer, Samuel Noah. *The Sacred Marriage Rite: Aspects of Faith, Myth, and Ritual in Ancient Sumer*. Bloomington: Indiana University Press, 1969.

Kristeva, Julia. "A Holy Madness: She and He." In her *Tales of Love*. Trans. Leon S. Roudiez. Pp. 83–100. New York: Columbia University Press, 1987.

Kugel, James L. *The Idea of Biblical Poetry: Parallelism and Its History*. New Haven: Yale University Press, 1981.

———. "On the Bible and Literary Criticism." *Prooftexts* 1 (1981): 217–36.

———. "On the Bible as Literature." *Prooftexts* 2 (1982): 323–32.

Landsberger, Franz. "Poetic Units Within the Song of Songs." *JBL* 73 (1954): 203–16.

Landy, Francis. "Beauty and the Enigma: An Enquiry into Some Interrelated Episodes in the Song of Songs." *JSOT* 17 (1980): 55–106.

———. *Paradoxes of Paradise: Identity and Difference in the Song of Songs*. Sheffield: Almond Press, 1983.

———. "The Song of Songs." In *The Literary Guide to the Bible*. Ed. Robert Alter and Frank Kermode. Pp. 305–19. Cambridge: Harvard University Press, 1987.

———. "The Song of Songs and the Garden of Eden." *JBL* 98 (1979), 513–28.

Lapson, Dvora. "Dance: Ancient Israel." *Encyclopedia Judaica*. 1971 ed.

Lehrman, S. M. "The Song of Songs: Introduction and Commentary." In *The Five Megilloth*. Ed. A. Cohen. Pp. 1–32. London: Soncino Press, 1946.

Leiman, Sid Z. *The Canon and Masorah of the Hebrew Bible: An Introductory Reader*. New York: Ktav, 1974.

———. *The Canonization of Hebrew Scripture: The Talmudic and Midrashic Evidence*. 1976. 2nd ed. New Haven: Transactions of the Connecticut Academy of Arts and Sciences, 1991.

Lerner, Gerda. *The Creation of Patriarchy*. New York: Oxford University Press, 1986.

Levine, Amy-Jill, ed. *"Women Like This": New Perspectives on Jewish Women in the Greco-Roman World*. Atlanta: Scholars Press, 1991.

Loewe, Raphael. "Apologetic Motifs in the Targum to the Song of Songs." In *Biblical Motifs: Origins and Transformations*. Ed. Alexander Altmann. Pp. 159–96. Cambridge: Harvard University Press, 1966.

Lord, Albert B. *The Singer of Tales*. Cambridge: Harvard University Press, 1960.

Luther, Martin. "Lectures on the Song of Songs: A Brief but Altogther Lucid Commentary." Trans. Ian Siggins. In vol. 15 of *Luther's Works*. Ed. Jaroslav Pelikan and Hilton C. Oswald. Pp. 189–264. St. Louis: Concordia, 1972.

Maccoby, Hyam. "Sex According to the Song of Songs." Review of *The Song of Songs*, by Marvin H. Pope. *Commentary* 67 (June 1979): 53–59.

Mandelkern, Solomon. *Veteris Testamenti Concordantiae Hebraicae atque Chaldaicae*. 2 vols. 2nd ed. 1937. Reprint. Graz: Akademische Druck- und Verlagsanstalt, 1955.

Margolis, Max L. "How the Song of Songs Entered the Canon." In *The Song of Songs: A Symposium*. Ed. Wilfred H. Schoff. Pp. 9–17. Philadelphia: Commercial Museum, 1924.

Matter, E. Ann. *The Voice of My Beloved: The Song of Songs in Western Medieval Christianity*. Philadelphia: University of Pennsylvania Press, 1990.

May, Herbert G., et al., eds. *Oxford Bible Atlas*. 2nd ed. London: Oxford University Press, 1974.

———. "Some Cosmic Connotations of *Mayim Rabbim*, 'Many Waters.'" *JBL* 74 (1955): 9–21.

Mazor, Yair. "The Song of Songs or the Story of Stories?" *Scandinavian Journal of the Old Testament* 1 (1990): 1–29.

McGinn, Bernard. "With 'the Kisses of the Mouth': Recent Works on the Song of Songs." *Journal of Religion* 72 (1992): 269–75.

Meek, Theophile J. "Canticles and the Tammuz Cult." *AJSL* 39 (1922–23): 1–14.

———. "Babylonian Parallels to the Song of Songs." *JBL* 43 (1924): 245–52.

———. "The Song of Songs: Introduction and Exegesis." In vol. 5 of *The Interpreter's Bible*. Ed. George A. Buttrick et al. Pp. 91–148. Nashville: Abingdon Press, 1956.

Merkin, Daphne. "The Woman in the Balcony: On Reading the Song of Songs." *Tikkun* 9 (May-June 1994): 59–64, 89.

Meyers, Carol. *Discovering Eve: Ancient Israelite Women in Context*. New York: Oxford University Press, 1988.

———. "The Drum-Dance-Song Ensemble: Women's Performance in Biblical Israel." In *Rediscovering the Muses*. Ed. Kimberly Marshall. Pp. 49–67, 234–38. Boston: Northeastern University Press, 1993.

———. "Gender Imagery in the Song of Songs." *HAR* 10 (1986): 209–23.

———. "'To her Mother's House': Considering a Counterpart to the Israelite *Bet 'ab*." In *The Bible and the Politics of Exegesis*. Ed. David Jobling, Peggy L. Day, and Gerald T. Sheppard. Pp. 39–51. Cleveland: Pilgrim Press, 1991.

Miller, Jonathan. "The Afterlife." In his *Subsequent Performances*. Pp. 19–72. New York: Viking, 1986.

The Mishnah. See Danby, Herbert.

Moldenke, Harold N., and Alma L. Moldenke. *Plants of the Bible*. 1952. Reprint. New York: Dover, 1986.

Momigliano, Arnaldo. *Alien Wisdom: The Limits of Hellenization*. Cambridge: Cambridge University Press, 1975.

Moore, Carey A. *Esther: Introduction, Translation, and Notes*. Vol. 7B of *The Anchor Bible*. Garden City, N.Y.: Doubleday, 1971.

Murphy, Cullen. "Women and the Bible." *The Atlantic Monthly* (August 1993): 39–64.

Murphy, Roland E. "Form-Critical Studies in the Song of Songs." *Interpretation* 27 (1973): 413–22.

———. *The Song of Songs: A Commentary on the Book of Canticles*. Minneapolis: Fortress Press, 1990.

———. "The Structure of the Canticle of Canticles." *CBQ* 11 (1949): 381–91.

———. "Towards a Commentary on the Song of Songs." *CBQ* 39 (1977): 482–96.

————. "The Unity of the Song of Songs." *VT* 29 (1979): 436–43.

Neusner, Jacob. *The Mishnah: A New Translation.* New Haven: Yale University Press, 1988.

O'Connor, M. *Hebrew Verse Structure.* Winona Lake, Ind.: Eisenbrauns, 1980.

Origen. *The Song of Songs: Commentary and Homilies.* Trans. R. P. Lawson. Ancient Christian Writers, no. 26. Westminster, Md.: Newman Press, 1957.

Orlinsky, Harry M. "The Canonization of the Bible and the Exclusion of the Apocrypha." In his *Essays in Biblical Culture and Bible Translation.* Pp. 257–86. New York: Ktav, 1974.

Ostriker, Alicia Suskin. *Feminist Revision and the Bible.* The Bucknell Lectures in Literary Theory. Cambridge, Mass.: Blackwell, 1993.

————. *The Nakedness of the Fathers: Biblical Visions and Revisions.* New Brunswick: Rutgers University Press, 1994.

Pagels, Elaine. *Adam, Eve, and the Serpent.* New York: Random House, 1988.

Pardes, Ilana. *Countertraditions in the Bible: A Feminist Approach.* Cambridge: Harvard University Press, 1992.

Parente, Paschal P. "The Canticle of Canticles in Mystical Theology." *CBQ* 6 (1944): 142–58.

Parmelee, Alice. *All the Birds of the Bible: Their Stories, Identification and Meaning.* New York: Harper and Brothers, 1959.

Patai, Raphael. *Sex and Family in the Bible and the Middle East.* Garden City, N.Y.: Doubleday, 1959.

Payne Smith, J. *A Compendious Syriac Dictionary.* 1903. Reprint. Oxford: Clarendon Press, 1967.

Pfeiffer, Robert H. "Canon of the OT." In vol. 1 of *The Interpreter's Dictionary of the Bible.* Pp. 498–520. Nashville: Abingdon Press, 1962.

————. *Introduction to the Old Testament.* 2nd ed. New York: Harper and Brothers, 1948.

Plaskow, Judith. *Standing Again at Sinai: Judaism from a Feminist Perspective.* New York: Harper and Row, 1990.

Pomeroy, Sarah. *Goddesses, Whores, Wives, and Slaves: Women in Classical Antiquity.* New York: Schocken Books, 1975.

Pope, Marvin H. *Song of Songs: A New Translation with Introduction and Commentary.* Vol. 7c of *The Anchor Bible.* Garden City, N.Y.: Doubleday, 1977.

Pound, Ezra, and Noel Stock, trans. *Love Poems of Ancient Egypt.* New York: New Directions, 1962.

Pritchard, James B., ed. *Ancient New Eastern Texts Relating to the Old Testament.* 3rd rev. ed. Princeton: Princeton University Press, 1969.

Rabin, Chaim. "The Song of Songs and Tamil Poetry." *Studies in Religion* 3 (1973): 205–19.

Rashi. "Commentary on the Song of Songs" (in Hebrew). In *Hamesh Megillot* (The Five Scrolls). The *Miqra'ot Gedolot* Commentary. Pp. 415–72. New York: Abraham Y. Friedman, n.d.

Rosenberg, Joel W. "The Garden Story Forward and Backward: The Non-Narrative Dimension of Gen. 2–3." *Prooftexts* 1 (1981): 1–27.

Rosenmeyer, Thomas G. *The Green Cabinet: Theocritus and the European Pastoral Lyric.* Berkeley: University of California Press, 1969.

Rosenthal, Franz. *A Grammar of Biblical Aramaic.* Rev. ed. Wiesbaden: Otto Harrassowitz, 1963.

Roth, Cecil. "Art: Antiquity to 1800." *Encyclopedia Judaica.* 1971 ed.

Rowley, H. H. "The Interpretion of the Song of Songs." In his *The Servant of the Lord and Other Essays on the Old Testament.* Pp. 195–245. 2d rev. ed. Oxford: Blackwell, 1965.

———. "The Meaning of 'The Shulammite.' " *AJSL* 56 (1930): 84–91.

Rozelaar, M. "The Song of Songs against the Background of Hellenistic Greek Erotic Poetry" (in Hebrew). *Eshkolot* 1 (1954): 33–48.

Rubenstein, Eliezer. *Ha-Ivrit Shelanu ve-ha-Ivrit ha-Qedumah* (Our Hebrew and Ancient Hebrew). Jerusalem: Ministry of Defense, 1980.

Rudolph, Wilhelm. *Das Buch Ruth, Das Hohe Lied, Die Klagelieder.* In vol. 17 of the Kommentar zum Alten Testament. Pp. 73–186. Gütersloh: Gerd Mohn, 1962.

Sappho. *See* Barnard, Mary.

Sarna, Nahum. "Bible: The Canon." *Encyclopaedia Judaica.* 1971 ed.

———. "The Interchange of the Prepositions *Beth* and *Min* in Biblical Hebrew." *JBL* 78 (1959): 310–16.

Sasson, Jack M. "Unlocking the Poetry of Love in the Song of Songs." *BR* 1 (Feb. 1985): 11–19.

Scheper, George L. "Reformation Attitudes Towards Allegory and the Song of Songs." *PMLA* 89 (1974): 551–62.

Schmidt, Nathaniel. "Is Canticles an Adonis Liturgy?" *JAOS* 46 (1926): 154–64.

Schneidau, Herbert N. *Sacred Discontent: The Bible and Western Tradition.* Berkeley: University of California Press, 1977.

Schoff, Wilfred H., ed. *The Song of Songs: A Symposium.* Philadelphia: Commercial Museum, 1924.

Scholem, Gershom. *Major Trends in Jewish Mysticism.* 1941. 3rd rev. ed. New York: Schocken Books, 1961.

———, ed. *Zohar: The Book of Splendor.* New York: Schocken Books, 1963.

Schulman, Grace. "The Song of Songs: Love is Strong as Death." In

Congregation: Contemporary Writers Read the Jewish Bible. Ed. David Rosenberg. Pp. 346–59. New York: Harcourt Brace Jovanovich, 1987.

Schwartz, Leo W. "On Translating the 'Song of Songs.'" *Judaism* 13 (1964): 64–76.

Scott, R. B. Y. *Proverbs and Ecclesiastes: Introduction, Translation, and Notes.* Vol. 18 of *The Anchor Bible.* Garden City, N.Y.: Doubleday, 1965.

Segal, M. H. *Grammar of Mishnaic Hebrew.* 1927. Reprint. Oxford: Clarendon Press, 1958.

———. *Mevo ha-Miqra* (Introduction to the Bible). 2 vols. Jerusalem: Kiryat Sefer, 1967.

———. "The Song of Songs." *VT* 12 (1962): 470–90.

———. *Torah, Nevi'im, Ketuvim* (Commentary on the Bible). 4 vols. Tel Aviv: Dvir, 1960.

Seiple, W. G. "Theocritean Parallels to the Song of Songs." *AJSL* 19 (1902–1903): 108–15.

Shea, William H. "The Chiastic Structure of the Song of Songs." *ZAW* 92 (1980): 378–96.

Simon, Maurice, trans. "Canticles Rabbah." In vol. 9 of *Midrash Rabbah.* Ed. H. Freedman and Maurice Simon. 1930. Reprint. London: Soncino Press, 1983.

Smalley, Beryl. *The Study of the Bible in the Middle Ages.* 3rd rev. ed. Oxford: Blackwell, 1983.

Smith, Morton. "Hellenization." In his *Palestinian Parties and Politics that Shaped the Old Testament.* Lectures on the History of Religions. New Series, no. 9. Pp. 57–81. New York: Columbia University Press, 1971.

Smith, R. R. R. *Hellenistic Sculpture.* London: Thames and Hudson, 1991.

Soulen, Richard N. "The Waṣfs of the Song of Songs and Hermeneutic." *JBL* 86 (1967): 183–90.

Speiser, E. A. *Genesis: Introduction, Translation, and Notes.* Vol. 1 of *The Anchor Bible.* Garden City, N.Y.: Doubleday, 1964.

Stadelmann, Luis. *Love and Politics: A New Commentary on the Song of Songs.* New York: Paulist Press, 1992.

Stanton, Elizabeth Cady. *The Woman's Bible.* 1895–1898. Reprint. New York: Arno Press, 1974.

Sternberg, Meir. *The Poetics of Biblical Narrative: Ideological Literature and the Drama of Reading.* Bloomington: Indiana University Press, 1985.

Stewart, Andrew. *Greek Sculpture: An Exploration.* 2 vols. New Haven: Yale University Press, 1990.

Stewart, Stanley. *The Enclosed Garden: The Tradition and the Image in*

Seventeenth-Century Poetry. Madison: University of Wisconsin Press, 1966.

Stillwell, Richard, et al., eds. "Ascalon," "Gadara," "Gaza," "Joppa (Jaffa)," "Marissa," "Ptolemais (Acre)," "Scythopolis." *The Princeton Encyclopedia of Classical Sites.* Princeton: Princeton University Press, 1976.

Stronach, David. "The Garden as a Political Statement: Some Case Studies from the Near East in the First Millennium B.C." *Bulletin of the Asia Institute* 4 (1990): 171–80.

Tannahill, Reay. *Sex in History.* New York: Stein and Day, 1980.

Tcherikover, Victor. *Hellenistic Civilization and the Jews.* Trans. S. Applebaum. Philadelphia: Jewish Publication Society, 1959.

Teresa of Avila. "Meditations on the Song of Songs." In vol. 2 of *The Collected Works of St. Teresa of Avila.* Pp. 205–60. Trans. Kieran Kavanaugh and Otilio Rodriguez. Washington, D.C.: Institute of Carmelite Studies, 1980.

Theocritus. *See* Gow, A. S. F., and Wells, Robert.

Trible, Phyllis. "Depatriarchalizing in Biblical Interpretation." *Journal of the American Academy of Religion* 41 (1973): 30–48.

———. *God and the Rhetoric of Sexuality.* Philadelphia: Fortress Press, 1978.

Urbach, E. E. "The Homiletical Interpretations of the Sages and the Expositions of Origen on Canticles, and the Jewish-Christian Disputation." In *Studies in Aggadah and Folk Literature.* Ed. Joseph Heinemann and Dov Noy. Vol. 22 of Scripta Hierosolymitana. Pp. 247–75. Jerusalem: Magnes Press, 1971.

Ussishkin, David. "King Solomon's Palaces." *BA* 36 (1973): 78–105.

Wagner, Max. *Die lexikalischen und grammatikalischen Aramaismen im alttestamentlichen Hebräisch.* Berlin: Alfred Töpelmann, 1966.

Waltke, Bruce K., and M. O'Connor. *An Introduction to Biblical Hebrew Syntax.* Winona Lake, Ind.: Eisenbrauns, 1990.

Waskow, Arthur. "The Bible's Sleeping Beauty and Her Great-Granddaughters." *Tikkun* 4 (March–April 1989): 39–41, 125–28.

Webster, Edwin C. "Pattern in the Song of Songs." *JSOT* 22 (1982): 73–93.

Wells, Robert, trans. *Theocritus: The Idylls.* Harmondsworth: Penguin Books, 1988.

Wenning, Robert. "Griechische Importe in Palästina aus der Zeit vor Alexander des Grossen." *Boreas* 4 (1981): 28–46.

———. "Hellenistische Skulpturen in Israel." *Boreas* 6 (1983): 105–18.

Wetzstein, J. G. "Die syrische Dreschtafel." *Zeitschrift für Ethnologie* 5 (1873): 270–302.

Whallon, William. "Formulaic Poetry in the Old Testament." *Comparative Literature* 15 (1963): 1–14.

White, John B. *A Study of the Language of Love in the Song of Songs and Ancient Egyptian Poetry.* Society of Biblical Literature Dissertation Series, no. 38. Missoula, Mont.: Scholars Press, 1978.

Williams, Ronald J. *Hebrew Syntax: An Outline.* Toronto: University of Toronto Press, 1967.

Winkler, John J. *The Constraints of Desire: The Anthropology of Sex and Gender in Ancient Greece.* New York: Routledge, 1990.

Wolkstein, Diane. *The First Love Stories: From Isis and Osiris to Tristan and Iseult.* New York: HarperCollins, 1991.

Wolkstein, Diane, and Samuel Noah Kramer. *Inanna, Queen of Heaven and Earth: Her Stories and Hymns from Sumer.* New York: Harper and Row, 1983.

Yoder, Perry. "A-B Pairs and Oral Composition in Hebrew Poetry." *VT* 21 (1971): 470–89.

Zakovitch, Yair. "Explicit and Implicit Name-Derivations." *HAR* 4 (1980): 167–81.

———. *Shir ha-Shirim im Mavo u-Ferush* (The Song of Songs: Introduction and Commentary). Tel Aviv: Am Oved, 1992.

Zeitlin, Solomon. "An Historical Study of the Canonization of the Hebrew Scriptures." In vol. 2 of his *Studies in the Early History of Judaism.* Pp. 1–38. New York: Ktav, 1974.

Zohary, Michael. *Plants of the Bible.* London: Cambridge University Press, 1982.

Index

Landsberger, Franz, 19 *n*
Landy, Francis, 22 *n*, 210
Lebanon, Mount, and area, 8, 122,
    148, 174, 176, 177–78, 188,
    203, 204
Leiman, Sid, 28 *n*
Lerner, Gerda, 167
lily, lilies, 14, 128, 148, 157, 173,
    188
love, 137
    power of, 5, 131, 213–14
    symptoms of, 7
    personified, 130, 153, 204–205
    vs. worldly riches, 218
lover (the Shulamite's), 138, 139,
    153, 154, 218
    his attractiveness, 138, 139
    as "brother," 6, 128–29, 209
    his companions, 6, 18, 179, 220
Luther, Martin, 31

Mahanayim, 199, 202
mandrakes, 124, 208
mare, as erotic metaphor, 39–40,
    144–45, 195
Margolis, Max, 33 *n*
marriage, 175, 214
Masoretic Text (MT), 36, 135, 184,
    186, 193, 200, 210, 211, 220
Mesopotamian art, 151–52
metonymy, 145, 206
Meyers, Carol, 159
Midrash, Midrashic usage, 161,
    166, 180, 201
Midrash Rabbah, 22 *n*
milk, 185, 186
Moldenke, Harold and Alma, 148,
    149
mother, 6
    house of, 6, 159, 210
    image of nursing, 128–29
    King Solomon's, 6, 22–23,
        165–66

the lover's, 6, 211–12
"mother's sons," 6, 141
the Shulamite's, 3, 5–6, 18, 19,
    128–29, 159, 209
as teacher of the arts of love, 6,
    210
Murphy, Roland, 19 *n*, 29 *n*, 135,
    143, 166, 192, 197, 199, 200,
    201, 207

nature in the Song, 9
necklace, 171, 172, 175
New English Bible (NEB), 37, 143,
    144, 151, 156, 162, 166, 172,
    183, 184, 189, 200, 221
New Testament, similar elements in
    the Song, 209, 214, 219
nidgalot (6:4, 6:10), 37, 191–92
night, 147, 157, 163, 173, 180, 221

oral transmission, 20
orchard, 176–77
Origen, 30, 31
'oṭeyah (1:7), 142–43
"our," as used by the lovers, 8, 147,
    153, 155, 208

parallelism, 191, 216
pardes (4:13), 24, 177
Passover Haggadah, 184, 190
pastoral elements, 8, 25–26
personification of abstract, 130, 204
Peshitta, 36, 138, 142, 163, 176,
    179, 210
Pharaoh, 145
Pharaoh's daughter, 10, 32, 34,
    163, 166
Philo, 31
place name symbolism, 203, 219
pools, 186, 202
Pope, Marvin, 29 *n*, 135, 142, 143,
    145, 147, 148, 150, 151, 154,
    155, 156, 163, 165, 166, 170,

saffron, 177
spikenard, 146–47, 177
spring, well, fountain, 176, 177, 202
springtime, 3, 19, 154
Stadelmann, Luis, 31 *n*
suitors, 214, 216
susati (1:9), 39–40, 143–45
Symmachus, 142, 168

Talmud, 163, 184
talpiyyot (4:4), 170–72
Tamar and Judah, 13, 142–43, 212
Targum, 31, 142
Tcherikover, Victor, 25 *n*
Teresa of Avila, Saint, 32
tesuqah (7:11), 206–207
Theocritus, *Idylls*, 25, 144, 157
Theodore of Mopsuestia, 32
Tirzah, city of, 188, 202
title of the Song, 137
Tower of David, 170–71, 172
Tower of Lebanon, 203
twins, 128–29, 169, 173

Ugaritic, 169
unity of the Song, 19–20

"veil," 5, 38-39, 119, 166–68

verb tenses, 39, 149, 152, 178, 205
vine, vineyard, 3, 6, 8, 18, 123, 141,
    147, 155, 156–57, 176–77,
    178, 192, 202, 207, 218–20
Vulgate, 36, 135, 142, 143, 144,
    176, 179, 200

wasf. See praise song
watchmen, 6, 18, 19, 158, 182,
    183
waw-conversive, 24, 191
wedding, 20, 22–23, 33–34, 161,
    163, 166, 175
wheat, 127–28, 201
"white and red," 184–85
wine, 127, 137, 148, 150, 176,
    179–80, 185, 201, 206, 211
Wisdom literature, 152
Wolkstein, Diane, 37, 158
women in OT, 4, 5, 21
word order, 146, 158, 161, 174,
    209, 218
wordplay, puns, 140, 154–55, 170,
    179, 204, 207, 208, 219–20

Zakovitch, Yair, 182
zamir (2:12), 154–55
Zohar, 32, 163

ABOUT THE AUTHORS

ARIEL BLOCH is professor emeritus of Near Eastern studies at the University of California at Berkeley. His books and articles deal with classical Arabic, Arabic dialectology, biblical and Modern Hebrew, Ugaritic, Akkadian, and Aramaic. His books include *Die Hypotaxe im Damaszenisch-Arabischen; Damaszenisch-Arabische Texte; A Chrestomathy of Modern Literary Arabic;* and *Studies in Arabic Syntax and Semantics.* He translated and edited *The Window: New and Selected Poems of Dahlia Ravikovitch* in collaboration with Chana Bloch. Among his awards are a National Endowment for the Humanities Senior Fellowship, the president of the University of California's Research Fellowship in the Humanities, and a National Science Foundation grant. At the University of California he taught courses in Semitic linguistics, including Arabic dialectology and Aramaic, and a graduate seminar on the Song of Songs.

CHANA BLOCH is a poet, translator, scholar, and literary critic. She has published three books of poems, *The Secrets of the Tribe, The Past Keeps Changing,* and *Mrs. Dumpty;* four books of translations from Hebrew: *A Dress of Fire,* by Dahlia Ravikovitch, *The Selected Poetry of Yehuda Amichai* (with Stephen Mitchell), *The Window: New and Selected Poems of Dahlia Ravikovitch* (with Ariel Bloch) and *Open Closed Open* by Yehuda Amichai (with Chana Kronfeld); translations of Yiddish poetry and prose; and a critical study, *Spelling the Word: George Herbert and the Bible.* Her awards include the Discovery Award of the 92nd Street "Y" Poetry Center, a Pushcart Award, the Poets & Writers Exchange Award, two National Endowment for the Arts fellowships, the Columbia University Translation Center Award, two National Endowment for the Humanities fellowships, and the Book of the Year Award of the Conference on Christianity and Literature. She taught Hebrew at the University of California at Berkeley, and is now professor of English and director of the creative writing program at Mills College, where she conducts poetry workshops and teaches courses on contemporary poetry, Shakespeare, and the Bible.

ABOUT THE TYPE

This book was set in Sabon, a typeface designed by the well-known German typographer Jan Tschichold (1902–74). Sabon's design is based on the original letterforms of Claude Garamond and was created specifically to be used for three sources: foundry type for hand composition, Linotype, and Monotype. Tschichold named his typeface for the famous Frankfurt typefounder Jacques Sabon, who died in 1580.

The Hebrew text was set in Narkiss, a typeface designed by Bezalel Narkiss.

IN SEARCH OF HERESY

BOOKS BY JOHN W. ALDRIDGE

After the Lost Generation
Critiques and Essays on Modern Fiction, 1920–1951
   (*Editor*)
In Search of Heresy

IN SEARCH
OF HERESY

*American Literature
in an Age of Conformity*

by JOHN W. ALDRIDGE

McGraw-Hill Book Company, Inc.
NEW YORK   TORONTO   LONDON

IN SEARCH OF HERESY

Library of Congress Catalog Card Number: 56-8166

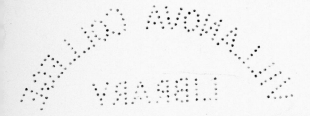

Published by the McGraw-Hill Book Company, Inc.
Printed in the United States of America

For my wife Leslie

ACKNOWLEDGMENTS

A MAJOR PORTION of the material of this book was first presented in the form of lectures delivered in the Christian Gauss Seminars in Criticism at Princeton University during the spring of 1954. Some of the same material, along with much of the remainder, later appeared in *The Nation, The New Leader, The New York Times Book Review, Virginia Quarterly Review,* and *Mandrake,* to the editors of which I am grateful for reprint permission. I wish to acknowledge special indebtedness to the members of the Seminars Committee at Princeton, particularly to E. B. O. Borgerhoff and R. P. Blackmur, for enabling me to undertake the work which made this book possible, and to them as well as to V. S. Pritchett, Sean O'Faolain, Alfred Alvarez, R. W. B. Lewis, and the other Seminars participants for creating an atmosphere of close critical attentiveness from which I gained stimulus, encouragement, and far more corrective instruction than I was able to put to use. My thanks are due also to the great editor and friend who suggested the title for this book. I owe, finally, a debt too personal for public definition to Mr. and Mrs. Samuel Blatt, and another equally great to my wife Leslie Felker Aldridge, whose warm devotion and moral courage have immeasurably enriched the isolation imposed by the writing of the book as well as that other, perhaps more permanent isolation which heresy imposes upon itself.

I should like to extend special thanks to the periodicals *New World Writing, Partisan Review,* and *The Paris Review* for permission to quote from the articles by Charles Fenton, Donald Hall, Allen Tate, Lionel Trilling, Delmore Schwartz, and William Styron. I want finally to thank the publishers for permission to quote from the following books: The Viking Press, Inc., for *The Adventures of Augie March,* by Saul Bellow, and for *The Liberal Imagination,* by Lionel Trilling; Albert and Charles Boni, Inc., for *Some Do Not,* by Ford Madox Ford; Houghton Mifflin Company for *The Heart Is a Lonely Hunter,* by Carson McCullers; The Bobbs-Merrill Company, Inc., for *Lie Down in Darkness,* by William Styron; Yale University Press for *Psychology and Religion,* by Carl Jung; Charles Scribner's Sons for *The Sun Also Rises,* by Ernest Hemingway.

J. W. A.

CONTENTS

IN SEARCH OF HERESY

INTRODUCTION

The choice of heresy

THE GREEK ETYMON of heresy is *hairesis,* which means a taking or choice. In English the word has come to mean an opinion or doctrine at variance with the orthodox or accepted. I suppose we do not need to speculate very long over the point that what for the ancient world carried the connotation of choice, the application of will to morals, has become for us a violation of law, incriminating will and morals alike. That is simply apt to happen in history when will loses supremacy as an instrument of moral choice: law replaces will; legality replaces choice; both replace morals. But it is true that we think in and act from symbols of language, and perhaps equally true that a symbol dies out in language when the act it symbolizes dies out in life. If heresy has lost the older connotation of choice, it may well be because the possibility of heresy as choice has receded from us. At any rate, I assume—and it is the assump-

1

tion underlying most of the essays in this book—that some
such recession has taken place and that we have suffered the
effects in nearly all the areas in which some purpose beyond
that of blind survival is required for the successful conduct of
life.

I do not know how to make this real to those who have not
already discovered it for themselves or who prefer to remain
oblivious of what they have discovered, but it is a fact of habitual daily apprehension for some, and examples of its reality
abound. Alfred North Whitehead gave one of the simplest il-
lustrations when he observed that the modern housewife, unable to buy cloth in a particular shade of blue and obliged to
content herself with whatever shade happens to be mass-
produced, is experiencing at the most immediate level the
effects both of enforced democratization of taste and of in-
fringement upon the democratic right of free choice, the two
together constituting one of the deranging paradoxes of life
in the modern world. The point is that the housewife cannot
commit a heresy in either sense of the word no matter how
desperately she wants to, for the means are simply not available. In time, of course, she ceases to want to, for the urge
toward heresy, like taste, atrophies unless allowed exercise:
she forgets her shade of blue along with her reasons for preferring it to all other shades, and begins to like the shade she
has no choice but to take. In loftier and more rigorous pursuits
we are all similarly diminished for lack of some special shade of
blue, and with an equally compromising effect upon our powers
of choice. It is the risk we are forever running as mass men in a
mass culture; it is the risk we can least afford to run as human
beings.

In a certain narrow sense, the political history of our epoch may be read as a study in the decline of choice-making ideological positions. What feudalism provided was a closed system of immutable choices; it left behind a predatory freedom hard bent on the search for limits within which its energies could be confined and put to work, within which choice could once again become possible on a scale of clear alternatives. The various forms which modern politics has taken—fascism, communism, monarchy, liberal democracy—supplied for a time both limits and scale; they represented at once crystallizations of choice and positions from which choice could be made and action taken, for they functioned to simplify and organize reality and to bring it within the compass of the mass mind and under the control of the mass will. Ultimately, of course, most of these positions hardened into dogma or they died out, and when that happened, those that survived as dogma ceased to be choice-making positions and became positions from which the choosing had all long since been done. In this form they could either enforce orthodoxy or foment heresy (in the newer sense of the word), stabilize themselves or give way to an altered version of themselves, but once stabilized they could no longer support choice because the alternatives necessary to choice had been canceled out by dogma.

At the present time we have limited and largely ceremonial monarchy, dogmatic Soviet socialism (which is one of the heresies of dogmatic theoretical communism), denationalized and, for the most part, disarmed fascism, and conformist capitalistic democracy (which is one of the heresies of liberal capitalistic democracy). Of these perhaps Soviet socialism alone has remained in force as both dogma and ideological position.

American democracy can scarcely be said any longer to constitute a dogma (a fact which has crippled our best efforts to
propagandize it abroad), nor can its conformism be called
an ideological position (a fact which has not at all crippled the
worst efforts of some of us to confer upon it the dignity of one).
It is a feature of our democracy that it has no dogma to enforce,
but neither does it enforce its conformism. It does not need
to because it produces conformism by leaving open to the mass
of people no alternative to conformism and, therefore, by removing from them the possibility of choice. This, I suspect,
is at the heart of that paralysis of will, that derangement of the
sense of future, which appears to be so prevalent today, especially among younger Americans. Our democracy in its current
form gives them neither a dogma which might provide a basis
for heretical action nor an opportunity to discover and choose a
politics or faith or way of life which would represent a heresy of
democracy. That is simply the certain shade of blue which our
political mass-production does not supply. But our present
way of life does supply conformity, conformity to the institutional, the corporate, and the civic interests, and so the young
people conform in ever increasing numbers, forgetting their
certain shade of blue and their reasons for wanting it, learning to want what there is to get.

In the case of the American intellectual, this condition asserts itself as a threat to morale and action alike, for it has
traditionally been the intellectual's task—assigned and con-
doned by no one but himself—to monitor the culture of his
time, to exercise within it his right of free choice, and upon it the
reprimanding influence of his dissent. But standing between him
and the performance of this task today are certain obstacles suffi-

ciently distinct from those facing the culture in general as to be called peculiarly his own. The American intellectual has first of all suffered the loss in recent years of the older sustaining ideologies and platforms of dissent: he became disaffected long ago with the revolutionary ideal of communism, which afforded him an angle of critical vision into politics during the thirties, and he has outgrown the naïveté which once enabled him to shout down on the head of American materialism from one of the posts of romantic disaffiliation like that of the Artist in Exile. One can in fact say that he has been uprooted or evicted from just about all the positions which formerly justified and ennobled the isolation of his role and which held out some respectable alternative to the state of being merely cooperative and pleasant required by mass society. The result has been that the intellectual, deprived of alternative, has grown increasingly vulnerable to the enticements of conformism, for while it is true that conformism at the present time is neither dogmatic nor enforced, it does have interests in the service of which the talents of the intellectual may be profitably put to use, and rewards to which his past innocence of reward renders him peculiarly susceptible. But above all, conformism has on its side the fact, perhaps more compelling for the intellectual than for the average citizen, that as a platform for action it is all there is: the margin of possibility for action beyond conformism has been cut down to nothing. The paternalism of the cultural institutions, the institutional values of money, status, security, and power, have filled and padded the vacuum left by the loss of the values of disaffiliation and dissent.

The absence of an active alternative to conformism is attested to not only by the emptiness of some of the recent novels of dissent but by certain others which affirm conformism the most strongly. One of the most popular of these, Herman Wouk's *Marjorie Morningstar,* never dramatizes the heresy of which the conformist values it insists upon are the dogma. Although Marjorie is attracted briefly by the "nonconformity" of Noel Airman, it soon becomes clear that this is merely an adolescent posture of Noel's and has behind it neither ideological conviction nor a vision of any way of life which can incorporate it. Similarly, the American intellectual is handicapped for lack of a nonconformist program of action. Both his professional function and his way of life are necessarily carried on within a convention impossible to distinguish from that of his conformist neighbor. In a society such as the one Sinclair Lewis satirized —an earlier phase of our own—in which conformism is based on strongly held ideas of respectability, personal honor, success, and civic virtue, which assert themselves in prudery, philistinism, and hatred of culture, an alternative is of course easy to conceive: a way of life incorporating simply the opposites of these values. But present-day conformism is not morally or ethically based, but rather emphasizes passive and amoral qualities—comfort, security, peace of mind—which do not represent a dogma nor suggest a heresy. (For further discussion of conformism in fiction see Author's Note, Essay Four.)

The essays in this book were written for a variety of different occasions and are not intended to constitute a formal or systematic inquiry into the conformist tendencies now dominant in the American intellectual life. If they had been so intended, I should have included with them a great deal of related material not here included. Yet each of the major essays has to do with aspects of the conformist development. In them, at times singly, at times variously, I have been concerned with such matters as the new liberal assent to mass cultural values (particularly the new egalitarian frenzy which may be observed among certain intellectuals who formerly prided themselves on their minority status, when such status was still serviceable), the movement of literary intellectuals into the universities, and their adoption of the values of institutional orthodoxy, and the dramatic possibilities which appear to be open to the novelist in the conformist culture of the present time. Much of the remaining material represents an effort, which I hope will be taken as tentative and exploratory, to define a relation between this problem of a culture's dramatic potential—deriving from the concerns which it deems to be morally valuable—and the kind and quality of fiction a culture produces. Essays Three, Four, and Five, in particular, may be read as a single unit of discussion centering in this problem. But lest I be accused of advocating under the guise of an attack on conformism a return to some of the orthodoxies of the past, I had perhaps better make it clear that I am concerned in these essays with the kind of orthodoxy which, because it is backed by morals, religious principles, and social codes of manners, helps to make possible the delineation of scene and character in fiction. I do not say that such an orthodoxy is right or wrong in any sense except the esthetic, for I do suggest that it undoubtedly serves the novelist better than a situation of conformism which is not morally or religiously motivated and is, therefore, likely to be less dramatizable.

The point of view from which I approach the new intellectual conformism rests on an ideal which—as I have already suggested—is now anachronistic, unworkable, and quite without

adherents, except for a few mavericks like myself who have not
yet learned to reconcile the contrary teachings of their heads
and hearts. I mean the ideal of creative independence and free
critical dissent which has come down to us in the central tradition of American thought and letters and which has energized
the work, even as it has debilitated more than a few of the
lives, of most of the writers whom we now consider to be important. Cooper, Emerson, Melville, Hawthorne, Twain, Whitman, Crane, Norris, Dreiser, Mencken, Faulkner, and Hemingway have all adhered to it in their several ways. Yet even in
them one can see that it was never pure, that it always existed
side by side with its opposite in a moral nesting of impeding
ambiguity. For it is clear that they wished to be accepted by
the institutions they attacked, by the society to which they
could not conform, that they longed to be loved by those
they hated and condemned, and, above all, that they expected
to be honored *for* their hatred and condemnation. But this has
always been the figure in the carpet of American literature, the
recurring case with writers both American and foreign, and it
is the case again with this book: its dissent is assent inverted;
it contains and affirms the dogma of which it is a heresy.

If this is a paradox, I suspect we had better embrace it, for
it may well represent our certain shade of blue, what is left to
us of the possibility of heresy as choice. For clearly the old easy
positions and solutions will no longer suffice. We will perhaps
do best to choose and submit to complexity and difficulty,
contradiction, paradox, and failure, to insist again and again on
the duty of the writer to be free, even as the range of his freedom grows daily narrower and his grasp on its meaning and
use daily more tenuous, to assert the need to oppose conform-

ism even though the culture presents no alternative to it, nor even a defensible "position" from which it can be opposed—to learn, in short, what another romantic once said it was possible only for the best of us to learn: how to hold two opposing ideas in the mind at the same time and still retain the ability to function. For it appears to be our fate, as it has been the fate of our literature as a whole, to have to hold together, without hope of resolution, the forces of dogma and heresy, conformity and dissent, hate and love, guilt and innocence, sin and redemption, and to create out of the holding itself the tension which brings art to life and life alive in art. What James's Dencombe saw as the truth of his own condition we have no choice now but to see as ours: "We work in the dark—we do what we can—we give what we have. Our doubt is our passion, and our passion is our task."

ONE

The situation of the American writer *

THOSE OF US who are now thirty or slightly older have already outlived the literary movement in which we grew up—the movement that came to fruition in the twenties, while we were still too young to participate in it, but that seemed destined for a time in the late forties to be given new vitality and purpose by writers our own age who were then coming out of the war. The great early figures of that movement—Yeats, Joyce, Gide, Shaw, Eliot, Pound—are nearly all dead now, their works and effects abandoned to the museums and the damp hands of classical scholarship. Later figures of the second rank like Scott Fitzgerald and Thomas Wolfe, whom we thought

* This essay was originally presented as a Christian Gauss lecture at Princeton under the title, "Thoughts on *Never* Being Bibliographed." The reference is to Edmund Wilson's famous essay. By echoing his style and tone in treating material very similar to his, I hoped to emphasize both the parallels and the ironic differences between the historical occasions of his essay and mine.

of, ten or fifteen years ago in college, as older but still active
contemporaries of ours, have already taken on the remote
character of minor deities out of some vanished Augustan
past. Of the best writers now in middle age and still capable
of serious work, only a very few have been able to develop at
all significantly those initial and, for the most part, narrow
insights into modern life which secured their place in the
literary world of twenty years ago. The one or two—I can
think of only Faulkner and Hemingway—whose later careers
have been something more than a falling off or merely a repetition of earlier promise are chronically under siege by hordes
of critics bent on sacking their establishments, picking over
their bones, and raising around their works sepulchers of
exegesis and bibliography. Some of the lesser known and,
one would suppose, more fortunate writers of the same age—
the one-book novelists and former poets—who sank into obscurity right after the twenties and for years were not heard
of again, have suddenly been rediscovered and crowned with
the notoriety of Civil War veterans and Titanic survivors for
having once belonged to the movement or figured in the mem-
oirs of someone who did.

The situation of the younger group of novelists is far different today from what it was seven or eight years ago when they
first began to appear. At the time a variety of circumstances
seemed to be coming together to produce an atmosphere both
exciting and liberating to new talent. The war had ended without that fatigued suspension of the will which followed after
1918 and gave rise to the earlier literature of nervelessness; and
there had finally come a break—sometime in the early forties
—in the tendency of the proletarian school to repeat itself

endlessly in novels rank with the outmoded economics of
Marx and Engels. The reading public, which, while the war
lasted, had been more or less content to subsist on the sweet-
nesses of Private Hargrove and William Saroyan, was now anx-
ious for a return to the sterner realities; and publishers were
finding it profitable to cultivate writers who, fresh from the hard-
ships of active service, seemed most likely to bring it about.
There began a rather grandiose and indiscriminate exploitation
of every literary effect, good or bad, in any way connected
with the war, of every young man with a combat trauma or
gripe that could be turned to print.

Twenty-five and thirty years earlier this kind of wholesale
speculation in talent had been a natural response to the upsurge of creative activity which came on in the twenties and
which quickly began to be exploited with the competitive zeal
normally associated with bull-market buying in Wall Street.
Publishers gambled on dozens of young writers in the hope
of discovering a new Sherwood Anderson or Sinclair Lewis,
and ended, in certain historic instances, by discovering Ernest
Hemingway, Scott Fitzgerald, and John Dos Passos, whose
successes over the years that followed were in large part responsible for the rise of the great serious reputations of such
houses as Scribner's and Houghton Mifflin. But now, at the
end of another war, with the precedent of early subsidy of
talent thus established and vindicated, what had formerly been
speculative became self-conscious, and there grew up a feeling
that literary renaissance and boom were known chemical
compounds that could be precipitated into being if only one
followed the formula of the past and paid enough money.

For the enterprising publisher of the forties this meant a

mechanical repetition of all the old conjuring tricks. Once again he bought up his stable of fresh young talent, although this time in the hope of discovering a new Hemingway, Fitzgerald, or Dos Passos; and it was not surprising that most of the writers he bought were those who, by an odd process of commercialized reincarnation, most closely resembled the masters whom he hoped to replace. Nor was it any more than inevitable that the ceremonies of first publication for many of these writers should seem to be patterned increasingly after those ancient rites of fertility in which the effigy of the dead god—or in this case the dead reputation—was cast into Hades to be born anew in the person of youth. After a while it became hard to avoid wondering whether the process of authorship was not really becoming one of ghoulish collaboration with the dead and dying, whether the first novel of Merle Miller or Robert Lowry was not in fact a new revision of *Tender Is the Night* done by Theodore Dreiser with the help of Compton McKenzie.

Yet in spite of the extremes of mercantile silliness to which it was occasionally carried, the quasi renaissance of the late forties had for a time an effect both exhilarating and wholesome on the younger writers themselves. It gave them enough money so that they were freed, very early in their careers, from the pressures of other work; and now that the war had ended, along with the restrictions which it had imposed on movement, it suddenly became possible with money to live the literary life once again, to throw big parties, to travel and settle abroad, to found magazines, with an ease and directness unknown since the twenties. It was in fact one of the most ironic features of the time that the commercial interests

which had generated and then exploited the prevailing atmosphere of assiduous trendmongering and ancestor worship had
also inadvertently brought about a condition in which both the
more serious and the more frivolous interests of the past could
actually for the first time in years be restored and developed.
The financial collapse of the thirties had led to a shrinkage
of nearly all the values of the intellectual life and had reduced
writers from their former high position as free producers to
the status of charity cases and wards of a welfare state. Their
Marxist concerns, moreover, had had the effect of temporarily
anesthetizing their sense of any purpose for art beyond that of
social relevance, just as, in the early forties, the official war-
time view of their "responsibility," huckstered by such new
patriots as Archibald MacLeish and Bernard De Voto, had
persuaded some of them to desert politics for propaganda.

But now, for those of the younger group who continued to
be benefited rather than stifled or debauched by the constant
iteration of the names and works of famous predecessors, the
flattering juxtaposition of earlier creative decades with their
own, there was set up a frame of mind and reference in which
it became natural once again to speak of a serious disinterested
calling of American letters and of a native tradition of excellence on which the beginning writer could take his bearings.
The promising young novelist with his first book completed
enjoyed not merely the customary guaranty of publication
provided him by the boom but the greater advantage of feeling himself launched into history and placed almost at once
in an established line of influence which perhaps he was
simultaneously appointed to carry on. While it was not always
obvious to him that his eminence had been concocted or that,

more often than not, he was being made simply the pawn of a publicity enterprise bent on exploiting the exchange value of the past, he was nevertheless given a sense of belonging, however tentatively, to a traditional hierarchy of peers to whom the practice of literature was a common craft and faith in its importance a common motivation.

In any case, by the end of the forties the opening phase of the postwar literary revival had run its course, publishing had settled down to a state of seemingly permanent inflation, and conditions became different again. The younger novelists who, three or four years previously, had written their first books in a spirit of confidence that they were entering on a new creative cycle and carrying forward an established creative tradition suddenly found themselves high and dry in a world where all they stood for seemed to have gone into eclipse and where they themselves had become premature anachronisms. Although they had, as a group, by now published a respectable body of work, including several novels of genuine distinction, and had among them such accomplished writers as Jean Stafford, Carson McCullers, John Horne Burns, Norman Mailer, Paul Bowles, and Truman Capote, they had largely failed to take the positions of authority and influence which had appeared to be opening to them only a short time before. In fact, the situation with which they were now confronted was such as to invalidate entirely the system of accession to power and prominence, the very possibility of reputation in the old sense, which had been the feature of the decades just past and on which, in the excitement of the immediate postwar years, they had come to pin their hopes. The modern literary movement had, in those years, lost nearly all its po-

tency as a reproductive and energizing force and had been
slowly absorbed into the universities, where its massive indig-
nations had cooled down to small fastidious tics experienced by
graduate students in the damp undercaves of libraries, and
where its great seminal ideas * had been frozen and crystallized
into churchly authoritarian dogma. The leaders and apostles
of the movement whom the younger group had thought of
as their natural and at least spiritually living mentors appeared now to have been embalmed and mummified like
ancient Egyptian priests and set up in niches to commemorate
the grandeur of a vanished cult, while their works had come
to be looked upon, not as models to be admired and imitated
but as sacred canonical treasures to be studied as objects of
research in the science of liturgics. Literature now was a
corporate body, official, institutionalized, and closed: the appearance of a new writer, the creation of a new work outside
the canon was not only irrelevant but irreverent, at best a
willful and rather nasty breach of etiquette, at worst very
nearly an act of heresy. Besides, the consolidation of literary

---

* It would undoubtedly be fatuous to attempt any categorical definition of
these ideas. They cannot merely be listed, for that is to burlesque history and
insult intelligence. Nor can they be purposefully discussed as if they enjoyed
some spectacular distinction not to be found in ideas underlying the literary
movements of other cultures and ages. But I do have in mind the special emphasis given in this century and the last to certain ageless assumptions about
the nature of literature and the role of the writer in society. One cannot begin
to distinguish the movement I speak of from others without taking this
emphasis into account, particularly as it shows itself in the metaphysical-
symbolist influence in poetry, the realist-symbolist influence in fiction, and
the formalist influence in criticism, this is to say, in the line of literary development carried forward in modern times by Rimbaud, Baudelaire, and
Flaubert and by Conrad, James, Joyce, Richards, and Eliot. If the modern
movement can be said to have a bias, it is in the direction of the impressionist
outgrowth of Romanticism. That, at any rate, is the feature which our best
criticism has recognized as the badge of artistic seriousness and worth.

power within the universities had progressed to the point where
the manufacture of new writers and works could be carried
out under the controlled conditions of the laboratory and the
tested and purified techniques of the masters injected like
plasma directly into the blood streams of apprentices, enabling
them to begin at once to write poems rich in ambiguity, paradox,
irony, symbolism, and tension, and short stories and novels incorporating James's device of the "trapped spectator," Conrad's concealed and multiple narrators, and Joyce's parallels
to the myth of Odysseus.

There was something suspect and vulgar now about a
writer who worked up his own materials or who retained more
than a speculative interest in the experience of his own time.
To the literary men of the academy he seemed to inhabit some
distastefully fetid underworld of subintellectual intrigue, a kind
of retarded bohemian cellar, where the cold, clear light of
Brooks and Warren never penetrated. But the independent
writer had what was, from the academic point of view, the
still more crippling defect of being unable or unwilling to keep
abreast of the current developments in his field. He thought
of himself, for example, as belonging to the avant-garde and as
carrying forward a tradition of free creative inquiry into the
spirit of his age; while the truth was that his entire conception
of the avant-garde—the conception of a community of intran-
sigent, revolutionary talents—had long since been outmoded
by the rise of a new academic avant-garde conceived in the
name of orthodoxy and dedicated to the principle that all
writers are created equal provided they conform to the rules
of the canon. As for the work of free creative inquiry into

the spirit of the age, it had been purged both of freedom and of creativeness and entrusted to a special commission head-quartered in the *Partisan Review,* where it became known henceforward simply as "Project X: *explication du Zeitgeist."*

The movement, finally, to which the independent writer naïvely felt himself to be still allied had not merely become institutionalized in the universities; it had passed into the receivership of the new avant-garde and been turned into capital for an official corporation of "experimental" literature, presided over by a board of director-critics, staffed by graduates of the literary workshops at Stanford and Iowa, and head-quartered in the *Kenyon* and *Sewanee Reviews.* Here the process of direct exploitation of the masters of the movement —which had begun in the universities with the creation of synthetic, junior-sized Joyces, Jameses, and Kafkas—was accelerated to the point where it passed into the large-scale production of hybrid and mutated forms of those special dramatic techniques which criticism had explicated out of the works of the masters. Thus, instead of reading James, the young avant-gardist read Percy Lubbock on *The Ambassadors* and made use in his novel of Lubbock's interpretation of James's use of "point of view"; instead of reading Faulkner, he read Richard Chase on the images of line and curve in *Light in August* and began distributing through his novel, at the rate of about three to the page (that being the "holy" number), images of line and curve. He discovered in time, of course, that for the successful employment of these techniques some subjects served better than others: some would symbolize, others would not; some met the official specifications as to "resonance, thickness, and depth," others were dangerously experiential and naturalistic and threatened to trap him into a single level of meaning or a failure to render or evoke.

There consequently grew up a special avant-garde etiquette of subject selection which became as restrictive in its effects on the quarterlies as the clichés and stereotypes imposed by the mass audience on the commercial magazines. A primary requirement was that a short story be presented against a background of sufficient complexity and dimension to make possible the objectification of theme through the natural elements of landscape and weather—a device made mandatory after the Robert W. Stallman researches into the work of Stephen Crane and Conrad. The best stories, therefore, were those set in such locales as the wild mountain country of the West and the decadent bayou and hill country of the South, where the majestic or baroque furnishings of environment could be made to serve as correlatives for the emotional responses of character. The situations themselves which could be expected to rise out of of these locales were naturally limited in kind. They tended to turn on the mechanism of the muffled psycho-religious epiphany—the canonical equivalent of Aristotle's recognition-reversal sequence—and to have to do with adolescent hayloft intrigues, the death of small pet animals on Montana ranches, the sadism of sinisterly precocious Mississippi children, the menopausal sex adventures of middle-aged gentlewomen with faithful old plantation retainers, and the sensibility crises of lonely young girls in Virginia boarding schools. Stories of this type appeared to result from the writers' calculated effort to make use of materials which were conceived by the academy to be "literary"—because rustic or bizarre—

and to have been drawn out of what few timid sorties into
"felt life" they themselves had had the opportunity to launch
prior to their matriculations in the workshops and graduate
schools.

As their memory of life faded, however, along with their
capacity to feel it, many of them began exploiting the world of
the academy itself; and there set in among them a species of
creative incest in which the relations which normally obtain
between writers and their experience were perverted into
relations with the agency which instructed or supported them
in the art of having relations with their experience. The prototypal result was the work of "in-group" exposé, the academic
conte and *roman à clef* such as Mary McCarthy's *The Groves
of Academe* and Randall Jarrell's *Pictures from an Institution,*
in which the dramatic interest centered neither in the "felt
life" nor in the quality of the rendered emotion—of which
there was usually none—but in the verisimilitude with which
known institutions and personages were represented and
satirized. And as these became in time increasingly easy to
identify, it began to be evident that there existed even a formal
avant-garde etiquette for scandal, a conventionalized snobbery
which limited the area of satirical attack to certain selected
institutions and personages—notably, to Bennington, Bard,
and Sarah Lawrence colleges, their faculties and presidents—
and which ruled out places like Columbia and the universities
of Chicago, Michigan, and Wisconsin as presumably fit for
investigation only in novels of a low naturalistic order or of
merely reformist intent.

By the same token, the avant-garde writers themselves
existed within carefully restricted lines of status and class.

In issue after issue of the quarterlies one read the same names at the heads of stories—Randall Jarrell, Mary McCarthy, Walter Van Tilburg Clark, Eudora Welty, Saul Bellow, Elizabeth Hardwick, Flannery O'Connor, Jean Stafford, Shirley Jackson, Katherine Anne Porter, Robie Macauley—and when the quarterly reviewers devoted their characteristically scrupulous attention to fiction at all, it was almost certainly to be to the work of these same writers. Those, on the other hand, who like Norman Mailer, Calder Willingham, James Jones, John Horne Burns, Irwin Shaw, Alfred Hayes, Gore Vidal, and Chandler Brossard, had come up outside the universities and had, for better or worse, remained free of affiliation except to their craft, were just as scrupulously ignored. They were apparently thought of as too unrestrainedly creative and, therefore, by an odd but typical logic, as insufficiently literary and serious. Their novels had to do with such subjects as war, race prejudice, sexual aberration, social maladjustment, neurosis, and insanity, or simply the way it was in 1945 or the winter of 1947, and these—now that the academy had attended to the burial of both the older realism and naturalism—were considered outside the province of the novel and suitable only as raw materials for sociologists, psychiatrists, and other case workers in merely human experience.

Besides, the novel now was a classic form; it had evolved beyond the point where it could be used easily, exploratively, or imperfectly, with any hope of adapting it to the conditions of new work. All one could legally do was produce small, mathematically perfect scale models of an institutionalized abstraction known simply as "novel," and then one had to be careful, for even in effigy the novel had at least to wear the

look of a strained and suffocating greatness. It consequently
came about that the majority of these younger writers, although they represented the only really fresh and independently
creative element to appear in the postwar generation, found
themselves cut off, at the outset of their careers, from both
the established avant-garde and the centers of the one respectable critical authority to which they might have looked for
guidance, understanding, and the means of serious reputation.

Meanwhile, in the literary market place a parallel situation
was beginning to emerge. The publishing boom, which had
been steadily gaining momentum through the five years following the war, had reached proportions by 1950 so fantastically beyond the power of any human agency to imagine or
control that one supposed the manufacture of books to have
been taken over in the night by some monstrous, self-operating,
perpetual-motion machine diabolically bent on conquering the
world by smothering its inhabitants beneath tons of print. One
was encouraged in this impression by the spectacle of the
publishers themselves, many of whom appeared to have been
converted into the captive host-creatures of an autotelic business enterprise whose original purposes had been lost in antiquity and whose sole remaining function was simply to keep
on endlessly and pointlessly running.

It seemed suddenly that all the old categories and relationships which had formerly guided and comforted one in one's
thinking about the production of books had gone into the
discard or had, like so many of one's old assumptions, simply
ceased after the war to correspond to reality—if, indeed, there
can be said to have been a reality after the war. It scarcely
mattered, for example, that books had at one time been the

results of the painful and loving efforts of intelligent men to communicate something which they conceived to be worthwhile, that they had been meant to *say* something, and by their saying to satisfy a very real and existing human need. Books now were simply disposable items containing a two- or three-hour supply of psychic maintenance; when they were used up, they could be thrown away like Kleenex. There was no longer any question of their satisfying a need, nor was it necessary any longer that they should. For a public accustomed from childhood to buying at the dictates of every passing acquisitive reflex, it was enough that books were offered on the market for sale, that they were simply *there* to be bought. They would undoubtedly still have been bought in large numbers if they had been nothing but bundles of blank paper sewn into gaudy covers.

In the midst of all this the writers of the younger group who had begun their careers during the first phase of the boom were caught up in conditions so radically different from those which prevailed at that time that it is no wonder many of them lost their bearings and, in some cases, after remarkable initial successes lapsed into silence or mediocrity. The rise of mass publishing had effectively brought to an end the period of innovation and discovery into which they emerged, and where they had formerly been made to feel special and chosen by virtue of being young writers upon whom the accolade of posterity was about to be bestowed, they now found themselves regarded simply as slightly older members of a transient, anonymous body of writers all of whom seemed equally young, equally talented, and equally forgettable. Not only had the traditional public image of the writer as a figure of glamour apparently faded along with the decline of interest in books, but there had grown up a widespread indifference to the fact of talent itself, and a feeling that fiction of whatever quality somehow no longer communicated any vision of reality which it was possible to respond to or recognize as true. Although novels of distinction were still being written, one could scarcely imagine a way in which they might have been received with even approximately the kind of immediate shock of recognition that accompanied the appearance of novels like *The Great Gatsby* and *The Sun Also Rises,* nor did there seem any possibility of their being preserved in the public consciousness long enough to be revived in ten or twenty years and accorded a similar place in the hierarchy of modern classical literature. The truth now was statistical and political; it yielded to the forces of tabulation and analysis, the devices of the survey, the corporate report, the personal interview and the house-to-house poll, rather than to imaginative synthesis. The works of Dr. Kinsey, C. Wright Mills, David Riesman, Susanne K. Langer, and other sociophilosophical thinkers were the substitutes for major fiction in the fifties and made use of insights into contemporary culture which would undoubtedly in any other time have found their most natural expression in the novel form.

There was, furthermore, a sense in which it could be said that publishing had by now evolved to the point where its business interests were no longer best served by the novelist of quality but by the second- or third-rate writer who could be counted on to turn out in large volume and at fast pace a kind of pseudo fiction, a species of high-grade, extremely serious hack writing—of which Herman Wouk's *The Caine*

Mutiny is one example—containing all the ingredients of the real thing but in diluted or homogenized form, so that it could be fed over and over again to readers without ever bringing them to the stage of satisfaction where they would cease to buy. Many of the first novels by the younger writers who were discovered in the early fifties belonged to this category—including a few, like John Phillip's *The Second Happiest Day,* which were singled out for special praise by critics on the ground of their "sincerity"—and that was perhaps one of the reasons for the falling off of interest in the younger literary generation as such. But as more and more novels of all kinds were published, each tended anyway, regardless of its quality, to be reduced in value to the level of all the others and treated in the same anonymous manner. And as the promotional agencies of publishing became increasingly petrified in their attitudes of soaring high encomium and the reviewing profession increasingly drugged on the volume of novels flooding into the market, there finally remained no method of distinguishing good from bad or of separating out the work most likely to be of more than passing interest.

In previous literary decades such as the twenties it had been possible—although one no longer knew quite how—for the novelist sooner or later to achieve a continuity of reputation and public success at least equal to the stamina and value of his work. One thought of the young Hemingway and the young Fitzgerald and of the inevitability of the process by which they rose, through regular stages of gradual growth and single successes, as well as instructive failures, to the positions of fame in which they finally became secure. But one also thought of those small centers of enthusiastic opinion—the magazines like the *Dial, Bookman, Hound and Horn,* the old *Saturday Review* and *New Republic,* and the columns and articles of men like Edmund Wilson, John Peale Bishop, Van Wyck Brooks, Stuart P. Sherman, and Burton Rascoe—where their names and books were not allowed to be forgotten, and of that initially small but receptive reading public which fancied that these writers were speaking to them and which in turn spoke back to them. One thought, in short, of the existence of certain sanctuaries where the memory of talent was preserved during the fallow time between the actual appearance of books. But now, in a time which seemed suddenly to have gone rotten with literature, the young writer of promise found himself in a situation in which he felt compelled perpetually to remake his public bed with each new work, until finally, in far too many cases, he became exhausted and was overcome with a desire just to lie down on the floor and go to sleep. With the appearance of each new book he was hustled forward to stand naked for a moment in the public gaze. He was extravagantly promoted and meanly or indifferently reviewed. For perhaps three weeks he was granted a sort of low-grade meretricious notoriety. But as soon as the reviews stopped coming in, he began to feel neglected, and in another month or so could consider himself lucky if an occasional literate reader remembered having seen his name.

Whatever his new book may have been, it stood small chance of being admitted to membership in a growing body of selected work which represented the accumulated literary achievement of his time. After the popular reviews had appeared, he did not, if he was typical, see his book discussed at length in the serious quarterlies, compared with the work of

his contemporaries, or assigned a place in the larger critical
order. There was no Ezra Pound or Ford Madox Ford to write
him letters of encouragement and advice; he had little or no
sense that what he had had to say had found an audience among
those of his own age who had shared in his own experience.
In a few months he was likely to be driven to conclude that
his only hope for literary salvation lay in the quick production
of another book, and then another and another and another,
through which he might possibly gain by siege what he could
not gain by honest stealth. But as the books came from him
at increasingly shorter intervals, with each one perhaps bearing the increasingly unmistakable marks of technical haste and
imaginative strain, he found himself going through the same
old process, only now there were mounting reasons why he
should slip backward two steps for every step forward he
managed to take. In the end, he was likely to have discovered
that in trying to build the public personality which his urge
toward status demanded, he had drawn irrecoverably upon
the creative capital which had been its sole justification and
had succeeded only in cutting status from under his feet.

One has heard it argued—most recently with that hysteria
of conviction which renders all conviction suspect—that the
tremendous expansion of the paper-reprint industry during
the boom years and the rise within the same medium of the
mass-circulation literary review have done much to reduce, if
not altogether to solve, the problems now confronting the serious writer. The large-scale manufacture of inexpensive re-
prints is said to have brought about in America a changed cultural situation in which the writer has been placed for the
first time in contact with vast sectors of the average reading

audience from which he had been formerly cut off; while the mass-circulation review has allegedly made it possible for him, again for the first time, to reach that audience with work of a new or an experimental kind which has hitherto been supposed unpalatable to it and, therefore, suited only to small-quarterly publication. It has been generally maintained that as a result of these developments the writer is now assured not only of the widest and most profitable market for his books but also of the chance to function up to his fullest capacity within that market without having to compromise his standards of artistic honesty and taste.

It is difficult to quarrel with these claims. One would prefer simply to accept them *in toto* as valid, for then one would be satisfied that the revolution for which, in one way or another, we have all so long been fighting had at last actually been won, and there would be nothing left to do but bury the ammunition, clear away the barricades, and settle down to work for the new coalition—as, in fact, many of our former colleagues of the underground have already been persuaded to do. But one is unfortunately still compelled to make distinctions, especially now in the face of a phenomenon which because of its enormous potentiality for good and the vastness of its implications for the future of our literature must always tend to appear to us in the shape of our wildest chimeras and to bedazzle us at every turn with the mirage of oasis. While it can hardly be denied that the rise to power of the reprint industry has profoundly altered the traditional relations between the writer and the mass audience as well as between the mass audience and the work of merit, it has yet to be proved that the lot of the writer has thereby, in a host of important respects, been appreciably bettered. There is much evidence for supposing, rather, that a number of partial and quasi satisfactions, backed by almost unbelievable financial returns, have been substituted for the real satisfactions which the writer has always needed to get from the circulation of his work but which appear to be farther from him now than ever before.

The abstract idea of mass audience has, for example, been allowed subtly to crowd out, by seeming to satisfy, the writer's constant need for a public. He has been handed sheaves of statistics indicating that the reprint sales of his books in the drugstores and on the newsstands have gone into the hundreds of thousands or millions, and he has complacently concluded that such figures represent the true magnitude of his readership and popularity. But what he does not know and cannot know, so long as the reprint system continues to operate on its present basis, is who his readers are and why they buy his books—whether they buy them because they are his or only because they just happened, while foraging among the racks, to come into titillating collision with their covers. By the same token, he does not know whether, if he publishes a reprint edition of another of his books, it will be bought by the same people who bought his last or will have to make its way with an entirely new set of readers.

And even if he is lucky enough to acquire readers specifically his own, the chances are that he will still come out the loser, for under the present distribution system, in which the wholesaler supplies his retail outlets in lot form rather than on the basis of individual orders for particular books, there is no way for readers to make their wants known or even to be certain that the works of their favorite author will ever again be available at a given outlet. The writer is thus placed in the most paradoxical of situations. Through the reprint market he gains access to an immense potential audience but never to an effective, articulate public. If his sales are at all typical, he achieves through that market the financial status of the established, successful writer but not the reputation, or the means of reputation, by which such status must be accompanied if it is ever to be real. He consequently finds himself with all his relations with his medium impoverished to the point where the only sense he has of his literary existence is that abstractly provided him by his sales reports and royalty checks.

The fallacy underlying the belief in the importance to the writer of an audience of sheer size is nowhere more clearly demonstrated than in the new mass-circulation reviews which have taken over the fallacy and inflated it into a first principle of editorial doctrine. Both *New World Writing* and *Discovery* —the two contenders in the field at the moment—have been represented by their sponsors as guaranteeing the writer all the freedoms that were available to him in the "little" magazines of the past along with the advantage of incomparably wider readership, hence, incomparably wider opportunities for acquiring reputation. Within the terms of the quantitative fallacy these claims are of course entirely valid; but once again one is compelled to make distinctions. The "little" magazines of the twenties and thirties came into being in response to the rise of a literary movement which was too revolutionary to win support in the existing commercial periodicals. Their audiences were always small, but they were vociferous and vocal, and they constituted the only kind of readership the serious writer ever really needs, a readership of peers and informed disciples through whom reputations can be initiated and preserved until such time as they are confirmed by the public at large.

New World Writing and *Discovery,* by rescuing the writer from what is conceived to be the obscurity of the small coterie public, have abandoned him to the infinitely more inpenetrable and permanent obscurity of the mass audience, where his influence is spread thin among thousands of inattentive minds and where his name is lost in the limbo of plenty. They have also placed him in circumstances which appear to have no purpose or objective, for it is characteristic of these reviews—as it is of so many of the products of our present drive to inflate still further by synthetic means the already bloated ego of literature—that they have no real cause to serve and no discernible demand to satisfy. They have grown up in response to no movement, and there is scarcely more than an academic sense in which it can be argued that they provide an outlet for work which would not have been acceptable—unless perhaps on grounds of quality—for publication elsewhere. They seem simply to have evolved out of a feeling that something approximating the "little" magazine probably ought to exist in our time and, by existing, might very well stimulate a movement or a fresh creative impulse to which it could then, albeit somewhat contrivedly, become a response. Such strained and self-conscious efforts to foment controversy as those recently made in *Discovery* by its editor, Vance Bourjaily, would lead one to believe this to be the case. But unfortunately, in choosing to make their way with the mass audience rather than with the coterie, these reviews have moved beyond the protection and support which the coterie alone can afford them and are brought up against a situation in which controversy can have no meaning or pertinence and in which new literature is simply used and discarded, without apparent motive or effect.*

---

* As the Age of the Paper Back continues, one fact becomes clear: the increase in volume of literary production has been accompanied by a decline in the possibility for development of any single literary reputation. This is especially true in the case of poetic reputations. In issue after issue of *New World Writing*, for example, the work of frequently talented new poets is introduced; yet one can already foresee a common doom for the talented and untalented alike. They are fated either to disappear or, perhaps worse, to go on endlessly and ineffectually appearing in *New World Writing*, gaining neither fame nor fortune. And this will be so because no one, certainly no constituted agency or body of readers, will ever single out for praise, quotation, or recollection this or that poem or line of theirs, and thus initiate around their names and work that slow accretion of interest which becomes reputation. It is a fact of no small concern that the names which dominate poetry at the present time—Eliot, Auden, Aiken, Williams, Thomas, Stevens —were all made famous by cultural circumstances of, at the very least, a decade ago, and that in our own decade we have no new comparably dominating name. We are being supported in poetry, in other words, as to a very large extent we are being supported in the novel, by men who were already masters when many of us were still in the grades. But we are by now familiar with the circumstances which made this odd situation possible—the shift of cultural interests which caused the modern literary movement first to be historicized, then institutionalized, then, most recently, democratized by those educational and critical agencies which sought to establish and indemnify a modern "movement" and which, in the case of poetry, derived much of their zeal from their worthy determination to educate the public out of its prejudice against the "difficulty" of modern poetic techniques. But whatever the causes, the shift occurred and the reputations were made. Today one cannot help but feel that the stock of the new poem or poet stands from the beginning at zero and is destined, barring a miracle, to remain at zero. It is not enough to suggest that the poet is perhaps not so good as Auden or Eliot. It is more to the point to admit that no one seems really to care enough to find out what he is. His work is presented with that of his fellows in such a magazine as *New World Writing,* and it at once becomes part of a "package," something to be read and discarded, but never used. The reader presumably tosses it aside with the feeling that he has "had" poetry for today, and that tomorrow or next week or next issue there will be other poetry and poets for him to "have." This is the final and most ghastly twist that can be given

It would be inaccurate to say that these conditions present themselves to the writer in the shape of a dilemma. That, in fact, precisely *is* his dilemma: that he does not and cannot know that he is in one. All the evils of his situation come to him wearing Yeats's mask of innocent virtue, and he has been so long accustomed to taking his satisfaction where he could find it—in the appearance of acclaim, the illusion of audience, the hypocrisy of status—that his need for the satisfaction to be gained from the real thing has atrophied and disappeared. In an earlier time one might have conceived this to be finally a question of integrity. But integrity implies the existence of a standard to be maintained, and its loss the existence of a temptation to which it can be sold. The irony and terror of the writer's dilemma today are that the question of his integrity can no longer be raised. In the name of what can he hold out? To which temptation does he have anything left to sell?

---

to Randall Jarrell's famous nightmare of the man who answered "Huh?" when asked if he ever read poetry. Today the man would answer "Yes."

TWO

The writer in the university

Now THAT THE larger initiating impulses behind the modern cultural movement have died out, we are beginning to find ourselves confronted, as sooner or later we had to be, with various illusions and manufactures—what Tocqueville would have called "hypocrisies"—of cultural and literary situations. We are also beginning to find ourselves confronted, as sooner or later we deserved to be, with manufactures of cultural and literary men to inhabit and maintain these manufactures, men, this is to say, primarily dedicated not to the disinterested creation of cultural works—poems, paintings, novels, symphonies, plays—but to the exploitative use of the cultural institutions which have been raised around the act of creating these works. This, I take it, is what happens in a time when the creative impulse flags, becomes institutionalized, then dies out from under the institution, taking with it the satisfactions

35

that formerly accrued from its use. The institution survives. But it survives solely as the public mode, the manufactured apparatus, of the creative impulse which launched it into being, and the satisfactions it provides become solely those which any and all institutions, cultural or otherwise, are able to provide— a little status, a little security, a little power—the hypocrisies of the original creative satisfactions.

The present cultural situation in America is everywhere alive with examples of this, of institutions which have lost their creative *raison* and have therefore substituted one or more of its various hypocrisies, bringing about that divorcement of action from impulse, existence from identity, emotion from response which is the feature of the castrating dualism of our time. The indisputable reality, to take one case, of that small but genuinely enlightened public on whose active response the artist could at one time count, and against whom he could define himself as real, has now been replaced—since it has ceased to be a reality—by a manufacture, a statistical construct, of a mass-consuming public whose existence is measured in numerals, the hypocrisy of audience, and whose capacity for response is computed in sales receipts, the hypocrisy of response. All the machinery of cultural production originally set up to satisfy the real demands of the initial small public has been gradually converted into an institutionalized apparatus designed to meet the largely hypothetical demands of the mass public. In the process, the popular arts have come more and more to resemble the canned and packaged goods obtainable at supermarkets: painters have taken to painting institutional abstractions of modernism, since modernism is no longer a movement or a creative mode but merely a fashion in window-dressing décor; writers have taken to turning out manufactures of novels, pretentious aphasia-inducing works with nothing in them but print, which the publishers nonetheless piously publish, the reviewers favorably review, and the public regularly buys—or just as regularly fails to buy—because the institutions of painting, writing, publishing, reviewing, buying, and nonbuying must all be kept going at whatever cost to reality, long after they have ceased to have any creative cause to serve.

All this is undoubtedly no more than the normal dirty politics of institutional survival. In the popular institutions it is perhaps of little importance, since there the amount of chicanery tends as a rule to vary inversely with the cultural value of the institution. But when one finds it becoming the habitual politics of mind for those who, as members of the intellectual classes, have the highest stake in the preservation of the serious values of the culture, it becomes a different matter altogether. I assume the institutionalization of the intellectual in America today to be an accomplished fact, his adoption of the hypocrisies of mass culture—conformism, assent to institutional values, distrust of creative values—to be the most unfortunate result of the process I have been describing. The attitudes of dissent and estrangement which the American intellectual formerly held toward the more exploitative aspects of his culture at least had the character of a deeply felt, genuinely emotive response. They were based not only upon a real dissatisfaction with real conditions in a real world but upon the promise held out by a socialist revolutionary ideal, the developing vitality of the modern cultural movement, and the continuing possibility of the free creative life. But with the corruption of this ideal, the decline of that vitality and freedom, the intellectual found himself in a position where it seemed he had no choice but to embrace all his former enemies, to accept for the real values in which he could no longer believe the manufactures of value which the culture could provide. And like most converts he became more assiduous in his faith than those to whom the faith was native. Because he could no longer love communism and the elite culture of Europe, he began to love democracy and the mass culture of America; and since anything less than total commitment was unthinkable to him, he felt obliged to love everything about America: equal rights, mass production, mass education, free enterprise, television, supermarkets, used cars, baseball games, Dr. Kinsey, President Eisenhower. He became with passion what he had formerly despised with reason. But as his testimonials of new faith and his confessions of old sins began to make clear, he could not honestly affirm with his emotions all the things which he had decided to affirm with his head. His protestations of love were poverty-stricken for objects worthy of love. His passion, like Eliot's version of Hamlet's hatred for his mother, was in excess of the real facts as they appeared, stronger than the capacity of the facts to call it forth, and so it lay on his conscience like a crime to muddle motive and stifle action—inexplicable, embarrassing, and suspect.

The formerly liberal journal *Partisan Review* has lately become the chief organ of the new intellectual orthodoxy. One is constantly being confronted in its pages by the spectacle of serious literary men, estranged from their former sources of creative value, frantically scurrying for cover beneath the skirts of the new American mother-symbol of mass egalitarian culture. Some of them, like Mr. Delmore Schwartz, have been driven by their urge toward womb immersion to the point where they have taken to issuing periodic self-immolating apologies in which they assert a pro-Americanism so extreme and calculated that it would make a native grass-roots fascist blush, and in which they claim ownership of more used cars, ranch-style houses, and television sets than the average citizen would find quite decent. Others have elevated the underlying metaphysics of this into a critical credo of even more sinister implications. One critic, for example, Mr. Leslie Fiedler, has devoted a large part of his recent book *An End to Innocence* to a detailed and at times extremely perceptive analysis of the major themes of American fiction, of which the dominant characteristic, running roughly from Cooper to James Jones, seems to him immaturity. In fact, it is I believe fair to say of Fiedler that he sees American fiction as one long documentary celebration of disguised adolescent homosexuality. Cooper's Chingachnook and Deerslayer, Melville's Ishmael and Quee-queg, Twain's Huck and Jim, the poems of Whitman, the novels of Fitzgerald, the suspiciously comradely soldiers of Hemingway and Jones, the ambivalent little boy-girls and girl-boys of Capote and McCullers—all are to him cases in point. By the same token, both the American conception and the American practice of the literary life are cloyed, he feels, with immature romantic fantasies: the myth of the writer as a madman, dope fiend, drunkard, and bum; the naïve success dreams of a Fitzgerald; the burly-boy antics of a Hemingway; the sentimental cult of experience which drove so many good writers into European exile, there to squander their time and talents, or which paralyzed them in infantile attitudes of defiance and rebellion, the old postures for killing the father.

Over against this view of the American writer Fiedler sets
the curative principle of maturity. He calls for a literary coming of age, a rise to full creative responsibility, which has precisely as healthy and right-minded a sound today as it had
when Van Wyck Brooks first uttered it more than thirty years
ago. But behind and beneath Fiedler's notion of maturity one
soon senses a complex of assumptions, unconscious and otherwise, which are not so healthy and which seem right only if you
adhere to a view of the right that negates both literature and
maturity. Maturity, it becomes clear, is predicated for Fiedler
upon the substantial figure of the urban orthodox man, the
figure which throughout his book affords him his post of observation and judgment upon the American literary scene. The
urban orthodox man is one who accepts calmly and detachedly
his full share of social and moral responsibility: he is a good
American, respectably married, a father, preferably of a large
and happy family, a jobholder, a churchgoer, an active worker
in community affairs, an owner of property; he may at the
same time be an intellectual, for his society is nothing if not
tolerant of small marginal differentiations, but he is not imaginative; he is certainly not so immature as to suppose himself
a writer, although he may be a professor, a teacher of writing,
or a part-time literary critic, one of the approved institutional
forms of the writer. In short, against the childishly extravagant,
socially disruptive values of the creative life Fiedler sets the
orthodox values of the socially conformist life, values which
appear to differ scarcely at all from those which the bourgeois
mind has traditionally opposed to the creative. But this is not
all; it is not nearly enough, for it throws too clean and in-

nocuous a light upon the simple ambiguity of Fiedler's position. His orthodox man is no ordinary Babbitt. He is more precisely literature's twilight man, the artist *manqué* turned literary intellectual. He is what remains after a creative movement has spent itself, the lone Alexandrian fishing beside the dull canal, and he has that deathly wisdom that comes with missed opportunity and *fin de siècle*. He sees in his wisdom that creativity is, after all, a dead end, that literature is at best an aberration, that mostly only homosexuals and romantics who are not mature enough to acknowledge that they are homosexuals practice it, and that really the only recourse for the normal man, the mature man, is assent to the orthodoxies of mass society. In an odd way he is himself a romantic, precisely as much of a romantic as those whom he condemns, but he is disillusioned. Deep down in his heart he hates himself for not being a writer, and he hates literature for having somehow got on without him. So he rationalizes the position he cannot help but take: he destroys literature by finding it homosexual and thus unworthy of his devotion; he exhorts writers to put aside their childish nonsense, to grow up, stop trying to kill the father, settle down and marry with the mother, so that there will be no more writers around to give him guilt feelings. By means of these subterfuges he purges himself of his literary obligations and is freed to affirm the various hypocrisies of creative satisfactions that are left to him to affirm—the institutions of the home, family, religion, community, the American way, and the *status quo*.

This affirmation is clearly Fiedler's end in view, and it seems to me to represent the chief danger of his position as a whole. Coming to us in the disguise of the disinterested ana-

lytical critic, the protector of serious literary values, he is yet
an underground campaigner for the new intellectual orthodoxy, for a literature of such sobriety and maturity that to
compose it no writer will ever have to leave the warm protection of the bourgeois womb. Near the end of his book he observes with a nearly audible sigh of middle-class contentment
that "our writers no longer go to Africa or the left bank to
escape from the dullness of America to a world of pure Experience; they are tourists or art historians or government
officials or holders of grants and fellowships, but they are
not Exiles." It seems to me obvious that the dullness of
America is as much if not more of a reality today than it
was thirty years ago when the famous exile movement took
place, and that if the present generation of American writers
are refusing to escape from that dullness, it may be because
they have themselves succumbed to it. Certainly one may wonder whether much of the pretentious mediocrity of recent
American writing may not be attributed to the fact that it
was produced by tourists, art historians, government officials,
and fellowship holders rather than by men of genuine talent
pursuing "pure Experience" in the immaturity of exile.

But Fiedler's passionate compact with orthodoxy has all the
earmarks of a metaphysical *mariage de convenance;* his heart
clearly remains with the values he scorns, and his scorn is
clearly a defense raised by his pride against the fact of his failure to make those values his own. This is one of the tragedies
of the literary generation to which Fiedler belongs: they all
in a sense suffer from the trauma inflicted upon them by the
decline of Bohemia, the disappearance in their time of the
possibility of the free creative life. Their orthodoxy, like that

of their political contemporaries, is the other side of their
thwarted urge toward heresy, the surrogate form of their disillusioned romanticism, their way of liking what they can get
after failing to get what they would have liked. I am thinking
of the writers who grew up too late to have an active part in
the literary movement of the twenties and thirties but who
nevertheless partook of its atmosphere and formed their first
attitudes on the views of art and the artist that were fashionable
at the time. As a second and entirely spectatorial generation,
they were deeply affected by the ideas of exile, iconoclasm,
and creative independence on which the movement had been
based, and they naturally took as their idols the men who
seemed to exemplify these ideas in their purest form, men like
Joyce, Lawrence, Pound, Eliot, and Hemingway, who together
comprised a sort of cultural-heroic abstraction of the socially
alienated but artistically dedicated writer. It was largely on the
basis of this abstraction that the younger group formed their
view of the writer and the literary life, and it was inevitable
that they should sooner or later begin to form a view of their
own future purposes as writers on the ideal which it held out.
But the world they came into after 1945 was not one in which
this ideal any longer had a place or function as a working creative premise. The small coteries with their independent
"little" reviews and special audiences, which had encouraged
and sustained the older writers in their attitudes of alienation,
had by then died out or been corrupted into self-parody; the
centers of literary power and prestige had shifted both from the
coterie and from the former open market of genteel publishing
to the universities, their journals and audiences; and the aging
masters of the exile movement had themselves become institu-

tionalized, their private lives turned into topics for research, their best works into standard sophomore texts. The deification of the movement furthermore had led everywhere to a deification of the act of writing, and in the process it had become an act divorced from all impulse, a thing which everybody, regardless of talent or need, had to learn to perform. Writers who had been good writers flocked to the universities to teach writing to students who were taking degrees in the art of being writers—the whole mechanism working at an increasing remove from that primary commitment to experience which first teaches the writer. The few writers, on the other hand, who remained free of the universities and who ought to have served as examples of the efficacy of the literary life, were paradoxically scorned when they were not simply ignored by those who taught, for in spite of all the apparent creative activity, it was generally thought doubtful that anything more of value remained to be done in literature. Besides, the independent writer in a very real sense constituted a threat to the security of the others. He persisted in doing what they lacked the courage and incentive to do; he was a living reminder of the fact that they had once wanted and had perhaps been able to do it. But above all he represented the last obstacle in the path to the final fulfillment of the institutionalizing process, which was the concentration of all literary power within the universities and the creation of a class of men as its legislators who had never written, had never intended to write, but who had been taught by writers exclusively to teach others to write. These men would devote their time to using and dispensing power and to exploiting the advantages accruing to them by virtue of the fact that they were ostensibly literary men, while at the same time they would not be required to take the risks they would have to take if they were really literary men. Against the possibility of such a manufacture, the independent writer stood as a recalcitrant symbol of genuine literary values and of the real world of letters where reputations were made on the basis of risks taken and work accomplished. In the universities, therefore, he was dismissed as a crank and a maverick.

Coming into such a situation the younger intellectuals of Leslie Fiedler's generation who had at one time entertained hopes of following the course of the masters had very little choice but to conform. For the most part, they too lacked the courage and incentive to become independent, but they had had, in any case, such limited experience of life outside the universities and been so steeped in the history of the movement's decline rather than in the metaphysics of its revival that they were not disposed to develop in a creative way. Besides, as their learning increased, the traditional forms and poses of creative action began to seem to them quaint and outmoded: exile was now clearly a dead end; starvation for one's art was no longer in order; rebellion seemed childish and unnecessary; there was no sense in the age of the opening of new literary frontiers; and the social and economic situation was such that everyone wanted marriage, a family, and the amenities, along with the money and security to maintain them. The result was, therefore, that the majority of the group succumbed to the closest existing version of the way of life which they had originally aspired to, and that was the manufactured literary life of the universities. They became teachers of writing and modern literature, and as time went on and their talents atro-

phied, they too came to hate the independent writer, and finally
the whole independent creative tradition which they had formerly worshiped, for they were secretly ashamed of the romantic
adolescents they had once been, and even more ashamed of the
way they had sold out their adolescent hopes. Their only salvation lay now in protecting the institution, in assenting to the
hypocrisies of value with which they had allowed the institution to replace those hopes, and so they began to occupy themselves with problems of academic status, advancement, and
tenure; they became critics and scholars, models of Fiedler's
orthodox man of maturity.

The careful self-protectiveness behind this pious assent to
orthodoxy is nowhere more starkly revealed than in the several
articles which have lately appeared on the subject of the movement of the writer to the universities. With the single exception, I believe, of Mr. V. S. Pritchett's short essay not long
ago in *The New York Times Book Review*—an essay which,
incidentally, was largely critical of the movement—these commentaries have all been written by writers who have themselves
gone to the universities, and so one may suspect them of bias.
But what is remarkable about them is how baldly, with what
a cynical attentiveness to the front row of the baccalaureate
gallery, they reveal their bias. They do not argue merely that
the university is a good place for the writer to be. They take it
for granted that the *only* really important writers are those in
the university teaching writing. Over and over again, for example, one sees them elevating Wallace Stegner, Theodore
Morrison, Allan Seager, and Mark Schorer—some of whom,
to be sure, are competent enough writers—above such men as
William Styron, Norman Mailer, Truman Capote, and con-

ceivably even Hemingway and Faulkner, not on the basis of any honest comparison of their respective merits, but simply because the latter happen not to hold memberships in the teaching fraternity. It is of course not hard to understand how this ranking system grew up nor how the general reading public might be led to accept it as the official guide to the assessment of reputations. Until around ten years ago the universities and the academic journals were given over almost entirely to scholars and scholarship, while criticism was in the hands of independent men of letters—men like Edmund Wilson, Van Wyck Brooks, Malcolm Cowley, and the younger Allen Tate and R. P. Blackmur—who were interested mainly in the independent writer. But since that time the most influential centers of critical opinion have been located in the universities and the journals where critics tend to know and to breed only their own kind, and where what little creative work is published is likely to be almost exclusively that of university writers, who, as a rule, lack means of publication elsewhere. The critics and writers who are dependent upon the journals for publication and knowledge of literary affairs are therefore bound to assume that the best writers are those whose interests are most like their own and whose work appears regularly in the journals. Then, by somewhat the same process that has promoted Faulkner and T. S. Eliot to the front covers of *Time,* a kind of low-brow flirtation with the high-brow institutional, it has become the university writers who write the literary surveys and analyses-of-the-year which appear in the popular review media—*The Saturday Review, The New York Times,* and the *New York Herald Tribune*—and which naturally have to do with other university writers, so that the public comes to believe that the universities alone are subsidizing American literature.

Mr. Charles Fenton, a Yale instructor and Hemingway scholar, is one of the newest propagandists for this view. In an article appearing in *New World Writing No. 7* he notes triumphantly that

. . . this phenomenon of the writer as professor is now a fixed and recurrent one. It is, indeed, no longer a phenomenon; it is fact. A first generation of writer-teachers, men like Theodore Morrison, Wallace Stegner, Robert Penn Warren, Horace Gregory, and Allan Seager, have now attained academic stability. . . . A second generation, far more numerous and, on the whole, less widely known as writers, though no less distinguished, has solidified and extended the invasion. Paul Engle, John Ciardi, Mark Schorer, Richard Wilbur, Peter Viereck, Randall Jarrell, Saul Bellow—all these and many more have consolidated the writers' beachhead in the universities. Now a third generation of young men who want to write are preparing themselves in the graduate schools for the academic assault. . . . Today there is scarcely an English Department in the United States which does not contain a practicing poet or novelist— or short story writer or playwright—who teaches a seminar or two in creative writing, perhaps a course in contemporary American literature, and, maybe, if his position is insecure and his chairman unfriendly, a section of Freshman English.

Fenton's charging military metaphors eloquently proclaim the message which his observations by themselves cannot confirm: that the salvation of American letters by the universities has now been accomplished. The best and most distinguished, albeit "less widely known" writers in the country have come down with a fine, healthy case of pernicious academia. *Requiescat in pace,* all you worriers and dissenters. The situation is well in hand.

Without at all intending to cast doubt upon the truth of the phenomenon Fenton describes or to disparage the talents of the writers he cites as examples of it—although a good case for disparagement might in certain instances be made—I should like to set more definite limits to his argument. Let us consider the university affiliations of some of the writers who automatically come to mind whenever one thinks seriously of contemporary literature. Among the poets who have been more or less regular teachers there are John Ciardi, Paul Engle, Richard Wilbur, Peter Viereck, Randall Jarrell, Karl Shapiro, Robert Lowell, Howard Nemerov, Horace Gregory, John Crowe Ransom, Allen Tate, John Berryman, W. H. Auden, Stephen Spender, and Archibald MacLeish, but of these Tate, Auden, Spender, and MacLeish did not settle permanently upon teaching until fairly late in their careers. Among the poets who are not teachers there are T. S. Eliot, the late Wallace Stevens, William Carlos Williams, Conrad Aiken, E. E. Cummings, and Robinson Jeffers, of whom the most distinguished are in markedly nonacademic professions: Eliot in publishing, Stevens in insurance, and Williams in medicine. The situation of the novelists is strikingly different. Saul Bellow, Robert Penn Warren, Mark Schorer, Wallace Stegner, Theodore Morrison, Randall Jarrell, and Robie Macauley may all be considered university novelists; but the ratio of partial or intermittent employment is somewhat higher among them than it is among the poets. Of the novelists who have never been teachers there are—to mention only the best-known names in a nearly infinite list—Hemingway, Faulkner, Dos Passos, Steinbeck, James Gould Cozzens, James T. Farrell, Carson McCullers, Paul Bowles, William Styron, Truman

Capote, Wright Morris, Gore Vidal, Norman Mailer, Calder
Willingham, Irwin Shaw, and James Jones.

These statistics perhaps prove only what one might have
suspected: that the majority of the most important older poets
and novelists have been able to live without teaching, and when
they have needed to work, the older poets at least have chosen
other fields; that the more commercially successful of our
younger novelists have done likewise; and that it has been
mainly the younger group of poets who have had to teach.
But certainly this gives us a far different view of the matter
from the one circulated by Fenton, and it serves to disprove
the primary implication of his remarks that the best of our
writers are teachers. It also disproves the argument with which
he attempts to make that contention inarguable: that the
economic situation of the serious writer is such that he has no
choice but to teach. It is of course true that since the decline of
patronage there have been almost no poets who have been able
to support themselves by their work. Very few of them in our
day have been as fortunate even as the distinguished poet
whom R. P. Blackmur describes as having devoted his entire
time to writing and still never having made more than three
thousand in a year, with an average over thirty years of five
hundred. But it is evidently still possible, in spite of the shrinkage in advances and reprint sales, for the average good novelist
to remain self-supporting. If many novelists are choosing not
to do so and are preferring to teach instead, I suspect the reason
is not economics but a failure of nerve coupled with a disaffection with the ideal of the independent literary life.

I do not wish, however, to seem unaware of the several distinctions which can and should be made in any sensible ap-

proach to this problem. One ought to take into account, for
example, the difference between the situation of the novelist
who published a first book, say, in 1947 and that of one who
did not appear with a first book until 1952. The novel of 1947
would undoubtedly have received its due share of critical
notice; it most certainly had a chance of at least being read,
and the writer of making at least a start on a following and
a bank account. At that time everyone was interested in the
direction the new postwar literature would take; publishers
were touting new novelists; and reviewers were attentive to
their work. But the novel published in 1952 came into an
atmosphere of saturation and relative indifference; publishers
were reducing their promotional outlays for first work; and
reviewers had grown perfunctory in their treatment of fiction
generally. The novelist, consequently, was likely to find himself published and quickly dropped, without having come
within hailing distance of either following or fortune, and
with no recourse other than teaching. When I speak here and
elsewhere of the younger group of independent novelists, I
refer to those who appeared right after the war in the advantageous time and who were fortunate enough to begin their
careers in the flush of some financial success which enabled
them to become at least temporarily independent of the necessity to take other work or to teach. But an interesting fact
about the younger university writers which Mr. Fenton himself acknowledges is that, for the most part, they are not writers
who have tried and failed to become independent and have
then gone into teaching as a compromise. Rather, they are
writers who have gone into teaching directly from college and
who have never experienced the struggles of the marketplace.

Mr. Fenton observes that it is this tendency which sets the younger university writers apart from the older. The latter nearly all came to the university after an early career of independent writing and took to teaching as a means of making a living while still retaining the orientation of literary men. The former have had a university orientation from the beginning and tend to look upon writing as the pedants of the old school looked upon formal scholarship, as primarily a means to academic status, fame, and power. Mr. Fenton assumes, nevertheless, that the threat of poverty is the main reason for the movement to teaching, and near the end of his essay he sets out to prove that the necessity for the writer to live by his work imposes a burden upon him which is ultimately smothering to his faculties and which a teaching job would remove. The example he uses is Dylan Thomas, who was badgered to the end of his life by debts and the distractions of petty jobs and who shortly before his death was reduced to begging for a loan of one hundred pounds from a wealthy former patroness. The spectacle is of course pitiable; it is a depressing coda to what we already know to be the tragic story of Dylan Thomas. But what Mr. Fenton seems to forget is that it was undoubtedly the threat of poverty which kept Thomas writing—just as it was the lust for wealth and position that kept Balzac writing—even though from time to time he may have had to set aside his serious work and turn temporary hack. The writer, on the other hand, who goes into teaching is likely to decline in productiveness as the economic pressure upon him is removed; and as he begins to enjoy the status advantages of his position, he is almost certain in the end to lose the need to prove himself as a writer. He now *is* a writer; that is how he came by his teaching job; and he will remain a writer in his own eyes and those of his society without any further writing effort on his part as long as the job lasts. This undoubtedly accounts for the low productivity of the university novelists whom Mr. Fenton mentions. It is one of their distinguishing features as a group that they are nearly all one-book men or men whose books are scattered sparsely over long stretches of time. Since they already inhabit what at least looks like a literary situation, they are relieved of the obligation to create a real one out of their own work. Under the patronage of the university they do not have to count on their writing to do everything for them. Their independent contemporaries, on the other hand, are forced to be fairly regular producers; they have no choice but to pay their tithe to posterity in work accomplished.

That Mr. Fenton's own academic commitments prevent him from recognizing this is made clear in his remarks on the type of writers to whom university life is *not* recommended. These, he says, are

. . . the writers for whom the academic world would be a catastrophe for reasons of temperament and attitude. The rich, angry vigor of Arthur Miller would be, well, unnecessarily overstimulated by departmental meetings and hierarchical jockeying. There are a few institutions which welcome the professional bohemian, but even the very loose academic structure of Bread Loaf was devastated by Truman Capote; the effect of a fully flowered exotic on an English Department—and it upon him—would be monumental. Nor would a university career seem appropriate for a productive, richly fertile and imaginative popular writer. Stephen Vincent Benét endured

the Yale Graduate School for six months and then fled to Paris.
Later he disciplined himself to attend symposiums and give lectures,
but he never became thoroughly at ease with the academic requirements. "God did not make me to be an influence," he wrote his
wife once from a two-week period of residence in a university writing program. "He meant me to sit on my rear and write."

Mr. Fenton is obviously trying to create the impression here
that it is only the freakish and emotionally unstable writer
who would not be acceptable in teaching, or, for that matter,
anywhere else in polite, respectable society. He makes use of
loaded terms like "temperament and attitude," "exotic," and
"popular" to fend off the real matter at hand, which is that the
writers he mentions would not and could not teach because
they are *real* writers. The crucial point is not "temperament
and attitude," for there are many other writers without marked
idiosyncrasies to whom teaching would be equally disastrous,
and for the same reason. Arthur Miller and Truman Capote
are, after all, serious, productive writers; Stephen Vincent
Benét was a serious, productive, albeit popular writer. As
such, their primary concern has been the perfection of their
talents and the discovery of the kind of experience, however
exotic, which will best provide them with material. They have
all been dedicated to sitting on their rears and writing, a feat
of spiritual athletics from which most of the university writers
have been in frantic flight.

Mr. Donald Hall, in an essay appearing in the same issue
of *New World Writing*, speaks of the university writer in a
tone of complacent self-protectiveness that is very similar to
Mr. Fenton's. After surveying the situation of the younger

generation of American poets, nearly all of whom are teachers, Mr. Hall observes that

. . . poets are ridiculed as teachers: the patronage system established by the universities supports many of the poets I have mentioned. Is there any reason why an opium den is intrinsically more poetic than a Senior Common Room? In this attack is only the romantic cliché of the poet as starving revolutionary—a cliché contradicted by the contemporary poet who lives in a suburb and lectures to undergraduates.

Once again one notices the strenuous effort to fend off the real matter at hand; the use of emotive words and extreme alternatives—"opium den" is opposed to "Senior Common Room" in an unreal, purposely weighted juxtaposition of values; "starving revolutionary" is made the arbitrary synonym for the serious writer; romantic clichés are used to contradict a romantic cliché attack. The real question which Mr. Hall strategically renders rhetorical and senseless is not whether "an opium den is intrinsically more poetic than a Senior Common Room," for the opium den is not, and to my knowledge has never been an alternative to the Senior Common Room. What poet since De Quincey has lived in an opium den? The alternative is the independent creative life, and that is always more poetic than any Common Room. It is so because it is a life dedicated wholly to the values of creative production, not to the manufactured and institutionalized equivalents of those values. One would suppose, furthermore, that there might still be some doubt as to just how thoroughly the lecturing, suburbanite poet of today contradicts the older romantic cliché. The new poet may have all the competence which Mr. Hall attributes to him (at least he ought to have, for he is, above all, a scholar of poetry), but the poets he admires, imitates, and lectures to undergraduates about are still those who, like Yeats, Eliot, Pound, Williams, Auden, and Stevens, lived the free creative life and who, in eschewing the suburbs and the lecture platforms, attained to a poetic vision of the age which he and his contemporaries have not yet been able to equal.

But Hall, Fenton, and Fiedler are all apologists for the new intellectual orthodoxy; they have to be because they are themselves fully committed to it. Mr. Hall's opium den would not be available to him even if he wanted to move in, and of course he does not want to. It is of much greater use to him vacant, for then he can say that nobody wants to rent it; everybody prefers the Senior Common Room. Everybody is right, of course. In the Common Room they risk having none of those clammily distasteful encounters with experience to which they would be subject in the opium den; they enjoy there all the benefits of creative calomel without any of the dangers; and as long as they remain there, they can take advantage of the various emoluments which the Common Room makes available to them in partial recompense, one supposes, for the damage it has done to their chances with posterity. There are, for example, in addition to the normal prizes of status, salary, and tenure, such extra inducements for the university writer as the literary fellowships sponsored by the *Kenyon* and *Sewanee Reviews,* which are both journals edited or controlled by other university writers. These fellowships were made possible through a grant of funds a few years ago from The Rockefeller Foundation and have since been awarded on a yearly basis at the rate of three at a time, one in poetry, one in fiction, and one in criticism. According to the published circulars, the fellowships are intended to stimulate fresh activity in these fields by providing a year's subsidy for young writers of exceptional promise and presumably of some real need. But what the circulars do not state are the qualifications beyond youth, talent, and need which the candidate is expected to possess. After reviewing the lists of successful candidates, however, one can easily deduce them. To receive a fellowship a writer must be either a university teacher of some experience or a fairly regular contributor to the *Kenyon* and *Sewanee Reviews,* preferably both. He must, in other words, be a member of the fraternity. Of the ten *Kenyon* fellows created since the inception of the program in 1953, six were university teachers, one was a recent graduate of Kenyon College, one was Director of Publicity at Kenyon College(!), one was a Junior Fellow at Harvard, one was an independent novelist, and all were contributors to the magazine. This kind of selection was made in spite of the fact that the *Kenyon* editors, in stating their own qualifications for selecting fellows, alluded pridefully to their "professionally wide acquaintance among American writers." It would appear either that they were mistaken or that they sincerely believe—as one suspects they do—that the really important American writers are in the colleges, graduate schools, and campus publicity offices. At any rate, among the nine *Sewanee* fellows created since 1953, the record was perfect: all were academics, and all were contributors. As to the quality of the fellows themselves one can only express an opinion. All we officially know about them is that they are supposed to be "distinguished

younger writers." They include Flannery O'Connor, George
Lanning, Howard Nemerov, Edwin Watkins, Irving Howe,
William S. Merwin, R. W. B. Lewis, Richard Ellman, Edgar
Bogardus, Douglas Nichols, Louis D. Rubin, Jr., Danforth
Ross, Edgar Bowers, James L. Dickey, Madison Jones, John
Hardy, Mac Hammond, Louis Coxe, and Walter Sullivan.
Of these Flannery O'Connor and Howard Nemerov in fiction,
Irving Howe, R. W. B. Lewis, and Richard Ellman in criticism,
and Louis Coxe and William S. Merwin in poetry have pro-
duced work ranging in quality from competence to excellence.
A little of it, but only a very little, might be called distin-
guished. Miss O'Connor and Mr. Nemerov are decidedly
minor younger novelists, even among younger novelists;
Messrs. Howe, Lewis, and Ellman, on the other hand, are as
promising as any critics of the generation now about forty;
Mr. Merwin, to my mind, is for his age a poet of real stature.
But nearly all of the others are virtually unknown outside the
quarterlies; some of them are barely known even within them;
and all are represented by only a few poems and scattered
short stories. It might be said, in short, that while they are
probably on the average all good enough people, they scarcely
constitute a fair sampling of the best younger talent in the
country, the kind of fair sampling which the quarterlies in
their present positions of power and influence ought to be
able to make and ought to take pains to make, particularly
when they are spending the funds of a national foundation.

But quality is obviously not a major factor in the selection
of fellows. What is far more crucial is the extent to which the
candidates, having met the official requirements, are able to
meet the various others imposed by the political interests of

the quarterlies themselves. These are all extremely complex
and hard to define, but it is possible at least to observe them
in action and to point to their influence in specific cases. Miss
Flannery O'Connor, for example, is, as I have said, a distinctly
minor novelist; yet she alone of all the fellows has enjoyed the
honor of receiving two *Kenyon* awards in fiction. The reason
presumably is that Miss O'Connor has lately become the official "younger Southern novelist" of the quarterlies. Her fiction
has to do, in the main, with simple Southern peasant folk set
against rustic Southern backgrounds, and for the academic
Northern intellectual what is Southern and rustic is synonymous with all that is original, serious, and true in American
letters. In a sense, Miss O'Connor does for the academic intellectuals what Truman Capote does for the pseudo intellectuals of the flossy New York fashion-magazine world—she
provides them with tone or chic, a little sprinkling of fake
old magnolia blossoms; she is the literary equivalent of the
Grand Rapids–Modern spider furniture which they display in
their living rooms along with the work of the most recently
modish, obscure nineteenth-century Provençal painter. Miss
O'Connor has therefore won a high place in the hall of quarterly fame. Another Southern novelist, equally young and infinitely more talented, Mr. William Styron, would not, on the
other hand, fare so well; in fact, it is doubtful if he would
fare at all, although it is not a matter of public record whether
he has ever been invited to apply for a quarterly fellowship.
Mr. Styron's *Lie Down in Darkness* is easily the most distinguished Southern novel of the present decade, his *The Long
March* one of the two or three distinguished novelettes of
the last thirty years. Yet Mr. Styron would be disqualified for

membership in the *Kenyon-Sewanee* hierarchy of "distinguished younger writers" on two serious counts: he has never published a word in either magazine, and he is crass enough to have enjoyed a certain small commercial success through his writings. By the same token, Mr. Saul Bellow, another outstanding younger novelist, would be excluded, for although he had at one time a very high standing in the quarterlies, both as a frequent contributor and as a subject of commentary, he has lately lost caste because of the popular success of *The Adventures of Augie March* and because he is suspected of devoting himself a bit too exclusively to "creative" work, a practice looked upon as somewhat beneath the serious intellectual mind. With the appearance of his fairly widely read novel *Pictures from an Institution* and his critical book *Poetry and the Age* Mr. Randall Jarrell, also a long-time quarterly favorite, appears to be about to suffer the same fate; one sees his articles now in *Mademoiselle* and *The New York Times Book Review*, and it is almost as if one had encountered him down and out on Skid Row.

In the areas of criticism and poetry the qualifications of institutional affiliation required of the fellowship candidate are even more rigid. The young critic ought, first of all, to be a scholar, preferably with a doctor's degree, and he ought, secondly, to be working within the new critical tradition, the tradition from which *The Sewanee Review,* somewhat late in its history, and *The Kenyon Review* from its beginnings received their guiding impetus. The present editors of both reviews—Allen Tate, Francis Fergusson, John Crowe Ransom, and Cleanth Brooks—all grew up in this tradition and won their early reputations by championing its cause in the face of the genteel romantic criticism of their day. But these men do not require of their younger contemporaries a similar rebelliousness; in fact, they do their best to discourage it. The present-day versions of themselves would be writing for present-day versions of the old *Kenyon* and *Sewanee Reviews*— if such existed—and these would, by definition, be severely critical of the present *Kenyon* and *Sewanee Reviews*. The new young Allen Tate, therefore, would hardly be awarded a fellowship. But luckily for them, the young candidates in criticism have shown no inclination to rebel. They have confined themselves to good, sound, scholarly works of research and exegesis, for they have known that only by conforming could they hope to move up through the successive stages of the critical life cycle into which the sanction of their elders could be expected to launch them—the cycle beginning with a *Kenyon* or *Sewanee* fellowship, running through a Christian Gauss lectureship at Princeton, a teaching appointment at one of the better Eastern universities, a place on the staff of the Indiana School of Letters, and ending in final triumph with an advisory editorship on the *Kenyon* or *Sewanee Review*. The candidates in poetry also anticipate a cyclical development, although it is better for them if they have completed as much of their cycle as possible before coming up for an award. Their cycle begins, as a rule, with graduation from one of the better Eastern universities and runs through a Rhodes scholarship or comparable work at Oxford, graduate study, a junior fellowship at Harvard, a *Kenyon* or *Sewanee* fellowship, a teaching appointment at one of the better Eastern universities, a Guggenheim fellowship, a Consultantship in Poetry at the Library of Congress, a place on the staff of the Indiana School of Letters, to an advisory editorship on the *Kenyon* or *Sewanee Review*. The only awards the skillful fellowship holder does not sooner or later find himself automatically in line for are the Pulitzer and the Nobel prizes, the one because it is given in part for popularity, the other because it is given almost wholly for achievement.

The Guggenheim fellowship program has traditionally been the sole source of patronage available to the independent younger writer. Yet contrary to the prevailing belief both in the public at large and among writers themselves, the Guggenheim Foundation has never done very much for the independent writer, young or old. From the time of its creation in 1925, its fellowship program has been principally devoted to the support of scholarly research projects in the sciences and humanities, although in a statement issued that year Simon Guggenheim said that the program was intended "to improve the quality of education *and* the practice of the arts and professions in the United States," and there has regularly been a clause in the official prospectus to the effect that the aim has been "to further the development of scholars *and artists* by assisting them to engage in research in any field of knowledge and artistic creation in any of the fine arts including music, under the freest possible conditions." It was apparently very much on Mr. Guggenheim's mind in the beginning that talented young men and women right out of college were being forced into teaching without first having the opportunity to engage, as he put it, in "creative work in their subjects," and it was his intention that the fellowships would be used primarily to provide them with such an opportunity. He also clearly intended the program to perform a similar service for younger creative artists, although the emphasis was initially placed on scholarship, and this emphasis has determined policy ever since. There is much evidence to indicate, however, that as the years have passed the program has gradually been transformed into something far different from what Mr. Guggenheim envisioned, and that it has all but abdicated its stated obligations to younger scholars and artists. Before the twenties had ended, the age limits of twenty-five to thirty-five originally set for candidates had been revised upwards to forty, and since then the revision has continued, until now the upper limit, while still officially only forty, is in practice apparently located somewhere in the hinterlands of senility. More and more scholars of all the mature ages have received fellowships with less and less regard for whether their projects have been creative, and the proportion of awards made to artists of whatever age has sharply declined. In 1932, 11 per cent of the total fellowships awarded went to creative writers alone; in 1933 writers made up 24 per cent of the total; in 1937, 11 per cent; in 1949, 6 per cent; in 1952, 5 per cent; in 1954, 3 per cent; and in 1955, 3 per cent. This decline has occurred in spite of the fact that the number of fellowships awarded has risen from forty or fifty in 1925 to 234 in 1955. Since the end of World War II, moreover, the Ford Foundation and the Fulbright program have opened vast new sources of subsidy for scholars, so that their need for Guggenheim support has been greatly diminished, while scholars in the scientific fields now have ready access to research funds provided by private industry and the Federal government. Once again, it is the independent writer, living from book to book without even the minimal security of an academic salary, who is forced to suffer.

One is tempted to conclude that the reason for this is that the members of the Guggenheim Selection Committee have succumbed to the prevailing belief that a writer is no good unless he is a professor, hence within the category of automatic subsidy. But it is much more likely that, since all the committee members are themselves professors, they just naturally prefer other professors, particularly older ones like themselves. When confronted with writers they obviously feel uneasy and rather out of depth. While fellowship winners in the other arts are chosen by a special advisory committee made up of professional workers in those arts, the writers are chosen by the regular committee, with the result that the selections tend as a rule to be somewhat ambiguous and erratic, ranging from one or two people of indisputable talent to several people of little or none. This is especially lamentable when dozens, perhaps hundreds, of good writers apply and are turned down annually. I know of one young writer, author of five serious novels and a distinguished play, who has applied and been turned down four times running. Another applied with the highest recommendations from some of the most respected men in his field and still was refused. What the Guggenheim Foundation desperately needs of course is an advisory committee composed of serious young writers, but to bring that about one would first have to scotch the cherished academic myth that a professor may be totally ignorant of the other arts but is always competent to judge the art of writing.

As for the scholarly projects which the Selection Committee deem worthy of subsidy in such numbers, it is difficult to speak of some of them without collapsing into burlesque. One cannot help wondering if such matters as "Trade in the ancient

Mediterranean as documented by stamped wine jars," "The legal rights of employees within Swedish labor unions," "The fungi of the Society Islands," "Studies in the history of the theory of the rainbow," "The auxiliaries of the Roman imperial army," "Studies of the anatomy of the Old World species of onions," and "French émigrés to Schleswig-Holstein" could really have been considered by the Committee to be creative enough and important enough to merit the awards which were made for them in 1954 and 1955. But T. S. Eliot perhaps gave the answer when he said:

> We assume . . . that we are masters and not servants of facts, and that we know that the discovery of Shakespeare's laundry bills would not be of much use to us; but we must always reserve final judgment as to the futility of the research which has discovered them, in the possibility that some genius will appear who will know of a use to which to put them.

It would seem that at least some of the Guggenheim scholars are engaged in the accumulation of laundry bills, and until the genius appears who will vindicate them in the enterprise, I see no reason for supposing it of greater intrinsic value to the world than the creative survival of a single gifted young writer.

In view of all this, it would appear that the American university today holds out to the writer an abundance of advantages, by which it would be less than human of him not to be strongly tempted. In addition to the opportunity for fellowship support and the normal academic rewards of security and status, it offers him membership in a closely knit, highly selective intellectual class, in which, if he obeys the rules, he will be able to spend the rest of his life in the company of friends and peers. This is not so simple as it sounds, for it does not mean merely that the writer in the university enjoys the close fraternity of a professional group with interests congenial to his own. It means that in the university he becomes part of a vast and complex social organism which very largely *is* the literary-intellectual life of America today. The academic world and the literary world are, for all practical purposes, synonymous in this country at the present time. The universities control literature, its agencies, and its functions in a manner and to a degree that have been unparalleled in Western culture since at least the eighteenth century. Not even the immensely powerful group movements of the more recent past—those at Bloomsbury, Oxford, Paris, Chicago, and New York—have been remotely as influential, for the power of the universities today is not a localized power; there is no activity however faintly literary that is not touched by it. The cultural life of New York, in both its central and its marginal activities relating to literature, is dominated by university professors: they edit and comprise the bulk of the contributors to the leading intellectual magazines; they make up the boards of directors of the philanthropic foundations; they serve as advisers to publishers, edit, and write introductions for books; they act as technical consultants and cultural performers in radio and television. The poems, stories, and novels that are most discussed are nearly always those which have first received endorsement in academic circles and which very often have been written by professors. Where at one time it was the independent writer, a Dreiser, an Anderson, a Thomas Wolfe, who occupied the seat of honor at intellectual gatherings, whose opinions carried the most weight with publishers and editors, it is now the man from Harvard or Columbia, the critic with the lead essay in the current *Partisan* or the lead poem. If literary reputations are made anywhere today, they are made among professors, and they are kept alive or allowed to perish by professors. It is probably no exaggeration to say that the best and most serious elements of the modern cultural movement, including all aspects of experiment and technical innovation as well as the properties of taste required to evaluate them, are now and have been for years under the sole custodianship of professors. There is simply nowhere else for them to be. The professor is the new cultural force, the leader, and god of the new aristocracy of the intellect.

Therein lies, it seems to me, the principal danger for the writer as professor. He inhabits a professional world crowded with daily reminders of his remarkable preeminence. His contacts with his students afford him a constantly renewing sense of creative fulfillment; his station in his class places at his disposal quantities of influence; his regular preoccupation is with literary values and judgments. In time he is likely to lose sight of the fact that the university is at best only a manufacture of a literary situation, an institutional construct raised over the dead forms of creative impulses, and to begin confusing the quasi satisfactions which he gets from the university with the real satisfactions which he can get only from rigorous application to his own work. But everything in his life operates to foment that confusion, for so long as teaching makes him feel that he is a writer and engaging in literary problems, so long as he enjoys as a teacher the authority and influence that would come to him as a writer, he will not be impelled to function as a writer. Besides, perhaps without being aware of it, he daily suffers a breakdown in the integrity of his writing consciousness. He makes use in the classroom of insights and emotions which he ought to be using in his writing, so that if and when he comes back to writing he tends to experience a crippling sense of having said it all before, of being about to commit self-plagiarism. He is also likely to find that only in a nominal way does he inhabit a literary community, that most of his colleagues are indifferent if not downright hostile to literary values, and that, as far as his physical environment is concerned, it seems to have no connection with him whatever. If he teaches at one of the larger Middle Western universities, he will probably come to feel that he is inhabiting a cultural outpost, a veritable arsenal of learning, in the middle of a wasteland hundreds of miles from the centers of art and literature, and that in spite of his professional prestige, as an ordinary man he is living among barbarians and peasants. He thus begins to suffer a second derangement, this time a derangement of his sense of the external world. He can neither accept that world nor wholly reject it; its values are not his, yet they are all he has coming in; so he anesthetizes himself against it as best he can, and cuts himself off from the emotional nourishment which he needs for himself and his writing. If, on the other hand, he assents to his predicament, denies that it is a predicament, and settles down to convince himself of its virtue, he risks moral suicide, for the lies told for the sake of expediency become, for the writer, the cancers of conscience. If he persists in holding out against it, he risks going sterile and losing the thing which gave him his reason for persisting. If

he escapes it altogether, he may yet be saved, but he opens
himself to the gravest risk of all, the risk of coming to grips
with his talent under the cold, pitiless gaze of posterity.*

* Since I am myself a writer who has gone to the university, I want to
make my position plain. I have been a university teacher for several years
and expect to continue as one. But I do not see that any purpose is served in
attempting to make a virtue of the necessity which impelled me to teaching
nor in remaining blind to the many dangers inhering in it for the writer. I am
specifically concerned in this essay, however, with the tendency now rapidly
accelerating in the intellectual world to endow the university with creative
powers and advantages which it does not and cannot possess, and I am particularly opposed to the development which has made the university the seat
of literary politics and power in our time and which has transformed so
many of our younger intellectuals into university apologists and literary
politicians.

THREE

The heresy of literary manners *

WHEN WE SPEAK of manners in the novel, I take it we have
in mind something more than the merely fashionable and something less than the merely fastidious. All those occasions on
which the term has been used with opprobrium or forced into
a loaded synonymity with Mme. de Staël's ceremonials at

* To be properly understood, this essay should be viewed in the context
of discussion and rather fierce debate which constitutes both its area of reference and the occasion for its polemical tone. The discussion, centering in
Partisan Review and the articles in recent years of certain of the editors, has
had to do with the question of literary values and manners, their meaning
and importance in the development, specifically, of American fiction. In its
course, certain statements relating to the question made by Mr. Lionel Trilling, myself, and others have been criticized and debated. It has seemed to
me that many of these statements have been misinterpreted and, in some
cases, grotesquely misapplied by the commentators, and that a further clari-
fying statement from me has been called for. This essay represents an attempt
at both a clarification and an extension of my views, made in the face of arguments relating literary manners to everything from drawing-room etiquette to
an undemocratic affirmation of class snobbery. I am hopeful that it will help
to indicate the extent to which such arguments have been uninformed.

court, Mrs. Vanderbilt's hypocrisies at tea, or Mr. Eliot's
"pleasing archaeological reconstructions," we must now assume to have been improper occasions, the work not of disinterested minds but of those in whom the very suggestion of
manners evokes nightmares of class distinction and minority
group, pogrom and ghetto, and whose willed misunderstanding of their meaning is politically requisite to a continued
rational engagement of contemporary life, the preservation of
what we tend to think of as the liberal-egalitarian or "whole"
view of reality.

I would suppose that the whole view, which opposes all
social and class distinctions, is precisely the one least calculated to yield up a satisfactory view either of reality or manners,
simply because in the hands of its recent proponents it has
shown itself to be no view at all, but a pathological refusal
to make those distinctions which must be made before any
view becomes possible. One can in fact say that the whole view
is, by its very nature, a symptom of the actual disappearance
of distinctions in all areas of our cultural and intellectual life.
A recognition of this disappearance as a fact to be lamented is
a necessary first step toward an understanding of the meaning
of manners in both literature and the social world; but it is a
step which the rigidity of his doctrine will not permit the whole-
viewer to take. For him, distinctions of whatever kind are
real only to the extent that he can come at them traumatically,
within the context of the great social revolution which, in the
last century, has been working for their overthrow; and it is in
the nature of his political commitment that he should suppose not merely that that revolution is still in progress but that
it is fast reaching a victorious end in the achievement of a class-

less and equalitarian America. This kind of America is the
chauvinist dream of the intellectual Left, in the service of
which—now that it is almost a reality—the Left has already
begun to abandon revolution in order to take up a protective
and Rightist position over its fruits. What the fruits are to be
protected from is quite simply distinctions, distinctions of class,
economy, and privilege, all of which have disappeared, or effectively disappeared, as a result of the revolution but which the
whole-viewer is continually afraid will be reimposed. Thus
manners, which he interprets as the etiquette-distinctions of
privilege, seem to him a threat of the very first magnitude. They
are seen, in his terms, as inseparable from the idea of class; the
idea of class is seen as inseparable from the idea of a suppressed
minority; the idea of a suppressed minority is seen as inseparable from the idea of the totalitarian state; and the idea of the
totalitarian state is seen as inseparable from the idea of totalitarian atrocity. One consequently finds oneself brought around
the traumatic circle of the whole view to the ghetto and pogrom once again and to the *Caine Mutiny* spectacle of some-
body's old-world mother being melted down into soap to be
used for washing the backs of dictators.

It would seem then that in searching out a sensible approach
to the question of manners in the novel one would do better to
cultivate the company of those whose maternal forebears suffered merely the boredom of an unredeemed Middle Western
gentility or, at worst, some momentary humiliation at the
hands of General Sherman's Light Horse. The traumas inflicted by totalitarian atrocity and by General Sherman may
not, in the first instance, be very different; but the variance
in the degree of their application to politics, and in the forms

which in politics they tend to assume, is infinitely wide. The one ends in a politics of craven receptivity to each slightest stirring of the democratic impulse, wherever and under whatever conditions it may be felt. That is the price atrocity always exacts from its victims before it kills them—abject gratitude for the right simply to remain alive up to the secret hour ordained for death. The other—perhaps because it is historically more remote—asserts itself in a stauncher politics, one that can afford to bargain because it knows that some brands of democracy are better than others and that for some it is possible to pay a higher price than life. The one issues from a psychotic necessity always to count our gains because our losses are too grisly to contemplate. The other issues from an equally psychotic necessity always to count our losses because our gains are too grisly to contemplate. The one measures our gains in the degree of our distance from the pogrom and ghetto. The other measures our losses in the degree of our distance from the truly human. The one is a politics of the whole view because it is backed by a knowledge of the atrocity that can be perpetrated in the name of distinctions. The other is a politics of the parochial view because it is backed by a knowledge of what can be lost when distinctions disappear.

Mr. Eliot, Mr. Tate, Mr. Robert Penn Warren, and the other leading proponents of the parochial view all know what we mean by manners because this latter knowledge constitutes the formative fact of their experience and the controlling bias of their intelligence. It does not matter that Mr. Eliot arrived at it by traversing the swamp of pre-Christian ritual and ascending the rock of the English church or that Mr. Tate and Mr. Warren came by it only because they could not

get the thundering hoofbeats of Sherman's Light Horse out of
their heads. It does not even matter that between the church,
Sherman, and the modern world there seems, for the rest of
us today, to be no immediate or necessary connection. The
single distorted image can sometimes speak to us in the full
language of its genre, and we do not need to know the whole
of reality (nor can we know it) if we know well the ground we
stand on. For Mr. Eliot, Mr. Tate, and Mr. Warren, the church
and Sherman are simply aberrations of vision. They are partial,
distorted, and blinding; consequently, they make vision possible. They are what happens to vision when it retreats behind
something in order to see; it sees less but less more clearly
and, because it is protected, it is not obliged to like everything
it sees. Mr. Eliot's Anglo-Catholicism and the early Agrarian-
ism of Mr. Tate and Mr. Warren may be considered the ideological abutments behind which their vision has retreated from
a reality it has not liked but with which the whole view, as it
has gathered force, has sought increasingly to make them
content, the reality of a world where the human condition has
been abdicated and where the forms of dramatic conduct—
what Susanne K. Langer meant, in part, by the term "charged
symbols"—have been lost. In one way or another, each of
these men has undertaken to say in precisely what this condition and these forms consist and in what circumstances
their loss is likely to result. Mr. Eliot throughout his career
has spoken frequently of tradition and, in esthetic terms, of
structure and convention—"any form or rhythm imposed upon
the world of action" that will "arrest, so to speak, the flow of
spirit at any particular point before it expands and ends its
course in the desert of exact likeness to the reality which is per-

ceived by the most commonplace mind." One has only to substitute "human conduct" for "world of action" to appreciate the ease with which esthetic convention calls to mind its moral and sociological counterpart. Mr. Tate in his essay "What Is a Traditional Society?" has said:

> In ages which suffer the decay of manners, religion, morals, codes, our indestructible vitality demands expression in violence and chaos; . . . men who have lost both the higher myth of religion and the lower myth of historical dramatization have lost the forms of human action . . . they are no longer capable of defining a human objective, of forming a dramatic conception of human nature; they capitulate from their human role to a series of pragmatic conquests which, taken alone, are true only in some other world than that inhabited by men.

And Mr. Warren has suggested that Faulkner's objection to the modern world is that it lacks the ability to set up "codes, concepts of virtue, obligations" by which man can "define himself as human," "realize himself in terms of his whole nature," and "accept the risks of his humanity." Whether one chooses Mr. Eliot's "desert of exact likeness" or Mr. Tate's "other world than that inhabited by men" or Mr. Warren's image of Faulkner's dehumanized world, each represents an assessment of the modern condition opposite to the one provided by the whole view, and each insists on the need for those restraining and defining forms, structures, rituals, patterns, and conventions of conduct which, in the imprisonment of its paranoia, the whole view is committed to denounce as totalitarian heresy.

Even Mr. Lionel Trilling, whose allegiance to the whole view is fortunately qualified by his deeper allegiance to the whole of the Western liberal-humanistic tradition, has recognized the necessity for the existence within a culture of forms and structures such as these and, in so doing, has repeatedly been attacked by those who, having always thought of him as one of themselves, could only conceive of his position as treasonous. In fact, it was Mr. Trilling who first, so far as I know, made explicit the connection between their presence in a culture and the presence in the novel of elements which we customarily take to be the ingredients of dramatic life. Summarizing his sense of these forms and structures in the metaphorical and rather heavily emotive terms "class" and "manners," he has said in his "Art and Fortune" essay:

> In this country the real basis of the novel has never existed—that is, the tension between a middle class and an aristocracy which brings manners into observable relief as the living representation of ideals and the living comment on ideas. . . . If American novels of the past, whatever their merits of intensity and beauty, have given us very few substantial or memorable people, this is because one of the things which makes for substantiality of character in the novel is precisely the notation of manners, that is to say, of class traits modified by personality. . . . American fiction has nothing to show like the huge, swarming, substantial population of the European novel, the substantiality of which is precisely a product of a class existence. In fiction, as perhaps in life, the conscious realization of social class, which is an idea of great power and complexity, easily and quickly produces intention, passion, thought, and what I am calling substantiality. The diminution in the reality of social class . . . seems to have the practical effect of diminishing our ability to see people in their difference and specialness.

Class, as Mr. Trilling conceives it here, is of course only one of the forms which a culture's drives and preoccupations may take, and for a full understanding of the meaning of manners, which he defines in an earlier essay as "a culture's hum and buzz of implication," it is undoubtedly necessary to take into account the more concrete, though less specifically sociological, insights of Mr. Eliot, Mr. Tate, and Mr. Warren. But what is important is that, through the seriousness of their combined approaches, these men have succeeded in elevating the question of manners to a level far above the merely chauvinist vigilantism of the whole view, to a level where it may be recognized for what it really is—an esthetic question of the widest possible pertinence to the dramatics of the novel, both historically and at the present time.

The most recent discussion of manners in the novel—Mr. Delmore Schwartz's in an essay called "The Duchess' Red Shoes" published in *Partisan Review* for January-February, 1953—was vitiated by its willful failure to take account of the question at any recognizable level of seriousness. At least one supposes the failure to have been willful, to have been compelled, this is to say, by Mr. Schwartz's prior commitment to the whole view, which blinded him to all except the most pejorative senses in which the idea of manners may be applied to culture. This, at any rate, is the charitable view of his performance.

But beyond charity there is another reason for granting him the honesty of his impulses. Mr. Schwartz is an editor of *Partisan Review,* a critic of promise, and a poet of some stature. He has a certain reputation in the intellectual world and a certain authority. In the past his opinions have been received by his peers for the most part with that tacit polite-

ness which, if it does not necessarily imply that they have always been respected, at least implies that they have been
found to possess the minimum merit requisite to be taken
seriously. Since no storm of indignation or rebuttal followed
on his discussion of manners, one must assume that in this
instance he was again taken seriously, that his observations
were generally accepted as fulfilling the requirements of intelligence and good taste laid down for observations of their
kind and that, furthermore, they were accorded hospitality
by at least the less discriminating of his peers. One may therefore fairly appoint Mr. Schwartz the spokesman for a body
of existing, though unarticulated opinion and conceive of his
performance as fairly illustrating the level of thought on which
ideas of an abstract nature may be acceptably explored among
intellectuals today.

The very first sentence of Mr. Schwartz's essay betrays his
uneasiness before what he obviously feels to be the personal
as well as ideological threat implicit in the subject of manners.
"Good manners," he says, "are very pleasant and literary criticism is often very *inn*eresting, to be colloquial. When, however,
manners become a major concept in literary criticism, that is
something else again: it is an *inn*eruption, to be colloquial
again." Taken on the first level, this deliberate descent to bad
grammar represents one of the oldest and cheapest tricks
known to rhetoric—the attempt to disarm one's opponent by
employing low linguistic comedy to disparage the seriousness
of his subject or to make it appear pompous. When the subject is manners, which Mr. Schwartz has vested interests in
thinking of as "good" manners, it thus becomes a stroke of the

sharpest subtlety to open an attack by making burlesque use
of bad manners and bad grammar, in quite the same way that
small boys express their feelings of inferiority and boredom in
polite adult society by covertly sticking out their tongues,
wiggling their ears, and making obscene gestures. But the
obvious uneasiness one senses in the tone of Mr. Schwartz's
remarks forces one to find in them deeper and more serious
implications. His bad grammar is not merely a rhetorical
trick—for, after all, there is as yet no debate—but a way of
further reducing the subject through an appeal to the new intellectual anti-intellectualism, the high-brow equivalent of the
fear of ideas and distinctions which, in egghead and middle-
brow circles, has taken the form of contrived affability and a
tense avoidance of argumentative tension. Ezra Pound exploited this kind of anti-intellectualism to great effect in his
correspondence, and for many of the same reasons that Mr.
Schwartz exploits it here. Bad grammar for Pound was a
subconscious expression of his contempt for his chosen medium
and of his desire to place himself on terms of easy fraternity
with his friends. Bad grammar for Mr. Schwartz is a somewhat
less subconscious expression of *his* contempt for his chosen
medium—as Mr. Paul Ramsey specifically charged in his rebuttal letter in *Partisan Review,* May-June, 1953—and of his
effort to win over his audience by waving in their faces what
Allen Tate, in commenting on Mr. Schwartz's essay, called
"the red herring of snobbery." What both Pound and Mr.
Schwartz are in effect saying is: "By God, we're all just a
bunch of ignorant bums here and, by God, we're proud of it.
At least we're *men* and not sissies!" Thus in his first sentence

Mr. Schwartz transforms what might have been a serious discussion of a serious literary issue into a crassly emotive smear
involving deeply submerged and highly complicated status
drives and taboos—including even the highly suspect masculine taboo against the seemingly effeminate—in his readers as
well as in himself.

Mr. Schwartz's subsequent outburst—"Yes, we have no
bananas. But all God's chillun got shoes"—is a further development of this approach; and when it is taken in conjunction
with the closing paragraph of his reply to Mr. Ramsey,
which was published in *Partisan Review* for May-June, 1953,
there can no longer be any doubt as to the quality of his
thinking or the sincerity of his motives. In this paragraph Mr.
Schwartz abandons all pretensions to subtlety and panders
to the lowest patriotic and conformist prejudices of his
audience.

My chief reason [he says] for writing as I did was, I think, because I do believe in literature, and in the social ideal proposed by
the Constitution, and often violated or unrealized. And also I believe that the future of literature, as of civilization, depends to some
important extent upon the realization of that social and human
ideal. And finally Mr. Ramsey finds the style of my essay coy, flip,
irrelevant, and precious at times. He may be right, but here too
being an American [the italics are mine] is relevant. Humor is a very
important part of American life and often the best way to get other
Americans to listen to you, which is the reason I naturally find myself using humor in writing criticism and in responding to critics.
Thus, I am merely *fulfilling the obligations of being an American*
[the italics are again mine] in trying to be funny, just as, for the
same reasons in part, I am trying to be truly an American in owning
two used cars, in owning a TV set, in expecting everyone to love
me, and in expecting everyone to admire my work and my 1949

Buick. I have also been a loyal Giant fan since 1921. This avowal of fact may explain very little to Mr. Ramsey. It explains a great deal to me and surely it will to other readers.

We may pass over such questions as why Mr. Schwartz feels Americans have to be funny, why he feels he himself has to try so hard to be both funny and American, and why he and so many other liberal intellectuals have felt called upon recently to protest their patriotism in terms which only the American Legion would understand and only Senator McCarthy would fully endorse. We may also pass over, although less easily, the tone of coy self-deprecation and inverted snobbery implicit in his enumeration of his middle-class material assets as well as the interesting fact that he is making a most strenuous appeal to snobbery of one kind in the name of an attack on snobbery of another kind. We may even ignore his final appeal over Mr. Ramsey's head to the red-blooded, baseball-loving Americanism of his readers. But what must bring us up short is his naked admission of a truth which has long been obvious but which has never before been made explicit in his own words: that his fear of the concept of manners, hence his psychological incapacity to deal with it as an esthetic concept, is based on his feeling that it has behind it some odious political doctrine threatening to the Constitution of the United States. Mr. Ramsey's "descending ladder of meanings," down which he has traced the frantic flight of Mr. Schwartz's logic from manners to good manners to snobbery to brutal and insane selfishness, may now be extended beyond brutal and insane selfishness to authoritarianism to totalitarianism to fascism and communism until at last we are brought back again to the suppression of minorities and the pogrom and ghetto—all hallucinated and distorted by the paranoia of the whole view.

By the end of the first section of his essay this compelled and ritualistic association of charged ideas becomes the fixed habit of Mr. Schwartz's discourse, so that all his subsequent observations appear like a series of desperate military maneuvers undertaken in defense of life, liberty, and the pursuit of happiness. This is particularly true of his efforts to preserve the sanctity of the American novel in the face of what he conceives to be aspersions cast by Mr. Trilling. In "Manners, Morals, and the Novel" Mr. Trilling began by defining manners as

. . . a culture's hum and buzz of implication . . . the whole evanescent context in which its explicit statements are made. It is that part of a culture which is made up of half-uttered or unutterable expressions of value. They are hinted at by small actions, sometimes by the arts of dress or decoration, sometimes by tone, gesture, emphasis, or rhythm, sometimes by the words that are used with a special frequency or a special meaning. They are the things that for good or bad draw the people of a culture together and that separate them from the people of another culture. They make the part of a culture which is not art, or religion, or morals, or politics, and yet it relates to all these highly formulated departments of culture. It is modified by them; it modifies them; it is generated by them; it generates them. In this part of culture assumption rules, which is often so much stronger than reason.

This [says Mr. Schwartz] is Mr. Trilling's broad definition of manners. Throughout his essay, however, he sometimes uses a limited and very different definition of manners, namely, the manners of particular social classes and groups in a given social hierarchy. It is by moving back and forth between his broad (and tentative) definition and his limited (and unexpressed) definition that Mr.

Trilling is able to hold forth *Don Quixote* as a true novel (here the broad definition works) while *The Scarlet Letter* (here it is the limited definition) suffers "from a lack of social texture" and is, like almost all American novels, not concerned with society at all. How can one say, in terms of Mr. Trilling's broad definition, that *The Scarlet Letter, Moby Dick,* and *Huckleberry Finn* lack social texture? The equivalent would be to say that *Walden* is not about society because it deals with a solitary individual. In the same way, again, it is only by using his limited definition and ignoring his broad one that Mr. Trilling can quote and agree with James Fenimore Cooper and Henry James on "the thick social texture of English life and the English novel" in the nineteenth century as opposed to the thinness of American life and the American novel; for in terms of his broad definition there was just as much social texture in America as in England; it was a different social texture as it was a different society and it was not the kind of social texture that James was interested in; but it had just as much of "a culture's hum and buzz of implication," etc., which Mr. Trilling says he means by manners.

Mr. Schwartz's dialectic here is complicated but not impenetrable. His strategy is quite simply to attribute to Mr. Trilling a definition of manners (the limited or "unexpressed" definition) which, in fact, Mr. Trilling never makes, then to show him as shifting confusedly between it and the definition (the broad definition) which he does make, and, finally, to show him as hoist on his own petard by arguing sophistically that this latter definition is invalid because it may be applied to any culture whatever. This is to say that any culture, by reason of the fact that it *is* a culture, will manifest a "hum and buzz of implication," hence, any culture, whether Pueblo Indian or Kwakiutl, has the same supply of manners as any other. The only difference in manners from culture to culture is a difference in kind. Thus, according to Mr. Schwartz, it is impossible to say, as Mr. Trilling does, that, in comparison with nineteenth-century England, nineteenth-century America lacked social texture; it simply had a different social texture, a different kind of manners, but one equally good for the novelist. By means of this process of specious inference, badly disguised as logical demolition, Mr. Schwartz endeavors to direct attention away from Mr. Trilling's real point, which is that there is a valid sense in which it can be argued that there *was* something lacking in the social texture of nineteenth-century America, that in some cultures the "hum and buzz of implication" *is* louder, more irritating, and more various than in others, and that a Kwakiutl culture, by reason of the complexity of its observed manners and the depth of their implication, will always serve the novelist at least potentially better than a Pueblo culture dedicated to the suppression of manners and the cultivation of uniformity.

An acceptance of these propositions makes it possible for one to deal effectively—although, in Mr. Schwartz's terms, heretically—with each of the questions he raises both in the section of his essay just quoted and in the section which follows immediately after it. "How can one say," he asks, "in terms of Mr. Trilling's broad definition, that *The Scarlet Letter, Moby Dick,* and *Huckleberry Finn* lack social texture? The equivalent would be to say that *Walden* is not about society because it deals with a solitary individual." It seems to me that one can say this quite easily. It is because these novels lack social texture, or the society out of which they were written lacked it, that they have to be so strenuously *about* something, that they have to depend for such a large part

of their dramatic existence upon the concrete physical event—
the act of adultery, the adventure at sea, the flight down the
Mississippi. If their society had been able to provide them with
sufficient social texture—a texture of manners compressed between the stratifications of class—they would undoubtedly
exist more completely within and for themselves, and the dramatic event would impose itself upon us not in the moment
of violence, the breach of suspense, or the revelation of sin,
but in the gradual penetration of what Mr. Trilling calls
"the illusion that snobbery generates," the gradual penetration, this is to say, of the structures of hypocrisy and self-deceit,
of pride and venality, which, in a complex, developed society,
provide some of the counters against which the creation of
true character in fiction becomes possible. The absence of such
a society in America, and the consequent moral isolation of
the individual, is presumably one of the things *Huckleberry
Finn* is about. That is the source of the tension and irony one
feels in the relationship between Huck and Jim floating on their
raft in the middle of the river and the life passing by them on
the shore. The social world of the raft is made up of the
niceties, kindnesses, little rituals of comradeship—the manners, if you like—which the boy and the man are able to in-
vent and, with no small difficulty, to maintain as they go along.
It is an inadequate world and, at times, an inadequate comradeship. But the world of the shore is worse, for it offers only
instances of raw violence, the dramatic substitute in American life and the American novel for a culture's full "hum and
buzz of implication," which, if it had been present in the
background of *Huckleberry Finn,* would unquestionably have
enriched the contrast between the two worlds. As it stands, the

novel is impoverished by the simplicity of that contrast, by
the necessary thinness of the implication of violence in a
culture where violence not merely substitutes for but very
largely *is* the "hum and buzz." In much the same way, a great
many of the heroes of American fiction appear to us thin and
self-enclosed and suffering in a vacuum, for, while we feel the
pain of their isolation most acutely and appreciate the an-
guished lyricism which their pain frequently inspires in them,
we almost never see precisely what it is they feel so painfully
isolated *from*. This, I think, bothers one even in Mr. Schwartz's
Walden, which really isn't, as he insists, about society at all.
It is about a solitary individual rationalizing his isolation from
society. Society itself is nowhere to be found. We have always
to take Mr. Thoreau's word that it exists, just as we have always to take Mr. Sherwood Anderson's word and Mr. Thomas
Wolfe's word and even, oddly enough, Mr. John Dos Passos'
word, and that is never enough. As for Mr. Schwartz's Henry
James, it is simply not true that he was not interested in nineteenth-century America. He was, on the contrary, very much
interested in it, and his novels are full of it, although the America to be found in them is naturally not the one that interested
Mark Twain. James had to discover his America in the form
that would make it accessible to his particular kind of sensibility, and that was in the form of a vestigial social class in
which the decay of a great mercantile culture had left behind
the proprieties, if not the substance, of human conduct, the
scarcely observable manners "refined," as Eliot said, "beyond
the point of civilization" out of which the tenuous felt life of
his novels is compounded. If James had failed to find such a
form, we should presumably have been left with nothing but

the magnificent sensibilities of his characters floating like
ectoplasm about their drawing rooms, and that too would never
have been enough.

A great deal of the misunderstanding which these questions of Mr. Schwartz's reveal—at least that part of the misunderstanding which is not deliberate and strategic—would
probably have been avoided if he had troubled to take into
account Mr. Trilling's more considered discussion of manners
in the later essay "Art and Fortune." If, however, he had taken
it into account, he would have deprived himself of an argument altogether, for in that essay Mr. Trilling makes it clear
to those who, like Mr. Schwartz, read "Manners, Morals, and
the Novel" superficially or in purely political terms that he
is not interested in "establishing a new genteel tradition in
criticism and fiction," although he fully understands that,
"where misunderstanding serves others as an advantage, one
is helpless to make oneself understood." What he *is* interested
in is the relation between the value preoccupations of a culture, especially as they take the form of money and class, and
the dramatic meaning which these preoccupations tend to
take on in the fiction which a culture produces. If, as he said
in "Manners, Morals, and the Novel," the primary work of the
novel is "the investigation of reality and illusion," specifically,
the penetration of the "illusion that snobbery generates" and
if the novel, in dealing with the questions of reality and illusion which are raised by the ideas of money and class, characteristically relies, indeed must rely, upon "an exhaustive
exploitation of manners," then we must come at the concept
of manners from the standpoint of esthetics and rule Mr.
Schwartz's approach entirely out of order.

The esthetic implications of Mr. Trilling's view of manners begin to assert themselves in the section of "Art and Fortune" having to do with the question that so disturbed Mr. Schwartz, the question of "substantiality" in its relation to the thinness of social texture in the American novel. Mr. Trilling said in "Manners, Morals, and the Novel" that "the novel in America diverges from its classical intention, which . . . is the investigation of the problem of reality beginning in the social field." He then went on to say that Henry James was "alone [in the American nineteenth century] in knowing that to scale the moral and esthetic heights in the novel one had to use the ladder of social observation," and he paraphrased the passage in James's life of Hawthorne in which James

. . . enumerates the things which are lacking to give the American novel the thick social texture of the English novel—no state; barely a specific national name; no sovereign; no court; no aristocracy; no church; no clergy; no army; no diplomatic service; no country gentlemen; no palaces; no castles; no manors; no old country houses; no parsonages; no thatched cottages; no ivied ruins; no cathedrals; no great universities; no public schools; no political society; no sporting class—no Epsom, no Ascot! That is, no sufficiency of means for the display of a variety of manners, no opportunity for the novelist to do his job of searching out reality, not enough complication of appearance to make the job interesting.

In the section on "substantiality" in "Art and Fortune"— passages of which I quoted earlier—Mr. Trilling completes this observation:

I think that if American novels of the past, whatever their merits of intensity and beauty, have given us very few substantial or memorable people, this is because one of the things which makes for substantiality of character in the novel is precisely the notation of

manners, that is to say, of class traits modified by personality
[or, he might have said, personality modified by class traits]. It is
impossible to imagine a Silas Wegg or a Smerdyakov or a Félicité
(of *A Simple Heart*) or a Mrs. Proudie without the full documenta-
tion of their behavior in relation to their own classes and to other
classes. All great characters of American fiction, such, say, as Captain Ahab and Natty Bumpo, tend to be mythic because of the rare
fineness and abstractness of the ideas they represent; and their very
freedom from class gives them a large and glowing generality; for
what I have called *substantiality* is not the only quality that makes
a character great. They are few in number and special in kind; and
American fiction has nothing to show like the huge, swarming, substantial population of the European novel, the substantiality of
which is precisely a product of a class existence. In fiction, as perhaps in life, the conscious realization of social class, which is an
idea of great power and complexity, easily and quickly produces
intention, passion, thought, and what I am calling substantiality.
The diminution of the reality of class, however socially desirable in
many respects, seems to have the practical effect of diminishing our
ability to see people in their difference and specialness.

I take it that no theory of the development of the novel
pretending to seriousness or any just estimate of the situation
now obtaining for the novel in America can safely be put forward without due allowance for the truth of these observations
of Mr. Trilling's. The idea of "substantiality" must cause us
to explore in a new and vastly more complicated way the old
question of how character shows forth to us from the page of
fiction, in what terms exactly do we see that it is *there,* as well
as the equally old and still more complicated question of
just what *has* happened to character in the course of the novel's
development, especially when we remember that it was once
so unmistakably *there,* surrounded and enclosed by its world
of physical sensation and material form, and remember too

that our sense of this world, its thickness and dramatic tone, grew out of the relation that literally existed in the social world of the novel's jurisdiction between character and those elements of being—of class, property, money, and birth— in which it found extensions and violations of itself. We remember the great, roomy world of Fielding and Smollett, Thackeray and Dickens, so crowded with variegated life, so thickly populated with personality, and it is like the world the neurotic knew before trauma put blinders on his psyche; while the novel since Dickens shows a deepening trauma and a progressive dislocation of character from its place in the social scene, with society tending to devolve into abstract social force and then into social change and finally into social injustice, with character thinning down into personality and then into sensibility and finally into nothingness, and with the novel itself moving, as Mark Schorer said, "more and more . . . toward the extremities of poetry and history . . . as the individual finds an ever diminishing social authority with which to identify himself," and experiences increasingly that dropping away of connection between his internal nature and the forms of his social existence, which is the feature of our modern neurotic state.

In Jane Austen one finds the dramatic consequences of this connection displaying themselves in a very pure form, almost at times in the very pure form of social stultification. In the world of her novels gentility is a condition of property. It is a virtue which the inherited possession of land makes mandatory; hence, in the landed it is not one of the attributes in terms of which character is made manifest, for, like certain kinds of respectability in society at large, it is simply something one comes into along with the ancestral estate, without moral effort or conscious application of the will. It nonetheless comprises the etiquette or convention, the standard of what is reasonably predictable or acceptable, in relation to which character, when it is aroused either to act or to will, is shown forth and dramatized. Bad behavior in a gentleman of property comes to us, for example, in the dramatic contrast between what he does and what he is expected to do, and it is in the degree of the contrast that we are able to measure his reality as a character. The man without property but possessing great *personal* gentility is dramatized, on the other hand, in the degree of the contrast between what he *is* and what he is expected to be, for within the terms of the equation "property equals gentility," the man without property is expected to be only vulgar. A third and favorite contrast of Miss Austen's, and one that provides the material for a large part of her characteristic irony, is the contrast between the gentility which the landed inherit with their property and the gentility which some of them possess as an ingredient of spirit and which frequently shows up the inherited kind to be no gentility at all. This latter kind is what sets Anne Elliot in *Persuasion* apart from her sisters and accounts in the end both for her success as a person and her success in making an advantageous marriage, while it is her suitor and later her husband Captain Wentworth's possession of the second kind—gentility without property—that supplies the material circumstances in which her success can be effectively realized. The baronet William Elliot is the type of the landed gentleman who behaves badly and whose badness is dramatized in his violation of the inherited decorum which insists that he behave with gentility.

The dramatic movement of the novel might be said to consist of the process by which each of the three characters exceeds or falls short of the standard of quality laid down by the size of his property holdings. William, through treachery, falls far short of his; Anne, through personal gentility, exceeds hers; Wentworth, through gentility of the same kind, manages without property far to exceed his and barely to equal Anne's.

It might also be said that this process is climaxed in each case by the "penetration" of the reality hidden behind Mr. Trilling's "illusion that snobbery generates," the illusion that masks William's treachery, that obscures Wentworth's true prospects, and that causes us in the beginning to underestimate Anne's character. And one penetrates this illusion in the way Mr. Trilling suggests one always penetrates it in the traditional form of the novel—through the author's "exhaustive exploitation of manners . . . of class traits modified" or, in the case of *Persuasion, enhanced* by "personality." One can also see how it is by virtue of their class traits, their moral arrangement on the scale of property, that the characters of *Persuasion* help give the novel "substantiality," for the obligations which property imposes upon them form the standard by which their actions as characters can be measured and dramatically analyzed. Without these obligations there could have been no *Persuasion* because there would have been no problem. Anne would simply have married Wentworth at once over the materialistic objections of Lady Russell—her objections *are* Anne's "persuasion"—and gone off with him into a life of romantic poverty, while William would have had no decorum to betray and no goal in the name of which to betray it.

One can undoubtedly say the same for the lovers in Charlotte Brontë's *Jane Eyre*. What gives the passion of Jane and Rochester its intensity and dramatic authority is the conflict between the obligations of self-respect and virtue imposed upon Jane by her religious and class background and the fierce demands of Rochester's privileged licentiousness as well as of her own newly awakened emotions. Each of the scenes depicting this passion is played out under the accusing eyes of Jane's stern Calvinist God or, literally, under the shadow of sexual guilt cast by Rochester's mad wife locked in the rooms overhead. And it is one of the compelling ironies of the novel that Jane's moral obligations to herself win out in the end over the passion to which they will not allow her to succumb; for in the end the Providence that destroys Rochester's health and sight also makes it possible for Jane to serve him as she wanted all along to serve her God, not as a lover—for which she never really had much talent anyhow—but as a loving attendant, and to be loved in return, not for her qualities of passion, but for her qualities of service. It is Jane who, after all, wins *Rochester* in the end, and on her own terms. "Reader, I married him," she exclaims on the last page, and the note of triumph in her voice should not escape us. *She has* married him, but only after God has obliged her, as it were, by rendering him impotent and enabling her to keep her vow of chastity in a marriage-become-hospital. Interpreted in this way, *Jane Eyre* may be taken as one of the coldest works of feminist polemics ever written; and it may be taken so, at the level of its deepest and most rewarding subtlety, because the moral obligations imposed by religion and class are there to provide the tension and the complexity, as well as the key to the conflict, in which its true meaning resides.

Raskolnikov's situation in *Crime and Punishment* is a very similar case in point. We are able to appreciate the enormity of his crime and to participate in the anguish of his guilt because the crime comes to us in the context of the morality which it violates, just as the guilt comes to us in the context of the morality out of which it derives. It is the material of participation and judgment which the novel provides through the ingredients of character, scene, and sensory language, rather than the material which we bring with us into the novel out of life, that affords us our angle of vision, that enables us to *see* into Raskolnikov and to assess both his crime and the quality of his conscience. As R. P. Blackmur, in speaking of the ingredient of character in this material, has pointed out, Raskolnikov's mother and his sister Dounia "represent the normal conduct from which Raskolnikov departs; they represent the order of society which he tears down. and envelops; it is them, their lives, to whom he gives meaning," and, one might add, it is they, along with Svidrigailov and Razumihin, in their different and opposite ways, who give meaning to *his* life, who by turns estimate and objectify the quality of his conscience.

All that I have been discussing up to now has had to do with the question of the availability of this "order of society," particularly for the novel of the past, and with the related question of the kinds of material—money, property, class, religious scruple—of which, from time to time in the novel, this order may be seen to consist. But it is time now to narrow the focus, to produce *exempla* out of familiar works which will more concretely illustrate just how these materials function, even within single scenes, to help make possible the dra-

matic delineation of character in fiction, particularly to help
produce those instances of tension, discord, and even, at times,
of outrage as well as those instances of contrast between appearance and truth, illusion and reality, in which the fullness
of character is most often shown forth. I have chosen, more
or less at random, two traveling scenes, both, as it happens,
coming at the beginning of novels, one from Dostoevski's *The
Idiot* and the other from Ford Madox Ford's *Some Do Not,*
and as a final example, the "Red Shoes" scene from Proust's
The Guermantes Way. The fact that the first two are traveling scenes in a sense makes the job harder, for to the novelist
the placing and motivating of character presented during travel
is very nearly a "whole-cloth" proposition. He is denied access
to the customary props of landscape and weather, on the one
hand, and of native domestic surroundings and the individualizing habits and routines of daily life on the other, and so is
forced to build character entire, really to *see* his Mrs. Brown,
as Virginia Woolf would have said, without the help of the
crowded Edwardian context which might otherwise have done
nearly all his seeing for him. He is, in fact, required to make
do—as these scenes show—only with such individualizing
effects as may be registered through speech, gesture, and dress
and the systems of value and belief which these may represent.
In societies and ages in which speech and dress tend to be
standardized and in which the prevailing system of value
dictates conformity or a promiscuous and therefore a mean-
ingless geniality, one supposes that the scene of travel in fiction would eventually disappear altogether, simply on the
ground that there would be little or nothing in the experience

of such a scene worth recording; in fact, if we now live in this kind of society and age and can accept some of our current novels as accurately reflecting the reality around us, it would seem that the only experiences now worth recording are those that transpire in psychiatric sanitaria, in the death cells of prisons, in the dim minds of infants, and in bed.

The Idiot opens on a note of incongruity, a situation of contrast between illusion and truth, in which our senses are at once caught up, momentarily deranged, and then set straight. Traveling in a third-class carriage of the Warsaw train now approaching Petersburg are two young men who *appear* to be poor but who begin almost immediately to pull away and move above their shabbiness of dress and their third-class accommodations as the narrative focus clears and as we are allowed to take note of certain as yet unassessable attributes of feature which seem to suggest that they are in some way distinctive as persons.

One of them was a short man about twenty-seven, with almost black curly hair and small, grey, fiery eyes. He had a broad and flat nose and high cheek bones. His thin lips were continually curved in an insolent, mocking and even malicious smile. But the high and well-shaped forehead redeemed the ignoble lines of the lower part of the face. What was particularly striking about the young man's face was its death-like pallor, which gave him a look of exhaustion in spite of his sturdy figure, and at the same time an almost painfully passionate expression, out of keeping with his coarse and insolent smile and the hard and conceited look in his eyes. . . . [The other] was a young man, also twenty-six or twenty-seven years old, above the average in height, with very fair thick hair, with sunken cheeks and a thin, pointed, almost white beard. His eyes were large, blue and dreamy; there was something gentle, though heavy-looking in their expression, something of that strange look from which some people can recognize at the first glance a victim of epilepsy. Yet the young man's face was pleasing, thin and clean-cut, though colourless, and at this moment blue with cold.

These descriptions represent the second phase of the developing contrast by means of which the two young men are in the process of being gradually individualized as characters. Seen initially within the stereotype of third-class status and poverty, which leads us to expect them to be mediocre, they are now seen as personally distinctive and, therefore, as personally superior to that stereotype. Then in the next few moments, as conversation between them begins, they declare their identities, and the contrast moves into a third phase: personal distinction within the appearance of poverty is reinforced by actual distinction of class coupled with actual poverty. Or, to put the matter differently, we have been led first to infer from their circumstances that the young men are mediocre; then they are described as having some personal worth even though they are poor. Now we are led to infer from the fact of their aristocratic heritage that they must also have the high social and material status which normally accompanies it, but that is proven wrong by the fact of their poverty. The blond young man is a *Prince* Myshkin, but he is the last of the Prince Myshkins and quite out of pocket. The dark young man, Parfyon Rogozhin, is technically heir to a fortune of two and a half million roubles—one recalls Mr. Trilling's comment that "every situation in Dostoevski, no matter how spiritual, starts with a point of social pride and a certain number of roubles"— but Rogozhin has been temporarily cut off by his family in punishment for a foolish indiscretion. As soon as this information is supplied us, the contrast moves into a fourth phase, the

phase of its greatest subtlety, and the young men are presented through the remainder of the scene not simply as possessing some personal worth in the midst of impoverished
circumstances but as possessing particular and opposite *kinds*
of personal worth which are displayed in their respective attitudes toward the fact that they are both *aristocrats* and in impoverished circumstances. Myshkin is the soul of modesty and
refinement. He answers Rogozhin's questions readily and
frankly, and he is decent to the petty official Lebedyev who
constantly intrudes upon the conversation. Rogozhin, on the
other hand, is arrogant and fiercely resentful of his present
predicament and refuses to speak directly to Lebedyev at any
time. It is the sharp contrast in their treatment of Lebedyev
which particularly points up the differences in character of
the two men, just as it is Lebedyev from whose angle of vision
we observe and measure them and their situation. He is, in
fact, the moral center around which the others revolve, for as
their problem is one of money, status, and, in Rogozhin's case,
social pride, so he represents the value system of class snobbery, political opportunism and influence to which, in men of
his type, these are generally vulgarized.

Such omniscient gentlemen [says Dostoevski] are to be found
pretty often in a certain stratum of society. They know everything.
All the restless curiosity and faculties of their minds are irresistibly
bent in one direction, no doubt from lack of more important ideas
and interests in life, as the critic of today would explain. But the
words, "they know everything," must be taken in a rather limited
sense: in what department so-and-so serves, who are his friends,
what his income is, where he was governor, who his wife is and
what dowry she brought him, who are his first cousins and who are
his second cousins, and everything of that sort. For the most part

these omniscient gentlemen are out at elbow, and receive a salary of seventeen roubles a month. The people of whose lives they know every detail would be at a loss to imagine their motives. Yet many of them get positive consolation out of this knowledge, which amounts to a complete science, and derive from it self-respect and their highest spiritual gratification.

Lebedyev, then, is of the world of quantitative measurement, of possession, connection, position, and power, the world that is always at the back of the novel and that evaluates and approves the character of Rogozhin as it evaluates and condemns—although not in our eyes—the character of Myshkin. It is what Lebedyev *knows* of this world, and there is nothing he does not know, that enables him to express and then to validate our astonishment as the illusion of poverty that surrounds the young men is gradually penetrated and their identity and true status are revealed. It is in terms of this knowledge, furthermore, that he is able to make the ironic and yet accurately qualitative remark about Myshkin's poor bundle of clothing which puts the scene into focus—"Your bundle has some value, anyway, . . . and though one may safely bet there is no gold in it, neither French, German, nor Dutch—one may be sure of that, if only from the gaiters you have got on over your foreign shoes—yet if you can add to your bundle a relation such as Madame Epanchin, the general's lady, the bundle acquires a very different value. . . ." This is the value that gives us our center, our post of observation onto the scene and that provides the snobbery that generates the illusion that Dostoevski penetrates. But if the elements of class and status of which Lebedyev's value is the hypocrisy were not there in the background of the novel and, by extension, in Dostoevski's moral world, there would be nothing to generate the illusion, hence nothing to penetrate, and there would be no way of dramatizing the scene so that we would move gradually downward through the illusion of class to the reality of class to the reality of character within class, which is the reality at the heart of the power and "substantiality" of the scene.

The dramatics, the characterizing factor, of the first scene in Ford's *Some Do Not* presents itself to us not in the *illusion* of class but in the bare fact. From the opening line to the end, class works consistently and simply to distinguish the characters of the scene from one another and then to document their differences.

The two young men—they were of the English public official class —sat in the perfectly appointed railway carriage. . . . The compartment smelt faintly, hygienically of admirable varnish—the train ran as smoothly—Tietjens remembered thinking—as British gilt-edged securities. It travelled fast; yet had it swayed or jolted over the rail joints, except at the curve before Tonbridge or over the points at Ashford where these eccentricities are expected and allowed for, Macmaster, Tietjens felt certain, would have written to the company. Perhaps he would even have written to the *Times*. . . . Their class administered the world. . . . If they saw a policeman misbehave, railway porters lack civility, an insufficiency of street lamps, defects in public services or in foreign countries, they saw to it, either with nonchalant Balliol voices, or with letters to the *Times* asking in regretful indignation: "Has the British This or That come to *this!*" Or they wrote, in the serious reviews of which so many still survived, articles taking under their care, manners, the Arts, diplomacy, inter-Imperial trade or the personal reputations of deceased statesmen and men of letters. . . . Macmaster, that is to say, would do all that: of himself Tietjens was not so certain.

Here in the two short opening paragraphs of the scene Ford provides us with the broad terms within which Tietjens and Macmaster are to be dramatized and contrasted. We learn exactly what, for members of the "English public official class," is customary and acceptable; therefore, we know precisely where to place, and how to assess, the two young men in relation to their type. Tietjens begins at once to pull away from the type and to set himself in opposition to it. "The train ran as smoothly—*Tietjens* remembered thinking—as British gilt-edged securities. . . . *Macmaster*, that is to say, would do all that: of himself Tietjens was not so certain." Macmaster, on the other hand, begins by being characterized *within* the type and then, because of the very strenuousness of his conformity to it, he gradually takes on particularity of character. The initial or typical contrast between the two men is shown at the outset in the difference of their physical appearance. Macmaster is

. . . smallish, Whig; with a trimmed, pointed black beard, such as a smallish man might wear to enhance his already germinated distinction; black hair of a stubborn fibre, drilled down with hard metal brushes; a sharp nose; strong, level teeth; a white, butterfly collar of the smoothness of porcelain; a tie confined by a gold ring, steel-blue speckled with black—to match his eyes, as Tietjens knew. Tietjens, on the other hand, could not remember what coloured tie he had on.

And, as it turns out, Tietjens does not need to remember or to care. Because of his secure position in his class, he can afford the luxury of personal untidiness just as he can afford the luxury of independence in thought and manner. But Macmaster is Scottish and of rather humble origin, and so must conform to the rules of class, must, in fact, continually exert himself to go the rules one better. It is as much the degree of his overtypicalness as it is the degree of Tietjen's undertypicalness that causes him to take on character; but we are able to see and to appreciate that character, and therefore to respond to the dramatics of the scene as a whole, only because we have before us, in the form of Ford's generic description, the pattern of decorum or manners which, in each case, character violates.

The "Red Shoes" scene from *The Guermantes Way* opens with the Duchesse de Guermantes inquiring of Swann whether he will be going to Italy with her and her husband in ten months' time. Swann replies that it will not be possible, that in ten months he will probably already have been dead for several months. Hearing this news while on her way to the carriage which is to take her and the Duke to dinner, the Duchesse stops in confusion.

Placed for the first time in her life between two duties as incompatible as getting into her carriage and shewing pity for a man who was about to die, she could find nothing in the code of conventions that indicated the right line to follow, and not knowing which to choose, felt it better to make a show of not believing that the alternatives need be seriously considered, so as to follow the first, which demanded of her at the moment less effort, and thought that the best way of settling the conflict would be to deny that any existed. "You're joking," she said to Swann. "It would be a joke in charming taste," replied he, ironically. "I don't know why I am telling you this; I have never said a word to you before about my illness. But as you asked me, and as I may die now at any moment. . . . But whatever I do I mustn't make you late; you're dining out, remember," he added, because he knew that for other people their own social obligations took precedence of the death of a friend and could put himself in her place by dint of his instinctive politeness. But that of the Duchesse enabled her to perceive in a vague way that the dinner to which she was going must count for less to Swann than his own death. And so, while continuing on her way to the carriage, she let her shoulders droop saying: "Don't worry about our dinner. It's not of any importance!"

The Duke has heard Swann's news, but his first concern is punctuality, and he urges his wife to hurry. But just as she is entering the carriage, he notices that she is still wearing her black shoes and demands that she change at once into her red ones. The Duchesse returns dutifully to her room, and the Duke asks Swann to leave before she comes down again and delays their departure further by resuming the conversation. The Duke explains that she is tired out already and "will reach the dinner-table quite dead" and that he too is dying of hunger.

"I had a wretched lunch this morning when I came from the train. There was the devil of a *béarnaise* sauce, I admit, but in spite of that I shan't be at all sorry, not at all sorry to sit down to dinner. Five minutes to eight! Oh, women, women! She'll give us both indigestion before tomorrow. She is not nearly as strong as people think." The Duke felt no compunction at speaking thus of his wife's ailments and his own to a dying man, for the former interested him more, appeared to him more important. And so it was simply from good breeding and good fellowship that, after politely shewing us out, he cried "from off stage," in a stentorian voice from the porch to Swann, who was already in the courtyard: "You, now, don't let yourself be taken in by the doctors' nonsense, damn them. They are donkeys. You're as strong as the Pont Neuf. You'll live to bury us all!"

What is most striking about this scene is the extent to which the code of manners of the Duke and Duchesse makes possible

their bad behavior to Swann, dictates it, in fact, and makes it
acceptable. It is because of their allegiance to convention that
they can be dramatized as unfeeling, that we are able to measure the distance between what they ought to do and what they
feel they *must* do or cannot help but do. Convention is the
point from which, in estimating the scene, we depart. Humanity is the point at which we arrive and they do not, and
that is the disparity which gives us our superior knowledge
and they their superior force of character. The Duchesse,

> . . . placed for the first time in her life between two duties as
> incompatible as getting into her carriage and shewing pity for a
> man who was about to die, . . . could find nothing in the code of
> conventions that indicated the right line to follow, and not knowing
> which to choose, felt it better to make a show of not believing that
> the alternatives need be seriously considered, so as to follow the
> first, which demanded of her at the moment less effort, and thought
> that the best way of settling the conflict would be to deny that any
> existed.

. . . *so as to follow the first,* the alternative of getting into
her carriage, the one alternative her code of conventions holds
open to her. That is Proust's comment on the grave limitations
of that code in his society, and that is the stroke of inhumanity,
of bad manners which enlightens the scene for us. We *see* the
Duchesse in her decision to renounce the show of pity and to
enter her carriage. Her decision, for better or worse, *is* her
characterization. If her code dictated a show of pity, we should
have humanity but no irony, for the irony comes to us in
the contrast between the dictates of true humanity and the dictates of a code which, while ostensibly designed to make true
humanity continuously possible, ends by making life frequently

cruel. The Duke's parting remark to Swann is given force by a variation of the same contrast. It comes, first of all, as the result of an afterthought, "simply from good breeding and good fellowship," a momentary acknowledgment of a higher etiquette than that of the code. But we already know that "his wife's ailments and his own . . . interested [the Duke] more, appeared to him more important . . . [than] a dying man," and so we are in a position to assess the hypocrisy of the remark and, through it, the hypocrisy of the man. The code of conventions or manners in the scene may be said, therefore, to constitute its binding and compulsive force out of which, when it is violated or when there is brought up against it a more transcendent necessity, conflict and drama are generated.

One is struck by how progressively rarer this has become in the novel with the passage of time, how, for example, in the more purely existentialist fiction of our own day as well as in the typical American novel of tradition, the heroes appear to suffer their guilt in a vacuum or even to suffer nothing which we can rightly call guilt, but only remorse or only self-hatred or, most often lately, only a kind of numbness and vacuity. Even Flaubert's Emma Bovary is partly vitiated as a character because, although the provincial towns in which she lives provide her with a motive for perfidy, they do not provide the active terms in which her perfidy is judged and condemned. It is significant that in a novel dealing with the favorite subject of gossip there should be no gossip, but only the barest peripheral intimation of it, the faintest whispering in the wings. Emma's world is simply not alive enough or concerned enough with life to be able to rouse itself to the task of malice. It is a dull, stupid, complacent world, a world of puff and pomp and provincial oratory, the world of the Homaises, the Rodolphes, and the Charleses. This is one of the reasons Emma despises it so and becomes perfidious, but this is also one of the reasons she is not so solid on the page as we would like. To be driven to do what she does she has to live in an impoverished world, but to be able to evaluate what she is driven to do we have to see her world as something other than impoverished. The same paradox perhaps accounts for Flaubert's failure with Charles, for Charles has to do for the novel what the towns cannot. He has to "represent the normal conduct from which [Emma] departs, . . . the order of society which [she] tears down and envelops," but the difficulty is that the normal conduct is conduct at a minimum, the near refusal to act which is the dullness of respectability; so Charles is required to be both dramatically present as a character and representative of a way of life which is not only undramatic but scarcely present at all; and this he cannot be or, at any rate, this Flaubert cannot make him be convincingly.

In our own novel in recent times there have been at least two instances of writers who have escaped the Bovarist vacuum by virtue of their commitment to social situations in which, for reasons of cultural lag or entrenched religiosity, a moral atmosphere or background remains accessible against which conduct may be posed in a dramatic way. Faulkner in the South works with an atmosphere so charged with guilt and aberration, a background so rich in natural complexity and violence, that it morally burdens his characters almost to excess, keeping them perpetually in a state of hyperesthesia and their conduct perpetually at the brink of melodrama. James T. Farrell, whose *Studs Lonigan* Mr. Trilling has singled out as be-

longing to that group of novels in which a "concern with manners is of their very essence," achieved a similar, though less
spectacular, effect in his early work by exploiting the atmosphere of Shanty Irish piety and hypocrisy in which he grew up,
the atmosphere which, through its ironic contrast with the situation of poverty that generates it, affords us the terms of moral
measurement for Studs Lonigan's gradual deterioration and
for Danny O'Neill's equally gradual redemption. It is interesting to see, however, that while Studs's deterioration is in the
strictest keeping with the logic which the poverty imposes,
Danny's redemption runs counter to it and forces Farrell to
attribute to him qualities of character which cannot be objectified through the naturalistic method and which, therefore,
seem to us excessive and inexplicable. The only *dramatic*
qualities of aspiration and transcendence which the O'Neill
novels do contain, furthermore, are those framed in the context of piety and hypocrisy, which means that when we cast
about for a justification for Danny's redemption, we cannot
help but find it in that context and assume that he too is pious
and hypocritical.

Mr. Morton Dauwen Zabel, in his excellent short study of
Graham Greene, could well have been thinking of Danny's
problem along with the problem of what I have been calling
the "Bovarist vacuum" when he said:

A criminal takes his dignity from his defiance of the intelligence
or merit that surrounds him, from the test his act imposes on the
human community. He becomes trivial when that measure is denied
him. . . . The hardship this imposes on the artist is obvious. When
felony, by becoming political, becomes impersonal; when the *acte
gratuit* elicits not only secret but public approval, its dramatist faces

the desperate task of restoring to his readers their lost instinct of values, the sense of human worth. . . . The Victorian *frisson* of crime was all the choicer for the rigor of propriety and sentiment that hedged it in. Dickens's terrors are enhanced less by his rhetoric than by his coziness. The reversion to criminality in Dostoevski takes place in a ramifying hierarchy of authority—family life, social caste, political and religious bureaucracy, czarist militarism and repression. The horror of "The Turn of the Screw" is framed by the severest decorum, taste, and inhibition.

And finally Mr. Zabel has said:

Where once—in James, Conrad, Dostoevski, in Dickens, Defoe, and the Elizabethans—it was society, state, kingdom, world, or the universe itself that supplied the presiding order of law or justice, it is now the isolated, betrayed, and finally indestructible integrity of the individual life that must furnish that measure. Humanity, having contrived a world of mindless and psychotic brutality, reverts for survival to the atom of the single man. Marked, hunted, Ishmaelite, or condemned, he may work for evil or for good, but it is his passion for a moral identity of his own that provides the nexus of values in a world that has reverted to anarchy.

It is in relation to a world of somewhat near this kind, in which by now I take it we all more or less recognize we live or have lived, that the problem of the "Bovarist vacuum" in fiction may be seen in its widest significance. This is to say that to see it best we must come at it not by beginning with Flaubert but by beginning now, with all that we know in our present moment of history, and moving back on Flaubert reflexively through the vast and discouraging stretches of the post-Flaubertian experience. But to perceive this world we must have lived with the perception in our bones, not as a fact of knowledge but as a fact of sense, and have retained a view of fiction, at least of everything in fiction that may be said to be *given,* up to and perhaps even beyond the instant genius begins its work, as the gauge of morals and morale of the world out of which it comes. By gauge I do not mean Stendhal's "mirror dawdling down a lane" or the literary counterpart of a photograph by Cartier-Bresson. I mean an instrument whose function it is to translate into its own system of measurement and its own scale of relationships the impressions that come in upon it from a reality of which the impressions are necessarily measured and related according to a different system and scale, or are not measured or related at all.

John Peale Bishop perhaps had in mind some such idea of fiction as this when he said, "It is the mark of the true novelist that in searching the meaning of his own unsought experience, he comes on the moral history of his time." Certainly, it is the "unsought experience" merely that the average fiction of a time is most likely to give us, unsought by the novelist and unwelcomed by us. And it is the "moral history" that we always want when we can get it and the novelist can get at it, and when it is there in his time to be got at in a form moral enough to give it a range and significance larger than history.

FOUR

Gray new world

THE IMPACT OF David Riesman's work over the past several years has been such that any general discussion of his ideas at this time must appear superfluous. It may be said with certainty that Riesman, for better or worse, is now in the public domain, and even though his "position" in the more advanced circles of the mind has been under sporadic siege, one cannot help but acknowledge the successes recently made by the hired legions of Time, Inc., in effecting his release into middle-brow adulation. Riesman has now, we may say, begun to suffer the typical fate of the good writer or thinker in America, particularly of the kind in whom talent has joined with a sense of the age to produce a meretriciousness nearly indistinguishable from the glow of prophecy. He has lived to see himself become, at the height of his career, a sort of myth-maker and culture hero of the leisure-oriented educated classes, the same classes which, a generation ago, took up Spengler, Ortega, and Freud, but which tend today not so much to fashion themselves on ideas as passively to consume them, without noticeable decrease of pallor. His key terms have become established as the common coin of the new cocktail-and-breezeway Bohemia—from which, ironically, the concepts behind some of them derive—and they have had bestowed upon them what in this country is the final proof of popular acceptance—the accolade of misquotation by the illiterately well-read. *The Lonely Crowd*, Riesman's core work, is now a best seller in the abridged paper-backed edition; the number of servants its author keeps in his Chicago house has been for several months a matter of public record. At the colleges the brighter students—in contrast to their elders—are forming themselves on his categories, quite consciously seeking "autonomy," and looking ahead to the time when they will be able to take a course in it. Others still brighter are discovering in "other-direction" a patent excuse for their silence and conformism.

Meanwhile, from the intellectualist camp the sniping continues. In the Autumn, 1954, issues of *Partisan Review* and *Dissent* Elizabeth Hardwick and Norman Mailer, reviewing Riesman's latest book, *Individualism Reconsidered* together charge him with a variety of offenses ranging from opportunism through conservatism to complacent optimism about the changing character of our culture. Mailer's discussion, which I take to be the most penetrating we have yet had of Riesman's whole "case," turns on the excellent point that what Riesman has given us is essentially a fiction rather than a sociological analysis of American culture, a creative image whose value

must be judged not by its truth to Reality—if such exists—
but as in a novel by the quality of the mind, and the depth
of the life, behind it. While in Riesman's case Mailer does not
assess either of these at very much, his point seems to me an
important one in putting us onto the primary fact about the
best of Riesman's work, particularly *The Lonely Crowd:* that
within its obvious and perhaps very narrow limits, it is wholly
successful as a work of the creative and intuitive intelligence.
The insights it employs differ in quality but not in kind from
the insights employed in any serious novel to achieve realism
or verisimilitude, and its success derives like a novel's from
the thoroughness with which it explores and dramatizes the
problems set by its subject. I imagine that this sort of success, in place of the sterner academic variety, is one of the
reasons Riesman has earned such a large share of dislike
among critics. Another may be that taken merely as sociology
such a book as *The Lonely Crowd* at once runs afoul of
our current mistrust of all programmatic definitions and set
formulas and our vastly inflated egocentricity, which causes
us to reject those definitions which take into account less of
life than we are daily bewildered by. But taken as a fiction
The Lonely Crowd presents us with a dramatic image of ourselves which we can respond to and learn from, just as we can
learn from the image of ourselves thrown back by the carica-
turing fun-house mirror of a first-rate novel of manners. It
does not matter that the image is not "true" and does not do
us justice. Neither are statistics and graphs "true," and certainly they never do us justice. What matters is that the image
has its own justice and that its very distortion may reflect

tendencies in us which in twenty or thirty years will become our truth.

In this sense, I believe *The Lonely Crowd* to be one of the most important literary expressions the present age in America has had, a book to rank in its implications for Western culture with *The Revolt of the Masses* and *Democracy in America.* It is a book, furthermore, which, because it is backed by a creative consciousness of high order, opens for us in a new way the old question of the relationship between literature and society, between the novelist and those portions of his material which we may take to be environmentally given, yet which from novelist to novelist are never seen to be precisely the same. I should like to argue that, in addition to its relevance to us all, *The Lonely Crowd* is a book which no novelist at the present time can safely ignore or wholly escape, for it may be read as a record of the disappearance from our culture of the social forms which have traditionally afforded the novel its dramatic materials.

What Riesman calls the "inner-directed" man has been the typical hero of fiction from its beginnings and of drama from antiquity. Whether we begin with Oedipus and Tom Jones or Odysseus and Don Quixote, we find the recurring source of drama in the conflict between the obsessive inner drives of the hero and the moral structures of his society which work to deny them fulfillment. One can in fact say that as the novel has evolved, its form has tended to imitate the movement of the "inner-directed" hero through the various phases of this conflict, as the curve of classical tragedy with its culminating recognition-reversal effect represents the archetypal imitation.

The "investigation of illusion and reality," which Lionel Trilling considers to be the proper business of the novel, quite literally depends upon the existence of some "inner-directed" ideal or dream that is so compulsive and blinding in its force that it causes the hero not to *see* or to refuse to *see* in time. Then, as a rule, the novel transports him, and us with him, through a body of experience which proves his illusion to *be* illusion and reality, as always, to be transcendent. When this proof appears, we have our moment of recognition and, nearly always, our moment of purgation, for the hero has by now clearly failed, fallen short, been duped, and so must go down in defeat. Or he has undergone initiation, conversion, and been reborn phoenixlike out of the ashes of his former self.

From the Greeks down, indeed, from Venus and Adonis and the early fertility cults down, we acknowledge this to be the pattern of our racial inheritance; it is in fact the pattern through which our minds naturally express our sense of the cycle and rhythm of life itself; and we recognize its recurrence again and again in the drama, the story, and the novel. It has given us in modern times some of our most memorable fictional characters—Emma Bovary, Lambert Strether, Raskolnikov, Babbitt, Axel Heyst, Jay Gatsby, Frederic Henry, Willie Stark, Willy Loman—and in the novel of the past, where it tends to be clearer because more firmly buttressed by the dramatizing agents of property, religion, money, and class, it has given us very nearly the whole of our formula for seeing and evaluating the reality around us. So completely has this been true that it is only with the greatest difficulty, the most painful renovation of our habits of insight, that we can discard its stereotype and see in the new reality around us the change which has rendered the stereotype invalid.

This change which, if Riesman is correct, has resulted in the rise of a new "other-directed" personality type, must cause us drastically to revise our conception of drama, just as it must drive the novel either to extinction or to the discovery of new dramatic effects. With the disappearance of "inner-directed" man the illusion generated by ideals also disappears, along with the dramatic action taken in the name of ideals, and drama of the traditional kind becomes impossible. What the new "other-directed" man apparently requires is the approval of others, usually of the others in what Riesman calls his "peer-group." But the difficulty from the standpoint of drama is that the need for approval does not express itself in the form of an ideal nor represent a basis for dramatic action. It is not a drive compelling the individual toward the realization of selfhood. It seems, in fact, to have no ideological basis whatever, but is simply the result of a vague, generalized feeling of anxiety. The need to please others does have, however, a very real though largely unrecognized practical basis. In a society in which, as Riesman shows, "inner-directed" traits are no longer required by industry and, therefore, no longer serve as criteria for the judgment of individual worth, a person's agreeableness or niceness becomes one of the main criteria by which he can be judged; his "personality" becomes his distinguishing or salable commodity. But "personality" in such a society does not mean a set of traits which particularize or set off an individual from others. The requirement that he be approved of by everyone forces the individual, on the

contrary, to suppress his particularizing traits—if he has any—
on the ground that someone, anyone, might not like them,
with the result that "personality" becomes, for him, innocu-
ousness and anonymity. What we are therefore faced with in
Riesman's gray new world is a situation in which the drives
have disappeared which might have caused the individual to
act dramatically and, at the same time, a situation in which
dramatic action is seen as a threat to the one kind of satisfaction which the society still considers worthwhile.

We ought also to take into account the parallel disappearance in Riesman's world of the older patterns of social class
as our way of life has become increasingly standardized, as
wealth has come to be distributed more widely and evenly,
and as aristocratic traditions have grown thin. One effect of
this has been to deprive the novelist of the means of distinguishing among characters through differences in their appearance and manners, social position, and breeding. He has
also been deprived of some of his oldest themes—the movement of the individual up and down the scale of class; his
struggle for wealth and prestige; his moral orientation toward
money, money not simply to buy *things* but to keep up the
family honor or estate, as one sees it dramatized in Jane
Austen, George Eliot, and Henry James; and lastly what Lionel
Trilling has called the theme of the "Young Man from the
Provinces." This is the young man of "provincial birth and
rearing . . . [who] starts with a great demand upon life
and a great wonder about its complexity and promise. He
may be of good family but he must be poor. He is intelligent
. . . but not at all shrewd in worldly matters. He must have
acquired a certain amount of education, should have learned

something about life from books, although not the truth." He should be in a position to move from a state of innocence to a state of knowledge, from "inner-directed" idealism, perhaps, to initiation in "other-directed" experience. Mr. Trilling mentions several novels in which the Young Man from the Provinces has figured as hero—*The Red and the Black, Père Goriot* and *Lost Illusions, Great Expectations, Sentimental Education,* perhaps *War and Peace* and *The Idiot.* And one can add to the list out of our own literature perhaps *The Leatherstocking Tales, Huckleberry Finn, The Red Badge of Courage,* some of James, *An American Tragedy,* some of Lewis, *Winesburg, Ohio* and *Dark Laughter, In Our Time, One Man's Initiation, Manhattan Transfer,* parts of *USA,* all of Fitzgerald and Wolfe, *The Wild Palms,* Farrell's Studs Lonigan and Danny O'Neill novels, and coming up to the present, *All the King's Men, Catcher in the Rye, Other Voices, Other Rooms, End as a Man, The Heart Is a Lonely Hunter,* and *The Adventures of Augie March.*

The novelist in the predominantly "other-directed" culture of today, however, is faced with a situation in which increasingly everyone tends to look, dress, and act like everyone else, to drive the same cars, to live in the same kind of houses, and, because of the power of the mass media, even to think the same thoughts. As for the Young Man from the Provinces, he is an antique figure, a literary stereotype of which the type in life can scarcely be said any longer to exist. The ignorant, domineering parents and community which he characteristically rejected in the name of his ideal, his illusion of life as it should be, have been replaced, for the most part, by parents of intelligence and understanding, and by a community which so closely resembles the city to which he formerly escaped that there is no effective difference between them. The Young Man himself, or his comparable type, is no longer provincial or idealistic. Dreams of glory, wealth, and adventure no longer obsess him. His future course is clear and realistic. The safe job with the corporation or university, the pretty wife and children, the prefabricated ranch-style house with the picture window, rumpus room, and breezeway, the Ford that looks like a Cadillac—these are the goals toward which his heroism is directed, his dramatic escape is made.

The movement which, in the last fifty years, the novel in America records is the movement gradually away from the "inner-directed" phase of our cultural development toward the phase of at least incipient "other-direction." In Dreiser, Lewis, Fitzgerald, Dos Passos, Wolfe, and Farrell one is repeatedly struck by how much the dramatic intensity depends upon the conflict between the rural and pioneer virtues of moral innocence, honesty, thrift, and fidelity, on the one hand, and the urban and modern attributes of knowledge, corruption, infidelity, and promiscuity on the other. One also recognizes just as often the conflict between the provincial drives toward material success and increased social status and the resistance put up against them by competition or prejudice or political chicanery. Lewis's Babbitt is what might be called an "inner-directed, other-directed" type. Like the "other directed" business man of today, Babbitt wants to be well liked, but the vastly important distinction to be made between the two is that Babbitt has strongly "inner-directed" reasons for wanting to be well liked. He wants success, wealth, and position; while today's business man usually wants merely security and, in his lonely isolation from the motives and springs of being, a constant assurance that he is accepted by others. Fitzgerald's Gatsby is a perfect example of the strongly "inner-directed" type dedicated to the fulfillment of his dream in a society already passing into "other-direction." Nick Carraway, furthermore, is the type of the provincial Young Man who, in the face of the corruption of this society, does Gatsby's learning for him, conducts his moral education by proxy. Jack Burden functions in Warren's *All the King's Men* in a very similar way. Willie Stark, the fiercely "inner-directed" man, dies unchanged and essentially undefeated, but Jack is initiated and undergoes conversion, is metaphorically reborn with a new father and mother, a new past and future, a future based largely on the virtues of "other-direction." The heroes of Farrell and Wolfe are nearly all drawn on the type of the provincial Young Man. Eugene Gant, George Webber, Studs Lonigan, and Danny O'Neill are simply confronted with experience, most of it for the first time, and the novels record their reactions, their progress toward moral fulfillment or destruction.

When we come to the thirties, however, we notice that the novels depicting the change from "inner-" to "other-direction" begin to be replaced by novels in which social scene gives way to social crisis and the portrayal of special social groups victimized by the Depression. Farrell's work overlaps this category, and the novels of Steinbeck and Caldwell are centered directly within it. Through the novels of the forties and World War II the social scene recedes still further, the Depression disappears, and there develops a preoccupation with social and psychological *problems*—the war experience, race prejudice, homosexuality, and insanity. Now in the fifties these subjects have largely faded out; the social scene is scarcely discernible; and there are signs in the novel of concentration upon rather thin childhood and domestic situations, in which the drama tends to center in a subtle psychic conflict between characters and in which occasionally a climaxing instance of violence effects in them a species of conversion—as happens in Jean Stafford's *The Mountain Lion*, Robie Macauley's *The Disguises of Love*, and Peter Matthiesen's *Race Rock*.

Not only does the reflection of the social scene in novels after the twenties and thirties seem repetitious following the appearance of such books as *The Great Gatsby* and *USA*, but the social scene itself, marked as it is by increasing "other-direction," tends to be less and less *worth* reflecting. It is quite possible, although it may well be brash, to argue that most Americans today literally don't *do* anything. Their goal is, in fact, a condition of life in which they will not be required to do anything ever again. This, I suspect, is what the poet John Berryman meant when he said that "a man can live his whole life in this country without finding out whether or not he is a coward." The novel has consequently been forced to concern itself with more and more marginal and aberrant subjects in its unceasing effort to keep alive and to discover fresh materials for drama. The movement from social manners to social crisis to perversion to the stunted domestic epiphany may be seen in this sense to represent the novel's adjustment to the gradual failure of dramatic possibilities in our culture.

It is perfectly true that the disappearance of "inner-directed" manners has been accompanied by the emergence of "other-

directed" manners, and that we are already beginning to experience the effects of the major shift occurring in our social
structure, the formation of new patterns of behavior and the
rise of new social classes. To take one example alone, one
notices how the transferral of power from solitary man and
class man to "man among others" has added a new intensity
and dimension to our *relations* with others. Where once power
and status depended largely upon a man's individual worth,
the perfection of his individual talent, or his place in his class,
it has now come to depend more and more upon the success
of his momentary contacts with persons of influence, on the
status which, in their presence, he is able to confer upon himself through his geniality or the breadth of his conversational
knowledge in one evening over cocktails. That is probably
one of the reasons why we place so much stress on the care and
maintenance of our personalities, and why one of the greatest
crimes a person can commit today is failure to *appear* to be
warm and friendly. In a society where everybody is competent, or competent enough, and nobody really knows what any-
body else's true status is, everything depends on the impression
one makes with one's personality. That may also be the reason
why we have evolved a whole new convention of speech, a
convention which allows us to assert ourselves to others provided we *appear* always to be deferring to them, a convention
which allows us occasionally even to express an unpopular or
disturbing opinion, but always provided we take great care
to express it to the accompaniment of the affected stutter or
the telltale circling finger—the false symbols of our uncer-
tainty and fallibility, our talismanic assurances to others that
we really don't know any more about this than they do, that,

after all, we're just average, common people like they are, and, above all else, that we love them just the same. The development which has substituted conversation for communion, contrived geniality for true fellow feeling, and political hospitality for honest friendship is, indeed, a symptom of cultural change. But the question we must ask, the question the novel always asks, is to what end are these new struggles for status directed, by what philosophy or ideal of life are they motivated, and what use does the individual make of this status when he finally gets it? If he does nothing with it but retreat into it and go to sleep, if its gain or loss costs him nothing or changes him in no way, then the novel too must retreat or simply be left by itself to contemplate the depths of its own vacuity.

AUTHOR'S NOTE

SINCE the "Gray New World" essay was written, the novels which implicitly or explicitly affirm the conformist values of the new mass culture have become numerous enough to constitute very nearly a distinct fictional category. Both at the time of its appearance and afterward, Herman Wouk's *The Caine Mutiny* was repeatedly attacked for its conformist propaganda. Of the several critiques Harvey Swados's devastating *Partisan Review* essay was undoubtedly the best, in that it rendered superfluous all further efforts to pin down the causes both of Mr. Wouk's peculiar offensiveness in the novel and his remarkable public popularity—the two being, as Mr. Swados shows, quite obviously identical. The same causes apparently operate to the same ends in the case of *Marjorie Morningstar*. At any rate, one sees Mr. Wouk displaying his familiar and by now thoroughly ritualistic biases. The young intellectual Noel Airman is portrayed with fitting repulsiveness and is made to end his pretentious literary career in deserved third-rate mediocrity. The heroine, after flirting with the gay Bohemian life and paying for it with her virtue, finally settles down to a nice, respectable, motherly middle age in Mamaroneck. But as in *The Caine Mutiny* the popular appeal of *Marjorie Morningstar* does not reside solely, or perhaps even primarily, in such tired and simplified dramatic norms. Whatever one may think of Wouk, one must never underestimate the complexity of the mechanism which has made it possible for him to contact his audience and compel their immediate attention on such a variety of levels of response. As the *Caine Mutiny* audience was allowed to participate vicariously in both defiance of established authority—the relieving of Queeg—and a concluding affirmation of its necessity—the defense of Queeg—so the audience for the new novel is given the initial thrill of vicarious sex and rebellion and the restoring and cleansing palliative of sober respectability. By means of this formula, which one can be certain is unconsciously arrived at, Wouk makes it possible for his readers to drain off their secret frustrations and, at the same time, to think of the draining as harmless since it occurs within the affirming hierarchy of conventional conduct which both Wouk and polite society equally respect. Through his novels they can enjoy the forbidden pleasures of dangerous living and, in the very middle of the act, be assured that pleasureless respectability is the only worthwhile way of life, in short, that they are right to like what they are stuck with. The reverse is true of the majority of modern American novels which, as *Life* editorialists never tire of pointing out, are filled with sex, violence, and corruption, but which disturb the average reader by suggesting that he is somehow living too dull a life or has missed something vital in his past. The great service which Wouk performs for the peace of mind of the American public consists in his attributing to dullness and mediocrity the moral and esthetic virtue which other writers normally reserve for the dedicated and richly imaginative life, and in so doing he has become one of the first American writers to give the public both the courage and the moral obligation to be ordinary.

Still another example of the conformist trend in fiction is Sloan Wilson's *The Man in the Gray Flannel Suit,* a novel which, for the usual reasons, a *Life* editorialist recently found pleasing for its "affirmative" qualities. These qualities are of course obvious throughout the novel and can be held accountable for its popularity. They consist of easy "affirmations" of the status quo, the joys of community service, family life, being happy and contented. But the novel is far more instructive when read as a testimonial of the new American conservative philosophy, the shifts that have lately occurred in our success goals, the drastic changes that have transformed our collective pursuit of the productive life. The novel is, in a very real sense, a thinly fictional portrait of Riesman's gray new world. The hero is caught in a dilemma which fifty years ago would have been inconceivable: he must decide whether to pursue success, power, and wealth at the expense of his personal happiness or to content himself with a small, subordinate job which will allow him to spend time with his family, his house, his front lawn, his car, and his community. The problem is of course not a difficult one nor very long in the solution. In fact, the novel dramatizes the solution before it is fairly under way. The hero's employer is a prototype of the old-fashioned tycoon, left over from the era of economic expansion before dictatorship and paternalism in industry succumbed to fraternalism and manipulation. And the employer is clearly no longer the sort of man one should take one's bearings on. With all his power, wealth, and prestige he is miserably unhappy, estranged from his wife and his daughter, incapable of finding meaning in his life. He is a tragic example to those who would think to aspire and succeed, the perfect witness of the cultural death of Horatio Alger. The only answer for the hero is happy compromise, and when he assents to it, he receives his reward; he *becomes* happy; his wife and children love him once again; he is recognized as a man of importance in his community; he begins to *live*. And so we find ourselves back where we started, in the good old Woukean world. It would be pleasant to be able to detect in it all some dark Republican conspiracy, but there is none. It was merely inevitable at this point in our national development, when we have grown accustomed to having what we want, that we should also produce writers like Wouk and Wilson who are able and willing to sell us what we like to hear.

FIVE

The society of three novels

I ASSUME THAT the questions concerning fiction which most urgently press upon us at this time are these: first, the question of the method by which serious works of fiction show forth their seriousness to us, enable us to recognize them as significant and dramatic, in the degree of their removal from mere lifelikeness; and second, the apparently, but only apparently, contradictory question of the relationship obtaining between the social milieu of serious fiction—the milieu in which the lifelikeness of the unserious usually begins and ends—and the milieu of artifice, implication, ambiguity, paradox, and irony which serious fiction may be said to constitute—the milieu which replaces lifelikeness, life unarranged, with an illusion of life rearranged and invested with order and newly displayed in the terms of significant form. I assume, further, that in seeking an answer to these questions we accept as something given, constant, and essentially impenetrable the factor of talent or genius, and that, therefore, we shall be concerned with only those elements which may be supposed to be available to talent or genius in the world outside the work and to come into fiction only after the operation of talent or genius begins. The problem of the "quality of the mind of the producer," as James put it, is a mysterious one, for we can know that quality only through the quality of the work it accomplishes, and cannot know what minds of quality in any time were unable to accomplish or how much more they might have accomplished had they had the advantage of a more congenial time. But what we can know is the kind of materials which in the past minds of quality seemed typically to need and which they seemed typically to exploit with best results, and we can then apply that knowledge to our own time. Our question, then, will not be the quality of the mind behind the work, but the quality of the world before the mind, and the uses which the mind seems able to make of that world. It is true that the quality of the mind behind the work may still be measured in our own time in the uses to which it can put the world it has before it, but this comes to us most often in one of those forms of damage and distortion, of disparity between content and force, insight and significance, which record all too clearly the consequences of creative power set loose amid paucity and required to make up too strenuously out of its own resources the dramatic materials that ought by rights to be provided by the world before it.

In attempting to formulate an approach to these questions I have selected for analysis three novels of recognized merit published over the last several years. They are J. D. Salinger's *The Catcher in the Rye*, Saul Bellow's *The Adventures of Augie March*, and William Styron's *Lie Down in Darkness*. I have chosen these novels not only because I believe them to be serious and, in their different ways, dramatically significant, but because each has enjoyed a certain notoriety and a certain position of esteem in the popular criticism of the day. It is by now taken for granted that a new novel of discernible merit—it being so rare and remarkable a phenomenon—will automatically be received in the market place with an amount of acclaim greater than it deserves and that a halo of nearly religious luminosity will tend to settle around it, obscuring its real nature in magnification of its virtue, so that it appears in time to exist in a condition of permanent moral elephantiasis. No one, as a rule, feels himself entitled to examine such a work after this ailment sets in—in fear, one supposes, of discovering the ailment to be merely psychogenic in origin— and since we have no higher board of criticism before which the work is required to pass, it usually proceeds on its way to distinction or extinction firmly capsulated and virginal. In the case of these three novels, which have already, at least officially, been sent on their way, I have intended to violate this practice, cut through the luminous halo enclosing them, and see them in a fresh perspective, first, in order to mitigate as much as I can the inflamed judgment imposed upon them by a criticism which is resigned to grading perpetually on the curve, and, second, in order to discover what facts they will yield to help us arrive at an answer to the questions which I raised in the beginning. In choosing these novels specifically, I have been guided, finally, by the assumption that each con-

ceals in its heart more than an ordinary obligation to the society in which we now live, each has to do with problems of
value and belief peculiar to this society, and each represents
an approach to the problem of dramatizing value and belief
through the notation of social manners.

Mr. Salinger's *The Catcher in the Rye,* like *The Adventures
of Huckleberry Finn,* is a study in the spiritual picaresque, the
journey that for the young is all one way, from holy innocence
to such knowledge as the world offers, from the reality which
illusion demands and thinks it sees to the illusion which
reality insists, at the point of madness, we settle for. But the
great difference between the two novels is the measure not
merely of the change in time and history of a cultural situation, but of the changed moral circumstances in which innocence typically finds itself in crisis and lends itself to drama.
The innocence of *Huckleberry Finn* is a compound of frontier
ignorance, juvenile delinquency, and penny-dreadful heroism.
It begs for the challenge of thugs, thieves, swindlers, and
feuds, and that is what it gets and delights in, takes such delight in, in fact, that even when the dangers become real and
the escapes increasingly narrow, we know it is all in fun, that
this is innocence living out its concocted daydream of glory in
which no one really gets hurt, and even the corpses climb
to their feet and dust themselves off at dinnertime. Still, in the
suspension of our disbelief, in the planned illusion of the novel
itself, the innocence and the world of violence appear to be
seriously and effectively opposed. The innocence is the raft
to which Huck and Jim, in flight from the dangers of the shore,
make their narrow escapes. It is the river itself, time, faith,

continuity, moving endlessly and dependably beside and between the temporary and futile altercations of men. And it is
the raft and the river together which give the innocence of
Huckleberry Finn its focus and breadth of implication, so that
it exists at once on the level of naïveté at which it responds
to adventure and on the level of maturity at which it lends
itself to allegory.

The innocence of Mr. Salinger's Holden Caulfield, on the
other hand, is a compound of urban intelligence, juvenile contempt, and *New Yorker* sentimentalism, and the only challenge it begs for, the only challenge it has left to beg for, is the
challenge of the genuine, the truly human, in a world which
has lost both the means of adventure and the means of love. But
it is in the nature of Holden's dilemma, his spiritual confine-
ment in this world, that he lacks a concrete basis, can find no
concrete embodiment, for the ideal against which he judges,
and finds wanting, the life around him. He has objects for his
contempt but no objects other than his sister for his love—
no raft, no river, no Jim, and no Tom. He is forced, consequently, simply to register his contempt, his developing disillusionment; and it is inevitable that he should seem after a
time to be registering it in a vacuum, for just as he can find
no concrete equivalent in life for the ideal which he wishes
life to embody, so the persons on whom he registers his contempt seem inadequate to it and unjustly accused by it. The
boorish prep school roommate, the hypocritical teacher, the
stupid women in the Lavender Room, the resentful prostitute,
the conventional girl friend, the bewildered cab driver, the
affected young man at the theater, the old friend who reveals
that his interest in Holden is homosexual—these people are all

truly objectionable and deserve the places Holden assigns
them in his secret hierarchy of class with its categories of
phonies, bores, deceivers, and perverts. But they are nonetheless human, albeit dehumanized, and constitute a fair average
of what the culture affords. They are part of the truth which
Holden does not see and, as it turns out, is never able to see—
that this is what one part of humanity *is;* the lies, the phoni-
ness, the hypocrisy are the compromises which innocence is
forced by the world to make. This is the reality on which
Holden's illusion is finally broken, but no recognition follows,
and no conversion. He remains at the end what he was at the
beginning—cynical, defiant, and blind. And as for ourselves,
there is identification but no insight, a sense of pathos but
not of tragedy. It may be that Mr. Salinger made the most
of his subject, but his subject was not adequate to his intention, just as Holden's world is not adequate to his contempt,
and that is probably because it does not possess sufficient humanity to make the search for humanity dramatically feasible.

Mr. Saul Bellow's *The Adventures of Augie March* is still
another study in the spiritual picaresque, a later form of
the traditional *bildungsroman* in which the *pícaro* or hero
is consciousness rather than swashbuckling rogue, and so is
required, as the rogue is not, to develop, deepen, strike through
its first illusion to the truth which, at the end of the road, it
discovers to be its fate. But *Augie March* begins with the
aphorism, "Man's character is his fate," and it ends with the
aphorism transposed "man's fate is his character." The learning is in the transposition. Man's fate is that he shall inherit, be stuck with, his character. The movement which the

transposition represents is the movement from the naturalistic to the existentialist, from what is determined to what is accepted or chosen. Augie at the end of the road simply comes into his destiny, although, as it happens, it is not the destiny, the alternative to the "disappointed life," for which he sought. It is the destiny which his character fated, and so, like the rogues of literature in the past, he is not changed but confirmed. I suspect we accept this in those earlier rogues because, having recognized their qualities of character at the outset, we turn our attention to the manner in which these qualities display themselves from adventure to adventure, and find there a confirmation of what we recognized. The emphasis is not on what the hero becomes but on what he does and the bizarreness and excitement of what he does. We know, besides, that his destiny, when it is achieved, will be a formula and a fake—a magical inheritance, a last-minute revelation of noble birth, the conquest of beauty, a "happily ever after." The drama is in the adventure, our interest in being titillated and duped. But the problem which immediately presents itself in the case of Augie is that while his adventures are formed in the pattern of the traditional picaresque, his character demands exposition through the developing form of the more modern *bildungsroman*. He is a Stephen Dedalus set adrift in a world made for Moll Flanders or a Jonathan Wild. As a man with a mission, he is required to impose his will on his experience, to subdue or be subdued, and so to change. But Mr. Bellow feels his obligation to the picaresque too strongly, particularly to the requirement that he who begins as a *pícaro* must end as a *pícaro,* and so we are left at the end with the mission unfulfilled, the will unimposed, the man unsubdued.

To have been an altogether successful adaptation of the picaresque form, the novel would have had to consist of a series of episodes recounting high adventure and intrigue, with an overlay of equally high comedy and social satire. We would then have been placed in the position to appreciate and find full satisfaction in the quality of the adventure and in the confirmation of what we already knew to be Augie's character as he engaged the adventure. But the adventure in the novel as it stands is neither high enough nor rich enough to be a justification of the whole, and we are struck more by Augie's isolation from than by his participation in the social scene of satire. That is, in fact, the necessity which the theme of the novel imposes upon him. He must be disengaged because he must hold out. As the novel develops, we begin to notice, furthermore, as we notice in *Catcher in the Rye,* that the social scene tends to become rarefied and increasingly inspecific. It is not a proper subject for the traditional picaresque satire of the foibles and frailties of class, although the novel does contain many excellent portraits of people. The class structure is simply not there to be satirized, except insofar as the status of individuals is related to money. What one sees is simply the rich and the poor, and these consequently become the poles of commitment between which Augie vacillates. It is interesting to see, however, that the novel in its early sections partakes of some of the dramatic advantages arising out of the racial and economic tensions of lower-class urban experience, a type of experience which in the twenties and thirties was much more common to our larger cities than it is now. The Depression experience alone, in fact, provides Mr. Bellow with nearly all the social and class materials he has, as well as with the perspective of under-privilege from which to judge those materials. But in the early sections we are plunged into a crowded and fully developed world, alive with discord and tensions. There are Augie's mother, his brothers Simon and Georgie, and Grandma Lausch, the Kinsmans, the Coblins, the Kleins, Bluegren and Clem Tambow, the Einhorns, the Commissioner, Kreindl, and Dingbat. But later on, as Augie matures, this world is left behind, the tensions slacken, the social scene becomes depopulated, and we move from a closely interacting mass of people to isolated personalities—the Renlings, the Fenchels, Cissy Flexner, Padilla, Mimi Villars, Hooker Frazer, the Magnuses, then Thea Fenchel, the millionaire Robey, Kayo Obermark, Mintouchian, Basteshaw, and finally Stella. And as this development occurs, the narrative slows and thins out, and Augie's pilgrimage becomes merely a horizontal and unmotivated progression through experience. It also becomes less and less clear precisely what Augie's real problem is. We know that he has, as he says, a lot of opposition in him and that he refuses to lead a "disappointed life." Like Holden Caulfield he wants a life in which he can accept the full risks of his humanity, but he also wants a specific fate and function, a destiny worthy of his talents and ideals. In David Riesman's terms, he appears, at first glance, to be an "inner-directed" man holding out against the conformist pressures of an "other-directed" society, but it would be truer to say that he is "inner-directed" in temperament but not in aim and that he is holding out against an "inner-directed" society of strongly ambitious and acquisitive aims, the kind of society which we had in this country up until roughly the beginning of World War II. Nevertheless, the point of Augie's life, the point of his resistance, and, therefore, his point as a character, are all strongly ambiguous. He holds out, but in the name of what we never really know.

There is a sense in which it might be argued that Augie both as a character and as a social type is an example of what happens when the individual loses, or is unable to find, a moral purpose, an "inner-directed" goal. All of Augie's adventures are, in a way, pragmatic conquests, attempts to confirm through the application again and again of the test of experience a truth and a vision of reality which ought to come from within and be imposed upon experience. His situation is such that he is able to see validity everywhere, particularly in the lives which those around him have settled for. But the problem he poses as a fictional character is that, as a man committed to nothing, he can have no dramatic centrality; his conflict with society can never be really intense or meaningful because there is nothing at stake, no price of spiritual opposition which might endow him with tragic or pathetic value. This, it seems to me, is the vitiating paradox behind him and his story as a whole. He is empty and without commitment and, in keeping with the rule of decorum and the truth of his social situation and Mr. Bellow's theme, he must be so. But his emptiness is his dramatic ruin, just as it is the ruin of nearly all the characters in recent American fiction. The force of the fall from innocence, of the failure of an heroic design, has given way to the surly spasm of futility and what has been called "the merely middle-class emotion of embarrassment."

It is perhaps because Mr. Bellow subconsciously sensed Augie's inadequacy as a character that he sought through his style to impose upon his material an almost fearsome significance, a disguise of acute profundity, allusion, and paradox, suggesting that behind or above the people of the novel there hangs a thick cloud of metaphysical, philosophical, and historical truth in relation to which their thoughts and actions have meanings more sublime than any that may appear on the surface. One can in fact say that it is the style alone that preserves the novel from the purely naturalistic stereotype, that keeps it from being simply a chronicle of the adventures of an educated Studs Lonigan. It is the style, in particular, which suggests through its images and metaphors that there is a philosophically informed dimension to Augie's development. It creates around him an aura of speculation and examination, so that throughout nearly the whole of his progress, we continue to believe that he is truly engaged in a struggle to choose among fantastically complicated metaphysical alternatives, and that at the end his revelation and ours will come. But as the concrete basis for Augie's development moves farther and farther away from the gaseous invertebrate metaphysic of the style, the style is forced to accomplish more and more, until finally it is required to create all the meaning out of its own resources and to state more meaning than exists in the subject or the scene to be stated.

In the opening sections of the novel the burden imposed upon the style does not strike us as excessive because the world which the style describes is crowded with action and people. There are nevertheless clear symptoms of the excess to come. Here, from the first chapter, is a description of Mr. Kreindl:

He was an old-time Austro-Hungarian conscript, and there was something soldierly about him: a neck that had strained with pushing artillery wheels, a campaigner's red in the face, a powerful bite in his jaw and gold-crowned teeth, green cockeyes and soft short hair, altogether Napoleonic. His feet slanted out on the ideal of Frederick the Great, but he was about a foot under the required height for guardsmen.

And here is one of Grandma Lausch:

She took her cigarette case out from under her shawl, she cut a Murad in half with her sewing scissors and picked up the holder. This was still at a time when women did not smoke. Save the intelligentsia—the term she applied to herself. With the holder in her dark little gums between which all her guile, malice, and command issued, she had her best inspirations of strategy. She was as wrinkled as an old paper bag, an autocrat, hard-shelled and jesuitical, a pouncy old hawk of a Bolshevik, her small ribboned gray feet immobile on the shoekit and stool Simon had made in the manual-training class, dingy old wool Winnie, whose bad smell filled the flat, on the cushion beside her.

All this is feverish and overdescribed. The style is aware of so much, so much more than it needs to be aware of, that we feel we are in the presence of monsters. Mr. Kreindl, in particular, is observed so minutely and horrendously that we are carried beyond him into a veritable thicket of gold teeth, strained necks, and green cockeyes. But at this point in the novel the observer is so close to the material, and the material is so thick that we tend to disregard these excesses. Later on, however, when the material thins out, the strain becomes noticeable and offensive. This is especially true of those passages in which the style, lacking the support of specific environmental detail, is required to bear by itself the weight of philosophical speculation. Here is an example from Chapter XXII:

I have a feeling [Augie says] about the axial lines of life, with respect to which you must be straight or else your existence is merely clownery, hiding tragedy. I must have had a feeling since I was a kid about these axial lines which made me want to have my existence on them, and so I have said "no" like a stubborn fellow to all my persuaders, just on the obstinacy of my memory of these lines, never entirely clear. But lately I have felt these thrilling lines again. When striving stops, there they are as a gift. I was lying on the couch here before and they suddenly went quivering right straight through me. Truth, love, peace, bounty, usefulness, harmony! And all noise and grates, distortion, chatter, distraction, effort, superfluity, passed off like something unreal. And I believe that any man at any time can come back to these axial lines, even if an unfortunate bastard, if he will be quiet and wait it out. The ambition of something special and outstanding I have always had is only a boast that distorts this knowledge from its origin, which is the oldest language, older than the Euphrates, older than the Ganges. At any time life can come together again and man be regenerated, and doesn't have to be a god or public servant like Osiris who gets torn apart annually for the sake of the common prosperity, but the man himself, finite and taped as he is, can still come where the axial lines are. He will be brought into focus. He will live with true joy. Even his pains will be joy if they are true, even his helplessness will not take away his power, even wandering will not take him away from himself, even the big social jokes and hoaxes need not make him ridiculous, even disappointment after disappointment need not take away his love. Death will not be terrible to him if life is not. The embrace of other true people will take away his dread of fast change and short life.

This passage does not raise a question of agreement or disagreement, but it does raise a question of the divisibility of theme and content. We can safely assume that we have here a statement of an important element of the theme which Mr.

Bellow supposed his novel to be developing. There is little evidence in the novel itself, however, that his supposition is correct. This is, in fact, the secret which the abstractness of the style reveals. It is abstract because there exists no specific emotional or social experience to give it body and concreteness. The style is forced to compensate for the insufficiency of the experience on which it is intended to comment by bringing into play such concepts as "truth, love, peace, bounty, usefulness, and harmony," and these, in their irrelevance to the comment of the action itself, testify to the excess of theme over content and the inability of content to meet the responsibility imposed on it by the theme. If Mr. Bellow could have been satisfied simply with the adventures of his hero, with the form which the picaresque tradition made available to him, he would have avoided this problem altogether. But as a serious writer with a strong sense of his responsibility to the issues of our time, he insisted upon trying to do more, and what more he tried to do is expressed in the imperfect union of his theme and his material, his philosophical intention and the incapacity of his material to body it forth; and that is as much a fault of his experience of his time as it is of his talent.

To come at this experience directly and to deal with it with complete success in the novel is perhaps beyond the power of any novelist now living. A more indirect approach appears to be necessary, an approach in which the amount of experience seen is limited by a parochial view, a knowledge of the world in small, which, if faithfully rendered and thoroughly penetrated, may be made to represent the modern world in large. It is the necessity for such a knowledge that probably explains why so many of our younger novelists are writing today out of the Southern experience and tradition. The South for the past several years has been in the phase of social and economic development in which it stands in a sense as an analogical miniature of the situation of America as a whole. It displays in extravagant form all the tensions, conflicts, and evolutionary processes which brought us to our present condition; and its peculiar virtue for the novelist is that, while these processes have, for the most part, worked themselves out elsewhere in the country, they continue to operate in the South and continue, therefore, to throw into sharply dramatic juxtaposition those elements of natural setting, traditional conduct, class disorientation, and personal morality which help to constitute the generalizing power of a literature. The agrarian background and traditional social arrangement of the South have given it an abundance of distinct class types, each with separate manners and histories, and to these have been added new types produced out of the belated Southern industrial revolution. Taken together, these tend to make for discord, bizarre and ludicrous relationships, incongruities of class displacement and propinquity, all of which are again productive of dramatic material.

In an early issue of *The Paris Review* Mr. William Styron was asked to comment on this general question of the South in relation to the state of literature at the present time. His interviewers inquired if he thought it was true that in most of the so-called Southern novels the reactions of the characters are universal. Mr. Styron replied that

. . . that universal quality comes far more from a single writer's mind and his individual spirit than from his background. Faulkner is a writer of extraordinary stature more because of the great breadth of his vision than because he happened to be born in Mississippi. All you have to do is read one issue of the *Times Book Review* to see how much junk comes out regularly from south of the Mason-Dixon line, along with the good stuff. I have to admit, though, that the South has a definite literary tradition, which is the reason it probably produces a better quality of writing, proportionately. Perhaps it's just true that Faulkner, if he had been born in, say, Pasadena, might very well still have had that universal quality of mind, *but* instead of writing *Light in August* he would have gone into television or written universal ads for Jantzen bathing suits.

Mr. Styron was asked next why he thought the Southern literary tradition exists at all.

Well, first [he said] there's that old heritage of biblical rhetoric and story-telling. Then the South simply provides such wonderful material. Take, for instance, the conflict between the ordered Protestant tradition, the fundamentalism based on the Old Testament, and the Twentieth Century—movies, cars, television. The poetic juxtaposition you find in this conflict—a crazy colored preacher howling those tremendously moving verses from *Isaiah,* 40, while riding around in a maroon Packard. It's wonderful stuff and comparatively new, too, which is perhaps why the renaissance of Southern writing coincided with the last few decades of the machine age. If Faulkner had written in the 1880's he would have been writing no doubt safely within the tradition, but his novels would have been genteel novels, like those of George Washington Cable or Thomas Nelson Page. In fact, the modern South is such powerful material that the author runs the danger of capturing the local color and feeling that's enough. He gets so bemused by decaying mansions that he forgets to populate them with people. I'm beginning to feel that it's a good idea for writers who come from the South, at least some of them, to break away a little from all them magnolias.

A few years ago *The Hopkins Review,* which was headquartered in Baltimore and had, therefore, a natural bias, con-

ducted a lengthy symposium on the situation of letters in the
South, parts of which were later published in book form under
the title *Southern Renaissance.* In the course of the discussion
the question of the source of Faulkner's genius was repeatedly
raised and, as might be expected, repeatedly answered in a
way that reflected most favorably on the advantages of his
Southern birth and upbringing. While I did not entirely sub-
scribe to some of the opinions that were brought forward, I
was sufficiently caught up in the spirit of the occasion to try
out the subject on a Southern friend of mine. "What is it that
Faulkner has?" I asked him. "Great talent, yes, but also close
and living contact with just about the only culture left in
America where people still have personality, still live by a sem-
blance of order and dogma, and are, therefore, easily translata-
ble into fictional terms. Or for another example, take Penn
Warren's *All the King's Men.* Go through it page by page
and try to decide where it gets its great quality of life. From
image after image, scene after scene, depicting the richness
and complexity and color and tension of Southern life pretty
much as it actually exists and, of course, as it impinges upon
and is dramatized within the sensibility of Jack Burden."
My friend countered with a question: "Where do you think all
this richness and complexity and color and tension *is?*" My
answer today would be: in the novel. That is the only place
it can possibly be if it is to exist and we are ever to get at
it. But where it began by being was in the quality and content of Penn Warren's creative imagination. *All the King's
Men* was simply the symbolic and verbal vesture of what that
imagination was able to imagine and project into artistic form.
But the creative imagination cannot exist and continue to

imagine in a vacuum, although as we look about us it may appear that a great many imaginations are struggling to do so. It must have access of a deeply generic kind to a body of living experience from which it can derive its dramatic energy and the materials for the images it produces. It must always form, with the raw shapes and appearances of the natural world, as well as with the structured and mannered life of men in the social world, a working partnership which does not differ fundamentally from the sort of partnership so vulgarly exploited by the imagination of the writer of cheap journalism.

This is to say that while I am absolutely certain that Charlotte Brontë wrote *Jane Eyre,* I am equally certain that nineteenth-century Calvinist England coauthored it. On the other hand, while I have good evidence for believing that a person named James Jones actually exists, I continue to believe, on the far greater evidence of his novel *From Here to Eternity,* that James Jones is really a pseudonym for the peacetime United States Army. As for Faulkner and Warren, I attribute the coauthorship of their novels to the South, which, aside from certain ailing portions of the moral universe of New England, happens to be the only section of the country left where, as I have said, there is still a living tradition and a usable myth, where there are still vestiges of an entrenched class authority upon which it is possible, to the great benefit of the novelist, for Northerners to encroach, and where, against the background of Spanish moss, scrub pines, broken-down shanties, and deserted mansions, the suffering of the Negro provides the framework of guilt so essential to our peculiar brand of modern tragedy.

One might in fact say that the only really new vitality to

enter the American novel since the war years has been provided by the South, particularly through the work of those writers who have been concerned with it in its relation to the experience of childhood. I suspect that there are a number of good reasons why this is so, not the least of them being the fact that many of the writers I speak of—Carson McCullers, for example, and Mr. Styron, Truman Capote, and William Goyen— grew up in the South and, now that they are in exile from it, have cause to remember that they had their most intense imaginative life there. In the South it seems that the sensitive child is faced early in life with a grim alternative: either he must live inside his imagination a great part of the time, or he must surely go mad. The South hurts him into the habits of mind congenial to fiction, precisely as mad Ireland hurt William Butler Yeats into poetry. This may explain why it appears that nearly every Southerner who preserves his sanity into adulthood emigrates to New York and becomes a novelist.

Of course almost any experience is dramatic to a sensitive child, and in times of crisis and confusion, when the mature world has become too muddled or frightened or hypocritical to be easily presented in fiction, writers have always taken advantage of the dramatic resources of childhood. But just any childhood will not do. Everything depends on where it is spent. One notices, for instance, how much better a novel Mrs. McCullers was able to make out of the childhoods of her little girls in *The Heart Is a Lonely Hunter* and *Member of the Wedding* than Mr. Salinger was able to make out of the gawky Northern adolescence of Holden Caulfield. Holden's irreverent sensibility is posed against a moral world of New York urban life which scarcely exists dramatically because it is neither very moral nor very tangible. But Mrs. McCullers's characters, however unsatisfactory they may be in other respects, are always located in a world. F. Jasmine in *Member of the Wedding* does little more than sit on a lap through a large part of the book, but at least the lap she sits on belongs to a Negro maid, and that anchors her in the center of a way of life. In *The Heart Is a Lonely Hunter,* Mrs. McCullers's finest novel, the girl Mick is not only anchored; she is hemmed in on all sides by characters out of native Southern life who are symbolic extensions of her central difficulty, which is loneliness. Unlike Holden Caulfield she has a whole set of suitable dramatic equivalents for her feelings. The stage for her is crowded with people, and around and behind them she has the great vitality, richness, and oddity of the Southern spirit and environment to react to and escape from. This same spirit and environment, furthermore, form the content of the magnificently sensitive prose in which her story is presented. The scene describing the deaf-mute Singer's train trip, for example, could not have been written without the South, if only because it is largely the South which the scene describes.

Outside the dirty windows there was the brilliant midsummer countryside. The sun slanted in strong, bronze-colored rays over the green fields of the new cotton. There were acres of tobacco, the plants heavy and green like some monstrous jungle weed. The orchards of peaches with the lush fruit weighting down the dwarfed trees. There were miles of pastures and tens of miles of wasted, washed-out land abandoned to the hardier weeds. The train cut through deep green pine forests where the ground was covered with the slick brown needles and the tops of the trees stretched up virgin and tall into the sky. And farther, a long way south of the town, the cypress swamps—with the gnarled roots of the trees writhing down into the brackish waters, where tropical water flowers blossomed in dankness and gloom. Then out again into the open beneath the sun and the indigo-blue sky.

This is no mere description of landscape. In the final sense, it is a moral commentary, and it is possible only in a place where landscape and the evil of the human heart still retain their primitive moral connection.

Mr. Styron, who is to my mind the most accomplished member of the younger group of Southern novelists, has repeatedly argued that his *Lie Down in Darkness* could have been set in any section of the country. He says in the interview from which I have previously quoted: "Only certain things in the book are particularly Southern. I used leit-motifs—the Negroes, for example—that run throughout the book, but I would like to believe that my people would have behaved the way they did anywhere. The girl Peyton, for instance, didn't have to come from Virginia. She would have wound up jumping from a window no matter where she came from." It seems to me that one reading of his novel is enough to convince one that Mr. Styron is quite mistaken. The Southern elements of the novel—particularly the elements of fundamentalist religion, regionalist guilt, and the contrast of races—are, in fact, so powerful that if anything they seem excessive to the motives of the characters and perpetually to overpower them. This is one of the ways in which *Lie Down in Darkness* differs from *The Adventures of Augie March*. In the latter, the action which Augie takes is insufficient to the philosophical motive which Mr. Bellow attributes to him. In the former, the characters are swept along by a complex of forces stronger than motive and beyond or beneath philosophy. The domestic tensions of misunderstanding and jealousy are only the ostensi-

ble causes of the disintegration of the Loftis family. Behind
them are larger and more insidious disorders. Behind Milton's
father-guilt and incest-guilt is the whole Southern blood-guilt.
Behind Helen's jealousy and Puritanism is the timeless
Southern gentlewoman madness, the madness that comes
from too much in-breeding, too much Negro fear, too
much sexual neglect. Behind Peyton's father-complex is a
century of paternalism and man-hatred and sexual masochism.
And all these drive the Loftises to ruin and give them a
dramatic size and intensity greater than in themselves they
have any right to possess. Around them, furthermore, is the
Southern environment, an environment crowded, as it is for
Mrs. McCullers, with objects and instances evocative of evil,
hence, expressive and correlative of their own evil.

 Halfway between the railroad station and Port Warwick proper
. . . the marshland, petering out in disconsolate, solitary clumps
of cattails, yields gradually to higher ground. Here, bordering the
road, an unsightly growth of weeds takes over, brambles and briars
of an uncertain dirty hue which, as if with terrible exertion, have
struggled through the clay to flourish now in stunted gray profusion,
bending and shaking in the wind. The area adjacent to this stretch
of weeds is bleakly municipal in appearance: it can be seen from the
road, and in fact the road eventually curves and runs through it.
Here there are great mounds of garbage; a sweet vegetable odor
rises perpetually on the air and one can see—from the distance
faintly iridescent—whole swarms of carnivorous flies blackening the
garbage and maybe a couple of proprietary rats, propped erect like
squirrels, and blinking sluggishly, with mild, infected eyes, at some
horror-stricken Northern tourist. . . . Below was a brackish creek,
foul with sewage and hostile to all life save for great patches of algae
the color of green pea soup, where dragonflies darted and hovered,
suspended from the sunny air as if by invisible threads . . . somewhere there had been a silly story about the creek—about a Negro

convict who had fallen into the stream and been drowned and who, since the body, mysteriously, was never recovered, had reappeared from the creek at night on each anniversary of his death, covered with scum and slobbering horribly at the mouth as he prowled the town in search of beautiful white women to ravish and to drag back to the unspeakable depths of his grave.

This is the natural material with which the South provides Styron. Through it he is able to respond to and project back into language those intricate relationships between fictional setting and human agony which, at least since Hardy's heath and Conrad's sea, have formed the heart of some of our finest novels. Opposed to this world, in the moral terms of the novel, is the world of the urban North, the world of discontinuity, loneliness, psychoanalysis, nervous breakdown, the world you are exiled to and give up your sanity to, the world in which the environment has nothing to do with the self or with feeling or with life. It is significant that it is after she marries and goes North that Peyton becomes overtly psychotic, undergoes treatment, then kills herself. It is also significant that the section of the novel having to do with her Northern experience is presented in the form of interior monologue. The environment now has no relation to the personal world. The only sense of identity one can get is through talking to one's self. This is the environment at the back of both *Catcher in the Rye* and *The Adventures of Augie March;* and it is perhaps only a slight oversimplification to say that had it been richer, more complicated, more personal, and more dramatic, those novels would have possessed a texture of scene and place more nearly in keeping with the texture of their portraits of people and their philosophical implications.

SIX

Hemingway: the etiquette of the berserk

I MUST CONFESS that I was unable to share in the generally wild enthusiasm occasioned by the appearance of Hemingway's most recent book, *The Old Man and the Sea*. It was indeed a remarkable advance over his previous novel, *Across the River and into the Trees;* and it had a purity of line and a benignity, a downright saintliness, of tone which seemed to indicate not merely that he had sloughed off his former emotional fattiness, but that he had expanded and deepened his spiritual perspective in a way that we could not help but find extraordinary. But one must take care not to push these generosities too far, if only because they spill over so easily into that excess of blind charity we all tend to feel for Hemingway each time he pulls out of another slump and attains to the heroism of simply writing well once again. It should be possible for us to honor him for his amazing recuperative powers and

149

his new talent for quasi-religious revelation and still be able
to see that it is not for either of these qualities that his new
book must finally be valued, but for the degree of its success
in meeting the standards set down by his own best previous
achievement as an artist. I have these standards in mind when
I say that *The Old Man and the Sea* seems to me a work
of distinctly minor Hemingway fiction.

I came to this conclusion after noticing, first of all, that the
style of the book, in spite of its antiseptic clarity and restraint,
is oddly colorless and flat, as if there were nothing sufficiently
strong within its subject to resist it at any point and provoke it
into fully alert dramatic life. In the best of the early Hemingway one always felt that the prose had been forced out under
great pressure through a tight screen of opposing psychic
tensions; and one read it with the same taut apprehensiveness,
the same premonition of hugely impending catastrophe, as
that with which it was written—quite as if one were picking
one's way with the author through an uncleared minefield of
language. But now the prose—to change the figure once again
—has a fabricated quality, as if it had been shipped into the
book by some manufacturer of standardized Hemingway parts.

It soon becomes clear, however, that this weakness of style
is merely a symptom of a far more serious weakness in the
thematic possibilities of the material itself. The theme of the
strong man—Harry Morgan, Colonel Cantwell, or Santiago—
struggling to survive amid the hostile pressures of a purely
physical world has never been the central theme of Hemingway's greatest fiction; in fact, when one thinks back over his
recent novels, one is tempted to conclude that it fails him
miserably as a central theme each time he tries to use it in any-

thing more ambitious than a short story. What has always served Hemingway best has been the theme of the shell-shocked, traumatic hero struggling through his code of conduct to preserve himself not from physical but from psychic destruction. This was the theme of his great early work; and it provided him with a formula for dramatic success on which he has never been able to improve.

In the relatively few years since American criticism began devoting serious attention to the contemporary novel, we have learned to be content with two standard approaches to the problem of Hemingway and the code of his hero. The first approach treats of the code as an index of Hemingway's moral perversion, his dumb-ox compromise with the demands of a healthily intellectual and ethical life. The second treats of it as an etiquette of burly fastidiousness by means of which his characters survive in a universe made monstrous by the death of all reasonable, beneficent gods.

For the purposes of rational discussion it should be possible to rule the first approach out of order, simply as an early superficial approach that was not very sensible. But when we come to the second, we discover ourselves in the predicament of having to grant it sense at the same time that we find it wanting in real sensibility. The fact of the matter is that the approach to the code as merely etiquette will kill us yet, if we do not realize soon that the code may be taken as etiquette only at first glance, that in the final consideration what is etiquette for the characters is for Hemingway the artistic convention or formula out of which his novels derive their richest and subtlest effects of dramatic irony.

When Wyndham Lewis observed that the typical Heming-

) is a man "things are done to," he was undoubtedly
, of the impression we get of that hero as we watch
fering and enduring through the course of the typical
Hemingway novel. But if we are to understand the operation
of the code as both etiquette and dramatic formula, we must
begin farther back than Lewis began and conceive of the
hero not merely as a man "things are done to" but as a man
to whom a great many things have already been done. This
is a more precise description of him as he appears to us at
the opening of the typical Hemingway novel; and it is here, in
the peculiar effects upon him of things already done, of suffering already endured, long before the commencement of any
suffering he may be required to endure in the novel itself, that
we discover our first clue to the mystery of the code.

For Hemingway's two best heroes, Jake Barnes and Frederic Henry, this antecedent suffering was the result of war;
and the effect of this suffering was first physical and then
psychic trauma. Jake is introduced at the beginning of *The
Sun Also Rises* as having been sexually mutilated by a wound.
At the beginning of *A Farewell to Arms* Frederic has already
spent two strenuous years at the front. Each has been initiated
by violence, Jake through direct physical contact with it and
Frederic through long vicarious association with it; and each
has made his separate peace, his private adjustment to the
problem of survival. Onto the background of incessant war
they have both learned to project an artificial system of checks
and balances, a kind of psychic radar screen composed of
propitiatory rituals and sacred signs, which, if rigorously
maintained, will preserve them at least temporarily from destruction. There is, of course, no ultimate escape from the

violence against which their defenses are raised; for it is both
universal and abstract, and it is completely unselective in its
choice of victims. "It kills the very good and the very gentle
and the very brave impartially. If you are none of these you
can be sure it will kill you too but there will be no special
hurry." All one can do in the face of such indiscriminate
killing is make certain that one is not very good or very
gentle or very brave; and, luckily, that is exactly the assurance
that the code provides.

Within the magic circle of the code Jake and Frederic are
permitted the luxury of retaining intact the values of a successful life. They may believe in love, honor, goodness, truth,
gentleness, dignity, and bravery; for these are actually the
values on which the code is founded. But the code is required
to function amid the harsh facts of reality; and the harshest
fact of all is that, however good these values may be in themselves, they can never with safety be openly asserted in a
world dominated by a lawless violence. Jake and Frederic
may possess these values, but only so long as they possess them
implicitly and say nothing about them, or are careful to express them concretely and only in ways that have been ritualized by the code—as, for example, in sexual intercourse, which
is ritualized love, or in simple, manly forbearance, which is
ritualized goodness and dignity, or in bullfighting, which is
ritualized bravery and a way of courting death with honor.
To assert these values openly, however, is to uproot them
from the concrete, physical circumstances of ritual and to
consign them to the realm of the abstract, where they will be
infected with the violence of the world and become destructive.
For Jake and Frederic the overt assertion of any one of the

implicit values of the code represents a giving of the self, a loss of will and consciousness, which is tantamount to death.

Dr. Carl Jung, in his book *Psychology and Religion,* has said that

. . . consciousness must have been a very precarious thing in its beginnings. In relatively primitive societies we can still observe how easily consciousness is lost. One of the "perils of the soul" is, for instance, the loss of a soul. This is a case of a part of the psyche becoming unconscious again. Another example is the amok condition, the equivalent of the berserk condition in the Germanic saga. This is a more or less complete trance, often accompanied by devastating social effects. Even an ordinary emotion can cause a considerable loss of consciousness. Primitives therefore cherish elaborate forms of politeness, speaking with a hushed voice, laying down their weapons, crouching, bowing the head, showing the palms. Even our own forms of politeness still show a "religious" observation of possible psychical dangers. We propitiate the fates by wishing magically for a good day. It is not good form to keep the left hand in your pocket or behind your back when shaking hands. If you want to be particularly propitiating you use both hands. Before people of great authority we bow with uncovered head, i.e., we offer our head unprotected in order to propitiate the powerful one, who might easily fall suddenly a prey to a fit of uncontrollable violence. In war dances primitives can become so excited that they may shed blood. . . . Primitives recognize the ever-lurking possibility of psychical dangers, and the attempts and procedures employed to diminish the risks are numerous.

"Even an ordinary emotion can cause a considerable loss of consciousness. Primitives therefore cherish elaborate forms of politeness, speaking with a hushed voice, laying down their weapons, crouching, bowing the head, showing the palms"— in short, reproducing in ritual form the quiescent attributes

of the sternly conscious mind. We may add to this what we know of other primitive practices designed to exorcise evil. Sir James Frazer, for example, speaks of the tribal custom of pantomime, in which, in the form of religious ceremony or dance, the event most dreaded by the tribe is represented as actually happening, but happening in a way which makes it acceptably familiar and therefore purgative of the fear that is attached to it in life.

Recognizing as we do the peculiarly instinctual nature of Hemingway's art, it should not come as too great a surprise to us to discover close parallels between his creative processes and those of primitive man. The code of his heroes is clearly the symbolic construction of a psychic barricade erected against one of the primary perils of his soul—the loss of consciousness leading to a lawless, amok, or berserk condition. His art, when it is truest and most organically his, is a pantomimic rendering of a series of events which result in the breakdown of this barricade and in the subsequent loss of consciousness which he so greatly dreads. When the breakdown and loss occur, the emotion of fear is purged and the full dramatic energy of the art is released.

Mr. Philip Young in his recent short study of Hemingway gives a psychoanalytical interpretation of certain of Hemingway's typical artistic effects which comes very close to the view I am attempting to develop here. Mr. Young takes as the generative moment of the Hemingway trauma the famous night of July 8, 1918, at Fossalta di Piave, the night of the big wound when, like his hero Frederic Henry, Hemingway felt himself die and his soul leave his body. "I died then," he later recalled. "I felt my soul or something coming right out of my

body, like you'd pull a silk handkerchief out of a pocket by
one corner." Mr. Young believes that from this moment dates
Hemingway's obsessive preoccupation with death, his need
to return compulsively, in violation of Freud's "pleasure
principle," over and over again to the scenes of his injuries,
and his tendency, furthermore, before submitting to death sym-
bolically through his heroes, to occupy himself with vicarious
dying—with witnessing and participating in many wars, many
feats of daring, many bullfights. Drawing on the authority of
Otto Fenichel's *Psychoanalytical Theory of Neurosis,* Mr.
Young goes on to demonstrate how the experience of the big
wound produced in Hemingway the traumatic and repetitive
mechanism of decorum and self-control which in his novels
takes the form of the code. "Trauma," says Fenichel, almost
in paraphrase of Jung, "creates fear of every kind of tension
. . . because even a little influx of excitement may have the
effect of 'flooding' the patient," or, in Jung's terms, causing
him to lose consciousness and go berserk. Nevertheless, "the
patient cannot free himself from thinking about the (traumatic) occurrence over and over again," as both Hemingway
and his heroes do. There comes a time, however, when the
trauma itself has done its damage, and when the patient "has
to find new and better ways of adaptation. This . . . consists
in nothing more than a complicated system of bindings and
primitive discharges," or, in Hemingway's case, in a process of
gradual mastery of the traumatic "excitation" leading to a
certain suppression and impoverishment of the personality and,
finally, to a state of what Fenichel calls "primitivation" and
Young identifies as Hemingway's familiar primitivism. Mr.
Young's approach is illuminating as far as it goes, but it does

no more than provide the terms for the analysis which I am attempting here to undertake. What it fails to do is bring Hemingway's traumatic experience fully to bear on the dramatic pattern of his novels and to demonstrate the central fact that Hemingway in each of his best novels returns compulsively to the circumstances which induced his trauma, reproduces in the form of artistic pantomime the loss of soul or consciousness, the psychic death, which he himself experienced in those circumstances, shows how this loss occurs in the symbolic terms of the breakdown of the code, and achieves, through the process, a purgation of his own sense of fear as well as the dramatic climax of his art.

We might well suspect this somewhat extraliterary view of the code if we did not have before us the evidence of the two novels of Hemingway's—*The Sun Also Rises* and *A Farewell to Arms*—which stand above all his others in quality because, in them, the code and the circumstances and consequences of its destruction are presented and objectified in the purest possible form. It is in them, furthermore, that, in strict keeping with the nature of the code, the destructive agent is most clearly seen to arise out of the overt and violent assertion of some value on which the code is actually based but which it is against the law of the code to affirm.

In *The Sun Also Rises* Robert Cohn, the man who behaves badly by daring to admit his feelings, is the bearer of the destructive agent; and it is part of the consuming irony of the novel that the feelings he dares to admit are exactly those which Jake and Brett would like to express if *they* dared and if Jake's wound did not make it impossible for them to do so. The wound may be taken as a symbolic representation of the taboo which the code has imposed upon such feelings. In a passage of dialogue between Brett and Count Mippipopolous early in the novel this taboo is somewhat obliquely suggested by Brett.

> "Doesn't anything ever happen to your values?" Brett asked.
> "No. Not any more."
> "Never fall in love?"
> "Always," said the count. "I am always in love."
> "What does that do to your values?"

The count replies that love, too, has a place in his values; but since love is forbidden in Jake's and Brett's values, the wound is there to prevent them from having it and to force their emotion into channels of expression which their values do approve—Brett into sexual promiscuity and Jake into manly forbearance.

In the beginning the Pamplona fiesta is another approved channel: the drinking is carefully ritualized; the talk is good; and the weather is fair, as it always is for Hemingway when life is being lived according to the rules. But as the excitement of the holiday grows more intense, as the drinking spills over into drunkenness and street dancing, and as Jake, Brett, Mike, Bill, and Robert Cohn are caught up in a mounting tide of uncontrollable emotion, the fiesta becomes a setting of nightmare violence, a frenzied correlative action, for the berserk behavior by which Cohn brings about the destruction of the code.

It is interesting to see that as this occurs, all the elements attending on such destruction are actualized in the form of concrete, dramatic events. On the morning the first signs of disaster appear, the weather changes, and it starts to rain.

Mike, to the great disgust of the *aficionado* Montoya, breaks the rules by behaving badly toward the bullfighter Romero. Cohn, after having been humiliated once too often by the un-feeling Brett, knocks down Jake and Mike and has a vicious fight with Romero. Immediately afterwards, a Spaniard is gored to death by a bull, not, significantly, in the ring where his death would be in accordance with the rules, but in the run-way leading to the ring. Coming back to his hotel after the fight with Cohn, Jake feels unreal, as if he were walking in a dream; and this, like the whole nightmare of the fiesta itself, symbolizes the dreaded loss of consciousness which accom-panies the death of the code or the psychic death of the self.

Walking across the square to the hotel everything looked new and changed. I had never seen the trees before. I had never seen the flagpoles before, nor the front of the theatre. It was all different. I felt as I felt once coming home from an out-of-town football game. I was carrying a suitcase with my football things in it, and I walked up the street from the station in the town I had lived in all my life and it was all new. They were raking the lawns and burning the leaves in the road, and I stopped for a long time and watched. It was all strange. Then I went on, and my feet seemed to be a long way off, and everything seemed to come from a long way off, and I could hear my feet walking a great distance away. I had been kicked in the head early in the game. It was like that crossing the square.

This is also a moment of insight and conversion, when illusion is penetrated and reality revealed. But it is more importantly a surrogate form of the moment of death, and it is scarcely an accident that the words Jake uses here echo those of Frederic Henry's description of his wounding, as well as Hemingway's description of his own wounding. At any rate, following on this scene, as Cohn, who has been the agent of the death of the code, leaves Pamplona in defeat, the gored Spaniard's funeral procession moves through the streets on its way to the railroad station. In this fashion the pantomime is completed, the fear is purged, and all the elements of the code ritual are thoroughly objectified in the art.

At the beginning of *A Farewell to Arms* Frederic Henry's relations with the war are strikingly like Jake's relations with Brett. As long as the war is fought according to the rules, it is essential to Frederic's psychic survival to be attached to it and to respect its values; but it is equally essential that he maintain his spectatorial role with regard to it and that he respect its values in his own way. He will do his job conscientiously; but he will not be brave or honorable or glorious or self-sacrificing. These are dangerous abstractions of the true values of war, and are "obscene beside the concrete names of villages, the numbers of roads, the names of rivers, the numbers of regiments and the dates." They are like love as opposed to sex, goodness as opposed to forbearance, nightmare as opposed to good clean daylight. They force the mind away from essential experience and make one uncomfortably aware of the violent world outside that sometimes haunts one in sleep. It is only by living within the code that one can remain intact and completely, safely awake.

But in the Isonzo bombardment the war itself becomes violent, breaks the rules, and wounds Frederic; and, characteristically enough, it is at the moment of wounding that he has the sense of losing consciousness or self which, like Jake's sense of unreality, is the objective equivalent of the breakdown of the code. "I tried to breathe but my breath would not come and I felt myself rush bodily out of myself and out and out and out . . . and I knew I was dead. Then I floated, and instead of going on I felt myself slide back. I breathed and I was back." Later on, in the bewildering chaotic convoy movement back through the mud and rain from Caporetto, the destruction of the code by insane violence is again objectified; and, significantly, it is the *carabinieri,* those staunch defenders of the abstract values of a military action now gone berserk, who force Frederic to take the plunge into the river which purges him of his connections with the war altogether.

After his wounding on the Isonzo and the simultaneous breakdown of the code, Frederic begins to affirm overtly his hitherto forbidden love for Catherine Barkley; and with the last of his obligations swept away in the river, the future is now clear for its complete fulfillment. But unfortunately, with the code no longer in force, there is also nothing to prevent the rampant violence of the world from destroying that love; in fact, in Hemingway's terms, this is fated to happen to all emotions that are pursued purely and for their own sake outside the limits of the code. So, in the closing pages of the novel, we are confronted with the irony for which the earlier dramatic manipulation of the code has prepared us: with the flight to Switzerland the lovers have won their freedom; but they have left behind the ritualized faith which alone can make freedom tenable, and so they are condemned. Catherine must die; and Frederic, who has already experienced one death and been reborn and rebaptized, must die again.

In the three novels just preceding *The Old Man and the Sea* the code, in the sense that I have described it up to now, almost entirely disappears; and with it disappears the whole pantomimic ritual in terms of which the destruction of the code was formerly symbolized in loss of consciousness or psychic death, and as a result of which the psychic death was formerly dramatized in concrete instances of violence and physical death. Through some premature sagging of Hemingway's creative muscles, what used to be a system of fine internal tensions working their way dramatically to the surface becomes, in these novels, a fatty tissue of dead matter lying inertly in the open.

Harry Morgan in *To Have and Have Not* is a comic facsimile of the earlier Hemingway heroes. He is tough, taciturn, hard-drinking, and sexually athletic; but where these attributes were, in his predecessors, the ritualized forms of inner virtues that threatened at every moment to become violently and destructively overt, they are in him simply part of the static military equipment with which he does physical battle with a physical world in the face of certain physical death. The destructive agent is centered not in him or in his personal surroundings but in the rich, in whom, for the dramatic purposes of the novel and the psychic purposes of the code, it has no right to be centered. Consequently, when Morgan is finally destroyed, he is destroyed on the outside only. There is no psychic death because there has been no psychic life; and what little emotion is purged is not Morgan's or Hemingway's fear of an abstract horror, but simply our own fear that a doom so mechanically instigated will be, as it is, equally mechanically sealed.

In *For Whom the Bell Tolls* the destructive agent is also centered in an outside force, although this fact is rather well concealed by Hemingway's skillful use of rhetoric, polemics, and interior monologue, as well as by the presence of displaced and largely inactive elements of the old code formula. There is, for example, the familiar theme of loyalty to the common cause of the group, a loyalty which manifests itself in the same old reticences and courtesies. There is also the trapped-love motif, the tenderness of which is deepened by the violence which crowds close around it; and there is even the device of the code violator—in this case, Pablo—who, like Robert Cohn, is meant to destroy the code and let the violence in. But the difficulty is that the code of the group—or, more correctly, the pseudo code—is set against *physical* and not abstract violence. It is physical death at the hands of the fascists which Jordan and the others face; and the only result of Pablo's treachery is to bring that death a little closer. There is, consequently, no more room for the full dramatic formula of the code to work than there was in *To Have and Have Not*— no moment in the action when the violation of the code can be objectified in the terms of a correlative physical nightmare.

In view of all that has been said about *Across the River and into the Trees,* it would seem pointless to say more, particularly when one is able to offer nothing beyond an endorsement of the prevailing, although perhaps not the fashionable, critical verdict. But it may be useful if I lend the emphasis of my present argument to one fact about the book—that in it the slackening process which began for Hemingway with *To Have and Have Not* reaches a sad and ludicrous conclusion; and all that was once hard, intense, and rigidly controlled disintegrates into blatant self-burlesque. The code—if one can call it that—is now literally and consciously the joke-etiquette and tipsy mumbo-jumbo of an imaginary barroom secret society. The trapped-love motif, with its great dramatic potential, has crumbled into the incestuous pawings of a lonely old man who has nothing better to do while he waits to die. The emotion which it used to be death to utter and which, therefore, played over the agonies of physical suffering and frustrated love with great irony, has been diluted and sentimentalized into the querulous self-pity of the infirm. All the fatuities of which Hemingway has in the past shown himself to be occasionally capable—in *The Green Hills of Africa* and *Death in the Afternoon* as well as in *To Have and Have Not*—are fully consummated before the embarrassed eye.

Finally, in *The Old Man and the Sea,* the purely physical takes over altogether; and we have nothing but the naked contest of strength and courage between the aged Santiago and the fish—a drama which, for all its delicacy and depth of execution, is as far below the standard of complexity set by the early novels as *The Sun Also Rises* would be if it consisted of nothing but the bullfights at Pamplona. As for the code, it has diminished to the merest remnant of what it was, is now simply a bit of worrying irritation in the old man's mind over the *hubris* which has driven him to go out too far.

One remembers a bit sadly in reading over this novel Edmund Wilson's comment of nearly fifteen years ago that Hemingway's creative fluctuations are like the workings of the Bourdon gauge which operates on the principle that "a tube which has been curved into a coil will tend to straighten out in proportion as the liquid inside it is subjected to an increasing pressure." At the time Wilson presumably meant the analogy as a compliment to Hemingway's recuperative powers; but today it lends itself to a different interpretation. The tube now, we might say, has long since withstood the maximum pressure it was made to bear and has at last straightened out completely and for good. The tense young man in dramatic flight from the black horror of trauma has faded into the exhausted old man relaxed in an attitude of crucifixion and dreaming of the clear daylight and lions playing on the African coast.

SEVEN

The question of Malcolm Cowley

THE HISTORICAL METHOD in criticism, which over the past several years Malcolm Cowley, among others in this country, has vigorously simplified into popularity, is not one we set much serious stock by, although its lineage is long and, for the most part, distinguished, and its influence in shaping mass standards of literary opinion has always been very great. Its primary appeal for the public mind undoubtedly stems from the fact that throughout its course it has interested itself steadily in something other than literature—in society rather than in art, in the psychology of the producer rather than in the work produced—with the result that it has come to represent a kind of epicurean YMCA for those who have aspired and failed to win membership in the international fraternity of taste.

In the introduction to his *History of English Literature,* published in 1863, Hippolyte Taine, one of the great early

French masters of the historical method, summarized its objectives in the phrase *the moment, the race, and the milieu.* This is to say that the literary work is to be understood as the product of the historical climate of the time, the cultural inheritance of the people, and the current circumstances of the society. In theory, what this represented for Taine, as well as for the members of his immediate circle—Michelet, Renan, Sainte-Beuve—was a system for reducing literature to its chemical components by bringing to bear upon it the methods of the new mechanistic sciences, which were then engaged in reducing the universe to absurdity. But in practice it represented a quasi-critical excuse for trading the rigor of criticism for the security of a ready-made metaphysical cliché into which almost any writer could be crammed and made to fit. Taine's Racine, for example, appears to us not as the dramatist of power whose plays we honor today, but as an effete seventeenth-century courtier who has been bled lily-white to conform with Taine's preconceptions of the seventeenth century. In a similar way, Taine chides Balzac for creating characters who act objectionably and, on occasion, obscenely, but whose sin is not their lack of verisimilitude but simply their failure to act in accordance with a standard of conduct acceptable to the genteel morals of Taine. The supreme question, the question which the best esthetic criticism would always ask: whether the *Comédie humaine* is a valid literary judgment of the contemporary situation, a satisfactorily realized work of art, Taine never gets around to asking, nor does his tradition as a whole know how to formulate it. It is a tradition which has been determined above all to systematize and, if need be, to revise reality to conform with its preconceived image of it; and as is the case with all totalitarian ideologies, what it has been unable to make conform it has exiled or spiritually castrated or simply suppressed.

This tendency in the historical method made it an easy victim of the compulsive philosophical shoplifting which passed for politics in this country during the twenties and thirties. What was desperately called for in those years was a politics capable of viewing all human endeavor, whether in public affairs or the arts, as the product of the interacting forces of history and economics, but one which at the same time held open the possibility that these forces could be brought under control and made subservient to the collectivist and humanitarian aims of the people. This had been the great sustaining vision behind the labor movement from the beginning, and it had reasserted itself in the traumatic idealism that grew up in the first years of the American Depression. Marxism had seemed at the time to provide such a politics in the field of government, and the historical method became its counterpart and, in a sense, its official technique in the field of ideas. The way had earlier been prepared not only by the teachings of Hegel, Marx, and Engels, but in this country by the work of writers like Charles and Mary Beard, Vernon L. Parrington, and to a certain extent, H. L. Mencken and Van Wyck Brooks, each of whom had imposed upon the past his private social, psychological, or moral "reading," cast always in the framework of the programmatic *reductio ad absurdum* of historicism. But by the middle of the thirties, as the full force of the Marxist influence made itself felt, even these staunchly doctrinal approaches began to seem mild and naïve

by comparison with the militant mulishness which shortly over-
came the thinking of the Left and which brought the exploitation of literature by politics to an apex of madness it has never
since been able to attain. Certain of the younger Marxist
critics, lacking the learning of their elders and grown impatient with a point of view which stressed only the reciprocal
relationship of history and literature, now began to trumpet
for a literature not merely reflective of the social scene but
charged with reformist comment upon it. The labor of ideological instruction which Taine had performed on the works of
Racine and Balzac critics like Michael Gold and Granville
Hicks now tried to perform on the works and works-in-prog-
ress of Hemingway, Faulkner, Thornton Wilder, and some of
the other distinguished writers of the time. While these writers
for the most part remained cold to both the threats and the
endearments of the Left, others of less conviction were more
seriously affected, and there grew up a whole genre of ready-
to-wear novels and plays featuring the prescribed stereotype
capitalists, who were always bad, and the crowds of decent,
clean-cut, idealistic workers who were always depicted at
the end marching triumphantly, their picks and shovels on
their shoulders, the Internationale on their singing lips, up out
of the valley of oppression into the ruddy dawn of the new
proletarian tomorrow. One can only speculate on how far this
foolishness might have been carried had there not set in, at
about the beginning of World War II, a disillusionment with
the ideal on which this and other revisionary tendencies in
the American Marxist movement had been based, the ideal
of the ultimate perfectibility of history or, as Edmund Wilson

put it, the belief in man's ability to "impose on the events of the present a pattern of actual direction which will determine the history of the future."

There also came to power during and immediately following World War II a different school of criticism formed out of rebellion against the historical method and taking to itself the biases of the later existentialist philosophies which were then forcing historicism into the discard. This was the esthetic school originated by Coleridge and by Taine's contemporaries Baudelaire and Gourmont and carried forward into the modern era by T. E. Hulme and T. S. Eliot. Younger critics like Allen Tate, R. P. Blackmur, and Kenneth Burke, who had come of age in the political atmosphere of the twenties and thirties and whose talents had early been warmed by the fires of controversy, bypassed the trap of *moment, race, and milieu* and following Eliot began to programmatize a conception of literature as existing in and for itself, to be properly approached through its own symbolic properties, its form and language. Meanwhile, the historical method steadily declined in authority and influence, becoming more and more the critical palliative of the mass reading public and the grubstake of those literary backwoodsmen who spent their time between trips across the wide Missouri haranguing novelists for failing to present a "true" picture of American life and the American business man, and who persisted in trying to hold the cracked mirror of naturalism up to a world which had ceased long before to exist in its terms. Of the best old historical critics only a very few managed to escape this kind of debasement and to continue working productively in the tradition which, in a sense, they had already outlived. Edmund Wilson was one of these, and Malcolm Cowley was another. Wilson, however, was from the beginning something of a special case, for while he remained essentially faithful to the principle of the historical method, his wide range of intellectual interests carried him well beyond its programmatic confines. Cowley, while he has been enriched by the tradition of Baudelaire, has remained intellectually and temperamentally the more resolute historian. In his two book-length works of prose, *Exile's Return* and the present *The Literary Situation,* it is possible to see that his weaknesses are, in very large part, those of the historical method itself, and that his strengths are those which he has brought to his prose out of the resources of his poetic imagination.

Exile's Return, first published in 1934 and reissued in revised and expanded form in 1951, was an autobiographical narrative of development cast in the framework of an historical account of the literary twenties and thirties. But it was first and foremost a work of personal history conceived imaginatively and poetically, with all the vividness of a deeply felt emotional experience. Although it had to do with trends and fashions of thought and conduct, with the moment and milieu of a literary movement, it was dramatized both by the vigor and complexity of the subject itself and by the intensity of Cowley's own participation in it. The trends and fashions were treated as if they were characters in a first-rate fiction—as, for that matter, were the real-life literary figures whose activities afforded the book its wealth of anecdotal material. And since Cowley's concern was not with ideas as such nor with the artistic properties of individual literary works, nothing in his subject defied his poet's talent for reducing experience to the simple, the

pictorial, and the concrete. No intellectual abstraction, no call
upon his powers of precise critical judgment, forced him to
expose the weakness which, on the occasion of his first book
of poems *Blue Juniata* published a few years earlier, Allen
Tate had found evident in him. "No American at present,"
said Tate in a *New Republic* review, "writes a more lucid
prose than Cowley, and yet it is now clear that prose, certainly critical prose, is not his true medium. His mind is bas-
ically concrete and unspeculative; he brings to facts and observations an even, emotional tone that is the mark of a genuine style; but in criticism Cowley's instinct for exact definition is not strong; and the necessity for a certain amount of
abstraction only violates the even tone of his style." It was
the poet in Cowley who was responsible for the lucid prose
of which Tate speaks, and it was because Cowley was able
through that prose to personalize and lyricize his historical
subject in *Exile's Return* that the book remained free of the
defects inherent in his essentially historical method.

But Cowley's handling of a similarly historical subject in
The Literary Situation gives rise to questions which cannot be
so easily or so pleasantly resolved. His subject now is the condition of literature and of the creative spirit in this country at
the present time, and, as his thesis demonstrates, that condition
is largely one of stasis and retrenchment and is thus not in
itself very stimulating. Cowley, furthermore, obviously does
not have a sense of being personally caught up in it or emotionally engaged with its issues. His experience of active emotional participation in the literary life apparently came to an
end with the period which he documented in *Exile's Return*,
and of late years he has retreated more and more into seclusion;

his point of view has grown increasingly elder statesmanish; and his tone has undergone a gradual change from the lyric to the avuncular. What happens now in literature clearly seems to him to be happening to other people and no longer to himself or his friends. His dilemma in this new book, therefore, is that he cannot, on the one hand, count on his subject to dramatize itself through its own dramatic properties, and because he feels no personal or imaginative connection with it, he cannot, on the other hand, count on his poetic gifts to dramatize it for him. He is also up against the difficulty that as his sense of involvement has faded, these gifts, which in the poet are always directly dependent upon such a sense, seem themselves to have faded, leaving him out in the cold with nothing left but a style. It is still the lucid style which Allen Tate admired, but it is no longer lucid in the same way. Where in the past it had the lucidity which the poet achieves in forcing his strong and complex feelings under tension into form, it now appears to have the lucidity of a simple and rather tired view of experience, of complexities shunned and tensions abdicated. In the face of this, Cowley has had in this book to fall back for support upon the only method of prose narration he knows, and that is the horizontal and classificatory method of historicism. Throughout the book he has substituted tabulation for analysis, an enumeration of trends for a definition of causes, categorical labels for critical insights, lists of book titles, statistics on the paper-backed publishing industry, a "natural history" of the personal habits of writers, for a comprehensive synthesis of the facts behind the literary situation today. Perhaps more completely than any other journalistic critic of his generation, Cowley had in his grasp the materials out of which such a synthesis could have been made, for whatever his shortcomings, he has at least *read* the literature of our time and has been required professionally to hold informed opinions on it. Instead, what we get from him is a kind of plodding intellectual peasantry, a rural stubbornness in the face of abstract ideas, a penchant for dropping into his private memory hole whatever he cannot assimilate to his method or fully understand, a compulsion to reduce everything to the hard oversimplicity of bedrock, a compulsion which blinds him to the possibility that bedrock is at best merely a foundation and at worst merely an affectation. His mask is that of the kindly old sharecropper of letters who happens to write when the weather is too inclement for plowing or duck hunting, and while this undoubtedly serves to endear him to the lower orders of his readership, it disserves him badly on those occasions when it is clearly a disguise to cover a certain laziness of mind and a certain queasiness before the moral combat of cognition.

Near the beginning of his book and at intervals throughout it Cowley makes use of another kind of mask which affords us our angle of vision into much of his material and which illustrates far more tellingly than his rusticity of tone the evasive attitude he takes toward his responsibilities as critic. This is the mask of the uninitiated foreign observer—Cowley's choice is a "cultivated Hindu sociologist"—who is stationed at the edge of the current literary arena and through whose innocent eyes Cowley invites us to view with him the spectacle unfolding in its center. By resorting to this mask Cowley provides himself with an excuse for shirking the job of careful and thorough discussion which, if he were doing the seeing through his own eyes, he would be expected to perform. Faced with the problem of exploring in detail the works and trends fundamental to the literary situation, the problem of really taking up the burden of criticism, he is now able through his Hindu proxy to escape into his preferred and more relaxed role of historian and statistician of the simple and the obvious. His typical method is to draw up lists of novels and then to create an illusion of definition by stating that twenty-eight of them have to do with the war in the Pacific, nineteen with homosexuality, and seventy-two with life in the urban slums. "I counted," he informs us at one point, "the romantic or tragic love stories in ten of these earlier books (war novels). Of the affairs that go beyond the category of merely Having Sex, there are four with Italians, two with Germans . . . , two with Frenchwomen (of whom one is half Javanese), one with a Tonkinese, one with a New Zealander, and one with a Japanese. . . ." It would be different if this kind of thing were supplementary to an examination of the real meaning and worth of these novels, but when it constitutes very nearly the whole of what Cowley has to say about them, I believe one has a right to complain. This same approach, or variations of it, vitiates almost to the point of absurdity all those sections of the book having to do with the literary situation as such. It is only in the chapters setting forth the "Natural History of the American Writer," where Cowley is not required to concern himself with more than simple statistics and categories—so many writers live in Connecticut; some writers drink six pints of gin a day, but only when they are engaged on very long work; most of the writers who are not teachers are employed at other jobs; a number of writers are homosexual; at least one is a sadist; a lot are normal—it is only in these chapters that he is as informative and entertaining as one would expect him to be throughout.

After thinking back over Cowley's critical career and setting aside those fine and definitive essays on writers like Hemingway and Faulkner which he has occasionally been able to do, one is forced to conclude that he has suffered increasingly from the effects of trying to simplify his ideas for the benefit of what he obviously considers to be a simple-minded reading public. It is now clear that after more than twenty years of unremitting industry spent in this endeavor, he has at last succeeded in attaining his objective. But we should also remember that Cowley really belongs to a literary period different and older than ours, the period he described so well in *Exile's Return,* when, as Lionel Trilling once remarked, "criticism existed in heroic practical simplicity." I suspect, however, that Cowley should be reminded now, at this crucial stage in his career, that criticism is no longer simple, and that its heroism consists today in facing squarely and intelligently the full complexities of the literary situation in which we live.

EIGHT

Ira Wolfert: the failure of a form

FOR SOME YEARS NOW Ira Wolfert has been building a reputation for literary competence of that rare high kind which
is so close to excellence that we must assess it rather as the
product of an aspiration strained beyond its means than as a
symptom of a talent which has found it more profitable to
cheat than to aspire. Although he has had perhaps more opportunity than most men, Mr. Wolfert has never cheated: the impulse behind his aspiration has remained holy. But it is none
the less true that his aspiration has been of such quality and
directed toward such ends that it has been doomed from the
start to exceed his creative grasp. He is the sort of man who
probably should never have come to the novel in the first
place. He is by nature ill-equipped for it, and perhaps because
he senses his inadequacy he is always trying to make it do
work it was never meant to do, at least in such hands as his,

or to twist it into some hitherto undiscovered form more congenial to his limitations.

What his limitations are must by now be notorious, for he
has displayed them to good effect in two novels before his
most recent one, *Married Men.* They consist, in brief, of an
averageness of mind, a mediocrity of taste, and an obviousness
of feeling, all of which have caused him embarrassment in
his dealings with the larger philosophical abstractions and the
finer complexities of human emotion and behavior. In at least
one of his earlier works, however, Mr. Wolfert was able to get
around his limitations by the simple strategy of doing nothing
to call them forth. When he wrote *Tucker's People,* his first
novel, in the early forties, he depended almost entirely on his
very superior journalistic gifts—his clear perception of environmental detail, his deep sympathy for and understanding
of the various dwarfed personality types which inhabit the
modern underworld, and his ability to exploit to great dramatic effect the shade of difference between a fictional account
and its constantly intruding factual basis.

Of all his gifts this last probably served him and the novel
to best advantage, for it made it virtually impossible for the
average reader to see the fiction except through the haze of
his emotional response to the social condition against which
the fiction was a protest. And the same was true of his reaction
to Mr. Wolfert's war novel, *An Act of Love:* he saw it as a
glorious confirmation of his most cherished conventional attitudes toward the patriotic fact of war as he was able to observe
that fact under the fevered and overblown circumstances of
1945. He did not recognize Mr. Wolfert's fatuousness in that
novel, or his oppressively manic view of the joys of dying

in battle—if he had, he would have been obliged to recognize them as his own, and that, in 1945, would have amounted to an act of subversion.

Mr. Wolfert's gift for exploiting the moment had seduced the reader into taking a meretricious view of fiction, precisely as it had enabled Mr. Wolfert to elevate meretriciousness to the level of a kind of low literature. I do not say that he did this deliberately; he simply happened to share the attitudes of the great mass of his public. But it did have the effect of forestalling for a long time the critical judgment of his powers as a novelist which we are now compelled to make. For now, in *Married Men*, he has chosen to present, in journalistic form and language but in the terms of a conception far beyond the range of his journalistic gifts, a body of material from which no meretricious influence of timeliness or popular interest can arise to help him.

Mr. Wolfert's material in *Married Men* is no less than the moral and industrial history of a certain imaginary sector of American life in the modern era; or, to put it another way, the novel represents an attempt to analyze on a major scale the politics of the relationship which once existed in this country between the structures of economic class and the structures of the self. That Mr. Wolfert has largely failed in the attempt, or that, in some respects, his is one of the most important failures we have suffered in the novel in recent years, is not for the moment our concern. What should interest us first is his method, for that is the form in which his failure is transmitted to us and the form which, in large measure, his failure takes.

The striking feature of that form is its enormous size: Mr.

Wolfert's failure consists partly in his compulsive inability to make it smaller. The novel runs to slightly more than a thousand pages; and we are told on the jacket that it was revised three times. There can, consequently, be no mistake about it: Mr. Wolfert thought he knew what he was doing and could do no less. But what he thought he knew must escape our immediate comprehension, for in this country, at least in recent times, such garrulity as his has come to be thought of more as an ailment than as a method—the affliction of writers who, having failed to capture their subjects in youth, must resort in middle life to chasing them down through pages of print.

In the European novel, where garrulity is very nearly the grand tradition, we are inclined to accept it or, more often, to ignore it because it is usually inseparable from some great sustaining subject, some vast generalizing conception of man in nature. Even when Dickens and Dostoevski were writing novels to order, which they were not at all above doing, they were careful to write them by the pound rather than by the yard. Their subjects, furthermore, were not something they pursued; they were something they had, as elderly Boston gentlewomen have their hats. But American writers tend to have material rather than subjects, impressions rather than conceptions, feelings rather than emotions; and what they are apt to feel most intensely about is merely themselves. In this respect Mr. Wolfert is no Thomas Wolfe. He is not in the least interested in himself. If anything he is closer, in some of his technical resources, to the Russians. He has a sense of dramatic scene and detail that is nearly Tolstoyan; he even shares somewhat in Tolstoy's great preoccupation with the mechanics of power and its effect on men. But he is what Tolstoy would have been if he had been drugged and imprisoned, chained to a desk and condemned to write endlessly long after he had ceased to think. And his novel is a kind of *War and Peace manqué,* what Tolstoy might have written if he had had merely all that material, all that sweep, and no suitable form in which to make of his material a truly meaningful dramatic subject.

The material of *Married Men* is of two kinds. There is on the one hand the massive narrative itself, documenting in endless detail the life histories of the characters against the background of the social and economic history which they and their kind collectively produce. On the other hand there are the countless tedious passages of seemingly interpolated philosophical and metaphysical discourse which are apparently intended to serve as the vehicle for Mr. Wolfert's idea or theme. Ideally, the material should be impenetrable to analysis of this sort. There should not be two kinds at all, but one. The body of the novel should consist of a single, fully objectified unit of dramatic meaning, complete in itself and demonstrating through its own symbolic and imagistic properties the philosophical implications which are intended to rise out of it. This is the great lesson we have learned in the novel since Flaubert and Henry James. But it is a lesson which Mr. Wolfert's experience and cast of mind do not allow him to learn. His narrative moves along like a vastly independent convoy laden with action, while his philosophy is made to race after it and weave in and out through it like a police patrol heavy with monitory intent. And what is more, the narrative and the philosophy have behind them two completely different and violently incompatible systems of perceiving and explaining the reality which it is the business of the novel to engage.

The narrative is oriented on the old-fashioned historical-naturalist premise, a belief in the efficacy of sheer horizontally accumulated detail to produce a convincing picture of reality. Its traditional literary form is the saga, chronicle, fake journal, and the kind of novel which has come down to us through Zola, Balzac, Norris, Dreiser, and Farrell. Its traditional technique is garrulity. Its traditional goal is not literature but the reproduction of life. Philosophically, it represents a rationale which has been untenable for the last fifty years; for the findings of nineteenth-century European scholarship on which it is based have been that long in the discard. It assumes a mechanical universe governed by natural law and force and a static view of human behavior as simply a chemical and ganglionic response to environmental stimuli; and that is not the universe we have inhabited or a view we have been able sensibly to hold since the appearance of Freud and the publication, in 1905, of the first Einstein papers.

The burden of Mr. Wolfert's philosophy, however, is existentialist, in the respect that it assumes a relative universe and a view of human destiny as an achievement of the responsible or "engaged" will operating within an order of time, space, and nature which is quite the opposite of the mechanical order of the naturalists. Its traditional literary form is the novel of introspection and sensibility, the novel of James, Virginia Woolf, Conrad, and Faulkner, where dramatic realization is as a rule achieved through the realization of a character's power of free choice, his attainment of selfhood.

The question it asks, the question that is asked over and over again in the speculative portions of Mr. Wolfert's novel, is: What can a man do to bring about such a realization in terms of his whole nature? But the question which the narrative asks is: How can a man gain sufficient freedom from the social and economic trap in which environment and chance have placed him to find out whether he has a nature? It is clearly the first of these questions which Mr. Wolfert wishes his novel to answer, or at least to raise; but he has chosen to raise it within the framework of a narrative technique which, by the very nature of the world view it represents, can provide an answer only to the second. The result is that, even as Mr. Wolfert raises his question, his narrative rules it out of order; even as he struggles to save the souls of his characters, his narrative damns them. It is only at the very end of the novel, through what we must interpret as a sacrificial act of self-sabotage, that he is able to impose salvation on them; but by then it is much too late.

The terms in which the characters are introduced to us, the only terms in which, given Mr. Wolfert's method, they can be introduced, are those of naturalist determinism. This is to say that they are seen as the passive victims of forces set in motion by the environment surrounding them—in particular, by the psychological environment created through their relations with their immediate families. In the case of each of the leading characters the directing compulsive force is Oedipal: each in his own way must kill his father in order to release the self-creating principle within himself. This might well have served as the scaffolding on which Mr. Wolfert could have constructed his existentialist novel if he had been able to persuade his narrative to cooperate. But the insight into the psychological nature of his characters which he gives us, largely through his expository passages, is obscured and finally vitiated by the contradictory motives which his narrative causes his characters to have. Wes Olmstead, his prototypal tycoon, is *shown* to be driven, not by an impulse toward creative selfhood, but by an ultimately self-destroying desire for wealth and power; and the vast industrial empire which he builds in the service of this desire comes to represent the ultimate in spiritual impoverishment for the men under him. Elizabeth, his wife, while also ostensibly motivated by a need to become "existent" as a self and as a woman, is *shown* to be motivated by impulses no less acquisitive than her husband's when she undertakes a political career.

It is perhaps because Mr. Wolfert sensed and sought to reverse the direction in which his narrative was taking him that he chose, at the last possible moment, to resolve his characters in terms of an existentialist destiny. Olmstead, at the end of his life and in complete contradiction of the facts of his nature as previously given, is made to develop a conscience and to work for the creative betterment of his men. Elizabeth later on is inexplicably released into womanhood by Olmstead's death and, even more inexplicably, by the suicide of Banty Springer, a former Olmstead employee whom she scarcely knows.

But Mr. Wolfert's last desperate efforts are not entirely wasted. The story of Banty Springer, which forms the long concluding section of the novel, is surely one of the finest pieces of sustained narrative writing to be produced by an American novelist in many years. It is like the scenes of Joe

Christmas's castration in Faulkner's *Light in August* and Axel Heyst's sacrificial death in Conrad's *Victory,* in the sense that it represents one of those rare and almost unbearably lucid moments when all the tensions and ambiguities and, in this case, contradictions which have been spreading through a novel and holding it back from climax suddenly release and resolve themselves in a single tranquillizing act of perfectly rendered drama. But with all its perfection, Banty Springer's story is still not enough to save the novel. The thick tissue of paradox and inconsistency which has grown up before it in the narrative has already crowded out the master design in which it might have taken a significant place.

In these times of indiscriminate praise and blame, one further distinction needs still to be made. *Married Men* may be a crashing bore and a nearly crashing failure. But even at its most boring it is always serious, and even in its failure it testifies in a major way to the high quality of Mr. Wolfert's intent, the continued purity of his aspiration. It also stands well above the majority of the novels which, in its size and form, it so much resembles and with which it is certain to be compared. I mean those voluminous provocations to aphasia which go by the publicity names of "saga" and "chronicle" and "epic" and "panorama" and which seem to prophesy, in their every line, the coming of that day when the publishing of books in America will at last have been delegated to a gigantic autonomous printing machine, whose business it will be to turn out great bundles of paper between gaudy covers, to be sold in the millions to an audience so anesthetized that it will no longer know or care that there is no print whatever on any of the pages.

NINE

The education of James T. Farrell

Reflections at Fifty brought together in 1954 what James T. Farrell considered to be the most interesting of the literary and occasional essays he had written in recent years. It is not an important collection, for Farrell is not an important mind, except by comparison with what in America we deem to be mentality in the creative artist, nor is his influence as a novelist or critic any longer to be very seriously reckoned with. He now has, to be sure, a kind of "place" in American letters; we judge him perhaps as the last of the *natural* writers in the tradition stemming from Norris and Dreiser; and recently he has taken on something of that curiosity or luxury value which writers in this country tend around fifty to come into by virtue of the fact—which we somehow never cease to find remarkable—that like Clark Gable and Gary Cooper they have managed to survive to that age. But one cannot say of

Farrell that he promises to share with us a productive old
age in the manner of Shaw or Mann, or that at some time
prior to old age we can expect him to resume work upon the
foundation which he began to build with *Studs Lonigan* and
has since incessantly begun to build over. We therefore find
him in this volume engaged upon a typical menopausal literary
effort: the consolidation of ideas and insights which he experienced to a greater purpose twenty years ago and which
represent a defensive position which is no longer under attack. The book nevertheless is an instructive document, the
record of an interesting, serious, and at times almost ludi-
crously earnest intelligence, and it instructs us best on those
occasions when it does not appear to know how much it is
instructing us in the way that intelligence educated itself, and
in the role which self-education played in shaping the attitudes, morals, and modes to which that intelligence gave expression in literature.

Self-education comes high in America, and Farrell has
paid for it—as in differing respects have Faulkner and Hemingway—with his whole career. Its cost to him consists in the
fact that the attitudes it has given him are largely provincial;
the morals are parochial; and the modes are pedantic, for it
appears to be the case with the self-educated literary man in
America that he tends always to confuse learning and pedantry and that in pursuing the one he will caricature the other.
This, I take it, was part of Henry James's point about Hawthorne. But for an intelligence of a different quality and
grain from Farrell's the cost is not necessarily so high. The
self-educated critic R. P. Blackmur, for example, is similarly
afflicted with pedantry; in some areas he has informed himself

to a degree that is very nearly saintly. But Blackmur's intelligence derives its great compulsive force from precisely its ignorance of what the formal limits and conventions of learning are, of just how much work it has to do in order to graduate at the head of its class. The result is that in the course of expiating his ignorance (which I am certain he always believes to be profound) Blackmur outmodes the conventions by exceeding them. His fear of flunking out flunks out nine-tenths of his contemporaries. Farrell's pedantry, on the other hand, is of a peculiarly low order and flaccid kind, the kind that caricatures itself because it is backed by a knowledge of what the conventions are and how to imitate them.

It becomes clear in reading over the prose in this volume that Farrell went to school, but it is just as clear that he went to school to the wrong teachers. His prose is a savage compound of jargon and rhetoric derived from French naturalist novels, the writings of William James, John Dewey, the Marxists, and the German philosophers, political manifestoes, and behaviorist psychology, and it appears to have got into the book by way of the dump truck and shovel. It has no rhythm, grace, warmth, or subtlety of style, and it is overlaid with a heavy-footed earnestness and zeal like that of a frightened schoolboy, pompous and popeyed, reciting a speech cribbed largely from the *Encyclopædia Britannica*. In content it is approximately vintage 1910. I do not mean that the questions it raises are necessarily no longer in force. It is rather that one no longer expects to see them discussed in quite this fashion and at this level. It is scarcely real any longer, for example, to observe of naturalism, as Farrell observes of it in one of these essays, that "it has been an attempt to meet and to reveal and to explore the nature of experience in the modern world." We now know that this is exactly what naturalism has consistently failed to do for the modern world and that that is the reason the best modern writers can no longer take it seriously. If they did, they would have to take seriously Newton on the nature of space and Spengler on the nature of Western society. But this is the nature of Farrell's provincialism, one consequence of his self-education, and we have no choice but to take it seriously.

The other consequence, his moral parochialism, is the quality which above all others has impoverished his imagination and concerning the nature of which, by word, tone, and unwitting confession, *Reflections at Fifty* is at times almost heartbreakingly informative. The more purely literary phase of his education Farrell apparently got from two men, Sherwood Anderson and Theodore Dreiser, about both of whom he has written here with honest admiration and feeling. What they passed on to him by precept and example was the great cranky lesson which had sustained them in their own mountainous dedication to their craft: the serious writer in America is a man besieged; lying in wait on all sides of him are forces of darkness and bigotry bent on stealing his virtue; he is a perpetual Penelope and at the same time he must serve as his own avenging Odysseus; his role must be one of unremitting, nerve-end vigilance. Anderson and Dreiser had early developed a paranoid revulsion to being touched; the cry of "Rape!" was forever on their lips; and if they wore their integrity a bit too enticingly high at the knee, it was because their right to integrity, their right to keep it or give it away, was constantly being challenged. And this was the crux of Farrell's educa-

tion in literary morals. Anderson and Dreiser taught him integrity; they took him aside and patted him on the head and
told him always to speak the truth, my son, and no harm will
ever come to you. They helped to develop in him the one
quality for which today we rightly do him honor.

But then Farrell stopped learning. He stopped right then and
there with what he had and set himself up in practice as a
writer of novels, a man of integrity, a speaker of the truth, all
of which he was. The one truth he had was the truth of his
early life on the south side of Chicago when he was Studs
Lonigan–cum–Danny O'Neill–cum–James T. Farrell, and
after the manner of an Anderson "grotesque," he made this
one truth his own. Then he began to discover that, just as his
teachers had warned, there were dark forces about striving
to keep him from speaking the truth. There were court injunc-
tions, hostile critics, leagues of frightened philistines. His integrity was being threatened, and all that he knew to do,
all that his education had taught him to do, was to speak the
truth again and again in novel after novel until the dark forces
either surrendered or were destroyed. It did not matter that it
was substantially the same truth he spoke each time. The important thing was that it was The Truth. He began to develop
a compulsion, a repetition compulsion. Finally it became a
fixture of his psychic life. He would sit in the midst of his own
entrails, weaving them all day into a tapestry which he would
unweave all night, just to keep the dark forces off guard. But
he never learned how to be his own Odysseus. Even in middle
age, while flying in a plane from Los Angeles to New York or
while talking with a Russian official in Vienna, he tells us that
his mind was not there, was not absorbing and recording

fresh experience; it was back in the childhood world of his first and only truth with "Old Tom and Mary O'Flaherty, Jim and Liz O'Neill, Aunt Margaret, Aunt Louise, Uncle Al, little Danny." The integrity that became an obsession, the integrity that made him an honest writer, has held fast to the truth, and the truth now holds Farrell fast, blocking his ascent into the greatness that might have been his. It has forced him instead deeper and deeper into his pedantry, his thick, almost scholastic preoccupation with every last physical detail of his world, until in his last novel *The Face of Time* we find even the details running out and the truth narrowing to the little circle of infancy and age. And above the monotonous drone of the language, doing its remorseless work of genealogy tracing and visceral bookkeeping, we catch the accents of a man nearly catatonic, telling over the catechism which he was taught would eventually get him to Heaven.

TEN

The function of the book critic

THIS IS TO ASSUME that the "book" critic, as distinct from the formal literary critic and the historian of ideas, may be said still to have a function, and I am by no means sure we are safe in assuming this. Certainly his function, if he has one, is not what it was in that distant and now somewhat overly memorialized day when, as Lionel Trilling remarked, "criticism existed in heroic practical simplicity, when it was all truth against hypocrisy, idealism against philistinism, and the opposite of 'romanticism' was not 'classicism' but 'realism,' which—it now seems odd—negated both." We no longer feel ourselves at home with such ideas, nor do our serious critics, the best of whom, by a fine irony, have been the ones responsible for depriving criticism—hence themselves—of those convenient verbal oppositions in terms of which its heroism was formerly

192

defined. We conceive of criticism far more snobbishly now; we know, we take pleasure in knowing that it is no longer heroic, practical, or simple, but is at least an institution or a mining operation if not the whole of literature itself.

Still, for the purposes of searching out a function for the "book" critic, the older, humbler conception should serve us best, even though we should be hard pressed to find anyone today able or willing to work within it; for a principal motive behind the search is to insist upon a recovery of some of the force of the older conception, the salvage of a little of the heroism, practicality, and simplicity. I assume it as axiomatic that criticism is capable of infinite extension beyond the carefully patrolled borders now set up for it, and that this extension should commence with the restoration to full usefulness of the critic whose business was once the disinterested discussion of books, past and present, within the matrix of taste and close judgment.

This is not to suggest that we substitute one mining operation for another. If it were, we should soon have to recognize that we were having to market a very poor ore indeed and be quickly out of business. But it is to suggest that we mine for a better ore in the same general area, keeping before us always the fact that what we are looking for must measure up to the change which has rendered conditions far different from what they were when we mined there in the past. This change consists not merely of technological advance; it involves a full-scale reorientation of the relationship which once obtained between literature and the public imagination, between the written word, the literary image, and the power of that imagination to dramatize itself, to find extensions and confirmations of itself, in words and images, the humanizing faculty of language.

I take it for granted that the integrity of this relationship has today very nearly broken down and that it was beginning to break down even in the age of critical heroism and simplicity. That is what gave criticism then its special urgency and force: its insistence upon bringing and holding together the strands of language and a public imagination which was no longer quite at ease with, or convinced of the necessity of, the union. But there nonetheless still existed in that age a sense of the reality of both language and literature in an audience of what Henry Ladd Smith once called "the superior few," and it was to this audience that the older type of book critic addressed himself. He wrote his reviews and essays for such journals of liberal opinion as the *New Republic* and *Nation;* he discussed books and ideas in a literate, intelligent fashion, and the "few" understood and responded, oftentimes vehemently, oftentimes boorishly, but they responded, because they too read and at their leisure discussed books and ideas in a cultural atmosphere, however thinning, in which both had a living relation to the daily conduct of life.

If we say that in recent years that relation has become increasingly tenuous or severed, we have to take into account the shift that has occurred in the public's position with regard to all works of serious art as well as the anesthetizing effects of mass education and the mass media, and we have to keep in mind also that it is not only to art that the public no longer fully responds but to most of the art substitutes which we like to hold accountable for the failure of responsiveness to art. Radio, the motion pictures, and television have all begun to suffer the same fate, which is to be subjected to a decline of public interest even as the mass of the public gives to them daily more and more of its time and concentration.

The shift I speak of issues at least partly from a dwindling of the public capacity for sustained attention in all areas, and this has something to do both with the atomization of the individual self under the stresses of modern life and with the retreat of the mass psyche from circumstances which threaten to overpower and "flood" it with more stimuli than it can safely absorb. The human mind, to paraphrase Eliot, cannot bear too much reality, and when it is asked to—which is the hourly request of our time—it does not automatically fall back into that fantasy state in which literature takes on its strongest appeal as a device for channeling and discharging the unwanted sensations. It is far more likely to sink instead into a slough of protective detachment and ennui from which neither literature nor any palliative substitute can be counted on to arouse it. Literature for the mass mind then becomes—if it becomes at all—a thing which one merely consumes like Seltzer in an unceasing, fretful search for relief from one's sense of inner disquietude, and not only is its original integrity as a humanizing organism destroyed in the process, but its basic nature is gradually altered until finally it is smoothed and pasteurized into simply another of the divertive products of a culture bent on entertaining itself to death.

The automation both of the materials and the capacities of mass response has caused the whole of our cultural potential to become polarized at the extremes of special cultural interest. The best and most serious elements are now centralized in the universities (an inevitable but dangerous development), the worst and most fraudulent in the market place of popular entertainment. The solid middle formerly provided by the "superior few" has fallen away, scattering the few among the many between and at the extremes, and depriving the intellectual world of a liaison point between the areas of practical affairs and ideas. As this has occurred, the standards furnished out of the older humanistic education of the few have become hallucinated and bowdlerized in a frenzy of commercialized effort to pander to the tastes and appearances of taste created by the diffusion of interests and appropriated by the new semiliterate mass. That portion of the mass, for example, which has acquired or likes to fancy it has acquired a taste for books is given the illusion of absorbing and advancing the "modern" through the attention regularly given in the fashion magazines to the décor literature of certain younger writers. That this "modern" had already become a cliché before it had had time to become serious is a fact of no concern to a public so sophisticated that it accepts—in company with half the visiting insurance salesmen from Seattle— the antiquated plays of Tennessee Williams as if they were in the very forefront of dramatic experimentalism, antiquated in the sense that they are concocted out of the scrap-basket materials of the naturalistic theater of the thirties and are merely the Broadway analogue of the sex-crime-and-violence films which the lower orders of the same public twitch and shudder at in the theaters across the street.

But the automation of mass response has had its most devastating effects upon the processes of cultural production itself. The products for which the educated tastes of the few formerly created a demand and which the continuous exercise of those tastes sustained at a high level of quality have now become promiscuously available on the mass market, and that portion of the public to whom all tastes are foreign has grown content to accept the advice of the market on nearly all matters relating to consumption. This is to say that the market has taken over from the public the primary and crucial act of taste along with the act of setting the standard of quality at which taste shall be considered satisfied. While in a society like ours this kind of paternalism may be educative, as it undoubtedly is in such areas as the cheap production of reprint literature, it has tended to breed a complacency and passivity, a spurious sense of things arranged and under control, both in the public mind and in the minds of those whose job is the custodianship of taste, the preservation of cultural morals. It is remarkably easy, for example, to conclude from the current proliferation of reprinted classics that ours is indeed an Augustan age, that literature is something signed, officially sealed, and delivered to us by the past, and that as long as we remember to take it out for dusting now and then, we are free to devote ourselves to humbler, less stringent concerns. The publishers perhaps unconsciously enforce this impression, for in the face of a compliant mass market and the prevailing confusion of standards, they often yield to the temptation simply to keep the industry going by publishing whatever the traffic will bear, regardless of whether their consciences will bear it or not. The reviewers, in turn, who would ordinarily be able and willing to separate out the good from the bad, are obliged—since they have nothing else—to accept what the publishers place on the market, and because they too must work to keep the industry going, they tend to treat the good and the bad with an

indiscriminate seriousness, hence, with an indiscriminate per-
functoriness, with the result that the good and the bad stand
about an equal chance of success and failure. The reviewer's
life quite literally depends upon this kind of compromise, for
with countless numbers of mediocre books at his disposal, he
is forced either to treat them seriously or to deny that he has
any justification for treating them at all. What usually happens
is that the conscientious reviewer will give himself the illusion
of integrity by singling out for overpraise some book which
looks serious or which, at any rate, contains elements he remembers as having been identified with the seriousness of certain books of the past, however dull and stereotyped they may
have since become. It is very nearly endemic to present-day
reviewers that in the absence of a renewing standard of critical
values they will eulogize the conventional and condemn the
original. The conventional they see as original, while the
original appears to them artificial or bizarre or phony. But
the precision of the reviewers' judgments is no longer a matter
of very grave concern, for the idea is, as I have suggested, quite
soundly established in the public mind that literature is a task
completed, its issues settled with a finality which renders the
reviewers' judgments academic, and that if one should ever
have occasion to refer to it, one should look not to current
productions but to the classics or, better still, to that sacred
bibliographical fount from which all good pocket-sized books
spring, the fabulous 1920s.

   This attitude is yet another result of the breakdown of the
public capacity for response to language, and it has undoubtedly had more to do than any other factor with the change
which has occurred in the American literary situation. We

look back today as upon some remote geological era to the time not so very long ago when books were able to touch and hold the imagination of the reading public, the great time of furor and controversy centering in such works as *All the King's Men, Raintree County,* and *Under the Volcano.* These are all novels of the 1940s, and it is perfectly true that since then the culture has entered on a period of consolidation and stasis characterized by the absence of those large, motivating ideas which usually serve in fiction to provide a link between the world of public affairs and the world of artifice.

But it is equally true that the 1940s represented the opening phase of the polarization of our cultural interests, the scattering of the "superior few," and the beginning of the recession of the public imagination from the symbolic arena of language. Both in those years and in the decades immediately preceding them literature stood in a much closer relation to immediate experience than it does today, and the agencies whose function it is to hold the life of literature in trust were still engaged —albeit with increasing desperateness—in monitoring the public taste. It is a fact of wonderment now that a critic of the stature of Edmund Wilson could succeed through the 1940s in influencing large sectors of that taste with a criticism both learned and urbane. But we should not forget that at the same time almost the whole of our literary intellectual class was still concerned with contemporary literature and was not above commenting upon it. The book sections of the *New Republic, The Nation,* and *The New Yorker* up to roughly the end of World War II constitute a record of the kind of communication that was once possible between serious criticism and the remnants of the literate public.

But the literary intellectual class today is centered for the most part in the small academic quarterlies; the serious critics are represented in their pages by essays on Dante and Melville; and what little time they devote to contemporary literature is usually given over to the writing of "Fiction Chronicles," package review-essays in which six or eight new novels are treated with a cold detachment befitting the low opinion in which new work generally is held. The counterpart of Edmund Wilson, should he appear today, would soon have the sense of shouting into a bottomless pit, for if a literate public still exists for the *New Republic, The Nation,* and *The New Yorker,* its members have grown apathetic to literary questions or too busy with their own affairs to respond to them.

As for the counterparts of the serious novels of the past, it is perhaps only emptily brash in these times to observe that we have had several, of which two of the most recent are, to my mind, William Gaddis's *The Recognitions* and Alan Harrington's *The Revelations of Doctor Modesto.* Both of these novels possess merits and idiosyncrasies remarkable enough to have aroused a storm of critical controversy and to have won them a fair public following had they been published ten or fifteen years ago, when an Edmund Wilson might have performed for them the service he performed for the younger Hemingway or a Malcolm Cowley for the neglected older Faulkner. Instead, they were allowed to pass from publication into oblivion with nothing in between to arrest their passage. *The Recogninitions* received indifferent to stupid notice in the leading New York literary supplements, and *The Revelations of Doctor Modesto,* in keeping with the policy currently governing the review of serious first novels, was accorded brief and insipid notice in the very back pages of *The New York Times Book Review*. One explanation may be that both books, like all serious novels, present an imaginative view of the truly contemporary world, while the mass of the public and most of the reviewers have never grown beyond the view which was fashionable in the 1920s. But whatever the reason, it is difficult to understand how the reward of reputation can ever come to the author of either novel, for there exists at present no agency able or willing to keep their names alive in the public consciousness until the time when they publish their next books. There is no assurance, furthermore, that when that time comes they will fare any differently, except that the chances are excellent they will run afoul of the prevailing hostility to second novels and be obliterated once and for all. Without at least a small receptive audience and a body of critical opinion capable of accepting the risks of its obligation to new literature, the publication of books must become for these writers what Allen Tate called "a series of pragmatic conquests which . . . are true only in some other world than that inhabited by men," or a nightmare experience such as Scott Fitzgerald described of "standing at twilight on a deserted range, with an empty rifle in my hands and the targets down. No problem set—simply a silence with only the sound of my own breathing."

It is evident, then, that at the moment we should be hard pressed to find a book critic upon whom to bestow the accolade of "function." Where in the present circumstances of society would he discharge a "function" if he had it? The older type of book critic has almost entirely disappeared with the shift of literary power from the open frontier of the "superior few" to the closed circle of the university; many writers who began their careers as book critics are now university critics performing in the quarterlies an altogether different function. In the market place we have many reviewers but no critic with an authoritative voice whose daily or weekly business is the close supervision and enrichment of taste. Our reviewers are free-lance writers, hack writers, professors who write, literary journalists, but not men of letters. They are neither committed with their whole minds to literary values nor educated in the history of literary ideas and movements. Their treatment of books is consequently superficial, arbitrary, and undisciplined. The serious weekly periodicals are no longer outlets for informed literary discussion; their book sections differ scarcely at all from those of the newspapers. The book critic with a desire to form himself in the older tradition is faced, therefore, with a choice between occasional reviewing and even more occasional quarterly publication, but if he wishes to concern himself frequently and at length with contemporary work, to discharge in full his responsibilities to new writers and reputations, neither will afford him the space he needs.

His only hope, and it is at best a scant one, is that out of the present cultural ferment will emerge a new audience composed, perhaps, of the younger people who are obliged today to bear in silence their disaffection with the state of literary affairs but who will one day be able to assert themselves. In the meantime, he will probably be forced to work in isolation and obscurity. If he goes under, he will at least have the satisfaction of knowing that the culture that bred him and gave him his function has gone under too, that the silence is at last complete, the targets are down for good.

INDEX

204

ABOUT THE AUTHOR

John W. Aldridge was born in Sioux City, Iowa, in 1922 but at an early age migrated with his parents to Tennessee and settled on a small farm. In 1940 he entered the University of Chattanooga as a county scholarship student, shortly became editor of the campus newspaper, and in 1942 was awarded a fellowship for study at the Bread Loaf School of English. Mr. Aldridge entered the Army in 1943 and served through the war with the XX Corps in Europe. Following his discharge he resumed his university studies at the University of California at Berkeley, where he became editor of *Occident*. He was graduated in 1947, and later in the same year he published in *Harper's Magazine* a controversial article on the new postwar generation of American writers. In 1948, Mr. Aldridge was appointed Lecturer in criticism and in 1950 assistant professor of English at the University of Vermont. In 1948–1950, he organized and directed at Vermont a yearly symposium on the current American novel, and in 1951–1953 he established the School of Modern Critical Studies, in which Allen Tate, R. P. Blackmur, David Daiches, and other writers and critics participated. In the summers of 1952 and 1953 he served also as director of the Fiction Writers Conference held at Putney, Vermont, and in 1953 he founded and edited with the novelist Vance Bourjaily the literary magazine *Discovery*. In 1953 Mr. Aldridge participated as a lecturer, along with Hannah Arendt, V. S. Pritchett, and Sean O'Faolain, in the Christian Gauss Seminars in Criticism at Princeton University. It was at Princeton that he completed work on the basic material for *In Search of Heresy*.

Mr. Aldridge's first critical book *After the Lost Generation* was published by McGraw-Hill in 1951. A year later Ronald Press issued a college textbook of criticism compiled under his editorship, *Critiques and Essays on Modern Fiction*. Since 1949, he has been a frequent contributor of reviews and essays to the

About the Author

Saturday Review, The New York Times Book Review, Partisan Review, Western Review, Virginia Quarterly Review, and *New Republic,* and in 1955 *The Nation* announced him as a regular contributor. Mr. Aldridge has lectured in universities throughout the country, including Boston University, City College of New York, Columbia, Princeton, University of Wyoming, Oberlin, and Skidmore. He has done research in literary scholarship for the Rockefeller Foundation, and is spending the current year traveling and writing in Europe.

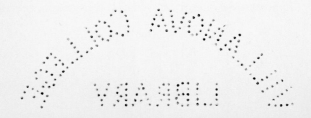